# faith and process

# faith
# and
# *process*

## The Significance of
## Process Thought
## for Christian Faith

# PAUL R. SPONHEIM

**AUGSBURG** Publishing House • Minneapolis

FAITH AND PROCESS

*To Mark, Rolf, and Scott*
*in whom is life*

# Contents

# Preface

Faith struggles to find words. This struggle takes place in sermon and Sunday school, in church college and theological seminary. As part of that struggle books are made. The words are often new ones, or the paragraphs and patterns in which they are placed are new. The pastor comes upon a sermon produced only a decade ago and shudders, "Did I really preach this?" It was a person of Christian faith who produced those words a few short years ago, and it is a person of Christian faith who expresses dissatisfaction over them now. How can this be?

It can be because faith is in process—in two senses. First of all, faith in God always exists in some particular human context. We do not cease being human and historical when we believe. Accordingly, our statements of faith are inevitably cast in the framework of some particular situation(s). As situations change, there will be a tendency for faith's speech to change, though there is no assurance that we will speak clearly what needs to be said to and in our particular time. To try to make our witness both timely and true is not an act of disloyalty to God. It is rather a prescription for new words.

Second, faith is in process in a more intrinsic sense. Hard as it is, the task of "applying" a given text to a new situation oversimplifies the work required of us. As students of the Bible know, there is no clearly-defined boundary between text and context. If this is true about the Word, may it not be true as well about the world? In any case, I am not the Holy Bible, but a human being who must make my way through life as best I can, claiming gladly whatever light may come to me. The Christian claims that the true light has shined and the darkness has not overcome it. But though the light is given, it is still the Christian who must see. So to see, to claim the truth that is there—that is struggle; it is process indeed. Faith seeks to know and to serve the truth with the Word in the world.

Thus faith does not resist the ongoing human quest for meaning. Rather, it offers its own warning against a reformation that does not continue, and it does not suppose that the realm of thought is an exception at this point. To recognize that faith must constantly seek to possess and express its truth is to recognize that Christians have cause to work with others. As Bernard Lonergan puts it:

> In brief, the world of the theologian is not some isolated sphere cut off from the affairs of men. But the static viewpoint inevitably leads to such isolation. By rejecting the static viewpoint, by conceiving theology as an ongoing process guided by a method, one puts an end to isolationism. The concern of the theologian is not just a set of propositions but a concrete religion as it has been lived, as it is being lived, and as it is to be lived. So conceived, theology has to draw on the resources not only of scientists and historians, but also of philosophers.[1]

It is in fact wisdom that we seek. We seek "the ability to judge soundly and deal sagaciously with facts, especially as they relate to life and conduct."[2] But "the facts" are not the private property of Christians. Faith need not pronounce reason pure in order to recognize that reality still presses upon the sinful self to be known. In this book I examine a particular view—or family of views—of the facts in the interest of "judging," "dealing with," "using." I believe Whitehead's view warrants such examination because of its intrinsic insightfulness and its extrinsic influence. But that remains to be seen.

Several steps are necessary. The first chapter establishes four specific categories under which faith may seek wisdom from the student of the world. The second and third chapters then present the world view in historical dress. The second chapter, which presents the descriptive vision of Alfred North Whitehead, is particularly important. It provides the basis for later constructive work and, indeed, for the criticism of such work on descriptive grounds. Chapter 3 introduces the vast literature in "process theology," employing the faith/reason distinction which is implicit in the authorization argued for in Chapter 1. In these chapters (as in the others) there is considerable comment on the work of other writers. While much of that is reserved for the notes in order to present a reasonably clean argument in the text, it is important to realize that a very lively debate exists within (as well as about) the movement of process thought. Only then, in Chapters 4 and 5, do I attempt a personal appropriation of certain resources available in process thought. It is only a beginning, and I make bold in the last chapter to advise you, the reader(s), concerning the principles and practice of such dialog, which I hope you will continue.

This quest is not easy. But its difficulty is matched by its importance and, perhaps, by its promise. Each of us will judge about that, of course. In any case it is clear that the Christian can pursue this quest calmly. Not everything depends on it. Whitehead himself knew and quoted the assurance, *Non in dialectia complacuit Deo salvum facere populum suum* ("It was not by dialectic that it pleased God to save his people").[3] We do not have to do better than that. Our faith may be "in process" twice over, but the One whom we worship is not the process we call world or the struggle which is faith.

In the making of this book I am in debt to many. Institutions do act, and I have been helped by them. The governing boards of Luther Theological Seminary generously supported a year of sabbatical study, and the Association of Theological Schools and the Division for Theological Education of the American Lutheran Church added supplementary assistance. The faculty and administration of the School of Theology at Claremont graciously welcomed me into that community. At Claremont the considerable resources of the Center for Process Studies—directed by John B. Cobb, Jr. and David R. Griffin—were made freely available to me. Back in St. Paul, in turn, the administration of Luther Theological Seminary generously provided financial assistance for the technical preparation of the manuscript.

Along the way people have gone to some pains to help me. John Cobb, Lowell Erdahl, Terence Fretheim, Ron Marshall, Lee Snook, Donald Sponheim, and Curt Thompson have read and commented on all or part of the manuscript during its basic development. Philip Hefner and Jonathan Strandjord provided final detailed criticisms. The book is better because of the varied criticism of these colleagues, though each of them might seek other changes. Beyond the actual work of writing I think gratefully of the stimulation provided by faculty and student colleagues and of that wise and good man, Bernard Meland, who with characteristic sensitivity guided my first extended encounter with process thought.

I am grateful as well to Roland Seboldt of Augsburg Publishing House for his initiative and support and to Roderick Olson for his work as editor. Alma Roisum, with her mind and her typewriter, has created some order from the chaos I have given to her. Sylvia Ruud has helped me try to capture in diagrams the flight of concepts. Cordell Strug has provided a way (back) into the book with his competent indexing.

The one in whom so much in our home holds together will understand that I dedicate this distillation of thought, this concatenation of categories, to our three sons, in whom is life indeed.

# KEY TO WHITEHEAD REFERENCES

*AI*   *Adventures of Ideas,* original copyright, 1933, Macmillan; renewed, 1961; Free Press edition, 1967.

*FR*   *The Function of Reason,* original copyright, 1929, Princeton University Press; Beacon Press edition, 1958.

*MT*   *Modes of Thought,* original copyright, 1938, Macmillan; renewed, 1966; Free Press edition, 1968.

*PR*   *Process and Reality. An Essay in Cosmology,* original copyright, 1929, Macmillan; renewed, 1957; Harper edition, 1960. I regret that the corrected edition of *PR,* edited by David Ray Griffin and Donald W. Sherburne (Free Press, 1978) did not appear in time for use in this volume.

*RM*   *Religion in the Making,* original copyright, 1926, Macmillan; renewed, 1954; Meridian edition, 1960.

*SMW*   *Science and the Modern World,* original copyright, 1925, Macmillan; renewed, 1953; Free Press edition, 1967.

*S*   *Symbolism, Its Meaning and Effect,* Macmillan, 1927.

# Part I

# Authorization

# 1

# Prospect: The Case for Faith's Interest in Metaphysics: Finding the Categories

## Christian Triadic Selfhood

To be a Christian is to be in relationship—to oneself, to the world, and to God. Of these relationships something must be said before counsel is sought for the people of faith.

While the *relationship to God* is the distinguishing one for the Christian, it is no more real than the other two. Yet it may be natural that the Christian will speak first of this relationship, for it entails the focus of Christian identity. To be Christian, after all, is to be consciously related to something quite definite, a center of purpose and power. In this relationship the Christian knows God as other than the self.

Two other claims are made concerning this God: (1) This Other—this God—is most emphatically *Other*. "Wholly Other" may not be a happy phrasing, raising as it does quite proper objections as to how one comes to know a "Wholly Other" at all. But the intention behind such linguistic overkill is clear enough and essential to the Christian. God is different in kind from us, categorically superior; to know God is to know One who is radically Other.[1] (2) This Other—this God—wills to bless. The Christian knows the gospel. God may be different from us, but this Other is clearly for us. To know this Other is good news. There is mystery enough about how this God can love the self—the Christian may

19

even combat severe doubt as to whether there is in fact such a loving God—but the Christian is not in doubt that this is claimed by the gospel.[2] Worship unites these two themes. Though we may respect, love, obey, and serve human beings, worship is rightly reserved for one radically different from us—God. Christian worship is adoration, thanksgiving, and praise that such a God is for us.

With any word so distinct and so good as this word of the gospel of God, it is not strange that the Christian's talk may be first and perhaps even only of that word. But there is another reality of which we must speak. The Christian is, after all, in the *world*. The Christian is related to that which is neither self nor God. However much the Christian may tend to talk of all that is outside the self as a circle with a single divine center controlling everything, the model of an ellipse with its two foci serves better.[3] Statements can be accurately made concerning the Christian person's relationship to that which is not the self which neither derive from nor provide the focus of faith. The Christian is caught up in the self-world relationship. The Christian is characterized appropriately as temporal and spatial. The calendar and the globe do not come to us as centered in God. The Christian self knows itself as located in a world, in some network of natural and social relationships. Even if one may want to say that there is a religious—even a "Christian"—aspect to all of these matters, it is not as such that they first have to do with the Christian. Rather these have to do quite simply with the Christian's location in a world and as such link this person with a host of other beings with respect to whom the adjective "Christian" does not apply. Thus one might speak of two communities, the world community and the Christian community, and no Christian can do other than hold membership in both cities. To say that a Christian self is related to that which is not the self is to speak of relatedness to God and to world.

The Christian is also *self-related*. While in its intimacy this relationship may tend to escape description, it calls out for recognition. We have spoken of a self related to God and world but not simply reducible to either. That self is not a mysterious cipher, a *deus ex machina* called in to account for transactions at this particular intersection of God and world. The self is rather what Kierkegaard called a "positive third" and as such includes within itself the structure of relatedness.[4] The self is related to itself, and that relationship, like the relationships to God and world, may be described in terms of knowing and willing. The self knows itself and acts upon itself. Self-consciousness and self-discipline are not imaginary phantoms, however infrequently they may seem to manifest themselves.

Thus to be a Christian is to be in relationship—to oneself, to the world, and to God.

God and world differ in how they bear upon the Christian self. It seems that the self quite simply *is* in the world, like it or not. Not only does the world invade the self relentlessly, so that the self must somehow deal with its agenda, but the self's very sense of identity seems to require the contrast with the ever-changing given of the world. God, on the other hand, is known to the self in claims: God *ought* to be believed, worshiped, enjoyed, served. Yet these distinctions are only matters of emphasis in the self's relationships. God's claims upon the self are accompanied by the strong sense that God's reality (like the world's) does not depend on the self's response. And the world (like God) impinges on the self not merely with neutral raw material, but with quite definite proposals—indeed, with a number of candidates, each campaigning for the self's worshiping response.

The Christian's relationships to God, world, and self are interrelated. That is so both with respect to how they are perceived by the self and with respect to what is perceived. The self regularly experiences the relationship to God through the relationship to the world. At no point—faith, morality, even ecstasy—does the Christian lose either self or world.[5] Moreover, what the Christian perceives turns out to be precisely God at work in the world.

In some ways the world seems to be the most comprehensive of the three, so that statements which may in truth be made of the world apply as well to self and God in that world.[6] Yet the Christian's stubborn sense of distinction between self, world, and God is not destroyed by this inclusiveness. The relationship between the whole (the world) and the parts (God . . . self . . . other beings) is, after all, a real relationship which supports subordinate relationships and distinctions. For example, within that subordinate network, place must be found to recognize in "world" all the "other others" to whom the self is related directly or indirectly.

Plainly, then, the self's relationships to self, world, and God are inextricably interrelated. Thus even self-relatedness cannot be isolated from world-relatedness and God-relatedness. Without the world I simply am not I. In that world there is no place for me to escape the call of God. This persisting reality of interrelatedness raises the question of just how God, world, and self are "together." The self seeks and senses a coherence, a connectedness in its relationships. Further talk of that must wait until later.

These rather abstract descriptions of interrelationships may take on a livelier and more convincing tone when we realize that we are speaking of inter*action*. There is action between the terms of the triad. There is, for example, something for the Christian to *do*—perhaps most fundamentally to believe God, to trust God, to enjoy God, to worship God. But though one is never done with that, there are other tasks impinging on the other relationships of the self. The Christian relationship to God lays claim in some way on self-relatedness and world-relatedness. In part it is a matter of replicating and extending the God-relationship. The church is end and means, celebration, but also service. While the God-relationship will not seek to evacuate the other relationships of their own content, it does impinge on them. The remainder of the self and the rest of the world are to be reached for this God of the gospel. The Christian is called to heed a word like, "Whatever you do, in word or deed, do all in the name of the Lord Jesus." Somehow the God-relationship is to qualify the others—inform, direct, integrate, or in some other way penetrate them.[7]

Responsive to this missionary thrust in the God-relationship, the Christian asks, "What help may be expected from self and world for faith's tasks?" After all, perhaps these other relationships are not only targets but also resources for faith. Insofar as God's work in the world is to be our work, it will be done by selves and in the world. At the same time, as the Christian turns in faith to probe the self and world, questions may be generated from these regions regarding the validity of the heady focus of faith. The question of the "fit" between God, world, and self-relatedness seems to be common property.

My topic is more specific. What has philosophy to do with and/or for faith? What commerce appropriately connects Jerusalem and Athens? As for philosophy, I propose a still narrower focus: the core discipline of metaphysics. I have in mind no occult flight from earth, despite the tendency to thus misappropriate the term. I suppose instead that Alfred North Whitehead is right in suggesting that metaphysics "seeks to discover the general ideas which are indispensably relevant to the analysis of everything that happens" (*RM* 7). Philosophers as varied as Aristotle, Spinoza, Hegel, Bradley, Weiss, and Pepper support that suggestion.[8]

Now suppose, further, that a convincing metaphysical description is at hand. What can that do for faith? How would such an analysis be relevant to the understanding of self, world, and God for the Christian characterized by these relationships and interrelationships? This, I suggest, is the question which haunts those who are caught up in the work of process theology. Most fundamentally, Whitehead's thought is a metaphysical vision out of which come—naturally, if not by sheer deduction—comments about aesthetics, education, philosophy of religion, and other more particular matters. Of course, the metaphysical scheme claims to be generated from particulars and tested by particulars, as we shall see in Chapter 2. The scheme may be outrageously deficient in some areas where attention to insights deriving from a particular discipline could lead to much needed repair. This possibility needs to be remembered and pressed. But such qualifications do not question the logical priority and centrality of the metaphysical task. Indeed great caution must be exercised in making ad hoc theological applications from specific discipline areas—whether Whiteheadian or otherwise—unless the underlying integrating vision of reality has been examined.[9] Despite the tendency to try for shortcuts, the meaning and worth of process theology depend largely on the significance of process metaphysics for faith.

The Christian's prospecting in the somewhat forbidding land of metaphysics, then, offers some promise. To understand self and world will matter to the Christian. We have already spoken of faith's designs with respect to these relationships. Faith hears a call to act toward self and world, and insight can advance action. But the Christian finds a more intrinsic authorization as well. This is true in two senses: (1) In analyzing self and world the Christian learns of the God-relationship since that is a relationship of the self through the world. (2) In the focus of faith itself—it is God of whom we speak—reality is claimed. Faith commits suicide, if it assesses itself as a "useful fiction." [10] Religious experience, religious tradition, faith—these are all aspects of a God-relationship, and as such claim to refer to one who is other than the self. The God known is claimed to be real prior to our experience, apart from our knowledge. If we cry in faith, "Let God be God!" to affirm independence of divine action, we should not deny that God exists before we come to know him through such action. This God who works in the real, who is known in the real, is himself real. So surely does faith ask about the metaphysical prospects quite for its own sake. The quest to understand the universal structure of reality is intrinsically important to a faith which claims a real relationship to a real God. This is not to promise success; for example, no convincing metaphysical analysis may be at hand. But the logic of faith welcomes the metaphysical effort.

Or is it possible that God's reality known to faith, and the reality of self and world known to metaphysics, are somehow two realms so utterly different that no connections occur? Might metaphysics matter for self and world relatedness, but be ruled inapplicable for God-relatedness? If the interconnections of the self's relationships did not cry "foul" at such a suggestion, the individual relationships severally would. In our relationship to the world we do precisely seek a "world," as Paul Weiss reminds us:

> Before, while, and after we specialize, we have and must have a grasp of the whole, vague, blurred, and even incoherent though this may be. To ignore that whole is to ignore our roots, to misunderstand our aims, to lose our basic tests. . . . Whether we wish it or not, we must, we do think cosmically.[11]

A metaphysics of the whole—with one part in principle excluded—will simply not do. In our relationship to God, moreover, we reject the suggestion that there is any reality so alien as to expel God altogether. One may put it this way:

> The Reformation said that the finite *is* capable of the infinite, that God is really here and he is here in such a way that the integrity of the world has not been abandoned or changed. Man should not fear the world in itself.[12]

The self related to God and to world is also related to itself. That self-related self is not some secret inner self sprung free from world and God. Must there not be some objective unity corresponding to the self's identity and continuity in the three relationships? If any principles, any categories, might prove relevant to understanding the self's relationships to God, world, and self alike—would they not be those we have called metaphysical?

What, then, can metaphysics—process or any at all—do for faith? The answer is best given in the doing, of course, but we seek to be clear about expectations at the outset. In fact, four prospects emerge:

1. A metaphysics of means for Christian ends: tactical wisdom.
2. A metaphysics of meaning for Christian claims: conceptual wisdom.
3. A metaphysics of meeting for Christian service: ethical wisdom.
4. A metaphysics of matter for Christian content: constitutive wisdom.

## Tactical Wisdom: A Metaphysics of Means for Christian Ends

Perhaps the least ambitious estimate of the contribution metaphysics can render to faith holds that some service is to be garnered as the Christian searches for means to achieve ends clearly in faith's view. (See Figure A, p. 26.) No metaphysical claim to identify these ends need be allowed here; the wisdom may be held to be merely tactical. But to reach even this limited claim four steps are required:

1. The Christian is called to be effective.
2. The Christian is called to be effective as a Christian in this world, that is, in the self-world relationship.
3. The Christian's intent to be effective in this world does not automatically secure that result. Some attention to means is in order.
4. An accurate analysis of the shape of reality will assist in the selection of means.

The first step in the argument seems nearly self-evident, but is in fact often resisted in the rhetoric of religion. That resistance seems to reflect a logic which threatens the human pole in the relationship to God. At least it seems difficult to speak meaningfully of a "relationship" between God and humankind if there is nothing for the human to do in any

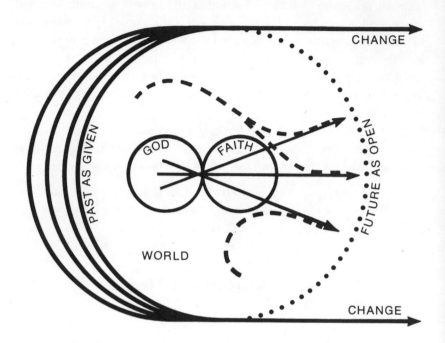

Faith receives motivation and ends from God (⟷)

Faith recruits means (- - - _ _ ⁄) in the world where service transpires

Means do not alter ends, but serve them (⟶)

**Figure A.  TACTICAL WISDOM:  Faith would serve God in the world. Metaphysics as servant.**

sense.[13] With the call to do comes the call to be effective. I shall argue later that the tendency to resist this call seems to reflect a misguided logic of disjunction which supposes that to attribute anything to the human role is to rob the divine—as if God's glory depended on our depravity— even our nothingness! In the discussion to follow I shall stress the impor- tance of affirming both independent *and* interdependent action on God's part with the result that human effort in principle poses no threat to God, since it is irrelevant in the first case and required (sought) in the second. Thus biblical scholars identify both a covenant of divine commitment and a covenant of human obligation.[14] But more of that later.

One might seek to grant the call for effectiveness and deny the "this-worldly" location of that effectiveness, thus challenging the second step in the argument for tactical wisdom. If this objection is not to be reduced to the aforementioned denial of the human, it is best put as the claim that the Christian is indeed called to act—but precisely and only *toward God*, i.e., in the self-God relationship. Kierkegaard may seem to be making this point at times in his rather isolating emphasis on the individual "before God" and in his insistence that the "opposite of sin is not virtue but faith."[15] Or Barth may suggest this theme in his tendency to reduce ethics to dogmatics.[16] Perhaps this objection is even more clearly at work in the common saying, "We are not called to be successful, but faithful."

Again, one suspects a logic of disjunction is at work in this objection so that success, efficacy in the world, is seen as tantamount to infidelity, lest God be robbed. Shall one, then, consider failure equivalent to faithfulness? If not, what human means may serve faith's desire to be faithful? What may the self bring from its store—if not from the "world"—to the self-God relationship? More important, this objection seems to run counter to the deep connection between faith and mission, as that pervades the biblical witness and Christian experience. Finally, it may be doubted that anyone quite manages to live this objection. Perhaps the Christian call to mission and the human inclination to efficacy combine to call the self back from its rhetoric.

Effectiveness does not follow from intention inexorably, as if fact were wedded to wish. One wonders why. For reasons I intend later to examine metaphysically, humankind seems particularly capable of confusion and prone to illusion. We can array ourselves against the flow of reality, perhaps not finally thwarting the shape of things to come, but surely significantly diminishing the positive influence of our intentions. While I have no desire to offer a self-mutilating sacrifice, it may be appropriate and accurate quietly to observe that in the church the presence of ineffectiveness, of stupidity, does not seem to fall below humanity's statistical norm. Even when the misguided piety that espouses failure is not at work, we in the church often seem singularly inept. I am not inclined to suppose that we lack a message of genuine power, but that we have failed to recruit means to release that power effectively.

Metaphysical reason can make a contribution to that process of recruitment, or at least that is the contention in the fourth step of our argument concerning tactical wisdom. Without singling out reason for exclusive commendation, we may join with Christians like Martin Luther, whose realism included not only a critique of reason's constructive pretensions theologically, but also an affirmation of reason's analytic competence instrumentally.[17] Nor is the service of God to be denied such instruments, unless we suppose, for example, that the translation of the Scriptures is a task for unlearned visionaries. In an ascending scale of likely importance, reason may be said to be useful to faith in "getting to know the enemy," getting to know the terrain held in common, and hence in the provision of means for reaching those folks on that land.

Metaphysical reason, more specifically, will make a contribution as it tells the Christian how the land lies in its most basic configurations. The root character of the discipline can be particularly helpful in aiding the work of demystification or debunking. Reality may get through to us the more readily if the topic under discussion is not the alleged all-mysterious acts of God or of some transcendental human super-ego, but the quite elemental meaning of any action at all. Distinctions can be made, nuances noticed, within that general frame of reference. Indirectly, metaphysics may make tactical contributions to faith, as it facilitates concrete contacts with other disciplines, serving as a bridge for that commerce while checking the other fields for their underlying presuppositions regarding the shape of reality.

All seems to go swimmingly in a metaphysics of means for Christian ends. Still, it is too neat somehow. Are ends one kind of thing and means another? Is there any commerce between the two? Any reciprocal commerce? Perhaps it is unrest of this sort that is beneath the familiar query, "Can the ends justify the means?" On the view developed so far, we seem required to reply, "Yes." But beneath the persistence of the question may lie a sense that the ends seem too remote from the means. Something more decisive needs to be at work in the means themselves. Without that we begin to wonder if we really have the ends in view in any effective way. We seem to seek some kind of intermediary between ends and means, some structure of connection which could carry a more intimate communion between what is Christian and what is human.

## Conceptual Wisdom: A Metaphysics of Meaning for Christian Claims

In the last lines we may have been calling for attention to a view of how things are, such that a framework could be found in which ends are applicable in the here and now and means can muster such connectedness as to be directed to an intended future in an other than arbitrary sense. Christianity intends such a framework and calls for such a view.

We have already emphasized the essential claim that faith places on reality.[18] Within that claim lies the insistence that there is cognitive content to faith. That content, the *fides quae creditur,* must not be eliminated from the act of faith, the *fides qua creditur.* The "how" of faith requires a "what." Even a Christian as concerned with subjective integrity as Søren Kierkegaard saw this:

> The Christian possible exists before any Christian exists, it must exist in order that one can become a Christian, it contains the determination by means of which it may be tested whether one has become a Christian. It retains its objective existence apart from all believers, while it is at the same time present in the inwardness of the believer. In short, here there is no identity between the subjective and the objective. Though Christianity comes into the heart of ever so many believers, every believer is conscious that it has not arisen in his heart.[19]

This Christian claim to cognitive truth turns out to be a matter of multiple claims. At the very least it is implied that these truths do not cancel each other out. There is some order, some coherence, then, in the claims of faith. That order may serve the making of a point that is materially paradoxical, but it is the order that rescues the paradox from the nonsensical.[20] The order need not be supposed to be mechanistic, yielding a method of simple deduction. In the faith we speak of freedom, persons and wills, divine and human. But the underlying descriptive order aims at something more than "atomistic" order. A stream of consciousness sort of truth will not suffice. The gospel truth is not just one thing after another. The human quest for coherence so pleads, and the Christian faith responds with its insistence that there is one God of Old and New Testaments, of creation and redemption. This God makes and keeps covenant. Perhaps for the time being we can identify such an intermediate degree of order as "organic." Within this order there are multiple interacting centers of organization defying prediction but yielding extended subordinate connection within fields of relationship.[21]

Joseph F. Wall illustrates the "blessed rage for order" which seems to be so internal to faith by asking the question, "Which of the following seems the worst conceivable state of affairs?"

1. There is no God.
2. There is a God, but this God is evil.
3. There is a God, but this God is an idiot.

That the third is the worst is suggested by Robert Sherwood's Irene, who says of God:

> Poor, lonely soul. Sitting up in heaven, with nothing to do but play solitaire. Poor, dear God. Playing Idiot's Delight. The Game that never means anything and never ends.[22]

The third may be rivaled by the second for some of us. Still, one must ascribe purpose to God, find order in God, before one can speak of a good or evil aim or bearing of the divine. Logically, at least, the issue of order seems the prior one. In any case, the God of whom Christians speak is no idiot.

This concern for order seems to be met by the content of revelation. The Scriptures do not speak of a lonely soul playing solitaire. Therefore, is seems idle to conduct formal skirmishes on the logically prior question of whether we know God at all. Yet the tendency to deny knowledge of God persists in religious circles. How shall one respond to this tendency? It helps little to score debating points by asking how one may know one cannot know God. It is better to read the entire Johannine declaration: "No one has ever seen God; *the only Son who is in the bosom of the Father, he has made him known.*"[23] This God seeks no sacrifice of intellect in holy ignorance; he comes to be known. One may insist ever so emphatically that the knowing is a matter of divine disclosure, not human discovery. But now that the revelation is here, what does it *mean?*

The meaning of Christian claims is most effectively expressed in terms of a view of reality which convincingly accommodates our being-in-the-world. After all, the claims are addressed to a self, who knows itself as one in relationship to God, world, and self. What difference does immortality of the soul make if I am just a body? How does forgiveness help, if choice—and so responsibility and guilt—are unreal? Utterances about the self-God relationship cannot "count" fully if they cannot "mean" in relationship to the self-world relationship.[24] Thus Christian claims invite the identification of some framework, some referential scheme of meaning in which they may be significantly heard. The faith seeks conceptual wisdom (see Figure B, p. 32).

Ian Barbour seems to be addressing this need when he calls for attention to the "models" embodied in myths:

> Models, like metaphors, symbols and parables, are analogical and open-ended. Metaphors, however, are used only momentarily, and symbols and parables have only a limited scope, whereas models are systematically developed and pervade a religious tradition. A model represents the enduring structural components which myths dramatize in narrative form. One model may be common to many myths.[25]

David Tracy shares Barbour's interest in models, but emphasizes that in faith we are not dealing with "picture models" but rather with "disclosure models":

> Technically, disclosure models do not provide an exact description of particular historical phenomena. They do provide intelligible, interlocking sets of basic terms and relations that aid us to understand the point of view expressed in particular historical positions.[26]

I do not suggest that the Christian claim must supinely submit to the tyranny of some regnant world view. Faith claims reality; it will not fail to state its case. But it *will* fail to state its case unless it reaches the human in some comprehensive view of how things are. If it does not play its normative role within some descriptive context, a rival view will rush in to occupy a house swept so clean.[27]

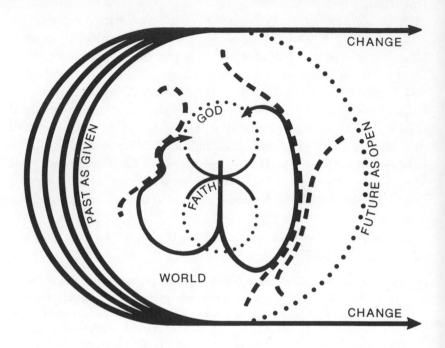

Faith knows God and seeks understanding in a framework
(– – – – – – –) provided by the world (where Faith and God are
to be found).

What Faith comes to say of God in the world does amplify and
order Faith's knowledge (new points for re-entry ··），
while preserving and serving its basic claims.

**Figure B.   CONCEPTUAL WISDOM:** Faith would understand
God in the world. Metaphysics as servant.

This quest for a descriptive framework for faith's claim suggests that:
(1) The Christian faith cannot make even its meaning fully clear,
much less make its case cogently, if it is strictly dependent on an eschatological point of reference such that at every crucial point we are left with
an appeal to the free action of a radically other God in the future. Such

an appeal must at least be based on a view of reality, for which such an "end" is a conceivable and perhaps even a winsome outcome.[28] Otherwise, who really needs the gift which that future holds? Happily, the Christian faith claims that we know more than the need for God.

(2) Nor can Christian claims make their case effectively if they are shunted off to the preserve of a particular language game. Rather they seek to intersect with what is known about the world which God and self have in common.

In this matter of framework or model the Christian cohabits with human insight which is not specifically Christian. Historical examples abound. The rich variety of the biblical witness often reflects differences of framework. Thus Paul may have stressed "even death on a cross" in the Christ hymn of Philippians 2 in order to rebuff the tendency to swallow up Christ's humanity in the mythical. On the other hand, the absence of a true passion narrative in Q may reflect a sapiential tradition in perfectly good standing in making its message the sayings of Jesus.[29]

Christians who stress the decisiveness of divine action still employ some human framework in stating the faith. That is well illustrated by Heiko Oberman's characterization of Luther's relationship to nominalism. While not deriving his faith from nominalism, Luther does drink deeply of the nominalistic liberation of secular experience from heteronomous authority and tradition. The link with Luther leaps out at the reader of Oberman's comment on nominalism:

> Contentwise we find characteristics of nominalism in an epistemology engendered by the new logic which relates experience and experiment in such a way that the individual—be it an inanimate object, a human being or an event—is understood in its own context as potentially new, original and unique before it is identified by classification into species. This epistemological stance, which one may well characterize as born out of hunger for reality, is part of a more embracing revolt against the metaphysical world of heteronomous authority and canonized speculation obfuscating, overlaying and distorting reality.[30]

Of historical examples, enough! But a point must be made about our current historical situation: from nearly every side Christian thinkers agree that today the meaning of Christian faith stands in particularly desperate need of a coherent and convincing framework of intelligibility.

Kent S. Knutson speaks of our time as one when "the fruit of Copernicus and Darwin has ripened on the tree." Of "modern man" he writes:

> . . . he affirms the temporal character of his existence and finds the other-worldly meaningless. Knowledge is understood to be that which is gained by human endeavor and is based on the exercise of man's rational faculties and his power of observation alone. Theology has doubtful credentials and belongs to the realm of the emotional, the poetical, and the illusory.[31]

This modern inquirer asks how truth is to be known:

> And the traditional answer which has been given in Western civilization—God—brings another question. What do you mean by that? Tell us, What does the word God mean? [32]

Some might claim that these statements emphasize the optimism of modernity in the current situation, ignoring the more significant emergence of post-modern realism.[33] Thus in his Nobel acceptance speech in December, 1976, Saul Bellow criticized his fellow intellectuals for poorly representing humankind. The Nobel laureate in literature challenged the optimism of fellow American William Faulkner's 1949 Nobel lecture in which he asserted that man would prevail. According to Bellow the human condition today is one where

> we stand open to all anxieties. The decline and fall of everything is our daily bread, we are agitated in private life and tormented by public questions.[34]

Our present pluralism may be such as to accommodate the presence of both the modern and the post-modern. If the post-modern were dominant, that would hardly help. An empty tomb of nihilism does not a resurrection make for Christian meaning-in-context.

The erosion of traditional schemes of reference is widely recognized. As one who has been greatly influenced by continental neo-orthodoxy Heinrich Ott might be expected to possess some immunity to the relativistic virus we are examining. Ott seems not in doubt about his commitment to Christian truth, but he most candidly laments the loss of framework for that truth:

In the sense that theological thinking orients itself toward that upon which it can lean, the salvation-historical thought category today no longer provides a reliable platform. I say "thought-category" quite consciously. It is not a matter here of the content of faith, but of the function of a category which was attributed to this content for a long time, of its function as a thought structure inside of which thought could go on. . . . This whole traditional procedure of theological reflection has become unbelievable today. The time of such a "Biblicistic dogmatics" is past. . . . What has become unbelievable is not the recitation of the content of faith (or as one says, the "saving facts"), as for example, of the cross and the resurrection of Jesus Christ, but only that such matters are discussed within the salvation-historical scheme. As if this framework still stood firm as the self-evident ontological or pre-ontological horizon within which every person moves and orients himself existentially! [35]

Nor has Roman Catholicism escaped. Andrew Greeley calls for a "new agenda," noting that "the old question was, Can you prove the existence of God? The new question is, Can you tell me who your God is?" [36]

Charles Glock places the matter of framework erosion in the context of the emergence of the counter culture:

The intervening variable, I shall here argue, is a cognitive one having to do with the way the world is apprehended and with whether or not and in what way that apprehension shapes and gives meaning to existence. [37]

He finds the counter culture to be grounded in "a new cognition" which challenged both the supernatural and the individualistic framework of traditional American religion:

The new cognition has its inspiration from science, including the social sciences. The sciences do not contribute a fully articulated world view, but one which, even in its unfolding state, comes in conflict with supernatural and individualistic modes of consciousness. The sciences, and here I refer especially to the social sciences, effectively deny that human destiny is entirely either in man's or in God's control. The possibility that both may be control agents is not closed out; but that they function as either of the old imageries would have it is not accepted. Insofar as they exert an influence, the sciences tell us, they do so in interaction with other forces—biological, psychological, sociological, anthropological, genetical—all of which have some influence in shaping human and social events.[38]

Both Greeley and Glock might still be interpreted as finding the problem of framework a matter of communicating what we Christians clearly understand to those who, regrettably, are outside the household of faith. But David Tracy appropriately drives the problem all the way home:

> My own suspicion is that those theologians who tell us that the problem is to render Christianity relevant to our contemporaries have profoundly missed the full dimensions of the present dilemma. For we are now our contemporaries, and our task is really to make our Christian self-understanding meaningful in our own life-styles and our own reflection.[39]

We are our own contemporaries; we are the outsiders! It is we who are threatened with a self sundered by a self-God relationship flying apart from a self-world relationship.

The problem is ours, then, and it is pervasive. One must, of course, be suspicious of attempts to universalize the intellectual's private trauma. Perhaps, after all, the anxious neighbor next door is seeking not being-itself, but another beer. But in this instance it seems more likely that the intellectual is simply articulating the underlying mood and mentality of the many. A frantic escape to a return to a religion advertising undialectical certitude does not manifest satisfying strength at the core, as much as it measures the degree of desperation in our time.[40]

I do not make bold here to address this problem; perhaps not even to identify it in detail. Our present task is to find the categories, not to fill them. For example, the basic issue of divine causality in our world (yes, precisely, "ours") will require analysis of causality as such before one can address faith's claims about divine action. I merely point here to the problem of the erosion or collapse of framework in order to ask programmatically, What help might reason give? What could count as conceptual wisdom? (1) We have already spoken of how reason might have a role in the matter of determining the inner coherence of the claims of faith. (2) In a somewhat more advanced, but still formal, role reason might serve as a kind of grammar, aiding in translation efforts as the theological practitioner, equipped with a developed capacity to recognize the formal features, the decisive notions, in a tradition, seeks "to discriminate among those many inevitable efforts to retell the story."[41]

But these roles seem both too restricted and too formal. The problem as identified by the aforementioned Christian spokespersons seems to require something more.[42] Something more material and more fundamental is needed. A metaphysical response holds promise of such help. (3) Metaphysics could make so fundamental (albeit formal) a contribution as to specify the conditions for any meaning at all.[43] (4) For material aid, metaphysics could provide the bridge of a general view of reality over which one could repair to other specific disciplines. (5) But the material and the fundamental only come together as we attend directly to a view of how things are, a view of reality.

It is not helpful to try shortcuts by frantic appeals to specific disciplines, all the while begging the question of the view of reality sustaining such presumed insights. It is essentially vacuous to conduct formal literary-critical end runs around the issue of framework collapse. What is the shape of things? How do things stand, or flow? What of self and other, mind and body? What world is there, for God or for me? The cry for a framework, for a model, may be more than a cry for metaphysical location since greater specificity is needed, but it cannot be less than that. In such location the formal concern for intelligibility and the material concern for plausibility come together.

Before one begins to try to find or make a framework, some preliminary remarks about method are in order. Contemporary self-understanding bears on method as much as on content. The method to be used in this effort will have to pass muster with that "morality of knowledge" which entails "a fidelity to open-ended inquiry, a loyalty to defended methodological canons, a willingness to follow the evidence wherever it may lead" including holding open the possibility that the faith claim itself will be placed in jeopardy.[44] But, on the other hand, the Christian engaged in this work cannot accept the all-too-mutually-convenient modern arrangement by which theology came to occupy what Richard Neuhaus calls the "sandbox of subjectivity":

> The dubious achievement of much modern theology—ranging in great variety from Barth to Bultmann—has been to legitimate the sandbox of

subjectivity. Such theology cannot be interfered with by reason's game, nor need it contribute to it. The fence must now be torn down.[45]

Obviously it will not do to have the theologian tear down the fence only to find the metaphysician constructing just such a barrier around this announced ally. Is metaphysics something more (other) than speculative exercise for solitary thinkers? Here perhaps help may be had for the metaphysician from the field of science. Writers such as Thomas Kuhn and Michael Polanyi have emphasized the subjective aspects of science.[46] But in disabusing the naive within and without the field of science of any supposed total objectivity, such writers seem to swing toward still another sandbox.

In a helpful response, Ian Barbour notes that while all data are theory-laden, rival theories are not incommensurable as if walled off from any assessment of competing claims. While comprehensive theories are highly resistant to falsification and criteria for falsification cannot be specified in advance in science, observation does exert considerable control over theory construction and maintenance. While there are no rules for choice between research programs, there are independent criteria of assessment— "simplicity, coherence, and the extent and variety of supporting experimental evidence (including precise predictions and the anticipation of the discovery of novel types of phenomena)." [47] While one cannot move uncritically from science to metaphysics, the direction of Barbour's response points the way for metaphysical construction as well.[48]

Another form of the subjectivity trap may be discerned in the historicist contention that metaphysics is merely a reflection of a particular cultural reality. At this point the response must face two ways. On the one hand, a metaphysical analysis is offered, admittedly from within an historically relative location, as a general vision which can guide us in understanding the past (including past metaphysical visions; accounting for them) and in anticipating the future. As such, metaphysics seems as crucial as it is difficult in a time of transition between more specific frameworks.[49] On the other hand, the presence of emphatically contemporary elements in a metaphysical sketch need draw no apologies from a Christian committed to the historical character of Christianity. Robert

Wilken has effectively argued that Christianity's commitment to history is not itself an unhistorical one:

> The Christian realizes that his history goes back to the time of the apostles, but he also knows that the Christian hope did not come to fulfillment in the age of the apostles; nor did it reach perfection at the time of Constantine, nor in the Holy Roman Empire of the Middle Ages, nor in the 16th century reformation, nor in the social gospel of the late nineteenth century, nor in the revivals of the American frontier, nor in the movements of renewal in our own day.[50]

Of course one may move to free the Christian commitment to history from imprisonment in the past so emphatically that other difficulties develop. But without denying the apostolic period special significance historically and without denying all historical periods importance by reference to a future created out of nothing, one may well insist that Christian truth claims rooted in the past and aimed at the future still must make sense to us today. To say such is not to confess that we are time-bound, but to claim that we are time-blessed; for the Christian is confident that the God who works now can speak now.

With these several methodological cautions at hand the quest for conceptual wisdom can begin, recognizing that specific metaphysical criteria still need to be identified and applied in connection with the actual task at hand. In the quest for conceptual wisdom as outlined here it is apparent that some assured Christian content is seeking form, however fundamental and material that need for form, for framework, may be.[51] Similarly the tactical wisdom regarding means sought in the previous section assumed that faith provides the Christian with the ends to be championed. In both instances faith has a content intact, whether that be mission or message. Faith seeks assistance along the way in acting and thinking effectively. Thus metaphysics can well be said to be the servant of faith in these instances. To speak so is not to demean the role of metaphysics; a servant does render service. But is it possible that the Christian may in some way put the question of content itself to the context? Could the philosopher become, as it were, colleague in a common work? We proceed to consider two forms—again bearing on acting and thinking—in which such help for the faithful may be available.

## *Ethical Wisdom:* A Metaphysics of Meeting for Christian Service

The Christian faith resists any tendency to cut the world free from its creator God. It is not merely that the Christian must live both before God and in the world. According to faith God himself continues to work in the universe. To say this is not to deny a cosmic effect to sin. But to deny God's continuing work can itself be an anthropocentric—a sinful— act, as Gustaf Wingren notes:

> To be surrounded by conditions and relations which have no connec-
> tion with the relationship to God, and to conceive of this relationship
> as being non-existent among those who are born, live, eat, beget chil-
> dren, and work, but who have not heard nor receive the historically
> given word concerning Christ, is in itself a tremendous declaration of
> independence of God and of fellowship with Him, and this declaration
> cannot be modified or balanced by statements affirming Christ's lordship.
> Creation does not mean that a knowledge of God is given, but that life
> is bestowed.[52]

God bestows life. The bestowal of life need not be supposed to be an utterly unstructured affair. If that structure can be discerned, per-haps I can come to know how I should order my own little theater of life. Perhaps God's purpose can be discerned in the structure. In any case the Christian wishes to learn of God from life for life. How do matters go? What do they suggest? What seem to be God's activities and purposes in the ongoing bestowal of life? We seek ethical wisdom.

For two reasons metaphysics may be particularly helpful in "reading" the work of God in the world: (1) God is not merely the creator of humankind, nor may it be supposed that his purposes are exhausted in that relationship. A metaphysics universal in intention (again, "the gen-eral ideas which are indispensably relevant to the analysis of everything that happens") has the scope and scale fitting the task.

(2) It may be that the effect of sin and the taint of subjectivity are par-ticularly prominent in the region of humankind. If we ask what God is about in creation, we have accordingly the greater reason not to limit our quest to the human realm. For a second reason, then, the range of meta-physical inquiry promises to be helpful. Wingren makes this second point with particular force:

FAITH'S INTEREST IN METAPHYSICS

> Creation itself is "purer" than man. Sin does not exist on the face of the earth, but in the heart of man. . . . Sin is "from within" (Mark 7:14-23). . . . It is therefore man who lacks purity. The Creation around man is purer than he is and constitutes no problem in the world which was made by God. What does constitute a problem is man, who lays hold on the things of creation and corrupts their proper functions by greed, theft, envy, and lust. . . . For this reason man discovers in Creation a greater purity and wholeness than exists in himself.[53]

Of course Wingren's point will be challenged, if it is argued that sinful intention is present farther down the evolutionary scale. His point may be qualified, if one holds that only the effect and not the intention of sin is needed to secure distortion. Still his appeal continues to carry weight, particularly if linked with a metaphysics which begins emphatically "from below," starting with energy events not as easily twisted by human purpose.

The Christian asks of life to learn of God—to do. We seek ethical wisdom. (See Figure C, p. 42.) It is not merely that the Christian hears God's call in the neighbor.[54] As we come to our world, we come to a world in which we believe God to be at work. We join with God to work in that world. Christians have realized that they are to work with others through whom God works, though they know him not. Believing God's will for the world to be one, we may study his creative activity in order to cooperate the more consciously and effectively. Kent S. Knutson strikes this note in writing of the meaning of the personhood which cannot be limited to Christians, but from which Christians can learn:

> Personal power is the name for that creative potential power God has given every man—the power of reason, the power of creative imagination, the power of reproduction, the power of organization, the power to analyze and criticize, the power to make decisions. Every family on earth, says Paul, is related to God's name and that means related to his power. Therefore we respect every other man and find ourselves responsible to cooperate with all other men, learn from all other men, because God has given the power of creaturehood to every man.[55]

Among other things, this suggests a lively interest in the "civil religion" of a land. Any tendency toward self-centeredness in that religion can be corrected not only by an appeal—for Christians—to a specific theological

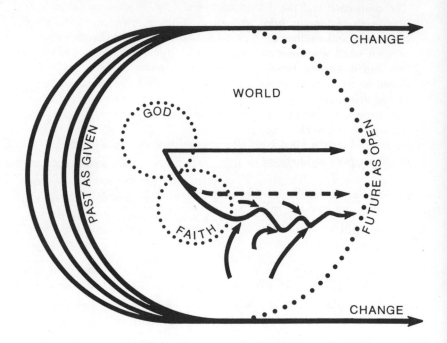

Faith holds that God is at work in the world (———▶).

Faith hears a call to join (follow) God in that worldly work
( ∿∿▶ ).

Faith studies the world to try to discern the work of God
( ⤳⤳ ), while keeping an ear cocked to hear whatever it
may be directly called to do (----▶).

**Figure C.  ETHICAL WISDOM:**  Faith would join God's work in
the world. Metaphysics as colleague.

tradition, but—for all persons—by relating the inevitable and narrowing
cultural cast of a particular civil religion to what God seems to be about
as suggested by the more universal scope of a metaphysical sketch.[56]

Some Christian thinkers have wanted to distinguish this cooperative
service in the world from a more distinctive Christian ethics. Yet the
distinction remains a relationship. So Wingren writes:

The connection and the distinction between natural law and the commandment of Jesus is from one point of view a reflection of another connection and another distinction. . . . Redemption gives more than creation when it restores creation. We are dealing here with a connection and distinction between natural and Christian, and both are reflected on the level of law or commandment. . . . This is what is meant by the accentuation, newness, and heightening of the law. The Christian attitude is that of a natural love for the neighbor which is thoroughly "of this world" and conveyed in the rough forms of men's daily vocations, but it is filled with a new willingness to *suffer* for the good of the neighbor and to do so with *joy*.[57]

Some such distinction and connection do seem right. One may not hear the call to suffer and die in attending to creation, though that realm has more than a little to say about both suffering and death. Still, one wonders whether the distinction is not too neat, too clear-cut. Gerhard von Rad points out the warning contained in the wisdom literature against too simple a distinction at this point:

The modern exegete is always tempted to read into the old texts the tensions with which he is all too familiar between faith and thought, between reason and revelation. . . . Against this, it can be categorically stated that for Israel there was only one world of experience and that this was apperceived by means of a perceptive apparatus in which rational perceptions and religious perceptions were not differentiated. Nor was this any different in the case of the prophets. . . . The experiences of the world were for her [Israel] always divine experiences as well and the experiences of God were for her experiences of the world.[58]

At the very least metaphysical analysis can bid to illumine the setting for Christian ethical action, as that pertains to such matters as the nature of agency, intention, responsibility, and the like. Whether a contribution to the identification of a specifically Christian ethic can be expected is not as clear. There all the subtleties of "how to derive ought from is" lie in wait.[59] If reality is characterized by multiple causality, and if non-divine causes can and do resist the divine intention, metaphysical specification of material ethical purpose will clearly be in jeopardy. But the formal contribution is not thereby rendered vacuous. The formal would only be imperiled, if God's continuing activity in creation were judged to be metaphysically insignificant. Moreover, if faith can accept the suggestion that

God has a distinctive metaphysical role, specific ethical candidates can be considered. Faith tells the believer to study the world to see what God may be doing. To learn of that is surely to come some distance toward knowing what we should be making with our lives. Attending to the unity of God, recognizing that "nature is less fallen than man," and believing that God's will for himself in the world is such as to give us bearings as well, we will begin such probing prepared to resist any tendency to undervalue the contributions. Once again, the task itself lies ahead.

These musings seem to represent a more advanced state of relationship with respect to Christian action than do the remarks introduced under tactical wisdom. The bearing of metaphysics on the Christian concern to act seems considerably more internal and potentially more significant. Metaphysics meets faith as colleague. One wonders if there may be a parallel advance in the area of Christian thought in comparison to the earlier quest for conceptual wisdom.

## Constitutive Wisdom: A Metaphysics of Matter for Christian Content

David Tracy proposes the following distinctions:

> A particular experience or language is "meaningful" when it discloses an authentic dimension of our experience as selves. It has "meaning" when its cognitive claims can be expressed conceptually with internal coherence. It is "true" when transcendental or metaphysical analysis shows its "adequacy to experience" by explicating how a particular concept (e.g., time, space, self or God) functions as a fundamental "belief" or "condition of possibility" of all our experience.[60]

In seeking conceptual wisdom or a framework the Christian is dealing with what Tracy calls issues of "meaning" and "meaningfulness." Now we ask, "What can metaphysics tell us of God?" The flow is primarily the reverse of that earlier indicated. We ask what "truths" or, if Tracy's definition is pressed in its most aggressive sense, what reasonable inferences about God can be generated by a convincing metaphysical analysis.

The flow need not be supposed to be altogether different in the two cases. We have seen that already in the quest for conceptual wisdom the Christian appropriates models which very materially fill out the intentions of faith. So, too, in this case it is not supposed that the Christian must recant in order to probe the metaphysical analysis for truth regarding God. But in the case now before us we are dealing with assertions whose conceptual justification and logical validity are generated metaphysically, even though faith may join reason in authorizing the agenda to be pursued. Moreover, the contribution has to do with the very content of faith itself. Such gifts could surely be said to be constitutive wisdom. (See Figure D, p. 46.)

What in principle may the Christian expect to gain from such inquiry? Or what may the Christian expect lies there to be gained in such inquiry for or even by the non-Christian? Let us begin with the first question. The Christian claims that God works in the world. If metaphysics is in fact able to turn up "general ideas which are indispensably relevant to the analysis of everything that happens," the fit is at hand as well for thinking about the worldly and real happening confessed as God's work. This is much the same kind of point made earlier concerning the quest for ethical wisdom, with the difference coming in probing the material for insight regarding the nature of God rather than Christian mission in the world. But in any case an available set of metaphysical principles could be applied usefully to any claim of divine action, quite possibly illumining aspects of that action not previously noted.[61]

It is even conceivable that metaphysics with its commitment to attend to reality may steward Christian experience and testimony. If faith is not free from the danger of letting its truth slip away, it may well hear its message spoken by a stranger in the camp. This would be the more likely if among faith's words is one which speaks of something which is true for all, bears on all, i.e., is "indispensably relevant to the analysis of everything that happens." While the original cognition and the fresh recognition would be matters of faith, metaphysics might well provide the intermediate momentum under its own initiative.

It may be observed somewhat parenthetically that no claim is being made here regarding divine action which is not "in this world." While our minds strain somewhat, it is not irrational to talk of God "before" this world, and perhaps even "after" or "beyond." Such talk would only be irrational if the idea of a limited world could be ruled out analytically as self-contradictory. That seems not to be the case. A metaphysics of this

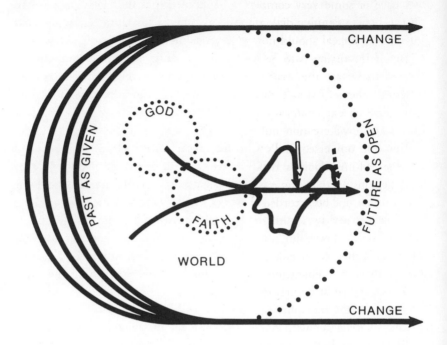

The project is launched jointly for Faith by God and world (>—).

The world may remind Faith of what it has forgotten (ᘔ⁄).

In the world Faith may recognize what it is seeking (⤵).

From the world Faith may receive a recommendation for what it seeks to say (⤴).

Figure D.   **CONSTITUTIVE WISDOM:**   Faith looks with and in the world to find God and understand God.

Metaphysics as colleague.

world, this universe, then, can give no direct guidance to one who would speak of matters beyond this range of reference. Such talk could not be based metaphysically, but would require an appeal to special experience or some very complex process of inference.[62] If we are seeking in this book a genuine dialog between faith and philosophy, the possibility of such an appeal should not be ruled out.

But if the dialog is to be genuine, such exceptional talk must be such as not to violate the structure of reality as analyzed within the metaphysical scheme. I should think this would mean, for example, that there would be no explanatory appeal to a God "before" this universe (as in the doctrine of creation out of nothing) to account for selected events within the universe. God's creation is not God and it is not nothing. Divine self-limitation is real limitation. This is not to deny that there may be considerable religious efficacy in such extrametaphysical reference, but it must not be accorded discriminating explanatory significance, else the fabric of reality is sundered. Furthermore, eschatological talk of God's action "after" this realm could not be granted inner temporal causal significance either. Such talk could presumably entail amplifying the metaphysical structure characterizing this realm, but such amplification would still respect that structure, just as the "realm beyond" receives the reality analyzed by the metaphysical sketch.[63] I shall return to these possibilities in the final chapter with reference to specific substantive suggestions.

We have spoken of how God's action in the world is metaphysically characterizable. As such, truth concerning that action might be held for faith in the earthen vessel of metaphysical reason. Is that action metaphysically discernible? Is it metaphysically distinctive, so that an adequate metaphysical analysis will in fact identify God's action? We need not require that the metaphysician name the name of God, but only that an adequate analysis identifies action which faith claims for God. We have seen that the Christian talks of God's continuing work as creator and extends that work to all that is real. This seems to be the best candidate in the grammar of faith for metaphysical identification. But the Christian who adopts a "traducianist" position, affirming that God works indirectly, through secondary causes, may be less optimistic.[64] If sin is present—perhaps even universally present—in such causation, the confidence wanes even more.

Still, the discernment of a general pattern in secondary causes may speak wisely to faith, especially if that pattern is such as to invite consideration of something more than secondary causes.[65] Perhaps in that constellation God may indeed be recognized. Care will still be needed in aligning that metaphysical principle with God. For example, it could be troubling if that principle seemed indifferent to moral distinctions. The Christian's faith in God as creator will maintain the interest in this kind of prospecting; the Christian's affirmation of a moral interpretation of holiness will provide the caution. On balance, the Christian has reason to be interested in the matter of the arguments for God and in the logically prior issue of the meaning of proof itself, as those issues can be approached within a metaphysical system.

But is such a metaphysical God the God of Abraham, Isaac, and Jacob? Yes, surely! Even the most earnest "second article Christian" will not be willing to give up creation altogether to some other God. We are dealing with the same God, then, but it does not follow that metaphysics and faith treat of identical content, as in Hegel's understanding of this rela-tionship.[66] Faith's talk of God is imbued with particularity which seems to resist metaphysical translation, as much as it requires metaphysical orientation. There is dialog in orientation. While I have been stressing what faith can learn, instruction flows the other way as well. Faith sees a vision which reminds the metaphysician that his sketch of reality should be such as to accommodate this possibility.

What we seem to be discussing are non-metaphysical aspects of God's nature or work as known to faith. Lewis Ford puts the matter this way:

> As long as God is understood to have totally unchanging characteristics which are necessary in all cases, then one ought to be able to know all there is to know about God by purely philosophical means. . . . If there is real contingency in the world, what happens in the world is not predetermined or pre-structured. God's experience of such a world cannot be pre-structured because it in turn is dependent upon what in fact happened. God's response to the world is thus contingent upon what happens in the world. Then the whole dimension of how God responds to his creation is something that philosophy cannot determine for us. This must be the domain in which we find revelation.[67]

It should be observed that while the question of whether contingent acts occur is a metaphysical question, the identification of particular contingent acts is not a metaphysical task.

It strikes me that Ford's observation can be understood in law/gospel terms. According to the Johannine prolog God gives life and light universally. His purpose derives uniformly from his singular creative will. While analysis may be hindered by intermediate causality, by rebellious response or by perceptive distortion, God's being and purpose for the world are metaphysically available to be known.[68] But Christian faith keys to something else as well. It speaks of the judgment of God. It tells of the issue, the end, of life. Any good word here will be truly gospel. The power of Paul's assurance in Romans is premised on the principle that judgment belongs to God. That judgment has been rendered in a particular work eluding metaphysical derivation:

> Who shall bring any charge against God's elect? It is God who justifies; who is to condemn? Is it Christ Jesus, who died, yes, who was raised from the dead, who is at the right hand of God, who indeed intercedes for us? [69]

It seems doubtful, then, that the gospel will be promising territory for metaphysical analysis, though it may be a promising field for confusion, if crucial distinctions are ignored.

Unfortunately, it is tempting to take this distinction too surely and too absolutely. Relationships remain to be mined. At the very least statements about the particular and contingent action of God cannot be in contradiction to the universal work of God as creator. And such particular action itself will be such that the general metaphysical principles continue to be relevant to its understanding, even if that action is not itself universal in character. Furthermore, we are invited to ponder the relationships between the general and the particular with respect to God. Christian faith badly needs a doctrine of God which integrates these aspects. With such a doctrine at hand it should be possible to analyze God's general activity within the metaphysical scheme to provide structural possibilities for the illumination of God's particular activity. We might come upon "hermeneutical hints" in the metaphysical scheme which could evoke an appreciative response from the particularity of Christian sentiment. In metaphysical analyses of the general structure of reality—including God's universal action—faith may well hear a recommendation which can guide it to a coherent account of its peculiar possession.

In such dialogical work the metaphysical contribution can truly be said to be constitutive, though not strictly determinative. It is faith which has here authorized a line of reflection that merges with an inquiry of worldly reason. While experiencing some surprise, the believer does not go into shock at this point. For faith not only knows that theology is human and therefore prone to profit from accurate metaphysical work. More than that, faith supposes that knowledge of the one true God at work in all that is real may illumine its particular treasure. Thus the self-God relationship comes to be superimposed on the self-world relationship with reciprocal illumination, though the two do not become one. Faith may come that far in process. And so that strange and wonderful phrase "process theology" may require of such a believer no less than the quest for wisdom that is tactical, conceptual, ethical, and constitutive.

# Part II
# Orientation

# 2
## Data: The Claims
## of this Metaphysics

### An Invitation to Abstraction

What is the real, the actual? What are person, world, mind, body? Where are they? Whence and whither are they? These questions interest the Christian—for any or all of the four reasons identified in Chapter 1. How lies the land on which we stand—the earth of which we are made—the world in which God works? To receive responses to these questions may be to find wisdom—whether tactical, conceptual, ethical, or constitutive. In this chapter we hear the proposal of process thought.

The point here is to get at the *meaning* of the metaphysical proposal; later we can ask what wisdom lies here for faith. We pause to consider process thought in its claim to describe the nature of reality. The lively brush of faith so quickly colors the canvas of perception, of understanding —whether in rosy hues or somber shades. Such coloring may caricature; at the very least it does interpret. Here, then, a deliberate effort is invited to hold back theological inquiry and evaluation in order to give description and analysis a fresh run at the faithful. Put on your shoes, for though God may be here, we come not to worship but to work.

Of course that distinction begs to be qualified—in three ways:

(1) The world of faith, of religion, is itself necessarily datum for metaphysical analysis and construction. Some metaphysical account must be made of this realm, though it is not faith which makes the account.

53

(2) If the student of reality finds metaphysical reason to speak of God—perhaps even linking such speech with the more particular utterances of the world of religion—that cannot be ruled out as inadmissible. The authorization and evaluation of such speech will be precisely metaphysical, descriptive.

(3) None of us—including Alfred North Whitehead—can be supposed to bracket belief, isolating it wholly from the process of describing reality, religious or unreligious. But we can seek to consider experience widely—including most certainly accounts of experience which differ radically from our own. We can imaginatively interrogate our own experience to seek to reduce to a minimum the privileged reading-in (or out) of religious convictions. Such a quest for objectivity is supported by the logic of Christian faith which pleads for some distinction between God and the world, between the real and the ideal, between that which is Christian and that which is not. Given such a distinction, an account of what is genuinely common to Christian and non-Christian should not be controlled by the interests of one of the partners.

In postponing any assessment of the significance of this view of reality for faith, we are in a sense abstracting, "drawing away," description as a work to be done and evaluated in its own terms. But abstraction is involved most fundamentally in the very task of description itself. If metaphysics or "speculative philosophy" is "the endeavor to frame a coherent, logical, necessary system of general ideas in terms of which every element of our experience can be interpreted" (PR 4), then the particular, the special, in our experience will not be of direct interest in its distinctiveness. (*Particularity* as such—that there are particulars and what it is to be such—will of course be a promising candidate for metaphysical consideration.)

Recognizing such metaphysical abstraction from particulars in their individual distinctiveness should not blind us to the crucial role particular experience plays in process thought. Indeed, Whitehead insists that "the elucidation of immediate experience is the sole justification for any thought" (PR 4). Experience is not self-evidently clear. Rather it invites analysis—"elucidation." A fuller consideration of both the "empirical side" and the "rational side" of metaphysics—with particular attention to criteria—awaits us, but even now a couple of Whiteheadian cautions deserve notice.

On the one hand, there is the matter of determining what will count for "experience." At the outset we should be concerned to cast the net as widely as possible:

> Nothing can be omitted, experience drunk and experience sober, experience sleeping and experience waking, experience drowsy and experience wide-awake, experience self-conscious and experience self-forgetful, experience intellectual and experience physical, experience religious and experience sceptical, experience anxious and experience care-free, experience anticipatory and experience retrospective, experience happy and experience grieving, experience dominated by emotion and experience under self-restraint, experience in the light and experience in the dark, experience normal and experience abnormal (*AI* 206).

The appeal to experience must be so formulated, for example, as to account for the influence on Whitehead of his reading, not only in mathematics and physics, but also in the Roman and Greek historians and in Dickens, Wordsworth, and Shelley.[1] It is apparent that care will be needed to avoid a narrow reading of "experience."

The universal scope of metaphysics poses a problem not only in the selection but also in the interpretation of data. For, as Whitehead observes:

> We habitually observe by the method of difference. Sometimes we see an elephant, and sometimes we do not. The result is that an elephant, when present, is noticed. Facility of observation depends on the fact that the object observed is important when present, and sometimes is absent. The metaphysical first principles can never fail of exemplification. We can never catch the actual world taking a holiday from their sway. Thus, for the discovery of metaphysics, the method of pinning down thought to the strict systematization of detailed discrimination, already effected by antecedent observation, breaks down (*PR* 6-7).

In response to this problem Whitehead proposes the airplane flight of imaginative generalization. This method

> starts from the ground of particular observation; it makes a flight in the thin air of imaginative generalization; and it again lands for renewed observation rendered acute by rational observation (*PR* 7).

Stephen Pepper writes in a similar vein of how world hypotheses depend on the construction of a "root metaphor":

> A man desiring to understand the world looks about for a clue to its comprehension. He pitches upon some area of commonsense fact and tries if he cannot understand other areas in terms of this one. This original area becomes then his basic analogy or root metaphor.[2]

Whitehead emphasizes that

> when the method of difference fails, factors which are constantly present may yet be observed under the influence of imaginative thought. Such thought supplies the differences which the direct observation lacks. It can even play with inconsistency; and can thus throw light on the consistent, and persistent elements in experience by comparison with what in imagination is inconsistent with them (*PR 7*).

It may be noted that Whitehead's choice of terminology bears the impress of the fact that our language also seems fashioned by the method of difference. The reader of *Process and Reality* is invited to choose between highly specialized usage of generally available words (as "feeling"), and the mysteries of an artificially constructed vocabulary (as "prehension"). When mastered, the artificial vocabulary seems to serve well enough and does not run the risk of readers substituting ordinary references for specialized usages. Still, there is the danger that the linguistic edifice will so impress with its splendor that internal coherence will replace the crucial test of experience. A middle way is proposed here too. I can do no better than offer a little of the one and a little of the other—trying, perhaps, to avoid the dangers of both by checking back against the deliverances of experience somewhat more overtly and frequently than the austere mind of Whitehead was inclined to do.

Metaphysical construction, then, starts with experience and seeks to serve experience. Abstraction is invited in the interest of concreteness. Thus a metaphysical sketch seeks to be "applicable" (meaning "that some items of experience are thus interpretable") and "adequate" (meaning that "there are no items incapable of such interpretation") (*PR 4*). Furthermore, "adequacy" "means that the texture of observed experience, as illustrating the philosophic scheme, is such that all related experience must exhibit the same texture" (*PR 5*).

Skepticism, discouragement—or even outrage—lie in wait when such bold intentions are announced. Whitehead did not understand a complete metaphysical system to be attainable even in principle.[3] But he knew what he was about and he has given us an open invitation to test his thought against experience.

We do focus very directly on Whitehead's thought in the pages that follow. To do so may seem to be an error of abstraction, for two reasons:

(1) Process thought is a many-splendored thing. A Whitehead who worried about the "fallacy of misplaced concreteness" might rest less than easy with a description which confidently spoke of a final position, a finished system.[4] Some effort will be made to incorporate the debate which goes on within the lively stream of process thought. But a gathered view is sought. Such can be offered for two reasons:

(a) There is a remarkable degree of agreement among process thinkers at the fundamental metaphysical level, despite striking disagreement on more particular, logically secondary questions.[5]

(b) Whitehead remains the normative and seminal thinker for process thought.

While others, notably Charles Hartshorne, reached process insights independently of Whitehead and fresh currents of initiative continue to appear, Whitehead's rigorous conceptual sketch remains a clarifying and efficacious point of common reference. This is not to claim that there are no disagreements about that sketch, but only that the identification and resolution of such problems continue to be matters of fruitful attention for current process thinkers.

(2) Whitehead's thought is not here drawn into intimate association with specific events in his life. Selective reference to his career will be made in relation to some aspects of his thought, but the basic analysis of the categories will not draw often upon an account of Whitehead's interesting career as mathematician, philosopher of science and metaphysician. I do not suggest that Whitehead's life and thought were isolated from each other. I am glad that competent sketches of his life are available to the student of his thought.[6] But I do propose that he offered his thought, not as an idiosyncratic diary, but as a description of categories bidding to illumine all experience. Thus reference to his life in a privileged, distinctive way would count against rather than for the fulfillment of the inten-

tion of his thought. Relative adequacy or deficiency in scope and interpretation of experience will of course concern us when we seek to assess how accurately Whitehead describes reality. Such testing lies ahead of us, as the plane essays a safe landing somewhere. At the moment, the more appropriate task is to locate the empirical runway from which this system gets its start. Given Whitehead's description of the method of imaginative generalization, we would seem to be asking two questions:

(1) What are the most *pervasive* elements in our experience?

(2) What are the most *primitive* elements in our experience from which, in turn, others may be derivable? [7]

## The Call of Experience

Whitehead offered a number of testimonies to what seemed most fundamental in experience. These statements are quite varied, differing, for example, in the degree to which technical language is employed. A gathered presentation of this testimony is attempted here. There is subtle risk in seeking some systematization *within* these statements as distinguished from the more candid risk encountered in constructing a system *upon* such materials. But the potential gains make the risk acceptable. We may find a more ready point of access to a way of thinking, to a way of viewing reality that might otherwise elude visitors to the austere abstractions of *Process and Reality*. Metaphysical construction, of course, remains to be attempted in relation to this material. When it is done, this somewhat primitive account—if convincing or as corrected—will provide a crucial basis for evaluation. Of course the distinction between metaphysical data and development is not altogether clean-cut. I have already started my metaphysical motor. But the airplane is still on the ground, taxiing about to get the feel of the runway.

In a characteristic statement written near the end of his literary productivity Whitehead speaks of a "vague grasp of reality, dissecting it into a threefold scheme, namely, 'The Whole,' 'That Other,' and 'This-Myself.' " He adds:

> This is primarily a dim division. The sense of totality obscures the analysis into self and others. . . . There is the vague sense of many which are one; and of one which includes the many. Also there are

two senses of the one—namely, the sense of the one which is all, and the sense of the one among the many. . . . We are each of us, one among others; and all of us are embraced in the unity of the whole (*MT* 110).

This insistence on vagueness is reminiscent of Whitehead's quotation from William James in *Process and Reality* (with all its categorical order) that "we find ourselves in a buzzing world, amid a democracy of fellow creatures" (*PR* 78). Vagueness does not defeat the quest to understand, but it surely qualifies it. We are driven to analysis, but rendered cautious at the same time.

Even this basic "Self, Other, Whole" formulation is simpler than experience warrants, for it contains as such no sense of time, of passingness, of process. That this sense must receive its due is the burden of a striking initial paragraph in a chapter of *Process and Reality* bearing, not surprisingly, the title, "Process."

> That "all things flow" is the first vague generalization which the unsystematized, barely analyzed, intuition of men has produced. It is the theme of some of the best Hebrew poetry in the Psalms; it appears as one of the first generalizations of Greek philosophy in the form of the saying of Heraclitus; amid the later barbarism of Anglo-Saxon thought it reappears in the story of the sparrow flitting through the banqueting hall of the Northumbrian king; and in all stages of civilization its recollection lends its pathos to poetry. Without doubt, if we are to go back to that ultimate, integral experience, unwarped by the sophistications of theory, that experience whose elucidation is the final aim of philosophy, the flux of things is one ultimate generalization around which we must weave our philosophical system (*PR* 317).[8]

Writing more abstractly, Whitehead says that this primitive experience is

> feeling from a beyond which is determinate and pointing to a beyond which is to be determined. But the feeling is subjectively rooted in the immediacy of the present occasion: it is what the occasion feels for itself as derived from the past and as merging into the future (*PR* 247).[9]

This passage introduces other notions in addition to schematizing "all things flow" in some kind of a three tense arrangement. One of these notions is the sense of the unity or identity of the self through the "flow" ("feeling from," "rooted in," "pointing to"). This is part of what White-head elsewhere identifies as the second component in "the complete problem of metaphysics" (*PR* 318). In the "Process" chapter in *Process and Reality* no sooner has he asserted that "the elucidation of meaning involved in the phrase 'all things flow' is one chief task of metaphysics," than he introduces "a rival notion, antithetical to the former." "This other notion dwells on permanences of things—the solid earth, the mountains, the stones, the Egyptian pyramids, the spirit of man, God" (*PR* 318). Characteristically Whitehead turns to what he calls the "utterances of religious aspiration" to find "a full expression of the union of the two notions in one integral experience":

> Abide with me;
> Fast falls the eventide (*PR* 318).

Whitehead attributes "solitariness" and priority to this self. Experience teaches that "life is an internal fact for its own sake, before it is an external fact relating itself to others" (*RM* 15). At the heart of the "life-for-its-own-sake" sense lies the experience of value, of worth:

> Our enjoyment of actuality is a realization of worth, good or bad. It is a value experience. Its basic expression is—Have a care, here is something that matters! Yes—that is the best phrase—the primary glimmering of consciousness reveals, something that matters (*MT* 116).

This value experience at the base of self identity does not exclude reference to others. Rather, this "actuality as something that matters, by reason of its own self-enjoyment," "includes enjoyments of others and transitions toward the future" (*MT* 118).

The "Self-Other-Whole" testimony of experience can be helpfully cast in "value" terms. Those terms include reference to discrimination:

> . . . our experience is a value experience, expressing a vague sense of maintenance or discard; and this value experience differentiates itself in the sense of many existences with value experience . . . and this sense of the multiplicity of value experiences again differentiates it into the totality of value experience, and the many other value experiences, and the egoistic value experience. There is the feeling of the ego, the others, the totality. This is the vague, basic presentation of the differ-

entiation of existence, in its enjoyment of discard and maintenance (*MT* 110).

This sense of discrimination depends on another distinction:

There are two contrasted ideas which seem inevitably to underlie all width of experience, one of them is the notion of importance, the sense of importance, the presupposition of importance. The other is the notion of matter-of-fact. There is no escape from sheer matter-of-fact. It is the basis of importance; and importance is important because of the inescapable character of matter-of fact. We concentrate by reason of a sense of importance. And when we concentrate, we attend to matter-of-fact. . . . The two notions are antithetical and require each other (*MT* 4).

In *Modes of Thought* Whitehead points out how the sense of importance is involved in personal interest, in the development of perspective, in the "zest for truth." These in turn involve selection, choice. For example:

. . . one characterization of importance is that it is that aspect of feeling whereby a perspective is imposed upon the universe of things felt. In our more self-conscious entertainment of the notion, we are aware of grading the effectiveness of things about us in proportion to their interest. In this way, we put aside, and we direct attention . . . (*MT* 11).

In *Adventures of Ideas* Whitehead examines language, social institutions, and human action to note the togetherness of "fact" and "importance": ·

A statesman, or a president of a business corporation, assumes the "compulsion of recent events" as laying down inexorable conditions for the future. He frames a "policy" upon this assumption and advises that it be "acted upon," thereby also assuming that the imposed conditions leave room for the effectiveness of "choice" and "intelligence." He assumes alternatives in contrast to the immediate fact. He conceives an ideal, to be attained or to be missed (*AI* 227).

The sense of importance which brings choice and selection to bear upon inescapable fact can also be seen in the reality of purpose:

The conduct of human affairs is entirely dominated by our recognition of foresight determining purpose, and purpose issuing in conduct. Almost every sentence we utter and every judgment we form, presup-

pose our unfailing experience of this element in life. The evidence is so
overwhelming, the belief so unquestioning, the evidence of language so
decisive, that it is difficult to know where to begin in demonstrating it
(*FR* 13).

How far have we come? Clearly we have come far enough to speak of
"an essential interconnectedness of things" (*AI* 227-228) [10] or to say that
"connectedness is of the essence of all things of all types" (*MT* 9). We
have found that the interconnectedness yields an organization involving
past, present and future on the one hand, and self-world, on the other.
The fact-importance distinction is another subordinate ordering theme of
wide generality. A passage in *Modes of Thought* attempts to bring these
themes together:

> . . . reflective experience exhibits three main characteristics which re-
> quire each other for their full understanding. There are the experiences
> of joint association, which are the spatial experiences. There are the
> experiences of origination from a past and of determination towards a
> future. These are temporal experiences. There are experiences of ideals
> —of ideals entertained, of ideals aimed at, of ideals achieved, of ideals
> defaced. This is the experience of the deity of the universe (*MT* 102-
> 103).[11]

In such a statement we may well be beyond the simple identification
of the pervasive and the primitive in experience. The striking "Space,
Time, and Deity" formulation is just that—an act of interpretation graft-
ed to the testimony ("there are . . . this is"). And it should be noted that
the reference here is to "reflective experience," involving a "vast gap" in
relating to animal existence (*MT* 102-103). Still this characterization will
function well as a summary of Whitehead's reading of experience. Thus
the experience of "time" is directly related by Whitehead not merely to
reflective human experience but also to contemporary physics with its
emphasis on "vector feeling," wavelengths and vibrations.[12] And Whitehead claims that "the sense of importance (or interest) is embedded in
the very being of animal experience. As it sinks in dominance, experience
trivializes and verges toward nothingness." [13]

While the Space, Time, Deity formula summarizes fairly well, omis-
sions occur. There is no mention of the "How" of the interconnected-

ness. Were we to consider that more fully, we would have to speak with respect to the self of how "the basis of experience is emotional" (*AI* 176) and of "the intimate sense of derivation from the body, which is the reason for our instinctive identification of our bodies with ourselves" (*AI* 226). With respect to the latter, Whitehead writes in a characteristic passage:

> In one respect the vagueness yields a comparatively sharp cut division, namely, the differentiation of the world into the animal body which is the region of intimate, intense, mutual expression, and the rest of nature where the intimacy and intensity of feeling fails to penetrate. My brain, my heart, my bowels, my lungs, are mine, with an intimacy of mutual adjustment. The sunrise is a message from the world beyond such directness of relation (*MT* 72).[14]

We will return to this theme below in the analysis of perception (cf. Whitehead's refrain: "we see with the eye" [*PR* 259, 267]). It will also bear upon his understanding of the human person, as will another theme neglected in this introductory presentation: the memory of our immediate past which may be said to be "our indubitable self, the foundation of our present existence" (*AI* 181).

It is appropriate to leave some of these themes undeveloped here in order to give them fuller attention in connection with specific aspects of Whiteheadian constructs. Such construction will benefit from close association with the deliverances of immediate experience—notably in such an area as the understanding of the human person. What has been here attempted is not a complete but a representative (and in that sense, accurate) presentation of the testimony of primitive and pervasive experience which calls to the one who would describe the shape of reality.

## To the Ultimate and Three Principles

On our way with Whitehead from hearing the call of primitive experience toward the task of metaphysical construction, we pause to remark concerning the formal nature of the "move" involved and the material assistance at hand for the move, especially in the American situation.

(1) The system we seek is to be logical and coherent. Whitehead seeks not only lack of contradiction,[15] but a scheme in which the fundamen-

tal ideas "presuppose each other so that in isolation they are meaning-less" (PR 5). "Incoherence is the arbitrary disconnection of first prin-ciples" (PR 9). Whitehead saw such incoherence illustrated in the two substance, body-mind dualism of Descartes. The very nature of sub-stance by definition ("requiring nothing but itself to exist") resists any coherent connecting of a substance body and a substance mind (PR 10). Turning to the empirical, we seek ideas which will bear on "every element of our experience." Of course any adequate view of the world will also seek to illumine more special configurations and draw upon less general principles to do so. Thus at a still very general level Whitehead distin-guishes between cosmology—the study of the principles applying to our "cosmic epoch"—and metaphysics, the study of the principles applicable to all cosmic epochs (PR 138).[16]

For two reasons I will not limit my discussion to what may be most properly "metaphysical." First, for most of its purposes, faith (which au-thorizes projects with the data) seeks simply to know what is real within the world given to it. Second, even the truly metaphysical remains an empirical matter. That metaphysical principles "cannot fail of exemplifica-tion" does not direct us to pure speculation but drives us to a rigorous testing of candidates in experience.[17] Later—especially in Part IV—we will consider the significance for faith of the possibility that the present universally applicable structure of reality may itself be subject to change. In the meantime we will discuss even the more specific principles within the cosmological scheme with attention to their exemplification of and relation to the most general principles which can be identified.

(2) While clarity is served by concentrating on Whitehead's rigorous work as a statement of process claims, it should be acknowledged that he undertook his metaphysical thought in a conscious relationship to that of others. Process and Reality is in one sense a conversation with European philosophy—and the conversation is sufficiently complex and compressed that the book is read with difficulty by those unfamiliar with that tradi-tion. While Whitehead often seems to be stressing the differences (to his advantage, of course), he does believe it is important

> that the scheme of interpretation here adopted can claim for each of its
> main positions the express authority of one, or the other, of some

supreme master of thought—Plato, Aristotle, Descartes, Locke, Hume, Kant (*PR* 63).[18]

It is the first-named of the giants with whom Whitehead particularly associates himself:

> . . . if we had to render Plato's general point of view with the least changes made necessary by the intervening two thousand years of human experiences in social organization, in esthetic attainments, in science, and in religion, we should have to set about the construction of a philosophy of organism (*PR* 63).

But important changes would be necessary—given the intervening two thousand years of human experience—and it was figures like Henri Bergson, S. A. Alexander, William James, and John Dewey who pointed the way for Whitehead. We have already taken Alexander's title, *Space, Time and Deity,* as a provisional organizing device used by Whitehead in relation to the deliverances of immediate experience.[19] And in the preface to *Process and Reality* Whitehead acknowledges his great debt to the other three thinkers and adds:

> One of my preoccupations has been to rescue their type of thought from the charge of anti-intellectualism, which rightly or wrongly has been associated with it (*PR* vii).

I shall not frequently introduce comparisons with other philosophers in this account, but as we move to Whitehead's philosophical constructions it may be noted that the work of Dewey and James on the American scene did materially aid Whitehead. I have in mind particularly the nature of philosophic method and think of Dewey's call to a work of *disintegration* in which a metaphysics functioning as a custodian of belief against the facts is exposed to attack.[20] I think of James' inquiries concerning what the "facts" may be—his denial of simple sensations, his stress on knowing as interaction, his insistence in probing the fuzzy "knowledge *of*" reality and his suspicion that simple and clear "knowledge *about*" reality may be the derivative work of abstraction.[21] In sum, there is the inclination no longer to trust reason as an untainted sovereign and rather to trust experience, even though it be a "buzzing multiplicity."

Experience may require analysis, but it is to experience that our analysis must turn.

What, then, shall we say as we try—aided by philosophic colleagues—to identify that which is truly fundamental in the call of experience? Whitehead says:

> The many become one and are increased by one (*PR* 32).

This is "the category of the ultimate." There are three component notions: "Creativity," "Many," "One." These are "involved in the meaning of the synonymous terms 'thing,' 'being,' 'entity' " and "are presupposed in all the more special categories" (*PR* 31). "Many" and "One" remind us of the chronicle of immediate experience in Section One of this chapter, and it may be seen that they respect the requirements of coherence by requiring each other. "Creativity" advances the meaning gained in the other terms by speaking of something more than a logical connectedness between the "many" and the "one":

> It is that ultimate principle by which the many, which are the universe disjunctively, become the one actual occasion, which is the universe conjunctively. It lies in the nature of things that the many enter into complex unity (*PR* 31).

We will be trying to clarify this notion in all that remains of this chapter. But already three notions seem to be involved: becoming, unification, novelty. As Whitehead puts it in another formulation:

> The ultimate metaphysical principle is the *advance* [becoming] from disjunction to *conjunction* [unification], creating a *novel entity* [novelty], other than the entities given in disjunction (*PR* 32).

Or, again:

> The many become [becoming] one [unification] and are increased by one [novelty] (*PR* 32).

Whitehead gathers these notions in a phrase, "the production [becoming] of novel [novelty] togetherness [unification]" (*PR* 32).

It might be said that the first of these three notions is a testimony to Galileo who challenges the conventional wisdom that motion is possible only when forces act and immediately ceases without them. Galileo showed that it is the force of friction that causes moving objects to stop and that in the absence of this force a body once set in motion would continue to move forever.[22] We shall see that to add unification and novelty as qualifications of becoming is to advance the discussion significantly.

While Whitehead offers several formulations of these notions, he does not essay any explanation as to why they are or should be ultimate. As John Cobb has remarked, the question why is there something rather than nothing is simply not Whitehead's approach to the metaphysical task.[23] Rather he contends that the ultimate notions "are inexplicable in terms of higher universals" or in the terms of subordinate categories. "The sole appeal is to intuition" (*PR* 32). But the appeal is accessible to discussion. Thus, if one were able to derive any candidate notion from a higher term, or to distinguish it from a more prevalent element in experience—a true universal—one would have refuted the candidate's claim to ultimacy. Moreover, it does seem possible to elucidate the meaning (if not explain the "givenness") of these categories by referring to certain principles of process thought. Three seem particularly helpful.

The "principle of process" states that

> *how* an actual entity *becomes* constitutes *what* that actual entity *is;* so that the two descriptions of an actual entity are not independent. Its "being" is constituted by its "becoming" (*PR* 34-35. Italics his).

In other words:

> It is fundamental to the metaphysical doctrine of the philosophy of organism that the notion of an actual entity as the unchanging subject of change is completely abandoned (*PR* 43).

Here "becoming" is emphasized most fundamentally; gone is the idea that change or movement is an optional state of affairs, as is suggested by Descartes' definition of substance as "an existent thing which requires nothing but itself in order to exist" (*PR* 79).

Whitehead's work in physics may echo in this conviction regarding "becoming." David Bohm points out that modern physics no longer is satisfied with an account of motion as the external displacement of essentially unchanged bodies through space:

... not only do the quantitative properties of things change in these motions (e.g., position, velocity of the various particles, the strength of the various fields, etc.) but so also do the basic qualities defining the modes of beings of the entities, such as molecules, atoms, nucleons, mesons ...[24]

Milic Capek concurs and ventures a hunch as to why this emphasis seems so hard to swallow:

Nernst's discovery of "zero energy," which appeared so paradoxical within the framework of classical science, becomes more intelligible when we realize that the conceptual separation of *motion* and *thing moved*, which is so strongly suggested by our macroscopic experience, loses its justification on the microphysical level. It is very probable that what was originally the distinction between motion and matter on the sensory level became later the distinction between *thing* and *event*, or *substance* and *process*, on the more abstract level. The disappearance of this distinction is even more conspicuous in wave mechanics; the discovery of De Broglie's waves shows that not only are material particles constituted by vibrations, but also there is a very limited chance to interpret these oscillations as vibratory displacements of corpuscular or subaethereal entities. "Events and not particles constitute the true objective reality" is the conclusion of Sir James Jeans, and thinkers so widely different as Bertrand Russell, Henri Bergson, A. N. Whitehead, and Gaston Bachelard agree with it.[25]

Obviously any adequate defense of this notion will have to address the issue of continuity, including that "on the sensory level." I have cited Bohm and Capek, not in such defense, but to provide alternative formulations of this strangely alien yet clearly fundamental sense of becoming. Basic qualities themselves change, events are real in the most primary sense. To speak of the ultimate one must speak of how "being is constituted by becoming."

Thus far, however, nothing would prevent us from conceiving of reality as simply composed of isolated, unrelated units of becoming. A philosophy student might think of Leibniz's windowless monads. A second principle is required, the principle of relativity:

that the potentiality for being an element in a real concrescence of many entities into one actuality, is the one general metaphysical character attaching to all entities, actual and non-actual; and that every item in its universe is involved in each concrescence. In other words, it belongs to the nature of a "being" that it is a potential for every "becoming" (PR 33).

Or, in still other words:

It is the one general metaphysical character of all entities of all sorts that they function as objects. It is this metaphysical character which constitutes the solidarity of the universe (PR 336).

Whitehead recognized very explicitly that this principle of relativity placed him in opposition to the Aristotelian dictum that a substance is not present in a subject: "On the contrary, according to this principle an actual entity *is* present in other actual entities" (PR 79).

This solidarity or unification was suggested to me by a TV clip citing a student testimony before a city council hearing on a "ban-the-can" ordinance: "What we now have with us we will always have with us." Whitehead does talk of "objective immortality" characterizing the process of becoming: Nothing ever quite dies. This principle sounds fantastic to us at first hearing. Ecological awareness, recognition that events on stars light years ago affect light and rain and so affect us, recognition that we co-constitute each other in human relationships—such features of our current consciousness may make it seem less fantastic. Further clarification will be needed, but even now it is clear that to say that every being is a potential for every future becoming is to show how unification joins becoming in the content of the category of the ultimate.

To affirm becoming and unification is not yet to affirm novelty. It is true that numerical newness is acknowledged ("another one") through these two notions. Perhaps, indeed, a kind of qualitative newness (a "different one") is available as well, if we say with Bohm that:

because of all the infinity of factors determining what any given thing is are always changing with time, *no such a thing can even remain identical with itself* as time passes.[26]

But the testimony of experience seems to call for recognition of a more fundamental qualitative novelty:

If we survey the world as a physical system determined by its antecedent states, it presents to us the spectacle of a finite system steadily running down—losing its activities and its varieties. The various evolutionary formulae give no hint of any contrary tendency. The struggle for existence gives no hint why there should be cities. Again the crowding of houses is no explanation why houses should be beautiful. But there is in nature some tendency upwards, in a contrary direction to the aspect of physical decay. In our experience we find appetition, effecting a final causation towards ideal ends which lie outside the mere physical tendency. In the burning desert there is appetition towards water, whereas the physical tendency is towards increased dryness of the animal body. The appetition towards esthetic satisfaction by some enjoyment of beauty is equally outside the mere physical order (*FR* 89).

To account for such novelty, such "appetition," several concepts are introduced. The most basic of them is "decision":

"Decision" cannot be construed as a casual adjunct of an actual entity. It constitutes the very meaning of actuality. An actual entity arises from decisions *for it,* and by its very existence provides decisions *for* other actual entities which supersede it (*PR* 68).

In this connection Whitehead formulates the "ontological principle" which

means that actual entities are the only *reasons;* that to search for a *reason* is to search for one or more actual entities (*PR* 37).[27]

Perhaps a schematic summary can be attempted.

## THE ULTIMATE

| (the production of novel togetherness) | CREATIVITY MANY ONE | (the many become one and are increased by one) |

Becoming: The Principle of Process: a being is constituted by becoming.

Unification: The Principle of Relativity: a being is potential for later becoming.

Novelty: The Ontological Principle: actual decisions provide true reasons.

The "fit" is not perfect. In schematizing we risk the loss of the togetherness, since "analysis of the components abstracts from the concrescence"

(PR 32). Yet these characterizations do seem to illumine what White-head takes to be the ultimate, though we must not let an orderly discussion of principles lead us to forget that reality is basically pluralistic. I have been citing passages in which there is persistent reference to "concrescence" and "actual entity." As the ontological principle has made most clear, it is of these units of becoming that the principles speak. Thus the view is said to be incurably "atomic." Since "all relatedness has its foundation in the relatedness of actualities" (PR ix), Whitehead could say quite simply in the preface to *Process and Reality:*

> The positive doctrine of these lectures is concerned with the becoming, the being, and the relatedness of "actual entities" (PR viii).

In that doctrine other categories come into play and now call for our consideration.

## Causation and Change

The principle of process makes clear that to speak of the fundamental unit of actuality is to speak of an occasion—a "becoming" which comes to constitute a being. The principle of relativity suggests that potential is provided for that becoming by the being of other actual occasions. This fluidity may seem to reduce reality to a shapeless jelly. Yet within the relatedness of reality the sense of self and other abides. As Stuart Hampshire has written:

> If I cannot doubt my own existence here, I also cannot doubt that there exist other things over there and away from myself. . . . When I refer to myself as doing something and as active, even if the activity is only that of directed thought, I make a contrast between that which I myself do and that which happens to me, a contrast that I would not understand unless something external to myself does sometimes impinge upon me.[28]

So far so good. Process thought adds two additional claims to Hampshire's basic description:

(1) The world is composed exhaustively of such experiencing processes (the ontological principle). As Whitehead says:

Just as "potentiality for process" is the meaning of the more general
term "entity," or "thing"; so "decision" is the additional meaning
imported by the word "actual" into the phrase "actual entity." "Actuality" is the decision amid "potentiality." It represents stubborn fact
which cannot be evaded . . . The Castle Rock at Edinburgh exists
from moment to moment, and from century to century, by reason of the
decision effected by its own historic route of antecedent occasions
(*PR* 68-69).

(2) All such experiencing processes (and we may begin to call them
with Whitehead "actual occasions") have self-reference. There is not only
a "What" to the relatedness of the occasions, but a "How" as well. I do
not only undergo change. I experience. Experience does not merely happen *to* me; it is *for* me; I am the subject of my act of experiencing. Whitehead proposes the term "subjective form" to refer to the "How" of relatedness. There are many forms by which one occasion may receive (we may
say with Whitehead "prehend" or "feel") another occasion. Among such
forms are "emotions, valuations, purposes, adversions, consciousness"
(*PR* 35).

Clearly a given event—President Carter's pardoning of draft evaders
but not deserters—will be received, "felt," very differently in varying
receivers. The form in which the subject receives the datum is a radically
personal matter. Yet Whitehead extends the sense of relatedness to include
subjective forms as well. We "feel feelings" of others—the mother does
feel her son's elation (the "How") over the pardon, not merely the news
(the "What") which he brings of the pardon. The mother's feeling the
feeling is not the son's feeling itself—no magical transfer is accomplished.
The son's elation is his—a self-relatedness. It is his alone. In this possession
there is a self-identity in solitariness. As such, that moment of the son's
feeling must be said to have "perished," when we speak of the mother's
experience (or indeed of the next moment in the son's experience). Still it
remains true that the mother experiences not only what the son experiences (the news of the pardon), but how he experiences (the elation).

Obviously the mother may receive, but not approve or share, her son's
elation. The subjective form from his experience vies in her with other
ways of receiving the same datum. Grief, guilt, and gratitude may bid
for dominance. Surprise ("I can't believe it") or resolve ("never again in

my family") may reign. But some peace will be made. The many will become one. What and How will come together in this one. Some elements in the data (the What) for the occasion may be inoperative ("negatively" prehended, as Whitehead terms it) in the unification.[29] A Choice of How will be made. The task of unifying all this in the occasion seems formidable enough. It is hardly a matter of happenstance. Indeed Whitehead feels called upon to say that the process of unification is guided by a "subjective aim" in the becoming occasion.

Occasions of experience themselves aiming and feeling—this may be more than one is prepared to swallow. Still it should be said that the problem Whitehead is addressing in these formulations is hardly his alone. In the passage quoted above Hampshire has implicitly posed the problem of how to account for the coming together of self and other which is so fundamental to existence. Whitehead accepts this problem as his explicit agenda:

> The perceptive constitution of the actual entity presents the problem, How can the other actual entities, each with its own formal existence, also enter objectively into the perceptive constitution of the actual entity in question? This is the problem of the solidarity of the universe. The classical doctrines of universals and particulars, of subject and predicate, of individual substances, of the externality of relations, alike render this problem incapable of solution. The answer given by the organic philosophy is the doctrine of prehensions, involved in concrescent integrations, and terminating in a definite, complex unity of feeling (*PR* 88-89).

How shall one get entities—self and other, and all the others—in the kind of relationships required to explain knowledge and action? It will hardly do to appeal simply to "practice" (Hume) or to "animal faith" (Santayana) (*PR* 230ff.). Whitehead did not invent relatedness, but he did take it with unusual seriousness in constructing his view of the world. In doing that he may still raise problems for us. We may wonder how an "incurably atomic" understanding of reality can show that a later unit cannot only feel "like" a former one, but even feel that prior reality immanent within itself.[30] Indeed the very generalized appeal to "feeling" may itself seem problematic. Thus with respect to this talk of occasions of experience themselves aiming and feeling, L. Bryant Keeling objects:

My contention is that there is no possible behavior on the part of an electron or the universe as a whole which is sufficiently analogous to human behavior to make it possible to apply the word "feel" in its ordinary sense to either.[31]

It is important to hear such objections and to remember them. But the metaphysical sketch requires fuller statement before evaluation can be reasonably undertaken.

In coming to speak of the self-relatedness of the actual occasion, of the subjective aim guiding the integration of data and subjective forms, we have come upon the ground of Whitehead's defense of the reality of *final causality*. He speaks of such final causality in a most comprehensive way. He can write with disarming simplicity.

The attainment of a peculiar definiteness is the final cause which animates a particular process . . . (*PR* 340).

Or he will amplify the point and say that the feeling (prehending) subject

is the purpose of the process originating the feelings. The feelings are inseparable from the end at which they aim; and this end is the feeler. The feelings aim at the feeler, as their final cause (*PR* 339).

Somewhat parenthetically, we may observe that Whitehead appropriates the distinction between the physical and mental (or conceptual) to formulate this concern to safeguard and clarify final causality. Thus he speaks of two "poles" in an actual entity. The physical pole receives what is given for it by its past. Through the physical pole *efficient causality* is at work. In turn, "the mental pole is the subject determining its own ideal of itself" (*PR* 380).[32] The juxtaposition of efficient and final causality is often a very explicit matter in Whitehead. In a characteristic passage he writes:

Explanation by "tradition" is merely another phraseology for explanation by "efficient cause." We require explanation by "final cause." Thus a single occasion is alive when the subjective aim which determines its process of concrescence has introduced a novelty of definiteness not to be found in the inherited data of its primary phrase. The novelty is introduced conceptually and disturbs the inherited "responsive" adjustment of subjective forms. It alters the "values," in the artist's sense of that term (*PR* 159).

Since all entities seek distinctive definiteness, all are characterized by mentality (*PR* 366).[33] Such an assertion is at least unconventional, and probably controversial. Exposition may be permitted to continue, if it is clearly understood that Whitehead does not identify consciousness and mentality. He considers consciousness a rare phenomenon. Obviously, he must be held accountable for an explanation of how consciousness does develop. That will be attempted later in this chapter.

While Whitehead surely does employ what must be said to be, at the very least, highly unconventional formulations in his defense of final causality, his appeal is to persistent themes in ordinary *experience:* novelty and responsibility. Again, however, he assigns those themes a scope and accords them a conceptual seriousness which is clearly unusual and may seem problematic. The scope of novelty is that required by an objective interpretation of the indeterminacy principle in modern physics which makes uncertainty or contingency a characteristic of what is there to be known, rather than accounting for such by appealing to the limitations of our knowing process. As such novelty carries with it a recognition of the irreversibility of time, as Capek points out:

> The impossibility of cyclical time follows from the affirmation of *real novelties* in the physical world. If every moment is irreducibly original by its own nature . . . then the irreversibility of becoming cannot be denied. For the theory of perpetual emergence of novelties clearly excludes the possibility of two identical successive moments no matter how long a time interval may separate them. Such identity, required by the cyclical theory of time, would deprive the later moment of the quality of authentic novelty which it should possess. Each moment in virtue of its own authentic freshness is unique and unrepeatable. Thus novelty implies irreversibility.[34]

As for responsibility, Whitehead writes:

> In our own relatively high grade of human existence, this doctrine of feelings and their subject is best illustrated by our notion of moral responsibility. The subject is responsible for being what it is in virtue of its feelings and is also derivatively responsible for the consequence of its existence because they flow from its feelings (*PR* 339).

I say that Whitehead *appeals* to responsibility. That seems a reasonable way to suggest what is at stake in the notion of final causality. It should be noted that the appeal is not without its difficulties. The appeal has been severely challenged—most pointedly, perhaps, by Edward Pols,[35] who would deny that the actual occasion is entitled even to the freedom claimed, given Whiteheadian categories—but also quite broadly by thinkers like Paul Weiss, who contend that even that freedom won't do to account for the responsibility of persons, as distinguished from the indeterminacy of occasions.[36] Again, before a response to such objections can be heard and assessed, other categories need to be in hand, notably those introduced in a later subsection of this chapter dealing with the understanding of the human person. In the meantime, Whitehead's appeals to novelty and responsibility remain significant claims in relation to his notion of final causality.

We introduced this section by noting that Whitehead announced that his philosophy was concerned with "the becoming, the being, and the relatedness of actual entities." We have been concentrating on the "becoming" of actual entities—on that process Whitehead calls "concrescence." But by the principle of relativity it is clear that as the actual entity achieves its definiteness of feeling in "satisfaction," it "perishes" in subjective immediacy only to bequeath itself in being (or as "superject," as Whitehead otherwise terms it) to instances of becoming in its future. The process of change from subjective becoming-for-oneself to objective being-for-others is termed "transition" by Whitehead. Thus he would speak of two kinds of change: concrescence and transition:

> The creative process is rhythmic: it swings from the publicity of the many things to the individual privacy: and it swings back from the private individual to the publicity of the objectified individual. The former swing is dominated by the final cause which is the ideal; and the latter swing is dominated by the efficient cause which is the actual. The oneness of the universe, and the oneness of each element in the universe repeat themselves to the crack of doom in the creative advance from creature to creature . . . (PR 229).

The recognition of transition is significant. Whitehead defends subjectivity, the "eternal now" of the moment of solitary becoming but without reducing the rest of the world to mere possibility, as some existentialists seem to do.[37] Both themes do call out for recognition in life. Thus Cecil

J. Schneer writes of both transition and concrescence in music and in history:

> The musical experience is a development, a process in time which is, triggered though it may be by waves, vibrations, pipes, numbers, nevertheless a purely subjective experience. . . . Like music, history is experienced in the present. The past is gone, the future is not yet. As in music, the impact of the momentary event is completely determined by the past. Our episode is meaningless without its background, its perspective, just as in music the note is of high or low pitch not in the absolute but according to whether the preceding notes were higher or lower. . . . The data, the documents, the chronicle of history are comparable to the wood, the resin, the catgut side of music. What is done with this becomes history or music—or else there is only the material gut and noise that existed in the beginning. I am not here drawing a contrast between music and science. Vibrations, wood, resin, even oscilloscopes are of no more intrinsic interest to the physicist than to the musician. To find in these a pattern, to link them through mathematics to fundamentals, to impose upon them an order of his own devising, is the main concern of the physicist. The resin and the catgut are the chaos of existence. To convert them to aesthetic experience is the province of music. To convert them to a theory of sound is the province of a Helmholtz. The death of a man, the ink on a parchment, the chip on a stone must somehow be converted into living thought to enter into our minds to interact with the experience of our past and to convert us subtly from the men we were into something different, more profound, more complex.[38]

While such a statement may tend toward overstatement, particularly in an idealistic vein, it does bring home graphically the two kinds of change so important to process thought. In speaking of these kinds of change we have spoken of the becoming and the being of actual entities, and—it would seem—of final and efficient causality, respectively. What has not been made clear is that in order to account fully for these processes, other causal factors must be specified.

## God and Creativity

The combination of efficient and final causality in which a significantly free becoming yields a being as given entails that:

"Potentiality" is the correlative of "givenness." The meaning of "givenness" is that what is "given" might not have been "given"; and that what *is not* "given" *might have been* "given" (*PR* 70. Italics his). It is evident that "givenness" and "potentiality" are both meaningless apart from a multiplicity of potential entities. These potentialities are the "eternal objects" (*PR* 72).

Eternal objects are "forms of definiteness" relevant to the becoming of actual entities, but not themselves exercising any agency in that regard. Are not such objects—however honorifically "eternal"—trivial or even superfluous, if they lack agency in time? It might seem so. Still, it is a significant claim that Whitehead makes for eternal objects in writing:

> The actualities constituting the process of the world are conceived as exemplifying the ingression (or "participation") of other things which constitute the potentialities of definiteness for any actual existence. The things which are temporal arise by their participation in the things which are eternal (*PR* 63).

By making this statement Whitehead exempts himself from a magical view of the process in which definiteness would be constantly created out of nothing. Rather it is the case that:

> The definite ingression into a particular actual entity is not to be conceived as the sheer evocation of that eternal object from "not-being" into "being"; it is the evocation of determination out of indetermination. Potentiality becomes reality; and yet retains its message of alternatives which the actual entity has avoided. In the constitution of an actual entity: whatever component is red might have been green; and whatever component is loved, might have been coldly esteemed (*PR* 226).[39]

Thus one might speak of the eternal objects as "formal causes" in the process of becoming.[40]

The creative advance is just that: creative, involving qualitative novelty. How do these new forms of definiteness come about? True, the self-determining actual entity chooses in the process, but how is it that the relevant novel potentials are presented to the one so choosing? The past actual entities bearing in on the subject cannot account for what by definition is precisely new. The eternal object as bare form is "neutral as to the fact of its physical ingression in any particular actual entity of the temporal world" (*PR* 70). Some agent seems required to bring together the particular actualizing choice and a specific possibility that is both new and relevant.

It is here that Whitehead formulates a concept of God within the metaphysical system:

> In what sense can unrealized abstract form ["the eternal object"] be relevant? What is its basis of relevance? "Relevance" must express some real fact of togetherness among forms. The ontological principle can be expressed as: All real togetherness is togetherness in the formal constitution of an actuality. So if there be a relevance of what in the temporal world is unrealized, the relevance must express a fact of togetherness in the formal constitution of a non-temporal actuality (*PR* 48).[41]

Thus to account for concrete novelty two steps are needed: (1) Whitehead speaks of a divine act by which the eternal objects are ordered so as to be relevant in the creative advance. (2) It is that ordering which is reflected in the initial phase of each entity when God offers to that emerging entity an "initial aim," a vision of what it can become by drawing upon the forms of relatedness represented by the eternal objects (*PR* 373-374).

At the beginning of this chapter I pleaded for an effort to hold back theological inquiry and evaluation in order to undertake metaphysical analysis so that the nature of reality might be given as thorough and honest a hearing as possible—precisely for the sake of the faithful. But among the qualifications of that plea I included this sentence, "If the student of reality finds *metaphysical* reason to speak of God—perhaps even linking such speech with the more particular utterances of the world of religion—that cannot be ruled out as inadmissible."[42] Whitehead seems to have brought us to just such a point in speaking of each actual occasion's dependence on a non-temporal ordering of possible forms of relatedness. Whitehead calls that ordering "primordial," meaning that it "is not *before* all creation, but *with* all creation" (*PR* 521. Italics his). The language and perhaps the logic of such a statement have a religious ring. Moreover, Whitehead emphatically links that ordering with the term God. While the appropriateness and fruitfulness of that linkage will concern us on more specifically theological grounds later, two considerations bearing on the linkage may be identified here in expounding Whitehead's own understanding.

(1) A monotheistic emphasis (as in the Judeo-Christian tradition) is suggested on metaphysical grounds:

> . . . by the principle of relativity there can only be one non-derivative actuality, unbounded by its prehensions of an actual world (*PR* 48). Unfettered conceptual valuation, "infinite" in Spinoza's sense of that term, is only possible once in the universe; since that creative act is objectively immortal as an inescapable condition characterizing creative action (*PR* 378).

That is, a second such act would be "fettered" by the reality of the first bearing upon it, according to the principle of relativity.

(2) This non-temporal actuality

> is here termed "God"; because the contemplation of our natures, as enjoying real feelings derived from the timeless source of all order, acquires that "subjective form" of refreshment and companionship at which religions aim (*PR* 47).

This second consideration anticipates both a fuller development of Whitehead's understanding of the actual entity to be termed God and the discussions of his descriptive understanding of religion to be introduced in the next chapter. Thus we return to Whitehead's employment of this notion in the metaphysical task of description.

How is this God, thus located metaphysically, to be understood in relationship to the other principal metaphysical ingredients? It is characteristic of Whitehead that he does not reject such a question, either by denying the reality of other fundamental metaphysical components or by exempting the metaphysical reality of God from comparison and analysis in relation to the other components. What are the other components? In his categorial scheme in Chapter 2 of *Process and Reality* he states that among a total of eight basic categories "actual entities and eternal objects stand out with a certain extreme finality. The other types of existence have a certain intermediate character" (*PR* 33). We have already noted something of how God is related to the category "actual entity"—including the fact that God is an instance of the category's exemplification (though as "non-temporal" God is not to be spoken of as an "actual *occasion*") (*PR* 135). More will follow on God's relationship to other actual entities. As for the other "outstanding" category, the "eternal objects," it may be argued that the notion of God functions as a check on the avowedly Platonic cast of the notion of eternal objects. While these "forms" do in a sense precede actuality and are "given" for God, they are clearly not an eminent or superior reality, for they require God as orderer and presenter, as well as the actual occasion itself as decider.[43]

Perhaps a more difficult task of metaphysical comparison confronts us in trying to understand how the notions of "God" and "Creativity" are related in Whitehead's thought. This task is complicated because the status of creativity in the metaphysical system is not a matter of consensus among students of Whitehead. While it is tempting to leave this matter as an internal affair for Whiteheadian scholars to settle, that will not do. Faith seeks to understand God within some view of reality, and some effort must be made here to understand a notion which seems to be featured so prominently in Whitehead's view.

As distinguished and insightful an interpreter of Whitehead as William Christian argues that for Whitehead creativity is a "pre-systematic" term, a "primitive notion," which "is superseded by the account of how actual entities come into existence by concrescence, in the categories of explanation and obligation."[44] Christian takes the "ultimacy" of creativity to refer to the underived and novel character of actual entities and proposes "originality" as an alternative expression.[45]

One can imagine overeager theological acceptance for Christian's claim. Reducing creativity to the activity of actual entities might seem to open the possibility of giving the metaphysically located God a greater role in the system.[46] If creativity is expunged as a possible source for the activity of actual entities, a gap in the existential adequacy of the system ("Why anything at all?") may be created which only a revealed God can fill.[47] While I seek the fullest possible metaphysical role for God and have already pleaded for openness to the concept of an activity of God which would not be metaphysically discernible,[48] at this point I must agree with those who challenge the descriptive adequacy of Christian's proposal.

In an attempt to identify the metaphysical role of creativity, we must not violate the ontological principle which declares that:

> every decision is referable to one or more actual entities, because in separation from actual entities there is nothing, merely nonentity—"The rest is silence" (PR 68).

Attending to this principle, one might be inclined to say with Christian:

> . . . creativity is not an entity. It is not to be found among the categories of existence. Much less is it an actual entity. Rather it is a name for a general fact, namely that the universe is made up of novel concrescences.[49]

What we do need is a full accounting of that "general fact." Whatever we are to say it will not do to suggest that creativity is "an external agency with its own ulterior purposes" (PR 339). But Whitehead can draw God, other actual entities, and creativity into highly explicit juxtaposition:

> The true metaphysical position is that God is the aboriginal instance of this creativity, and is therefore the aboriginal condition which qualifies its action. It is the function of actuality to characterize the creativity, and God is the eternal primordial character. But of course, there is no meaning to "creativity" apart from its "creatures," and no meaning to "God" apart from the creativity and the "temporal creatures" and no meaning to the temporal creatures apart from "creativity" and "God" (PR 344).

Somehow, without violating the ontological principle, Whitehead wants to say

> that every actual entity, including God, is a creature transcended by the creativity which it qualifies (PR 135).

In classifying creativity as a "pre-systematic" notion, Christian has correctly noted that this notion seems to be of a different logical order from that of actual entities and eternal objects. Lewis Ford and William Garland have noted that as well, but have a different view as to how the logical orders are related. Ford and Garland have both argued that room may be found in Whitehead for "second-order" reasons. Such reasons are not subordinate to actual entities as reasons, but, as it were, prior to them. Actual entities are the "first" (order) reasons why anything is, but we may push behind them to a different order of reasons.

As Ford puts it, the ontological principle

> precludes creativity from being the reason for any particular thing being what it is, but it may serve as a second-order reason or explanation why "actual entities are the only reasons." [50]

Similarly, Garland distinguished between "empiricist explanation" which appeals to actual entities as the reasons for the particular features of the world and "rationalistic explanation" which appeals to principles as the reasons which account for the universal, the generic features of reality.[51] So Ford, noting that the "many actual entities merely taken disjunctively do not constitute a final unity," proposes:

> If the reason cannot be found in the many, it must be sought in the creative process itself, for these constitute the necessary and sufficient reasons for that actuality. The creative rhythm of the one and the many accounts for the on-going process of transition and concrescence, and no other factors need be introduced.[52]

Recognizing, then, that creativity and actual entities are notions of differing logical order, one will not appeal to creativity as a substitute for causal explanation, "first-order" reasons.

Are there, then, distinctive roles to be assigned to creativity in metaphysical explanation—such that the task of metaphysical comparison with God is significantly posed? I believe there are three such: (1) the connection between causally linked occasions, (2) the unitive connection within a particular occasion, (3) the connection between causally unrelated occasions.

(1) Whitehead does affirm the reality of "transition" which should not be overlooked, despite the more frequent stress on concrescence:

> ... we desire to make explicit the discovery of the two kinds of fluency, required for the description of the fluent world. One kind is the

fluency inherent in the constitution of the particular existent. This kind I have called "concrescence." The other kind is the fluency whereby the perishing of the process, on the completion of the particular existent, constitutes that existent as an original element in the constitutions of other particular existents elicited by repetitions of process. This kind I have called "transition." Concrescence moves towards its final cause, which is its subjective aim; transition is the vehicle of the efficient cause, which is the immortal past (*PR* 320).[53]

Again—looking to "transition"—he can write:

It is inherent in the constitution of the immediate, present actuality that a future will supersede it (*PR* 327).

Thus "creativity" becomes particularly apparent in the transition between the actual entities to which the ontological principle refers. This notion finds scientific support beyond Whitehead. While contemporary physics rejects the idea of time as a container indifferent to events, it does not lose sight of succession. Thus Milic Capek writes:

The order of events constituting the causal chains (world lines) is the same in every frame of reference. The irreversibility of world lines is a *topological invariant. There are absolute successions in the world, although there are no absolute juxtapositions.* Because the "world" (a misleading word!) is nothing but the texture of the causal lines, the irreversible character of the latter is conferred upon world history as a whole.[54]

(2) With respect to the emerging concrescence:

the fundamental inescapable fact is the creativity in virtue of which there can be no "many things" which are not subordinated in a concrete unity. Thus a set of all actual occasions is by the nature of things a standpoint for another concrescence which elicits a concrete unity from these many occasions (*PR* 321-322).

In describing this process Whitehead comes to speak of a "pre-established harmony," as the drive toward unification deals with the data felt (formulated in the category of subjective unity) and the subjective forms of the feelings (formulated in the category of subjective harmony) (*PR* 41, 389-390).[55] Out of all the ways in which the many can be felt as one a unifying choice will be made; the spark of unification does not light only to sputter and die. But how can one be so confident? In this respect William Christian very aptly says of the emerging concrescence:

> *That* it is to be actual is wholly determined, so to speak, by the ultimate creativity of which the new occasion is an original embodiment. "Creativity" is the self-causation of the novel occasion.[56]

(3) There is "width" to the creative advance. This is true with respect to the "real potentiality" for becoming. Thus Whitehead speaks of an "extensive continuum" which is:

> a complex of entities united by the various allied relationships of whole to part, and of overlapping so as to possess common parts, and of contact, and of other relationships derived from these primary relationships. . . . This extensive continuum expresses the solidarity of all possible standpoints throughout the whole process of the world . . . all possible actual entities in the future must exemplify these determinations in their relations with the already actual world (*PR* 108). Extension, apart from its spatialization and temporalization, is that general scheme of relationships providing the capacity that many objects can be welded into the real unity of one experience (*PR* 105).

We shall have reason to observe the importance of this concept in Whitehead's theory of perception in the next section. At this point we may settle for a further observation with respect to any two contemporaries— that is, two occasions which do not stand in a strict relationship of succession. With respect to such contemporaries, Whitehead writes:

> there is a "unison of becoming" constituting a positive relation . . . The members of this community share in a common immediacy; they are in "unison" as to their becoming (*PR* 189).[57]

Again the contemporary physicist, while repudiating the homogeneity of a time flowing uniformly, will speak of "transversal extension" to time:

> Becoming is always extensive. . . . Relativistic space is neither the timeless space of Newton nor the Cartesian or Russellian succession of perishing instantaneous spaces, each of which is miraculously recreated at each moment. It is a reality which is not only foreign to duration, but inseparable from it.[58]

Capek likes the analogy of the dynamic structure of polyphony:

In a contrapuntal composition two or several melodically independent movements, whether harmonious or dissonant, are going on. The component melodic movements, besides each being unfolded successively, are also in a certain sense *beside* or *alongside* each other, and this relation "beside" is analogous to the relation "beside" in space.[59]

We have noted that Whitehead announced that his philosophy was concerned with "the becoming, the being, and the relatedness of actual entities." Perhaps one could say that the ontological principle does (at least causally) account for the "becoming" and the "being" of actual entities. But the concept of creativity is required to account adequately for the "relatedness" of entities. Thus Whitehead could say that "the ontological principle is the *first* stage in constituting a theory embracing the notions of 'actual entity,' 'givenness,' and 'process' " (*PR* 68. Italics mine).

Thus, after what may seem to have been a rather considerable detour needed to deal with the status of the notion of creativity in relation to the ontological principle's emphasis on actual entities, we return to the task of trying to understand how the notions of God and creativity are related to each other in the metaphysical sketch.

Whitehead has made clear his goal of metaphysical coherence:

> God is not to be treated as an exception to all metaphysical principles, invoked to save their collapse. He is their chief exemplification (*PR* 521).

To realize this goal he seeks to show that:

> God is an actual entity, and so is the most trivial puff of existence in far-off empty space. But, though there are gradations of importance, and diversities of function, yet in the principles which actuality exemplifies all are on the same level (*PR* 28).

In pursuit of this goal Whitehead moves in *Process and Reality* to speak of dimensions of God which did not characterize the earlier discussions (in *Religion in the Making* and *Science and the Modern World*).[60] He speaks of a "consequent nature," constituted by God's "physical prehensions" of actual entities in the temporal world. Thus both God and non-divine actual entities have both mental and physical poles. Furthermore for both God and non-divine actual occasions the integration of the poles yields a distinct result for the ongoing process, which we have found Whitehead calling the "superject." Just as through the principle of relativity an actual entity bears some relationship to every item in its universe, even if that be a negative one—the many have become one—so in the "consequent nature" God bears such a relationship *positively* to the whole universe at any moment. Whether we express this by saying that all that is is "felt" by God, or even claim that all is preserved or "saved," we touch here a notion to which Whitehead and others have attached great religious importance. I shall present this issue for consideration in Chapter 3 in connection with the theological appropriation of Whitehead. At this point the concern is to notice that the "consequent nature" is dictated by attention to consistency and—more than that—that God's "feeling" the entities of the world concretely brings "flesh" and specificity to the functioning of God as primordial with respect to the divine giving of the initial aim.[61]

Clearly, then, Whitehead intends the notion of God to reveal the same principles bearing on the same "natures" as may be found to apply to all other actual entities. But just as clearly, the "order" of the poles is reversed in that with God "the ideal realization of conceptual feeling takes the precedence" (*PR* 134). Whitehead is very clear about this point:

> Any instance of experience is dipolar, whether that instance be God or an actual occasion of the world. The origination of God is from the mental pole, the origination of an actual occasion is from the physical pole (*PR* 54).

While it is difficult to know just how to add up this combination of continuity and discontinuity, it seems important that the discontinuous element (the reversal of the poles) is introduced in the service of a full accounting of the otherwise prevailing order. If that introduction does manage to preserve the formal features of reality (becoming, unification, novelty; the principles of process and relativity, the ontological principle), I would judge that the coherence of the system has been preserved. Beyond this chapter we will be asking whether or how far what he wishes to say metaphysically is of importance theologically.

If the notion of God coheres with other elements in the metaphysical sketch, it should be possible to ask more precisely: What is the relationship between God and creativity? Four statements seem relevant:

(1) God is clearly not "Creativity-Itself"; rather, creativity is the more encompassing concept with God as an extraordinary instance. To state so flatly that there is a category or reality encompassing God and other entities may seem strange, but the believer will instinctively (and, I shall argue, correctly) choose that option over a pantheism which collapses the distinction between God and the non-divine. To identify God within a more comprehensive metaphysical category—as was done in the four "wisdom" diagrams in Chapter 1—need not be to denigrate God, unless sheer size is considered a criterion for worship and evil dismissed as irrelevant. But I have strayed into theological considerations well ahead of time. Whitehead is making a metaphysical point in writing:

> In all philosophic theory there is an ultimate which is actual in virtue of its accidents. It is only then capable of characterization through the accidental embodiments, and apart from these accidents is devoid of actuality. In the philosophy of organism this ultimate is termed "creativity"; and God is its primordial, nontemporal accident (PR 10-11).[62]

(2) While all actual entities are "at once a creature of creativity and a condition for creativity" (PR 47), God in his primordial nature bears a unique relationship to creativity: God "at once exemplifies and establishes the categoreal conditions" (PR 522). This suggestion will be considered and evaluated further when we reach the theological agenda of the doctrine of creation. Here it may be sufficient to ponder its metaphysical import with Lewis Ford:

> The formative elements need no explanation for their being, but the act which brings them together and creates the being of their togetherness exemplifies in its very nature the determinate generic relatedness appropriate to all actualities which the metaphysical principles express; concrescence as the harnessing of creativity to unify the many, prehension as the means of relating actuality to actuality and actuality to possibility, subjective aim as the means of directing concrescence, etc. All of these principles might have been ordered differently than they are, even though that particular ordering is universally binding on all actuality. The reason why they are ordered as they are lies in God's pri-

mordial decision, but this decision need not be looked for outside of the system it articulates. The integrity of God's decision is to be found in its own obedience to the rules it establishes.[63]

To "establish and exemplify" is a heady mix of notions, but it is not an incoherent one. While full theological evaluation must be delayed, this strikes me as a strong metaphysical statement of divine priority.

(3) While creativity seems the more comprehensive of the two notions, God shares with other actual entities a direct causal role denied to creativity (by the ontological principle), and is distinguished from the other entities—as well as from creativity—by the unique functions assigned to the primordial nature.

(4) God's universally present aim seems significantly to give a specific character to creativity. While the description of the ultimate requires the notions of order and novelty—if the many are to become one (order) and be increased by one (novelty),

> "Order" and "novelty" are but the instruments of his [God's] subjective aim which is the intensification of "formal immediacy." Thus God's purpose in the creative advance is the evocation of intensities (*PR* 135; cf. *PR* 424).

The content of God's aim cries out for clarification, which Whitehead provides by referring to the kind and degree of coordination in the coming together of the actual entity. Issues remain. We shall seek to probe the ethical import of this specification in Chapter 5. We shall have to ask how in the unity of God this specification is related to being able to say both

> The primordial appetitions which jointly constitute God's purpose are seeking intensity, and not preservation. Because they are primordial, there is nothing to preserve. He, in his primordial nature, is unmoved by love for this particular, or that particular; for in this foundational process of creativity, there are no preconstituted particulars. In the foundations of his being, God is indifferent alike to preservation and to novelty. He cares not whether an immediate occasion be old or new, so far as concerns derivation from its ancestry (*PR* 160-161).

and

> His tenderness is directed toward each actual occasion, as it arises (*PR*
> 161).

But it seems clear that Whitehead intends to associate a more specific aim
with God than is required by the sheer structure of creativity itself.

In a rather puzzling formulation Whitehead speaks of God as a "derivative notion" (*PR* 46). Whiteheadians debate among themselves as to
whether, with respect to the system, God should be said to be necessary
or contingent—or even impossible.[64] I shall address the question of metaphysical impossibility in this chapter's closing section on evaluation. The
issue of necessity is posed most forcefully by the work of Charles
Hartshorne to be considered in the next chapter in connection with the
theological appropriation of process categories. I believe it best to consider
even the most general metaphysical principles to include a dependence
upon empirical reality so that alternatives are rationally conceivable.
Within the system God shares contingency with the metaphysical principles themselves. Within those principles God is introduced to meet a
metaphysical need. Since the categories structuring the need possess a
logical priority to the notion addressing the need, the notion of God
may aptly be said to be a "derived" notion.[65] Once again, the theological
import of such a metaphysically derivative status for God—as well as the
intrinsic meaning of the concept of God itself—requires distinct theological assessment. But such assessment is hardly possible until other
"derived" notions are presented to fill in the descriptive sketch. I have in
mind notions which in turn have immediate interest to the believer.

## Humankind and Human Culture

Clearly it will not do to substitute the category "actual occasion,"
whenever we wish to speak of a human being. In such a substitution
the reach of language would be too wide (stretching from the human all
the way down to electronic pulsations) and too short ("Surely we mean
more than *that* by human being!"). While the people of faith may not
wish to separate the human self from the natural world, some distinction
at this point seems required. In this section I will try to show how White-

head accounts for the human selfhood—ontologically and epistemologically—and indicate that he did come to make rather amply developed
remarks regarding human culture. While some of his metaphysical emphases seem to make the account of the human person difficult, his account
of human culture accords well with his metaphysical scheme, thus providing a broad and coherent basis for evaluation.

In the previous section I argued that Whitehead's emphasis on atomism
in the ontological principle should not be understood to exclude a systematic role for "creativity" in the metaphysical view. Moreover, the
very emphasis on the "atoms," the actual occasions, is so formulated as to
require their relatedness—as the principle of relativity makes clear.[66]
As Whitehead writes:

> Atomism does not exclude complexity and universal relativity. Each
> atom is a system of all things (PR 53).

Thus Whitehead comes to speak of a "nexus," a togetherness of actual
entities:

> Actual entities involve each other by reason of their prehensions of each
> other. There are thus real individual facts of the togetherness of actual
> entities, which are real, individual and particular, in the same sense
> in which actual entities and the prehensions are real, individual, and
> particular. Any such particular fact of togetherness among actual en-
> tities is called a "nexus" (PR 29-30).

This togetherness can be spatial or temporal and is usually both in the
realities of ordinary experience: rocks, plants, people. In analyzing these
realities, Whitehead pairs this specialized term, "nexus," with a highly
specialized usage of the ordinary term "society." A "society" is a temporal nexus in which some characteristic is present which is derived by
prehensions of previous generations. If the society is purely temporal so
that the derivation is strictly serial, we have an instance of personal
order, or an "enduring object" (PR 50).

To speak of a human self is to speak of life. How does the account
made available thus far accommodate the notion of "life"? Whitehead
seeks to do so by referring to the degree of mental spontaneity characterizing the society. Typically we are speaking of a complex society—a

"structured" society—which includes subordinate societies within itself. If the occasions constituting these societies are not characterized by mental initiative, the society is said to be inorganic. Such societies deal with the conflicts in the emergence of the occasions "by eliciting a massive objectification of a nexus, while eliminating the detailed diversities of the various members of the nexus" (PR 154). But in a living society mental initiative is exercised

> to receive the novel elements of the environment into explicit feelings with such subjective forms as conciliate them with the complex experiences proper to members of the structured society (PR 155).

This description of life would apply to a living cell, but an account of a living human being requires greater complexity.[67] Such a living society includes more than one subordinate nexus—some living, some not. Such a subordinate nexus may be said to be "entirely living" when all of its member occasions manifest mental spontaneity. Indeed the structured society may in practice be said to be living, when just such a subordinate "entirely living" nexus is "regnant" or "dominant." Differences in the degree of coordination and spontaneity permit Whitehead to distinguish between the inorganic, the vegetable, the animal and the human.[68]

Thus does Whitehead account for "person" and for "life." Yet they are not together, as the phrase "a living person" would require. "Person" speaks of continuity, of tradition; "life" of spontaneity, of originality. Indeed Whitehead seems to ridicule any effort to find the continuity of person in life:

> Life is a bid for freedom: an enduring entity binds any one of its occasions to the line of its ancestry. The doctrine of the enduring soul with its permanent characteristics is exactly the irrelevant answer to the problem which life presents. That problem is, How can there be originality? And the answer explains how the soul need be no more original than a stone (PR 159).

Thus an entirely living nexus may be said to be "non-social," lacking what characterizes a society of actual entities—namely the dependence upon actual entities sharing a common defining characteristic; depending instead upon a complex environment provided by the animal body, and unable to survive without that environment (PR 159-160).[69]

Yet an entirely living nexus "may support a thread of personal order [that is, a directly serial form of "social" order] along some historical route of its members" (PR 163).[70] While there is no ground to posit any such order in the case of single cells, of vegetation, and of the lower animals—according to Whitehead—there is such central direction in the higher animals (PR 163-164). More certainly still, "our own self consciousness is direct awareness of ourselves as such persons" (PR 164). This living person depends on the immediate environment provided by the non-social entirely living nexus. It represents a "canalizing" of the originality in depth and character. Here a balance is struck as continuity and originality come together (PR 164). Thus

> life is a passage from physical order to pure mental originality and from pure mental originality to canalized mental originality (PR 164).

Common sense—while not infallible—rightly clings to this "canalization of the creative urge" as a stubborn fact. Whitehead speaks of us being "carried" on by our immediate past of personal experience so that

> it remains remorselessly true, that we finish a sentence because we have begun it. We are governed by stubborn fact (PR 197. Italics his).

In the less technical language of Modes of Thought a summary is presented:

> The one individual is that coordinated stream of personal experiences which is my thread of life or your thread of life. It is that succession of self-realization, each occasion with its direct memory of its past and with its anticipation of the future. That claim to enduring self-identity is our self-assertion of personal identity (MT 161).

This self-identity is limited and intermittent. In the face of this, one should resist the temptation to seek "another mentality presiding over these other actualities (a kind of Uncle Sam, over and above all the U.S. citizens)."

> All the life in the body is the life of the individual cells. There are thus millions upon millions of centers of life in each animal body. So what needs to be explained is not dissociation of personality but unifying control, by reason of which we not only have unified behavior,

which can be observed by others, but also consciousness of a unified experience (*PR* 165).

Precisely! That is what needs to be explained and of course the question does occur as to whether Whitehead can offer a persuasive explanation within the categories of unity we have been examining. While that question will be considered in this chapter's closing section on evaluation, it is in order here to offer at least a gathered listing of the instruments available to process thought with respect to the unity of the human self: its identity and its continuity. Four seem to emerge:

(1) Whitehead's most direct appeal is to the inheritance of a common character through the successive occasions—a complex eternal object. John B. Bennett comments:

> If we emphasize the valuations as definitive of the series, then we are urging that personal identity is a function of the continuity of the purposes, appetitions, or, more generally, dispositions which characterize the person. . . . There are patterns of behavior which identify us as the persons we are. There are fundamental valuations which distinguish us and thereby separate us from others.[71]

(2) The actual connectedness of the occasions—rather than commonality of character—seems to be what is stressed in Whitehead's observation that

> we—as enduring objects with personal order—objectify the occasions of our own past with peculiar completeness in our immediate present (*PR* 244; cf. *PR* 54).

Whitehead has not developed this theme of "peculiar completeness," but John B. Cobb, Jr. has suggested the theme of the immediate objectification of the mental poles of noncontiguous occasions:

> I do experience immediate prehensions of former mental experiences, sometimes with considerable vividness. . . . This understanding of personal identity explains our sense of responsibility for our past acts. We remember, or can remember, those experiences from the "inside." Hence we identify ourselves with them.[72]

(3) Since the occasion aims not only at the present but at the "relevant

future" as well, it is possible to speak of the self's identity in anticipation, in intention.[73]

(4) William Gallagher has directed attention to the relationship between the dominant society of personally ordered occasions and the other occasions in the brain which support it. Must we suppose the one to include the others or to survey the others instantaneously? But does the unity of mental life suggest either such a hierarchical image or so harried a one? Gallagher has offered an argument for considering the supporting nexus to be more social than Whitehead seems to grant:

> It is necessary to broaden the notion of "living person" so that historic routes of occasions are admitted, which are neither physical objects nor dominant routes. Without such an interpretation, it makes no sense to speak of any organization of the wealth of inheritance from the avenues of the body, as Whitehead clearly does intend. . . . [74]

Gallagher attributes much of the canalizing of novelty to these threads of inheritance which are more closely tied to the reiterative aims of the body. With such ordering in place, Whitehead can say serenely of the final strand of personal unity in experience:

> It toils not, neither does it spin. It receives from the past; it lives in the present. . . . Its sole use to the body is its vivid originality; it is the organ of novelty (PR 516)

While Gallagher's speculations seem to account for continuity more than for unity, there are interesting supporting materials for such continuity to be found in the more habitual forms of behavior: inattentive speech, motor habits and (lower down) biorhythms, the reticular system, balance, centers of appetite.[75]

Whitehead says that what is common to successive identity "is an eternal object or, alternatively, the nexus of successive occasions" (PR 162). In understanding the self, shall we speak of its continuity or of its becoming? In either case it is clear that the human self is radically relational—to itself, to other selves, and to lower levels of organization. A casual inspection of Whitehead might compromise this relational character of the self in favor of the "solitary," of which Whitehead surely does speak. After all, is not emotion rather basic in the unified stream of personal experience? Indeed it is, but the self does not become a subjective castle or prison, inasmuch as emotion is itself relational in this view. The "world" is there for the self in emotion and may be experienced in differing ways. In the next chapter these options will be seen to bear theological potential, as we confront the topic of "structure" of human existence, of Christian existence, of Christ's existence. A common element in the human experience of the world is language:

> . . . the mentality of mankind and the language of mankind created each other. If we like to assume the rise of language as a given fact, then it is not going too far to say that the souls of men are the gift from language to mankind. The account of the sixth day should be written, He gave them speech, and they became souls (*MT* 40-41).[76]

Does this discussion adequately account for the unity of the human person? It is certainly not self-evident that it does. I delay an evaluation of this sensitive point until we have before us Whitehead's discussion of a closely related issue: human perception. But first let us sum up. Personal identity is a form of genetic identity. It is clearly in time. As such:

1. It is partial. (I am not totally identical with myself fifty years ago or with myself yesterday.)
2. It is discontinuous. (Identity is won in the rush of becoming; I must become myself, though we need not assume that there are "gaps" between the units of becoming.)
3. It is cumulative and irreversible. (You can't go home again, or even stand still.)
4. It is temporal and physical. (It is not merely my traits that are temporal. While the mind may particularly fashion a future, the body preserves what is past.) [77]

Early in this chapter we noted that the witness of experience emphasized a dissection of reality into "This-Myself" and "That Other" (as well as "The Whole"). Thus far in this section we have been trying to understand Whitehead's account of how there is a self. That account has not been without its difficulties. Still another lies ahead. The self knows the other; accordingly, it behooves us to consider that knowing, that perceiving process. In particular we must face the fact that we do not seem to perceive discontinuous becoming—electronic occasions or even coordinated streams of experience.

To account for the apparent knowledge of brown tables and gray stones, of objects in a present world, Whitehead bids us begin with the fundamental fact of relatedness. Knowledge is a form of relationship. The paths and the pitfalls of human knowing have to do with distinctions and connections between relationships.

(1) The most fundamental kind of knowledge is precisely the reception of the (past) world that bears in upon us in the creative process: "The crude aboriginal character of direct perception is inheritance" (PR 182). Whitehead terms this the consciousness of the "causal efficacy" of the external world, and suggests that for our clearest examples "we must have recourse to the viscera and to memory" (PR 186). In this mode of perception there is strong emphasis on the body, recalling that the emerging occasion receiving the world originates with the physical pole. Thus Whitehead will say:

> The feeling of the stone is *in the hand;* the feeling of the food is the ache *in the stomach;* the compassionate yearning is *in the bowels,* according to the biblical writers; the feeling of well-being is in the viscera *passim;* ill temper is the emotional tone derivative from the disordered liver (PR 181. Italics his).

While the physical pole is basic in the concrescence, Whitehead's analysis of an actual occasion allows for an elaborate process of supplementation en route to the unification of data in form which constitutes the "satisfaction" of the occasion. In that process of supplementation the "mental" pole is dominant. Consciousness occurs at a late stage in this process through feeling the contrast between what is given and what might come to be. Thus—given this account of the place of the poles in the developing concrescence—it is to be expected that causal efficacy is not emphasized in consciousness, since

> those elements of our experience which stand out clearly and distinctly in our consciousness are not its basic facts; they are the derivative modifications which arise in the process (PR 245).

Yet there is consciousness of causal efficacy, perhaps most noticeably in situations where "ordinary" sense perception is inhibited:

In the dark there are vague presences, doubtfully feared; in the silence, the irresistible causal efficacy of nature presses itself upon us; in the vagueness of the low hum of insects in an August woodland, the inflow into ourselves of feelings from enveloping nature overwhelms us; in the dim consciousness of half-sleep, the presentations of sense fade away and we are left with the vague feeling of influences from vague things around us (*PR* 267).

This notion is so crucial in Whitehead's thought that yet another passage characterizing perception "in the mode of causal efficacy" may be cited. This mode

. . . produces percepts which are vague, not to be controlled, heavy with emotion; it produces the sense of derivation from an immediate past, and of passage to an immediate future; a sense of emotional feeling, belonging to oneself in the past, passing into oneself in the present, and passing from oneself in the present toward oneself in the future; a sense of influx of influence from other vaguer presences in the past, localized and yet evading local definition, such influence modifying, enhancing, inhibiting, diverting, the stress of feeling which we are receiving, unifying, enjoying, and transmitting. This is our general sense of existence, as one item among others, in an efficacious actual world (*PR* 271).

(2) But what of that which *is* clear in consciousness—again our brown tables and gray stones? To account for that we must introduce the derivative mode of "presentational immediacy" and the mixed mode of "symbolic reference." What is clear in consciousness is not a past world (the "inheritance" of causal efficacy), after all, but a present world with which metaphysical explanation must deal:

the immediate present condition of the world at some epoch, according to the old "classical" theory of time—a theory never doubted until within the last few years. . . . Some measure of acceptance is imposed upon metaphysics. If the notion be wholly rejected no appeal to universal obviousness of conviction can have any weight; since there can be no stronger instance of this force of obviousness (*PR* 190-191).

Whitehead would not reject the obvious, but he must explain it. How does a becoming self stumble upon stable objects in knowing a fluid world? Three steps may be distinguished logically.

(a) Presentational immediacy is perception which occurs at a late stage in the concrescence; as a matter of fact it seems to be significantly present only in quite complex occasions. But as so "derived" it would seem to be limited with causal efficacy to the knowledge of the past, even if the very immediate past. Yet Whitehead claims knowledge of the present. How is that possible? Whitehead's approach to this difficulty is by appeal to the "unison of becoming" of which we spoke earlier in describing the role of "creativity" in the system.[78] While the occasion cannot "inherit" the contemporary world, it joins the other actualities in that world in drawing on a common fund of real potentiality, a common past. That common past, caught up in a "unison of becoming," constitutes a common contemporary world to be known. Within the "width" of the unison of becoming spatial location can be meaningfully known. Thus the contemporary world is "immediately presented" as a continuum capable of division, though no direct knowledge of the actual divisions is in hand. But we know *there*—out there, over there.

(b) Furthermore, in the process of mental originality the occasion selects certain patterns ("eternal objects") in what is physically given in causal efficacy and "projects" them into the bare extended world immediately presented to it. Thus presentational immediacy is perception of *"gray, there."*

(c) Finally, given the common datum in both modes, it is possible for the two to come together in the mixed mode of symbolic reference—between causal efficacy and presentational immediacy. We perceive the "gray *stone* there":

> The two modes are unified by a blind symbolic reference by which supplemental feelings derived from the intensive, but vague, mode of efficacy are precipitated upon the distinct regions illustrated in the mode of immediacy. The integration of the two modes in supplemental feeling makes what would have been vague to be distinct, and what would have been shallow to be intense (*PR* 273). [70]

Symbolic reference may work both ways, but

> is chiefly to be thought of as the elucidation of percepts in the mode of causal efficacy by the fluctuating intervention of percepts in the mode of presentational immediacy (*PR* 271).

Error in knowing occurs not in either of the pure modes, but in the mixed mode when the body provides for the perception of the contemporary world content which has not in fact been carried forward in the form proposed. That is, error is risked in the shift of "stone" to "gray, there" in the knowing process. "Stone" itself is reached, whether erroneously or not, by what Whitehead calls the process of "transmutation" in which a pattern common to the members of the nexus is mentally selected for emphasis and applied to the nexus as a whole, instead of to the actual entities making up the nexus (PR 384-389). In that the act of selection of the pattern is a mental and so an original or novel act, the risk of error is present.

Now it is not at all clear that this will do as an account of the "self-knowing-in-the-world." But as a final expository act it is of interest to cite F. David Martin's intriguing effort to associate the various modes of perception with various arts:

> The percepts of music, because they are presented successively, awaken in us the desire for tracing out the temporal curve that is coming. The possibilities ahead draw our attention to the future. On the other hand, the present so completely dominates our participation with paintings, especially abstractions, that both future and past, 'although not irrelevant, are kept at the fringe of our attention. The percepts of painting, because of the allurement of their sensuousness and their nonsuccessive presentation, draw us into an unusual unification within the "here-now." In our participation with literature, however, the inheritance of the past fills in the present with exceptional plentitude.[80]

While the "fit" is hardly perfect, Martin's effort does draw the intricacies of the Whiteheadian scheme into overt relationship with the broad realities of cultural experience. Whitehead did that himself, as well. It remains for us to consider some of the principal themes in his comments, particularly in relationship to the metaphysical categories which we are attempting to understand in this chapter.

The attention to time generally and the principle of process in particular may be discerned in Whitehead's recognition of the transience of cultural achievement. In fact in *Adventures of Ideas* he specifically introduces the principle of process (along with principles of finitude and individuality) in commenting on the reality of adventure which is one of the five qualities which a civilized society is said to exhibit (*AI* 274ff.). As David Hall puts it:

> The aim of experience at balanced complexity is achieved *temporally* and, therefore, *temporarily*.[81]

The metaphysical insight that becoming is not a single stream flowing continuously at a standard rate into which events must be fitted seems to be respected in the rhythmic character Whitehead attributes to cultural development. Thus he argues that education should be aligned to the natural three stage growth process of romance, precision, and generalization.[82]

In an early section of this chapter I associated the principle of relativity —that each being becomes real potential for every later becoming—with Whitehead's emphasis on unification in his characterization of the ultimate. Perhaps the most persistent witness to unification or the principle of relativity in his cultural analysis is his own use of the history of culture. While the austere paragraphs of *Process and Reality* seem to eschew such reference (save for largely formal—analytic—reference to the history of philosophy), Whitehead's other writings are replete with references to Western culture. These are not merely references to the history of ideas. He specifically criticizes the Renaissance for being too Greek in its appropriation of the past, and himself appeals to such apparently non-rational factors as rainfall, floods, trees, coal, and iron (*AI* 7). Other cultural aims joining adventure are truth and beauty. These also remind us of the relativity principle. Truth involves a "facing of the facts" bearing in upon us and beauty the unification of a many characterized by discord, breadth, and intensity.[83]

The ontological principle's emphasis on the actual occasion and the associated valuing of novelty can already be heard in the theme of adventure and its underlying principle of individuality. Romance in education is rooted in the joy of discovery. Not surprisingly in discussing the means for cultural advance Whitehead gives considerable importance to individual freedom in thought and action, tolerance and the like. W. Widick Schroeder thus seems on target in his attempt to develop a Whiteheadian sociological approach to be located somewhere between Weber's freely acting individual and Durkheim's constraining world.[84]

In like manner in his cultural comment Whitehead stresses the bipolarity of events. That seems to hold true in his understanding of art which is both a cultural aim and a cultural means. The Janus-like flexibility of symbolic reference suggests that art turns the abstract into the concrete and the concrete into the abstract (*AI* 281-283; cf. *SMW* 199-200). More broadly, A. H. Johnson notes Whitehead's tendency to resist the movement from polarity to polarization:

> . . . he stresses the mutually interrelated phenomena of change (novelty) AND endurance (routine); fact AND value; vagueness AND clarity; freedom AND compulsion; reason AND emotion. This exemplifies his general *organic* approach to any problem.[85]

Perhaps this sense for complexity was reflected in an "appeal to sanity" which Whitehead issued on the eve of the Second World War:

> In the confused sociological topics which constitute international relations, there are no clear issues. Such premises are either before their times or behind their times, and only rarely with their times. Sometimes they have no contact with temporal events.[86]

There does seem, then, to be a good general fit between the metaphysical sketch and the cultural comment of Whitehead on the level of general principles. That much can be said without examining the metaphysical status of such cultural entities as a school of art, or a political tradition. Were we to do that we should have to examine how eternal objects function as cultural aims and, indeed, how transmutation functions to constitute social realities themselves.[87] Those issues are crucial in Whitehead's thought and they do bear upon his cultural analysis. For example, it seems too simple to say (with Johnson):

> . . . if actual entities are capable of manifesting certain types of behavior, it is possible for a society (of actual entities) to act in the same fashion.[88]

But these problems are not uniquely matters of culture analysis. It seems better to consider them in an attempt at general assessment of the view of reality here proposed.

## An Interim Assessment

In the brief comments just made regarding Whitehead's cultural comment all of his stated "aims of civilization" were mentioned (adventure, truth, art, beauty), save one—peace. To aim at peace is to base one's life on devotion to the ideal of a harmony in which moral rightness triumphs (*AI* 289). Whitehead's discussion of peace is drawn to the theme of transcendence and culminates in an appeal to what readers of the last part of *Process and Reality* will recognize as the "Consequent Nature" of God. Thus religion itself becomes a cultural force—a matter which did not receive comment in the section just completed. I have chosen to reserve Whitehead's comments on religion to the next chapter which deals with the appropriation of process metaphysics for the interest and needs of the faithful. That is admittedly risky, since clearly the realm of faith is one with which metaphysics itself must reckon. But Whitehead's description of religion seems difficult to distinguish sharply from his religious proposals. Thus the two may well be discussed together in beginning to consider what one shall say of and to faith from this perspective.

Just as I have reserved discussion of Whitehead's thoughts on religion, so have I tried in this chapter to limit the discussion of the notion of "God" to its metaphysical role. For both of these reasons this attempt at assessment must be considered an "interim" one. As we attempt in later chapters to interact with this viewpoint theologically, the way will be made for a more complete assessment—one in which the claims of faith regarding the shape of reality can be considered. Still, the believer does not have a monopoly on reality, nor—it may be supposed—on the understanding of reality. That case was argued in the first chapter. It seems possible therefore to attempt a preliminary evaluation of this viewpoint without explicit reference to the claims of faith. It seems desirable to do so in the search for a warrant for calling the people of faith to further interaction with this particular view of reality. With a process view before us now—at least in outline—we ask, Does this seem to be true to reality as we know it?

This assessment cannot be rendered in simple quantitative terms, as by passing an evaluative ballot among contemporary philosophers. Complete metaphysical consensus cannot be required or expected. A number of reasons for rejecting such a standard may be mentioned.

(1) We began this chapter with a discussion of the difficult method of "imaginative generalization" which is needed when the "method of difference" does not serve adequately. Conscientious and careful students of reality may still differ in judgment.

(2) Moreover, there is the essentially inexhaustible character of the task of description to which Stuart Hampshire bears witness:

> Description of reality is essentially inexhaustible. It is in principle impossible that we should ever come to the end of it and complete our description. This is true, not only because we cannot set limits to reality or give a possible sense to the words "I have identified all the things that there are"; but, more strongly, because we cannot even give sense to the words, "I have identified all the things that there are in this room." The inexhaustibility lies in the nature of description and identification, however restricted they may be.[89]

The judgment regarding which data are really crucial is one which may well divide philosophers.

(3) Still more troublesome, the selection of perspective or "root metaphor" in terms of which selection of data and generalization from data are to occur seems to retain some element of arbitrariness.[90] David Tracy argues that the great philosophers were well aware of such difficulties:

> . . . philosophy—at least among the great classical philosophers as distinct from their "schools"—has always recognized itself as "problematic." When one states—as Aristotle does—that the "first principles" of philosophy cannot strictly be proved, but can be indirectly validated (through the self-contradiction which their denial involves), then one has a rather exact grasp of the meaning of a properly "problematic" discipline.[91]

I cannot offer even so sure a validation, since I have emphasized the empirical character of metaphysical construction, acknowledging that alternative systems are conceivable and indeed can make some claims upon experience.

If metaphysical consensus is not available (for any or all of these reasons—or others) will faith lose interest in this endeavor? I think not.

Faith is more interested in the doing of the metaphysical task—that the work is under way—than in the delivery of a finished system. Faith knows intimately the reality of disagreement within its own camp and it does not take this as an indication of the futility of inter-faith dialog. Since the claims of faith are themselves metaphysical data of a sort, faith may well be more suspicious of metaphysical uniformity than of metaphysical diversity. Faith will not join those who find such diversity to be a sign of the futility of the task.[92] The goal sought—to understand what is real— even if it be conceived in a less than final or absolute fashion is no more difficult than it is precious.

What then shall we require of Whitehead qualitatively? How shall we proceed to evaluate his work? While philosophic criteria cannot be clean-ly separated from philosophic position,[93] the four criteria earlier identified —applicability, adequacy, consistency, and coherence—do not seem idio-syncratically Whiteheadian. In thus appealing to "rational" (consistency, coherence) and "empirical" (applicability, adequacy) criteria, Whitehead resembles Antony Flew who—while writing from a different perspective than process thinkers—pleads for coherence and fidelity to experience broadly and fairly understood as metaphysical criteria.[94]

I shall emphasize particularly the empirical criteria. But what counts as "experience"? I find David Crocker's list helpful:

a. Perceptual and introspective experience and the common sense con-cepts by which we formulate or interpret such experiences.
b. Moral, aesthetic, and religious intuitions and their embodiment in practical activity, works of art, and religious experience.
c. Well-founded scientific theories and the hypothetical constructs of theoretical entities postulated in such theories.
d. The insights and illuminating concepts of other speculative philoso-phies.[95]

Since the last two items themselves represent constructive interpretive work, the appeal to experience seems to be on more sure common ground in stressing the first two items. Thus other intellectual disciplines function like other metaphysical views, probing the rational adequacy of White-head's views by appealing—with and against him—to the deliverances of immediate experience. Debates about flight patterns become important precisely in relation to the ground from which one takes off and which

one would see the better.[96] Does, then, the view from Whitehead's metaphysical airplane fit the ground on which we stand?

Significant criticism and defense of Whitehead's metaphysical sketch
focus on the complex monism his thought represents. His mode of thought
is essentially monistic in that one mode of relatedness (causal efficacy) is
the basic principle explanatory of all that is—rocks, molecules, persons,
institutions. In his own terms, his intent is precisely metaphysical in that
one set of principles shall be sought "in terms of which every element of
our experience can be interpreted" (PR 4). But that monism is characterized by considerable complexity, involving several kinds of components and striking differences of degree in the manner of their combination. Criticism either seems to attack the monism, arguing for a fundamental duality in reality,[97] or the pluralism internal to the monism.
While Whitehead could not consistently satisfy both kinds of objections
by any conceivable emendations, the critiques still deserve independent
attention.

Causal efficacy's emphasis on organic relatedness—on an entity's relationships being constitutive of but not exhaustive of its reality—seems
strongly supported in the reading(s) of experience available in other
disciplines. Even two decades ago Peter F. Drucker could comment:

> Every discipline has as its center today a concept of a whole that is
> not the result of its parts, not equal to the sum of its parts, and not iden-
> tifiable, knowable, measureable, predictable, effective or meaningful
> through identifying, knowing, measuring, predicting, moving or under-
> standing the parts. The central concepts in every one of our modern
> disciplines, sciences and arts are patterns and configurations.[98]

Or, perhaps softening the emphasis on final causality somewhat, one
could note the congeniality of Whitehead's thought to general systems
theory, as represented by Ludwig von Bertalanffy and Ervin Laszlo.[99]
An understanding of natural wholes that are self-adaptive and even self-
creative, displayed hierarchically in a cosmic environment, will ring right
for the student of Whitehead. Again, Hartshorne can cite the "notable
agreement" between Gilbert Ryle and Whitehead on the point that

> the "introspection" by which our own experiences are given is not a
> mysterious function additional to perception and memory. It simply is
> memory, especially in its very short-run and most immediate form.[100]

The notion of internal relationships, then—in non-reductive wholes, in systems that are constitutive rather than merely summative, in human memory—fares well enough today, when we ask of the shape of reality. Intellectual disciplines seem to have followed the direction given to Whitehead by immediate experience's vague grasp of reality as a totality with internal distinctions. The difficulty comes down the road in the character and range of that relatedness. The issue focuses when we consider the similarities and differences between what is human and what is not.

Generally (though not universally) it is granted that human relatedness is not exhaustive of selfhood—as Drucker put it, "the whole is more than the sum of its parts." We have seen that one of Whitehead's principal devices for rendering this conviction is to insist that there is a "How" of private feeling in the "What" of public relatedness. In the coming together of an entity there is "for-itself-ness," which is not severed from the external relationships, since it is precisely how that which comes together is "received," or "felt." Whitehead's emphasis that "life is an internal fact for its own sake, before it is an external fact relating itself to others" (*RM* 15), is at least a conceivable way of rendering intelligible the frequently asserted notion concerning the "more" characterizing the human whole.

But of course Whitehead will not limit this point to humankind. We have already noted Bryant Keeling's strong objection to the universal extension of the concept of "feeling."[101] John Lawrence echoes that objection in an article bearing the forthright title, "Whitehead's Failure":

> What reason is there to assume that every concrete individual is like a human in being a "subject of experience"? Or alternatively, what justification can be offered for the generalized application of concepts like memory, emotional affect, sympathy, anticipation, etc., which are prominent in Whitehead's analysis of human experience?[102]

Can Whitehead be faulted for spiritualizing — humanizing — nature? This question elicits a two-fold response: (1) One may acknowledge that Whitehead may well have been too enthusiastic in the application of such terms as "feeling," since what we are speaking of in the matter of universal subjectivity is clearly not human subjectivity. To prefer the extension of ordinary meaning for "feeling" to the invention of a new vocabulary ("prehension") is still to risk distortion. (2) One may argue that the range of reference for subjectivity does not proceed from an analysis of human becoming (however much it may ring true in that respect), but from an elucidation of all becoming. If the process of reality leading to unification is productive of novelty, how shall that be understood in a most rudimentary fashion? Subjectivity, for-oneself-ness, serves to that end. It is, as it were, the inner core of the reality of change noted outwardly in novelty.

How does the argument go? One may begin with the view that the indeterminacy of which physicists write characterizes not only our measure of reality, but the reality itself.[103] What if all realities—human beings and electronic vibrations alike—are such as to elude exact measurement and defy total predictability? If this be granted, the advance to universal internal relatedness seems less ambitious than if we thought of inert particles moved only by external force. Motion is productive of a novelty which has an ineluctable contingency about it. It seems reasonable to posit some element of internal agency. In every actual entity there is something that acts and is acted upon. Now we are in a position to recognize that it is conceivable that every such entity is not only objectively novel, it is subjectively real. At once, it is new for the other and real for itself.

No sooner is that response made than a new battle is joined. For it is precisely cosmic categories of this type which raise the question of the adequacy of Whitehead's monistic thinking to account for the distinctiveness of human life and experience. If such metaphysical sweep does not claim too much for nature, it surely says too little of humankind! Critics who make this charge read Whitehead rightly, as a characteristic passage in *Adventures of Ideas* makes clear:

> Any doctrine which refuses to place human experience outside nature must find in descriptions of human experience factors which also enter into the descriptions of less specialized natural occurrences. If there be no such factors, then the doctrine of human experience as a fact within nature is mere bluff (*AI* 184-185).

That Whitehead is not bluffing cannot be doubted! But it can and has been doubted whether he finds anything—or enough—in human experience which is distinctive. Even so friendly a reader as Ian Barbour writes:

With regard to the higher levels, it may be questioned whether Whitehead's account of the continuity and identity of the human self is satisfactory.[104]

Three issues may be distinguished: (1) With respect to the "inter-weaving" of efficient and final causation in the actual occasion, is genuine freedom available? (2) With respect to the atomistic character of reality, can the freedom (and identity) of a human self be accounted for by reference to an occasion (even if free) at any given point in time? (3) With respect to the atomistic character of reality, can the continuity of the human self—as implied in intention and responsibility—be accounted for by the connections between occasions over a "stretch" of time?

(1) While Whitehead seems to want to talk of the emerging occasion's freedom to modify the initial aim given to it (by God), he may not be able to do this convincingly if he holds to the view that occasions happen "all at once" so that to speak of stages in concrescence is not to speak temporally. This objection has been made in an intricate argument by Edward Pols. [105] Still more basic in Pols' position seems to be the elimination of any systematic basis for an agency to function within the occasion in the modification of the subjective aim. Does Whitehead's "final causality" operate out of nothing? To respond I would argue that Whitehead is saved from an appeal to an ex nihilo freedom within the occasion by reference to the principle of creativity. Pols has considered this and found it wanting:

> It would appear, then, that creativity, divorced from the ordering given it by one of its creatures—God—is a "mere" activity. The word "creativity" merely expresses the fact that some indeterminate creature must always emerge, and that the universe is never complete. It does not designate any active power exercised by the subject as such.[106]

I wrote earlier of how creativity works in both transition and concrescence.[107] Here I contend that creativity accounts for the *provision* of the power of indetermination, while the occasion itself accounts for the specific *exercise* of that power so provided. That does seem to reduce the offense of the ex nihilo quality, though it does not remove the mystery of material choice. Furthermore, the freedom is exercised precisely *within* the emerging occasion—with a settled world already given for it. Thus it would be inappropriate to speak of this succession involved in the modification of the subjective aim *within* the occasion as temporal, if that term is to be reserved for the transition *between* occasions. Such a distinction seems consistent with Whitehead's work and is invited by a remarkably explicit passage in Whitehead's essay entitled "Time":

> Supersession is a three-way process. Each occasion supersedes other occasions, it is superseded by other occasions, and it is internally a process of supersession, in part potential and in part actual. . . . *Time is concerned primarily with the physical poles of occasions,* and only derivatively with the mental poles. But the linkage between the physical and the mental pole of an occasion illustrates the truth *that the category of supersession transcends time, since this linkage is both extratemporal and yet is an instance of supersession.*[108]

Whitehead's interweaving of "efficient" and "final" causality is undeniably complex, but it does seem paralleled in other accounts of choice—as in Søren Kierkegaard's thought where one needs to say *both* that that which is chosen does not exist and comes into existence with the choice *and* that that which is chosen exists, otherwise there would not be a choice.[109] Of course Kierkegaard adamantly opposes talk about such "choosing" in entities which are not human. We need to turn to the issue of the freedom of the self. But it is worth nothing that the mix of efficient and final causality found in process thought is not in principle idiosyncratic. Indeed one might argue that the interests of coherence are better served with Whitehead where the elusive character of freedom is found to be a factor in all reality and is given systematic anchorage in the principle of creativity.

(2) Can a microscopic analysis of atomic occasions—even if they are found to be free—account for our virtually indubitable experience of self-identity, including the freedom of that self? Gallagher's hypothesis helpfully contributes subordinate centers of unity, drawing on the importance of inheritance from the body.[110] David Crocker tries to account for the unity of experience by stressing that the interval between successive occasions is so infinitesimal as to elude consciousness.[111] Indeed Whitehead went so far as to speak of the contiguity of occasions:

The notion of the contiguity of occasions is important. Two occasions, which are not contemporary, are contiguous in time when there is no occasion which is antecedent to one of them but subsequent to the other. A purely temporal nexus (e.g., a self) is continuous when . . . each occasion is contiguous with an earlier occasion (*AI* 202).

Still Whitehead's "process self" seems to run counter to our ordinary perception of ourselves. That perception needs critical attention. If Whitehead's demotion of sense perception can be found to be convincing, it will remove part of the force behind the appeal to a more substantial self. He draws support in that effort from writers who can hardly be classified as process thinkers. For example, A. R. Louch, understanding himself to be following the lead of Wittgenstein, writes:

> Describing and appraising are not opposed ways of examining or commenting on the world; rather, one way of viewing and describing the world is by means of appraising, that is, moral and aesthetic categories. This hypothetico-deductive account of explanation has force only so long as one is prepared to accept an atomistic (e.g., sense-datum) account of what is to be observed. In rejecting this account of explanation, I have also rejected an atomistic metaphysics.[112]

Perhaps that "solid" substance I see is not so surely to be identified as my "self." Nor will it do—when threatened with the disappearance of a material substantial self—to retreat dualistically to an inaccessible inner "spiritual" substance. At least such an appeal would have to get past the critiques of contemporary linguistic philosophers like Strawson and Malcolm, as well as empirical testimony to the interweaving of the physical and mental.[113] As Whitehead puts it: "No one ever says, Here am I, and I have brought my body with me" (*MT* 156).

Yet, while weighty objections can be raised against the alternative conception of a more substantial self, some uneasiness persists about the adequacy of Whitehead's account. Perhaps the issue is better focused by attending to the matter of the continuity of the self. Perhaps the key to a fuller selfhood lies not in trying to find some block-like ego—whether physical or mental—outside of time. Rather it may be right to recognize the soundness of the stress on temporality but go Whitehead one better by stressing the linear continuity of the self, as difficult as that may seem to be within the categories of his atomistic theory.

(3) Continuity in time seems a promising key to selfhood, since we regularly associate the human with such matters as having intentions, acting purposefully, and assuming responsibility for one's actions.[114] We have already noted that process thought can offer the occasion aiming not merely at the present but at the "relevant future" as well.[115] David Crocker has written a detailed account of how Whiteheadian categories can account for intendings, intentions, and intentional actions—stressing the theme of the subjective form of purpose in relation to propositions and projects for the relevant future.[116]

What process thought does not seem able to offer is some continuity in becoming for the string of intending occasions, as if there were a whole that did not depend on the parts. Edward Pols, for example, claims just that for his alternative view:

> . . . since we are claiming that there is a power "relation" between the unity of the act and the multiplicity of the infrastructure: we represent the act as a power so permeating the spatiotemporal manifold of the infrastructure as to unify it—the unification being precisely the full concreteness of the act.[117]

Pols specifically opposes his view to Whitehead's epochal theory with its "atomistic assumption that discrete time-units are of the smallest possible size only." [118] Pols is clearly right in finding his view different from that of Whitehead. It follows, of course, that he has a different problem—to show how the larger wholes and the "infrastructure" of particulars are connected. Should one prefer the one problem to the other?

As an "interim" assessment of this point, three conclusions seem warranted: (1) Even if some greater unity and/or continuity must be claimed and can be found for the self, that need not be in defiance of what Whitehead's analysis contributes, but can be inclusive of it. Whitehead's statements about becoming, about body-mind interweaving, etc., do describe, even if they do not exhaust, the self. (2) Whether more needs to be said of the self than Whitehead seems able to say cannot be determined, given the agenda of this book, without specifically considering the claims the people of faith feel constrained to make regarding human selfhood. Part III considers certain of these claims. (3) Speculation can be welcomed which might advance this topic beyond Whitehead's own work. In that work itself there seems to be some movement in this direction. Thus, while the analysis of "life" in *Process and Reality* stresses originality at the possible expense of order, Whitehead offers a more balanced account in *Adventures of Ideas:*

> In so far as the mental spontaneities of occasions do not thwart each other, but are directed to a common objective amid varying circumstances, there is life. The essence of life is the teleological introduction of novelty, with some conformation of objectives. Thus novelty of circumstances is met with novelty of functioning adapted to steadiness of purpose (*AI* 207).

One speculative advance on Whitehead is John Cobb's employment of the concept of regional inclusion to understand the relationship between the regnant society of personally ordered occasions that answers to the concept of a "soul" in Whitehead's thought and the other occasions in the brain which support the regnant society. Another is William Gallagher's effort to provide intermediate levels of organization for the presiding occasion. One wonders whether the continuity provided by the reality of creativity might yield something on the topic of the self that emphasis on the atomism and the ontological principle cannot.

What we have said thus far might amount to the charge that Whitehead's monistic thinking obliterates the distinction between an animal kingdom and humankind, between nature and history. Blur it, it does. The issue is, of course, how radical a distinction is desired or required. It may be relevant to consider briefly the comments of other disciplines involved in this distinction. Whitehead's most copious support comes from the natural sciences—especially physics. While Whitehead has been challenged by physicists who would follow Einstein's more deterministic tendencies,[119] there seems to be broad support for his views. Thus David Bohm writes of degrees of stability and autonomy at each level of physical organization[120] and Errol Harris writes:

> Each stage is produced by a sort of "self-enfoldment" of the structure characterizing the prior stage, producing in unbroken series: first energy, then mass, then atoms, as successively more intricate, more closely integrated and more stable patterns of self-manifestation of the primordial process of activity, in which the continuum of events is space-time.[121]

In addition to Whitehead's own considerable attention to history, Whiteheadians have tried to apply process metaphysics to historical method to
overcome difficulties in both analytical and genetic theories of explanation.[122] Moreover, Toynbee can write in a way that invites, if not requires,
Whiteheadian underpinnings:

> My guess is that patterns in the past, insofar as they are real—and,
> though this is very controversial, I believe them to be real—are pat-
> terns due to a certain amount of uniformity, of regularity in the work-
> ing of the subconscious part of the human psyche, whereas the element
> of unpredictability, which I think is the dominant element, comes
> from the freedom of choice that we have on the conscious and volitional
> level of our minds.[123]

The ecologists, drawing history and nature together, would seem
strongly to support Whitehead's monistic approach. J. B. Bennett suggests
three reasons for that support:

> The first reason involves the notion of a system. The basic systematic
> principle of ecologists is that people can never do merely one thing.
> This principle of interdependence is given vast systematic extension
> in Whitehead's thought. The second reason involves some of the spe-
> cific ways Whitehead's systematic philosophy has of clarifying the
> claim that man and nature are ultimately of one community. The third
> reason involves the sense in which nature can be regarded as possessing
> value, independent of man, and the sense in which moral categories
> can be considered to extend to it.[124]

Perhaps, then, a case can be made that Whitehead's abstruse lines do in
fact manage rather well when confronted with the "empirical" criteria
of applicability and adequacy. But what of consistency and coherence?
Among the significant criticisms of Whitehead's thought which charge
incoherence, several amount to objecting to the pluralism of components
in the system. Thus Pols objects to the attempt to introduce several kinds
of agency, when the eternal objects are actually the determinative force
in the system.[125] Sherburne proposes a "Whitehead without God," finding functions assigned needlessly to God in the system.[126] And Weiss
objects to the pluralism of orders involved in the reversal of the poles with
respect to God.[127]

A key element in each of these issues is the status of creativity. I have

already suggested that creativity functions to support the self determinative power of actual occasions, resisting the sovereignty Pols finds for
eternal objects. I can readily agree with Sherburne that creativity functions
as the ground for the givenness of the past and wonder whether claiming
too much for God in some Whiteheadian interpretations may have ob-
scured the legitimate roles discussed in the expository section of this
chapter.[128] I have already suggested how the reversal of the poles is introduced in the service of a full accounting of the otherwise prevailing order
and that the principles of process and relativity and the ontological principle are preserved in that introduction. Again, these are the basic principles which elucidate the reality of creativity. Without denying that
serious issues are raised by each of these challenges, it seems possible to
draw these objections to Whitehead's pluralism into a later discussion
when it must be asked whether the juxtaposition of creativity and God is
acceptable to Christian faith. That discussion lies ahead.

I submit that Whitehead's metaphysical sketch deserves the attention
of Christians who find their faith calling them to quest for wisdom—
tactical, conceptual, ethical, or constitutive—as to how things are. I do
that on the basis of the defense that can be assembled against the charges
put to his thought, the corroborating support of other disciplines, and—
most basically—because the reading of immediate experience that underlies this system rings true to me.

Self and other, fact and value, flow and identity—of these is my life
composed. Whitehead has the terms right. He has thought them together
well. In the vague totality one can speak of many becoming one and of
increase by one(s). The farther one goes in abstraction—through the principles of process and relativity and the ontological principle and on to the
rich subordinate resources—the less sure one may be. In that necessary
work of explication the support and criticism of philosophical colleagues
and of other disciplines are significant. Much of that work remains to be
done, and an assessment such as I have attempted can only be an interim
one. But I suggest Whitehead's promise for the people of faith is such that
they should join in that work.

My suggestion is hardly novel. There already exists a multitude of
efforts to speak of faith claims in relation to this view of reality. I have
offered a somewhat full sketch of the view precisely in order to invite your

independent reflection with respect to the concerns of faith. But it would be folly to undertake that task without any regard for the work of others. Such attention should not be uncritical. Those others may or may not share one's own reading of the claims of faith at particular points. They may or may not share with Whitehead his process reading (as here interpreted) of the shape of reality. That remains to be seen and is worth seeing.

# 3

# Projects: A Sketch of Recent Theological Appropriation

## Religion in Whitehead: The Quest for Justification and the Two Natures

To understand the novel order which confronts us, Whitehead speaks of God "in his primordial nature."[1] To be, to become, in the process of "novel togetherness" is to have to do with God, as that reality responsible for giving the emerging concrescence its "initial aim." Clearly, if this is an accurate metaphysical assessment it applies to humankind. But, while on this account to be human is thus to be in relationship to God, it is not as such to be in *conscious* relationship with God. Nonetheless people do consciously worship, love, serve, fear . . . God! Can the indisputable fact of religion as a human phenomenon be synthesized with the metaphysical function(s) assigned to "God"? At the very least, Whitehead as a metaphysician is obliged to offer an interpretation of religion within his metaphysical system.

As matters turn out, the claims of religion lead Whitehead to considerable amplification of a theme suggested metaphysically. That theme, "the consequent nature of God," figured in the metaphysical analysis of Chapter 2 as an offering to consistency and as an informing-enabling of the otherwise barer primordial valuation of possibility.[2] God's timeless valuation is able to bear upon (the "superjective" aspect) the world with freshly relevant purpose through the knowledge present to God as consequent. Together the "consequent" and the "primordial" provide the basis for Whitehead's own constructive work in religion and for the choices which have confronted and characterized efforts to appropriate this metaphysics theologically.

In religion we are driven beyond (within?) the metaphysical universals to the realm of the particular, the concrete, the historical. Already in 1925, in *Science and the Modern World,* Whitehead had recognized the elusive character of contingency:

> There is a metaphysical need for a principle of determination, but there can be no metaphysical reason for what is determined. . . . The general principle of empiricism depends upon the doctrine that there is a principle of concretion which is not discoverable by abstract reason. What further can be known about God must be sought in the region of particular experiences, and therefore rests on an empirical basis (*SMW* 178).

Similarly, at the very end of his metaphysical description in *Process and Reality* (1929) Whitehead, turning directly to the "nature of God," acknowledges that:

> any cogency of argument entirely depends upon elucidation of somewhat exceptional elements in our conscious experience—those elements which may roughly be classed together as religious and moral intuitions (*PR* 521).

But, while Whitehead may in a sense be beyond the metaphysical in dealing with what is stubbornly "particular" and "exceptional," he will not permit his analysis of religion to take a holiday from exemplifying the principles of the metaphysics to which he has come:

> In the first place, God is not to be treated as an exception to all metaphysical principles, invoked to save their collapse. He is their chief exemplification (*PR* 521).

Whitehead offers a view of religion, particularly in *Religion in the Making* (1926), which not only seeks to avoid metaphysical violations with regard to the subjective (human religion) and objective (the nature of God) dimensions of the phenomenon. That view seeks as well to understand religion as aiming at metaphysics (*RM* 31). Yet Whitehead would resist an Hegelian tendency to identify faith as philosophy for people with low I.Q.s. Whether he can manage the delicate maneuvers required by this complex of relationships and distinctions remains to be seen.

"Justification is the basis of all religion" (*RM* 15). But what lies within that phrase so familiar to religious ears is a dialectic of the inner and the outer.

> Religion is the art and the theory of the internal life of man, so far as it depends on the man himself and on what is permanent in the nature of things (*RM* 16).

On the one hand, the inner is emphasized. Whitehead's statements here range from the epigrammatic "You *use* arithmetic, but you *are* religious" (*RM* 14. Italics his) to the abstract "Religion deals with the formation of the experiencing subject; whereas science deals with the objects, which are the data forming the primary phase in this experience" (*PR* 24). This emphasis yields the controversial formulation that "Religion is what the individual does with his own solitariness" (*RM* 16). It offers examples:

> The great religious conceptions which haunt the imaginations of civilized mankind are scenes of solitariness: Prometheus chained to his rock, Mahomet brooding in the desert, the meditations of the Buddha, the solitary Man on the Cross. It belongs to the depth of the religious spirit to have felt forsaken, even by God (*RM* 19).

The "solitariness" emphasis has been popularly attacked as a view which isolates the individual from other human beings. If that were true, it would be a striking development in a metaphysics which so emphasizes relationships as to be hard pressed to develop a concept of the individual. Surely at the outset at least such criticism must soften in the face of the other side of Whitehead's dialectic: "What is permanent in the nature of things."

It is here, with the outer side of the dialectic, that the metaphysical is most obviously involved. The scope of faith's concern is universal. As such it will intersect with the universal claims of metaphysics. Indeed, Whitehead even claims:

Rational religion appeals to the direct intuition of special occasions and
to the elucidatory power of its concepts for all occasions. It arises from
that which is special but it extends to what is general. The doctrines of
rational religion aim at being that metaphysics which can be derived
from the supernormal experience of mankind in its moments of finest
insight (*RM* 31. Cf. *PR* 23).

Whitehead seeks to hold the two sides together, claiming of "rational"
religion that "because it is universal, it introduces the note of solitariness"
(*RM* 47). Filling out the connection, he writes:

. . . universality is a disconnection from immediate surroundings. It is
an endeavor to find something permanent and intelligible by which to
interpret the confusion of immediate detail (*RM* 47-48).

Or more concretely:

Now, so far as concerns religion, the distinction of a world-conscious-
ness as contrasted with a social consciousness is the change of emphasis
in the concept of rightness. A social consciousness concerns people whom
you know and love individually. Hence, rightness is mixed up with the
notion of preservation. Conduct is right which will lead some god to
protect you; and it is wrong if it stirs some irascible being to compass
your destruction. Such religion is a branch of diplomacy. But a world-
consciousness is more disengaged. It rises to the conception of an essential rightness of things. The individuals are indifferent, because unknown (*RM* 39-40).[3]

The value judgments in such a paragraph make it apparent that "religion in Whitehead" will not be a matter of pallid neutrality. In fact, he
seeks in religion an answer to a deep problem which emerges within
the metaphysics itself—the problem of "perpetual perishing." It is this
reality of perpetual perishing which makes the notion of personal continuity of becoming the truly difficult one that we found it to be at the
end of the last chapter. As Whitehead puts it:

The process of concrescence terminates with the attainment of a fully
*determinate* "satisfaction"; and the creativity thereby passes over into
the "given" primary phase for the conscrescence of other actual entities. . . . Completion is the perishing of immediacy: "It never really is"
(*PR* 130. Italics his).

If the concrescence as subject cannot really *be,* it can hardly be supposed to *abide.* It is to this fundamental but rather cheerless notion of perishing that the issue of justification is addressed. But before turning to that problem and the resources available in (to) religion, it remains to say something more of the origin and development of the human religious dynamics.

Whitehead speaks of four factors in religion: ritual, emotion, belief, rationalization *(RM* 18). This order is generally that of their emergence in history, even though it may be "untrue to affirm that the later factors are ever wholly absent" *(RM* 18-19). Of the origin of religion, it is difficult to be clear. It is thought to lie in ritual:

> Ritual is the primitive outcome of superfluous energy and leisure. It exemplifies the tendency of living bodies to repeat their own actions. Thus the actions necessary in hunting for food, or in other useful pursuits, are repeated for their own sakes; and their repetition also repeats the joy of exercise and the emotion of success *(RM* 20).

Thus ritual produces emotion which in turn spurs ritual. But we have not yet reached the origin of religion, specifically. Play and religion illustrate the same dialectic of ritual and emotion. Whitehead comments:

> . . . an habitual ritual may diverge into religion or into play, according to the quality of the emotion excited. Even in comparatively modern times, among the Greeks of the fifth century before Christ, the Olympic Games were tinged with religion, and the Dionysiac festival in Attica ended with a comic drama. Also in the modern world, a holy day and a holiday are kindred notions *(RM* 21).

Two notions seem essential in distinguishing the "religious quality" in emotion: universality and rightness. A passage from *Process and Reality* can serve to close up our work of definition and introduce the matter of development in its reference to universality:

> Religion is an ultimate craving to infuse into the insistent particularity of emotion that non-temporal generality which primarily belongs to conceptual thought alone. In the higher organisms the differences of tempo between the mere emotions and the conceptual experiences produce a life-tedium, unless this supreme fusion has been effected. The two sides of the organism require a reconciliation in which emotional experiences

illustrate a conceptual justification and conceptual experiences find an emotional illustration (*PR* 23).

Given this understanding of religion, it is clear that the progressive development of the polarity of solitariness and universality will be valued. This holds true of the way in which religion functions:

> Rational religion is religion whose beliefs and rituals have been reorganized with the aim of making it the central element in a coherent ordering of life—an ordering which shall be coherent both in respect to the elucidation of thought, and in respect to the direction of conduct towards a unified purpose commanding ethical approval (*RM* 30).

The value of solitariness/universality not only bears on the life of believers; it reaches out to impose an order of value on the content of the faith as well. Thus Whitehead writes that

> [religion] runs through three stages, if it evolves to its final satisfaction. It is the transition from God the void to God the enemy, and from God the enemy to God the companion (*RM* 16).

As religion develops, then, the universal is no longer understood to be indifferent or even hostile to the individual's solitary self. This linkage permits the individual to launch criticism of less advanced forms. Thus Whitehead applauds the Hebrew prophets in whom "rational criticism was admitted in principle":

> The appeal was from the tribal custom to the direct individual intuition, ethical, metaphysical, or logical: "For I desired mercy, and not sacrifice; and the knowledge of God more than burnt offerings," are words which Hosea ascribes to Jehovah; and he thereby employs the principles of individual criticism of tribal custom, and bases it upon direct ethical intuition (*RM* 35. Cf. 17).

In sum, while Whitehead argues against the uncritical association of religion and goodness, calling religion "the last refuge of human savagery" (*RM* 36), it is clear in which direction he would have the power of religion develop:

> "Strait is the gate, and narrow is the way . . . and few there be that find it." When a modern religion forgets this saying, it is suffering from

an atavistic relapse into primitive barbarism. It is appealing to the psychology of the herd, away from the intuitions of the few (*RM* 28).

I have drawn very extensively on Whitehead's discussion in *Religion in the Making,* since that discussion is conducted with a helpful concreteness of phrasing and example lacking in much of *Process and Reality.* But much remains unclear as yet. It is clear, I take it, that religion permits and requires metaphysical backing. It permits such, since it does not withdraw behind a "special religious sense" (*RM* 119). It requires such, for if in religion the solitary seeks the universal,

> a rational religion must not confine itself to moments of emotional excitement. It must find its verification at all temperatures (*RM* 53).[4]

But it is not clear, for example, that to find a universal God is to find a companion whose goodness you seek to imitate (*RM* 40). Nor, more basically still, is it clear that in finding the metaphysical one finds the second qualifier of religious emotion: rightness. Why suppose the "permanent in things" to be the "right"? To address such questions we need to ask of the God who might justify—the God primordial and consequent.

In Chapter 2 I cited Whitehead's comment in *Process and Reality* concerning the "refreshment and companionship at which religions aim" (*PR* 47).[5] This comment occurs in one of the very few passages in that book, before Part V, in which Whitehead refers to both the primordial and the consequent natures of God. On which nature shall the emphasis be placed with regard to justification?

(1) On the one hand, it seems clear that one can align this concern with God as primordial. That seems to be the clearer emphasis in the immediate passage in question, since Whitehead emphasizes "real feelings derived from the timeless source of all order" (*PR* 47). The religious quest for justification through relationship to the "permanent" here focuses on order:

> The order of the world is no accident. There is nothing actual which could be actual without some measure of order. The religious insight is the grasp of this truth: That the order of the world in its whole and in its parts, the beauty of the world, the zest of life, the peace of life, and the mastery of evil, are all bound together—not accidentally, but

by reason of this truth: that the universe exhibits a creativity with infinite freedom, and a realm of forms with infinite possibilities; but that this creativity and these forms are together impotent to achieve actuality apart from the completed ideal harmony, which is God (*RM* 115).

This order is more than descriptive; religion intuits "a rightness in things, partially conformed to and partially disregarded" (*RM* 65. Cf. 60). Thus Whitehead links religion with a sense for the "quality of life which lies always beyond the mere fact of life" (*RM* 77). Following this line of emphasis, one would be sure to distinguish God from creativity,[6] and note the particularity of God's aim:

> "Order" and "novelty" are but the instruments of his subjective aim which is the intensification of "formal immediacy." Thus God's purpose in the creative advance is the evocation of intensities (*PR* 135).[7]

The emphasis in such "justification" surely falls on God as primordial. I have already suggested that it is this "aspect" of God which is the most directly accessible metaphysically—even if one may feel drawn to speak of a "consequent" nature for purposes of consistency (with statements about all other actual entities in their physical/mental natures) and in order to add specific temporal knowledge to the otherwise bare primordial valuation. Still, the metaphysical emphasis is on the primordial nature. Thus in *Science and the Modern World* God is simply the "principle of limitation" and *Religion in the Making* speaks of a third formative element (along with creativity and the ideal forms):

> The actual but non-temporal entity whereby the indetermination of mere creativity is transmuted into a determinate freedom. This non-temporal entity is what men call God—the supreme God of rationalized religion (*RM* 88).

Does such a God, given metaphysically, give what is sought in religion? I believe one could quite legitimately speak of a sense of justification here, as the believer identifies with the will, the law, of God. However, without judging those themes at all pejoratively, one may wonder if by them we may reach the "refreshment" and "companionship" at which Whitehead finds religions to aim. Those words carry warmer, more personal tones. This discrepancy becomes the more apparent if the religious person on self-examination should come to find nonconformity to the law. To say "lex semper accusat," or even simply "lex accusat," is not to attack the law, but it hardly suggests companionship or refreshment. We shall be considering in Chapter 5 several contributions the concept of God as primordial can make to faith. But here we are pondering Whitehead's association of justification with "companionship" and "refreshment." These words seem to rhyme better with what Whitehead came to write about God as "consequent."

(2) While the concept of God as consequent is available in *Religion in the Making* (*RM* 85, 150), it is in the highly compressed fifth part of *Process and Reality* that Whitehead provides a poetic and pregnant major statement of God as "the great companion—the fellow-sufferer who understands" (*PR* 532). That statement is addressed to a problem:

> The ultimate evil in the temporal world is deeper than any specific evil. It lies in the fact that the past fades, that time is a "perpetual perishing." Objectification involves elimination. The present fact has not the past fact with it in any full immediacy. The process of time veils the past below distinctive feeling (*PR* 517).

We are dealing here with material of considerable importance to Whitehead and his theological heirs. Yet, regrettably, neither the problem nor the solution is clear. It is clear that on grounds of metaphysical consistency Whitehead speaks of God's consequent nature:

> . . . by reason of the relativity of all things, there is a reaction of the world on God. The completion of God's nature into a fulness of physical feeling is derived from the objectification of the world in God (*PR* 523).

There most surely are questions to be considered regarding the relationship between the natures. We intend to consider them later. But Whitehead's intention to affirm a consequent nature for God cannot be questioned, as Chapter 2 already made clear.[8] But what is not clear is what, exactly, is the problem to be so solved, and how the consequent nature may be supposed to help.

"Perpetual perishing" does not conflict with "objective immortality." Indeed, by the principle of relativity "the 'perishing' of absoluteness is the attainment of 'objective immortality'" (*PR* 94).[9] To perish subjectively is to become objectively a potential for every subsequent becoming. What, then, is the problem? The problem seems to be either (a) conflicts in the realm of potential being lead to subsequent elimination by selection, so that the entity's being is not carried forward in its wholeness, or (b) in the process of being carried forward, the entity's subjective immediacy (as a feeling for itself) is lost (even if no reduction of objective being—a—should occur). Following Lewis Ford, we may call these (a) the perishing of being and (b) the perishing of becoming.[10]

Is the problem of "perpetual perishing" (a) that my contributions so conflict that some (much) of me does not live beyond my moment in the sun? or (b) is it that my very self—as real in self-awareness—only flickers to die, however much may be contributed by that frail career to the cosmic process? That the problem is the perishing of being (a) seems suggested by certain references, crucial in the development of the argument for the consequent nature. Thus Whitehead writes:

> The nature of evil is that the character of things are mutually obstructive. Thus the depths of life require a process of selection. . . . [Moreover] The evil of the world is that those elements which are translucent so far as transmission is concerned, in themselves are of slight weight, and that those elements with individual weight, *by their discord,* impose upon vivid immediacy the obligation that it fade into night. "He giveth his beloved—sleep" (*PR* 517-518. Italics mine).

If this is the problem of perpetual perishing, Whitehead would seem justified in saying that "there is no reason, of any ultimate metaphysical generality, why this should be the whole story" (*PR* 517). Accordingly, God as consequent could receive

> every actuality for what it can be in such a perfected system—its sufferings, its sorrows, its failures, its triumphs, its immediacies of joy— woven by rightness of feeling into the harmony of the universal feeling, which is always immediate, always many, always one, always with novel advance, moving onward and never perishing (*PR* 525).

In this view God would seem to deal with conflict in a way already suggested by life's capacity to go beyond "massive objectification" (involving elimination of detail) in a creative new synthesis.[11]

Now such a God could verily "justify" one's life—in a way quite different from that involving identification with the ever sure will of God found in the primordial nature. The value of life, the worth of achievement, the beauty and poetry of existence are in God fully and forever! Still, if overcoming perishing means simply objective (but complete) preservation, one may wonder whether such a message is not more grim than good. In fact, Whitehead does seem to suggest more than preservation, since he writes:

> The prehension into God of each creature is directed with the subjective aim, and clothed with the subjective form, wholly derivative from his all-inclusive primordial valuation (PR 523).[12]

So the receiving seems to involve ordering, perhaps even a selection of sorts. Thus he acknowledges:

> The revolts of destructive evil, purely self-regarding, are dismissed into their triviality of merely individual facts; and yet the good they did achieve in individual joy, in individual sorrow, in the introduction of needed contrast, is yet saved by its relation to the completed whole (PR 525).

We cannot here pause for analysis and assessment of this aesthetic determination of good and evil. We will be doing that in Chapter 5 where we try to discern what ethical wisdom can be found in Whitehead's view of reality. But what should be noted is that the power of God as consequent is not without qualification. While he can use "what in the temporal world is mere wreckage," his judgment remains merely "a tenderness which loses nothing that can be saved" (PR 525).[13]

Nonetheless, on this account God's work has undeniable religious significance. It may be asked whether any competing religious vision can do better. In any case Whitehead himself tried for something better—namely, the victory over the perishing of becoming (b). This interpretation seems strengthened by the way in which the earlier uses in *Process and Reality* of the phrase "perpetual perishing" seem to refer to subjective perishing intrinsic to the entity's gift of itself in transition. Thus time as perpetual perishing is taken to mean that "no subject experiences twice" (PR 43. Cf. 94).

It is not clear how Whitehead could claim—if this is the meaning of perishing—"that there is no reason, of any ultimate metaphysical generality, why this should be the whole story" (*PR* 517).[14] After all the perishing of becoming seems fundamental to the thoroughgoing atomism of his philosophy. Yet he can write as if he recognizes that impediment, defiantly:

> The concept of "God" is the way in which we understand this incredible fact—that what cannot be, yet is (*PR* 531).

Often Whitehead will drive these two notions of perishing together, as when he writes:

> The perfection of God's subjective aim, derived from the completeness of his primordial nature, issues into the character of his consequent nature. In it there is no loss [against the perishing of becoming?], no obstruction [against the perishing of being?] (*PR* 524).

Can he have it both ways? I find I must agree with Lewis Ford's double judgment:

> Unfortunately, Whitehead never made explicit the differences between the perishing of becoming and the perishing of being. The perishing of (subjective) becoming is natural and inevitable in the creation of (objective) being. Being, however, persists in being what is except insofar as it is eliminated by means of negative prehensions. The physical unification of past being by temporal actual occasions requires negative prehension, both for spatiotemporal perspectival elimination and for the evasion of past evil. But in God there is no loss or perishing of being since he positively prehends all that is prehendable. In this sense immediacy is retained . . . , but not the original subjectivity of that immediacy.[15]

Yet process thinkers continue to seek some triumph in Whitehead's categories over the perishing of becoming. Could not some such triumph be found in God as consequent receiving perfectly the subjective form of my immediacy of becoming? Lewis Ford himself joined Marjorie Suchocki in pondering this possibility:

> The subjective form of my experience is not objectified as part of the content of God's experience, but becomes the subjective means whereby God has that experience. Now it becomes problematic: whose experience is it, mine or God's? It is God's materially, in that the activity of sub-

jective unification is his, mine having perished. But it is mine formally, for I am the author of that particular way of experiencing that situation. The experience is mine, reborn in God. As we may put it most succinctly, God's experiencing through me is the same as my experiencing in God.[16]

The argument seems to try to stretch continuity of form into identity of "matter," of subjective immediacy. Moreover, even if some such argument can be made, the "justifying" value of a triumph over the perishing of becoming is not quite clear to me. On a popular level eager appropriators of Whitehead may suppose they have found here a philosopher's witness to personal life after death. Two difficulties block the way:

(1) The perishing and the victory would apply to entities, not yet so clearly to the societies of entities which we have found human beings to be. Yet Whitehead seems to address this objection in a remarkable passage:

> Each actuality in the temporal world has its reception into God's nature. The corresponding element in God's nature is not temporal actuality, but is the transmutation of that temporal actuality into a living ever-present fact. An enduring personality in the temporal world is a route of occasions in which the successors with some peculiar completeness sum up their predecessors. The correlate fact in God's nature is an even more complete unity of life in a chain of elements for which succession does not mean loss of immediate unison. This element in God's nature inherits from the temporal counterpart according to the same principle as in the temporal world the future inherits from the past. Thus in the sense in which the present occasion is the person *now*, and yet with his own past, so the counterpart in God is that person in God (*PR* 531-532. Italics his).

While this is boldly drawn, the analogy would still seem to leave us short of the kind of personal continuity claimed as a religious value.

(2) The meaningful assertion of personal life after death depends on a framework of categories—a complex including human relationships, self-body-time and the like. At least Christian faith has called for such a cosmic reference for its hope beyond death. Moreover, it may be asked

whether Whitehead's "self" is not so intimately part of its relational (temporal/social) context as to defy intelligible translation to some purely spiritual life if such could be found. Thus both the faith and the system suggest that even if the powerful and poetic visions of the last pages of *Process and Reality* could yield a triumph over the perishing of becoming (against the metaphysical grain), we would not yet be in the clear regarding the immortality of the person.[17]

Finally, it may be doubted that this is the kind of issue upon which metaphysics may be expected to rule. At least in *Religion in the Making* Whitehead ventured such a doubt regarding the relationship of metaphysics to belief in personal immortality:

> The doctrine here developed gives no warrant for such a belief. It is entirely neutral on the question of immortality, or on the existence of purely spiritual beings other than God. There is no reason why such a question should not be decided on more special evidence, religious or otherwise, provided that it is trustworthy (*RM* 107).

In this book's last chapter I shall return to this question, and others, which involve again the issue of the relationships between the disciplines.

The religious quest, then, is for justification. In this quest the self will be formed in relationship to "a righteousness in the nature of things, functioning as a condition, a critic, and an ideal" (*RM* 62).[18] Out of these three, two emphases offer themselves: God's primordial will for the world (condition and ideal) and God's consequent judgment of the world (critic). These categories may still seem somewhat other than what the religiously sensitized person may expect to hear when the word "justification" is mentioned. We may, of course, have defined justification in too narrowly religious terms. In any case I am convinced that there is wisdom available here for the people of faith to appropriate in their quest to understand God's justifying action. I shall be about that task in Chapter 5. Meanwhile, as it turns out, Whitehead's notions of the "primordial" and the "consequent" tend to organize the rhythm of much recent and current theological appropriation of his thought. Before examining that material under this schematic analysis, it may be helpful to convey some new sense of the range and scope involved.

## An Historical Comment: The Many Become One and Are Increased by Many

I have stressed the central significance of Whitehead for process thought. But I have also noted how Whitehead very explicitly draws together the insights of other thinkers. It is this latter role which Bernard Meland stresses:

> His literature is so complete in itself as a summary view of all that pre-ceded his efforts that he is generally taken to have been the instigator, and thus the one seminal voice expressive of this new age of thought. It is truer to say that he was the systematizer, and comprehensive formu-lator of seminal insights furnished by a host of scientific, philosophic, and religious thinkers who preceded him and by contemporary philos-opher-scientists, especially in England, who comprised what was then known as a movement in organismic philosophy.[19]

If it was a "many" which came together in Whitehead's formulations, verily a multitude emerges from that moment! In this chapter I seek to characterize the *theological* appropriation (already narrowing the scope) by an interpretation which keys substantively to the "natures of God" and methodologically to the distinction/relationship between faith and reason. Many other interpretive clues are available, of course. My choice of interpretive framework inevitably grants more attention to some figures than to others. In this brief historical interlude, which deserves a name no more grand than "comment," I am obliged to step aside from that interpretive clue to indicate—almost by way of sheer chronicle—something of the range of figures involved, together with some literature which may be consulted to correct the distortion which may be present in my perspective.

Perhaps the most direct way to approach this "many" is simply chrono-logically. Thus one could well say that the work of theological appropria-tion is now in its third generation. As first generation figures Charles Hartshorne, Henry Nelson Wieman, Bernard Meland, and Daniel Day Williams demand mention. Hartshorne served as Whitehead's assistant at Harvard, even though he was not strictly Whitehead's student. In the next section I shall seek to show that his work yields expansively to the two natures/two methods interpretive scheme, even though his handling of these matters differs importantly from Whitehead's. According to

Meland it was Wieman who was instrumental in introducing White-head's thought to the University of Chicago. There, drawing on the momentum provided by the empirical school of thought stressing close attention to experience (figures like Shirley Jackson Case, Shailer Mathews, George Burman Foster, and Gerald Birney Smith), the White-headian viewpoint came into vital ferment and issued in the first major strand of theological appropriation.[20] While Wieman, always uneasy with the speculative splendor of Whitehead's thought,[21] came to move away from Whiteheadian categories, two other Chicago faculty—Daniel Day Williams (after 1955 at Union Seminary, New York) and Bernard Meland—continued to draw upon Whiteheadian insights, though with considerable independence. Both men will be discussed in the next sections of this chapter.

In the second generation of theological appropriation the names of John B. Cobb, Jr. and Schubert Ogden stand out. I defer a discussion of the substance of their work to the next section. But it may be noted here that they represent both the continuation of the Chicago tradition (as alumni carrying the concern to be faithful to the deliverances of experi-ence) and its dispersal to Perkins School of Theology (Ogden) and the School of Theology at Claremont (where Cobb directs the Center for Process Studies). These schools may be said to have replaced the Uni-versity of Chicago as the leading academic center(s) of process theology. Their graduates form a third generation of scholars taking their place alongside the other two.[22]

This account may seem to imply that the "many" trying to do theology with at least one eye on Whitehead were American and Protestant. Mainly they were. But both points need qualification. North American soil has seemed more receptive to the seeds of process thought—not the least to the hybrid theological variety—than has any other. Indeed, some might argue that the crop was already there, ripe unto harvest, since process theology simply gathers up the energetic concerns of the people in this place: the frontier mentality, the pragmatism, the experimental optimism.[23] But qualifications are required, if we are not to defy geog-raphy. Already in the early years Whitehead's thought exercised some influence in England, as reflected in the work of William Temple (*Nature, Man and God*, 1935) and Lionel Thornton (*The Incarnate*

*Lord*, 1928).[24] More extensive is the work of W. Norman Pittenger, who has brought a Whiteheadian approach to a great range of doctrinal and ethical questions. In the area of doctrine his most important work is *The Word Incarnate: A Study of the Doctrine of the Person Christ*.[25] In ethics his study of sexuality is particularly striking.[26] Whiteheadian theological essays continue to appear in England, though in a significantly lesser degree than in America.[27] Such work there seems to be even less well supported in the philosophical faculties than is the case on American terrain.

On the European continent the headwinds facing process thought blow back any discernible progress. One may, of course, cite generally congenial parallel viewpoints such as those of Nicholas Berdyaev and Piet Schoonenberg, but such have not functioned to support a concerted effort to appropriate the thought of Whitehead theologically.[28] The paucity of translations of Whitehead deters any such appropriation, though a number of essays by American Whiteheadian scholars are available in non-English sources.[29] Alix Parmentier's *La Philosophie de Whitehead et le Probleme de Dieu* stands out as a major study by a French scholar, whose Roman Catholic devotion and careful Whitehead scholarship come together in an uneasy but promising mix.[30]

The Protestant dominance in process theology faces a marked challenge in the rapid development of Roman Catholic interest in the work of Whitehead and Hartshorne. From the early work of Walter Stokes, S.J., of Fordham University, to the "fundamental theology" of David Tracy of the University of Chicago, an expanding band of Catholic studies has appeared.[31] Bernard Lee's *The Becoming of the Church* illustrates the tendency of Roman scholars to work for a synthesis of the thought of Whitehead and Teilhard de Chardin.[32]

Lutherans, who join Roman Catholics in a strong confessional orientation and hardly seem to fit well within the general "Protestant" classification, are represented by a very slim stream of published writings, though several faculty members in Lutheran seminaries and colleges reflect in their teaching their work with senior figures in process thought.[33] I am suggesting in this study that Lutheran commitments in the area of theological method make it natural that they will seem rather ponderous and slow of foot in any race to claim Whitehead for the church, but that these same commitments open the way to very sizable contributions—in ways tactical, conceptual, ethical, and constitutive.

Before breaking off this general comment on the range of the work of theological appropriation in order to pick up again my interpretive theme, some further reference should be made to such works as a more extensive literature summary by John Cobb and David Griffin, three collections of writings edited, respectively, by Ewert Cousins; Brown, James and Reeves; and Bernard Lee, and to three general introductions by Robert B. Mellert, Norman Pittenger, and Cobb and Griffin.[34] I make no attempt here to rival these works as chronicles and collections, but do make bold to examine the work of theological appropriation ·in the light of issues already emerging in the discussion of religion in Whitehead.

## Two Natures and Two Methods:
### (I) *Intellego ut credam*

Charles Hartshorne is a major philosopher of this century in his own right, and a good case can be made for the contention that he came to his principal positions in essential independence from Whitehead.[35] Nonetheless, his work has been associated with Whitehead by its readers—and indeed by Hartshorne himself. As a figure within the movement of process thought Hartshorne is responsible for developing several distinctive themes. Several of them cluster around *the consequent nature of God* and *the place of reason* in conceiving the relationship between God and humankind.

Whitehead's explicit statements about the consequent nature of God may well be "too little and too late" in his system to command much attention metaphysically, though some of them at least can claim broader implicit support. Hartshorne would address that deficiency. In 1943, responding to a charge by Stephen Lee Ely that Whitehead's God is not the God of religion, Hartshorne wrote:

> Whitehead has sometimes spoken as though not much religious character can be imputed to God by a purely secular philosophy. It appears, however, that he has in recent years come to feel more than at first that such terms as "love" in relation to God have a good technical foundation. The theory of the "consequent nature" of God, at first neglected

or half-developed, has in fact made this inevitable. . . . My own feeling
is that to attempt to separate the God of Whitehead's system from the
God of love which he certainly does at times speak of would serve no
purpose and would weaken both the systematic and the religious aspects
of his philosophy. . . . God, even the god of the system, does things for
the sake of value, and what would be the value of dropping values once
realized? [36]

Whether for reasons "systematic" or "religious," Hartshorne comes to
speak eloquently of "the divine relativity," inclusive of all that is. The
systematic argument goes like this: (1) In general we understand nature
socially, recognizing that relationships are internal and constitutive; being
is constituted by becoming. If we can show that this applies to God, the
divine relativity would be at hand. (2) "The higher one goes in the scale
of nature the more obviously do the social aspects assume a primary
role." [37] "Human nature is social through and through." [38] (3) The direction thus indicated (in the first two steps) is reinforced by "logical analysis" which "shows" "that the social in its most general sense is definable
as the synthesis of all the universal categories." [39] (4) The all-related or
all-inclusive one may appropriately be spoken of as the supreme being,
since "the very notion that there is a better than the totality self-contradictorily posits a supertotality inclusive of the value of this 'better.' " [40]
     Within this argument Hartshorne is assuming that "a category so
completely ultimate for thought and life as relation (or as felt quality)
can, it seems, be assigned null value only in the case of 'nonentity.' " [41]
That the category of relation applies to God can be justified independently
of the systematic argument. Hartshorne appeals to the realm of faith:

> God is conceived socially before he is conceived absolutely or as perfect.
> God is the highest ruler, judge, benefactor: he knows, loves and assists
> man; he has made the world with the design of sharing his bliss with
> lesser beings.[42]

But in reflecting on that divine sociality theologically, the tradition has
neglected the divine relativity. But what God would be worthy of worship? As we consider that question we come to see that the neglect of the
theme of the divine relativity is not justified by our human experience.
Just as we extend the meaning of "relation" in an eminent degree to God,

so we probe those human relations and find that to be affected (in that sense passive) is as such neither good nor bad:

> . . . we view persons as defective because they are too exclusively "passive" to the influences of others; but no less may persons be depreciated for their wooden "inflexibility," their mulish stubbornness, their inadaptability, unresponsiveness, or insensitivity—all faults that imply insufficiently subtle and versatile passivity towards others.[43]

Of course, within the divine sociality Hartshorne does not fail to speak as well of an "independence which is admirable":

> In ethical character one should be as independent as possible of other contingent beings. . . . God then, an object of piety, will be in highest degree, or utterly, independent of our actions and fortunes for the preservation of his holiness of will. That is, he will promote the highest cosmic good, come what may.[44]

Moreover, God is distinguished from us in that

> he, unlike us, is never confronted by a world whose coming to be antedates his own entire existence. There is no presupposed "stuff" alien to God's creative work; but rather everything that influences God has already been influenced by him, whereas we are influenced by events of the past with which we had nothing to do.[45]

Thus Hartshorne speaks of a "dipolar" deity, perfectly expressing both the causal (active, eternal) *and* the effected (passive and temporal).[46]

On balance it is certainly possible to recognize this line of thought as one which generally parallels the "two natures" of God—primordial and consequent—which we have found to be so important to Whitehead. Indeed as late as 1976 Hartshorne himself says that he had less trouble than most in reading Whitehead on the two natures since "I was already in this tradition." [47]

Nonetheless a number of significant changes in emphasis occur:

(1) In developing the consequent nature of God Hartshorne tends to minimize the role of the primordial nature. Specifically, he jettisons the complex apparatus of the "eternal objects" and, accordingly, the primordial ordering of such. While Hartshorne does affirm the absolutely time-independent character of the fundamental metaphysical categories, he

clings to the contingency of particulars. Griffin well summarizes the threat the doctrine of eternal objects poses at this point:

> The doctrine of eternal objects is a needless complication of the philosophy of process, and even compromises the ultimacy of creative process. It makes the process seem to be not genuinely creative, but to involve only a shuffling of eternal realities, making the temporal world a mere duplicate reality.[48]

(2) What Hartshorne does retain as a "second nature" to the consequent is the sheer abstract divine essence. That abstract essence is less than and indeed contained within the concreteness of God as actual (consequent). But in itself it is necessary and provides the basis for a sustained effort by Hartshorne to restate the ontological argument for the existence of God. While Hartshorne freely grants the Kantian point that "existence is not a predicate" in the case of the "modality of contingency," he argues for another modality—necessity:

> Why is the divine essence equivalent to existence? Because this is the most abstract individual nature there is, and because what is deduced is equally abstract, merely that the most abstract nature is somehow actualized, no matter how. . . . God by existing interferes with no other individual in his class. There could be no other. . . . Thus the existence of God is not a possibility *competing with other possibilities*. Such competitiveness is the very meaning of contingency.[49]

(3) Hartshorne argues that what "Anselm discovered" was that God either necessarily exists or necessarily does not exist. Non existence would apply, if the concept of God were self-contradictory. A classical concept of divine perfection which effectively denied the divine relativity would constitute such self-contradiction. But if the perfect God is defined as the "self-surpassing surpasser of all," self-contradiction is avoided and the necessity of existence for the divine essence is at hand.[50] God surpasses himself in that he constantly includes within himself the novel growth of the temporal process.

(4) Hartshorne does grant:

> Such a proof could not give us God as a concrete actuality. The concrete divinity can only be contingent and empirical. Thus the particular

actual world which presents itself to the divine experience, hence the particular character of the divine experience itself as receptive of the world, is knowable, if at all, empirically only.[51]

Nonetheless, a major portion of his life's energy has been poured into the case for God, drawing upon logical analysis to prove God's existence —or, more broadly—to argue for particular conceptions of God. The God whom reason recognizes is not another God alongside the one whom faith worships. *Intellego ut credam.*

(5) Hartshorne's emphasis upon the consequent nature leads him to appropriate the term *pan-en-theism* to say that all things (including God as abstract) are within God as concrete. (God's becoming includes God's being.) But since both God and that which is not God are free, are individual, it will not do simply to say that all things are God (pantheism).

I pause to comment. Hartshorne's distinction between pantheism and panentheism depends on the relative independence of individuals, which Hartshorne takes to be a matter of metaphysical necessity. Yet, ironically, some pressure is exerted against this point. That may be true of divine freedom. Clearly, given the necessary and a priori character of metaphysics for Hartshorne, it will not do to speak with Whitehead of God as "freely establishing" the metaphysical conditions.[52] Perhaps more significantly, the independence of non-divine individuals seems in some jeopardy. One can speak of Hartshorne's view as an expression of the idealistic assumption: to be is to be known by God. William Lad Sessions finds this theme already in Hartshorne's doctoral dissertation in which the whole volume is occupied with

> the attempt to show that "reality" or "being" has meaning only in terms of (valuational) experience, that to be real is equivalent in meaning to being related to mind—not finite but infinite or perfect mind.[53]

This threat to the independence of non-divine individuals can be illustrated by referring to Hartshorne's treatment of the triumph over perpetual perishing. On the one hand, Hartshorne offers a powerful development of the preservation of *being:*

> We must remember that the divine omniscience overcomes the seeming

fragility of achievement and renders it immortal. Thus each moment of true salvation is a thing of beauty and joy forever in the divine life.[54]

But—on the other hand—Hartshorne seems to argue that even the "perishing of becoming" is overcome in the divine life. Subjective awareness is not lost. It is only we who are finite who must in receiving the other let that one's subjectivity slip from us.[55]

Now Hartshorne does not seek to accommodate any notion of continuing individual initiative in a future state:

> Though we do not forever continue to serve God, our temporary service is everlasting in a sense which I find deeply satisfying: whatever enters the treasury of the divine life is at once where moths cannot corrupt and thieves cannot break through nor steal. And we can in this life be aware of ourselves as already immortal elements in deity, and so by Love we participate now in our immortality. The triumph over death as our triumph is now, not in a magical future.[56]

If non-divine independence is not all that important in this life, perhaps our subjective presence even now in God will solve the problem of perpetual perishing. Clearly, Hartshorne finds his life "justified" by the divine relativity:

> What is the inclusive value of human life? . . . Is it the "glorification" of God defined as so completely absolute that it must be beyond our power to contribute to his greatness? A new era in religion may be predicted as soon as men grasp the idea that it is just as true that God is the supreme beneficiary or *recipient* of achievement, hence supremely relative to all achieved actualities, as that he is the supreme benefactor or *source* of achievement, and in so far nonrelative to its results.[57]

More basically, still, self-determination is fundamental to the becoming of any entity. That seems absent in the "divine treasury," and may even be in some jeopardy apart from that. Thus Hartshorne can speak of the divine lure as "an irresistible datum" and seems to find the consequent nature determinative of non-divine decisions:

> Only he who changes himself can control the changes in us by inspiring us with novel ideals for novel occasions. We take our cues for this moment by seeing, that is, feeling, what God as of this moment desiderates.[58]

This threat to freedom causes one to wonder whether Hartshorne may have "simplified" Whitehead's metaphysical system at excessive cost. With the realm of eternal objects gone, the sense of alternative possibilities is diminished. Moreover, the appeal to God as the most abstract (inclusive) being (and hence the ontological argument) may deny the notion of creativity the prominent role it plays in Whitehead's thought where it is the more comprehensive category with God as an extraordinary instance.[59] And if the previous observation is correct that the freedom of God is imperiled as well, the religious appeal that remains may well be to the sheer metaphysical point (available to unaided reason) that God receives all that is as distinguished from the query as to *how* God receives—i.e., with what disposition. Yet the language of religion is still employed, but under the auspices of necessity. In a remarkable passage Hartshorne holds love and reason together:

> . . . only an all-loving deity whom all may love can provide individuals, even though vicariously, with permanent achievement for their effort. This is so not because of contingent features of our world, but because in any world God alone could and would be universally loving, universally lovable and everlasting.[60]

Has Hartshorne, then, simplified Whitehead's system at excessive cost? On the face of it wondering about that seems at least impudent, if not plain silly. Of course divine freedom is limited (necessarily, Hartshorne would claim) by human freedom. But can one charge him with placing both human and divine freedom in jeopardy? I am not sure. I do find tendencies in his thought that point in the direction I have indicated. These tendencies would support the strong emphasis Hartshorne gives to reason. We find that emphasis in Hartshorne's:

(1) arguing for the logical superiority of dipolar theism,

(2) making a claim for the necessary existence of God,

(3) making much of that claim, despite the acknowledged contingency of the concrete God,

(4) claiming a triumph over subjective perishing, while actually providing a notion which seems to amount to a triumph over objective perishing—is the missing connection that to be (even "to become") is simply to be *known* by God?

Religion is at work here; justification is sought. But the controlling method seems to be *intellego ut credam* (I understand in order to believe). Reason has the first role, and perhaps the stronger. So much so, that an enthusiastic study of Hartshorne poses the possibility of some telescoping in the interest of economy:

> Since the concrete God is reality itself for Hartshorne, why not call it concrete reality and forget religious dressing? The obvious rejoinder is that theological history carries much intended by the concept of concreteness: for example love. But why not secularize love, or perhaps accept the thesis that love is already secular? The only significant reason for keeping a theological dressing may be that communication with theologically saturated culture requires it as a practical measure. Hartshorne's God can be understood and defended in secular terms, but is culture sufficiently secular to make such a move practical? [61]

I do not want to suggest that Hartshorne would accept such a severe streamlining. I have only wished to suggest that a full metaphysical account of freedom bids us pause when the distinction between reason and faith seems in jeopardy: to know the metaphysically real may not be to know God (or only God, or all of God), to know God is not necessarily to worship God, to be known by God is not necessarily to be loved by God.[62] Can one permit oneself such hesitations and still find a robust role for reason in the service of the human quest for justification?

One way to do so would be to speak of the relationship to God as a matter of faith, to be sure, but at the same time to argue for the universality and inevitability of such faith. If reason be identified with the public, the universal, one would still be saying: *"Intellego ut credam*—in probing to the depth our common humanity we find the true faith. This seems to be the position of Schubert Ogden. The continuity and contrast with Hartshorne is subtle. When charged with trying to present "a tight argument for the existence of God," Ogden responds:

> Although Hartshorne has developed some such proof of God's existence the simple truth of the matter is that I have never done so . . . my argument is not so much a demonstration of *the reality of God* as an argument that, if we are human at all, we unavoidably *believe in God*.[63]

What is the faith for which Ogden makes such strong claims? It is "an original confidence in the ultimate significance of life" which underlies

not only religious faith, but moral and scientific concerns as well.[64] This
confidence is as important to the secular self as it is to the Christian person. That convergence is not to be supposed strange, since both secularity
itself and "the new metaphysics" (to which Ogden will be appealing)

> trace their origin to the distinctively Christian understanding of exis-
> tence, especially in its Protestant form.[65]

We unavoidably believe in God. Ogden maintains this position against
apparent evidence to the contrary. No critic manages a full-fledged atheism of both "heart" and "head"; even to commit suicide is to affirm the
significance of death.[66]

Surely there is here a quest for justification—of human concern and
effort. And the justification seems sought through the "consequent nature" of God. While there is talk of God as the beginning as well as the
end of all things, it is the outcome of life upon which the stress is placed.
Ogden has accepted the challenge Whitehead found in perpetual perishing. God as consequent makes it possible to replace the grim slogan, "For
so he giveth his beloved—sleep" with "the primal word that our lives are
accepted unconditionally into God's life." [67]

If the primal word speaks so universally, can it still possess the particularity of Christian faith? Ogden's claim is

> that *Jesus is the truth of human existence made fully explicit,* meaning
> by this claim that the possibility of faith working through love that
> Jesus re-presents to us through the Christian witness of faith is pre-
> cisely our own authentic possibility of response to God's grace.[68]

The two steps needed to reach this conclusion are (1) to show that the
christological issue is directed to the theological question, "Who is God?",
(2) to show in turn that the theological (God) issue is directed to the
question, "What is the ultimate meaning of our existence?" [69] We should
not let the many keep us from seeing the one. Ogden takes these two
steps with unabashed determination:

> The claim "only in Jesus Christ" must be interpreted to mean, not that
> God acts to redeem only in the history of Jesus and in no other history,
> but that the only God who redeems any history—*although he in fact
> redeems every history*—is the God whose redemptive action is decisively
> re-presented in the word that Jesus speaks and is.[70]

The argument can be buttressed by appealing to the view that in the New Testament the christologies are the variable while a theological anthropology is the constant.[71]

Since we do already trust in the ultimate meaning of life, it will be precisely in *re*-presenting that primal word to us that the ministry of Jesus resides. To buttress this claim Ogden extends Bultmann's understanding of "radical demythologization" as the parallel to the Pauline-Lutheran doctrine of righteousness by faith alone without the works of the law:

> The tragedy of Protestant theology is that it has so seldom fully envisaged the radical implications of the Reformation principles *sola gratia— sola fide*. Although, beginning with the Reformers themselves, the one point has been well made that man is saved through faith alone in complete freedom from "works," the corresponding point about the saving action of God has almost never been grasped. It has rarely been seen that God saves man by grace alone in complete freedom from any saving "work" of the kind traditionally portrayed in the doctrines of the person and work of Jesus Christ.[72]

One might demur by appealing to the historical givenness of the Christ event. It is not really that God was or was not free to be gracious apart from the event of Jesus—Christian faith flows from grace acted and active in that event. But such a response is not really to the point, given Ogden's metaphysical approach to the matters of faith. Empirical, historical particulars such as the career of Jesus are simply not to the point when we ask what must unavoidably be believed.

Thus Antony Flew mistakenly appeals to the empirical reality of evil against the theist claim, not recognizing that

> neither the theist nor the atheist is able to comply with the rule of empirical falsifiability in advancing his respective claim.[73]

More specifically,

> the empirical facts of evil, however "undeniable and undenied," can never disprove the existence of God, if the idea of God itself is genuinely coherent and free from contradiction. What gives rise to the supposedly insoluble problem of evil is a self-contradictory notion of God's omnipotence as including all the power there is. . . .[74]

Similarly, it will not do for an historian of religion to appeal to the empirical evidence of cultural differences against Ogden's universal primal faith, or the skeptics to mutter about the priority of "animal *dis*-trust"—outside the Midwest at least.[75] The believer

> knows that his foundational assertions, at least, are strictly metaphysical, he also knows that they cannot be factually falsified, not even in their determinate form, since no evidence can count against them unless all evidence does.[76]

While Ogden does move to acknowledge that "some of the claims of the historic Christian witness of faith are clearly subject to factual falsification"[77] in that they are not strictly metaphysical, that concession is a guarded one:

> Although human existence is entirely factual or contingent, and so in principle different from the strictly necessary existence of God and, in a suitably different sense, of the world as well, it nevertheless has a unique primacy, which insofar entitles it to be included among the subjects of metaphysical understanding.[78]

With Ogden we seem very much still in Hartshorne's orbit. Reason is leading us to foundational truths which are decisively "represented" to the believer in the Christ. The dynamics of emphasis in the God-humankind relationship are somewhat altered, to be sure. Ogden, following Bultmann, seems to put the stress on the inevitability of human faith in the movement from christology through theology to anthropology. But to get straight the logical character of the foundational assertions of faith is to understand the strictly metaphysical character of God's existence.

Two other writers may help to fill out that orbit somewhat: David Ray Griffin in *God, Power, and Evil: A Process Theodicy* and David Tracy in *Blessed Rage for Order: The New Pluralism in Theology*. Griffin directly associates himself with Hartshorne's view of the necessary character of metaphysical principles and dismisses the "omnipotence fallacy" on the metaphysical grounds that "world" necessarily requires freely interacting, mutually limiting powers (including God).[79] One should not, then, rage against God for the misuse of that metaphysical freedom to which there is no conceivable alternative. Tracy follows Ogden's clue regarding "the basic faith in the final meaningfulness of an authentic life which secular-

ity itself has articulated with such power."[80] He appeals particularly to
the concept of limit. Universal and elemental features of human existence

> can be analyzed as both expressive of certain "limits-to" our ordinary
> experience (e.g., finitude, contingency, or radical transience) and dis-
> closive of certain fundamental structures of our existence beyond (or,
> alternatively, grounding to) that ordinary experience (e.g., our funda-
> mental trust in the worthwhileness of existence, our basic belief in order
> and value).[81]

Of this approach—present in such diverse figures as Hartshorne, Ogden,
Griffin, and Tracy—one may ask, "Would it do, if it were true?" Two
kinds of questions, then:

(1) Descriptive questions: Is it true? Is this approach right in arguing
for the strictly necessary character of metaphysical principles? Even if it
is, has it rightly identified them? I have already expressed myself in
favor of a more empirical, descriptive metaphysical account, following
the suggestions of Whitehead.[82] I am not able to see that a Spinozistic
*uni*verse without multiple centers of power is incoherent, though I contend it to be highly inaccurate.[83]

(2) Prescriptive questions: Even if true, would it do? Does this approach sufficiently "possess the particular" of faith? Can (does) this
God who can be had metaphysically meet my religious need? Can he
justify me? Both kinds of questions, though perhaps especially the second, are important to a second trend in the effort to appropriate the
insights of process thought for theology.

## Two Natures and Two Methods:
### (II) *Credo ut intellegam*

Whitehead's advice was to seek simplicity, but distrust it.[84] Perhaps
to claim a strictly necessary God or a truly universal faith is to simplify.
Then there are those students of Whitehead distrustful of such simplicity.
An early and continuing voice of caution has been Bernard Meland's.
This caution does not apply merely to thought about God. Rather it ap-
plies to the description of reality generally:

> . . . reality continually exceeds and eludes the formulated notions by
> which we seek to grasp or articulate its concreteness.[85]

Accordingly, we should be modest in what we claim for our concepts,
including those of the master himself:

> His [Whitehead's] systematic formulation . . . becomes a formidable
> resource for all who can avail themselves of his technical structure of
> thought. But to use this magnificent resource as a closure upon thought,
> compelling all other insight to be brought within its purview or reject-
> ed as being irrelevant to rational experience, is to profane this vision and
> to forfeit creative stimulus of its imaginative venture.[86]

Such a softening of our confidence in reason does serve to make room
for faith. But the concepts of the faith do not possess immunity to ambiguity. Indeed the work of theological thought faces fresh problems:

(1) History is morally ambiguous. Meland knows and speaks words
like "love," "forgiveness," and "creativity," with regard to history, but
knows as well

> that we are born into a world of insensitivity, terror, and cruelty, a
> world of narrow loyalties and strife, of bitterness, self-striving, pride,
> and competitiveness. In short, we are born into a situation of sickness
> and health, of growth and decay, of hope and despair.[87]

(2) In trying to understand the events behind the gospel story we must
stress

> that real novelty, real mystery, was encountered in the historical pro-
> cess.[88]

(3) No individual can set out without presuppositions to inspect the
world or God, for a communal perspective functions as a "structure of
experience":

> Within any nation's or community's history, then, the present moment
> of time is laden with qualitative meaning so complex in character, being
> the living distillation of decisions and resolutions of ages, so profound
> in implication for all existence and for all present events, that no single
> center of consciousness is equal to discerning its burden and its oppor-
> tunity. Each new generation comes into an organized inheritance

greater in depth and range than the perceptions of any living person who is a member of it. Thus people live in a context of feeling and awareness that is always beyond their grasp emotionally or cognitively.[89]

Yet, if speak we must and will, what shall we say? Meland is elusive at this point, partly because he understands the witness of faith to be so fused with cultural resonances as to defy the clarity of isolated dogmatic utterance. God's word—and the word about God—is simply never heard by itself. Yet it is clear that "the root-metaphor of this Judaic-Christian drama is the covenant relationship between God and man." [90] Thus Meland acknowledges that through all his writing runs a "concern with an elemental sense of creaturehood." [91]

In the terms of our earlier discussion, the objective referent for Meland at times seems to be neither God as primordial nor God as consequent, but causal efficacy or creativity itself. As late as 1976 Meland defends this theme, noting that

> in process thought creativity and the redemptive act do convey common qualities of tenderness and negotiability.[92]

Yet, when we approach the theme of the Suffering Servant, it must be seen that the redemptive act "partakes as well of a new dimension of renewal and hope." [93] Here we seem beyond the expectations consonant with creaturehood:

> The individual self, with all its hoped-for possibilities and failures, its pride and pretensions, must find access to the deeper reality of its individuated existence in the communal ground of God and other human beings, in relationships that offer grace and sustaining love.[94]

Here we are beyond a reasoned recital of the necessary structure of existence. Faith reaches out for justification.

Meland's pensive suggestions are paralleled in somewhat bolder relief in the thought of Daniel Day Williams. Williams affirms the particularity of the Christian perspective in three ways:

(1) Faith keys to *particular experiences,* while "philosophy which generalizes about all experience may very easily neglect the significance of particular experience." [95]

(2) Faith requires the *particularity of mythical expression*. While some of Christianity's mythical utterances can be helpfully translated into such literal speech as metaphysics provides:

> . . . there is a mythical expression here which goes beyond anything that we can literally express, and which therefore is beyond the reach of validation through the dialectical process. The myth presents our memory and our evaluation of the events which we believe contain revelation. It is a loss to the Christian faith when we insist on discarding all its expressions of faith which we cannot translate into rational prose.[96]

(3) The people of faith speak of *particular acts of God*—both at the margins of time, as it were ("acts of creation and of eschatological judgment and deliverance") and within time ("We say God sent his Holy Spirit at Pentecost. He spoke to Jeremiah, he heals diseases . . . .").[97]

This particularity of experience, expression and claim suggests that faith cannot be derived from or reduced to metaphysics. Faith claims independence in origin and existence. Yet, along with this independence, Williams would affirm an interdependence between theology and philosophy. He does so by recognizing that the Christian perspective is precisely that, a perspective. It follows that

> . . . whatever we see, or believe, or think, our own peculiar angle of vision is involved and hence may be corrected or enlarged by reference to another perspective.[98]

Since "the validation of the concepts of any perspective can never be achieved wholly within that perspective," the test of truth becomes

> . . . the capacity of an interpretation of the world to become more inclusive, more coherent, more adequate through a continuing discussion, criticism, and reformulation in contact with other interpretations of the ever widening range of human experience.[99].

Williams offers an explicit theological rationale:

> . . . Christ does not transform human thought as an isolated and absolute truth; rather as the word become flesh, that is, as a meaning which accepts the risk of proving itself with the whole process of human truth-seeking.[100]

While Meland stresses the way in which faith and world view are subtly interwoven in what is given (as in the "structure of experience"), Williams seems to call the people of faith to a rather more deliberate and active use of reason. Faith and reason are sufficiently distinct to permit that. The vision of faith reaches out through reason to seek understanding. While I have been quoting from an early essay (1948) in examining Williams' reflections on the theological method, his career well demonstrates the "dialectical process" of faith and reason of which he speaks. He can be found with mathematicians, scientists, and philosophers contributing a festschrift to Charles Hartshorne or at work with the likes of H. Richard Niebuhr and James Gustafson on *The Purpose of the Church and Its Ministry* and *The Advancement of Theological Education.*[101]

Nor may the two sides of Williams be neatly sorted out in any of this work. They are together, as the dialectic requires. That is most apparent in his major work, *The Spirit and the Forms of Love.* So together are they, indeed, that it is difficult to fix the character of the appeal or argument. I suspect that process metaphysics largely controls his luminous discussion of the categories of love: individuality, freedom, action and suffering, causality and impartial judgment in loving concern for the other.[102] Yet it is surely Christian faith which causes him to inquire how "God's healing grace has become decisively present in Jesus Christ," to know that "the cause of Jesus' suffering is sin and the human predicament" and that the defeat of sin and death "in the Servant's death on the cross is the atonement."[103]

The two strands come together in Williams' intention to

> . . . hold that God's capacity to involve himself in the suffering of his creatures and of his incarnate Son is the supreme manifestation of his divinity. His suffering is the exhibition of his perfection, which is not that of impassible Being but of love which cannot be impassible.[104]

Here we seem to have Hartshorne's appeal to the consequent nature of God combined with the stubborn particularity of the Christian event ("his creatures . . . his incarnate Son"). Along with this, one finds Williams resisting Nygren's disjunction between eros and agape in a way which seems to place considerable emphasis on God's primordial quest:

> If God loves the world enough to give his son, does this mean that there is a calculated value in the result? All such language seems

strangely out of place. The action of love is always the action of the
spirit, creatively moving out to the other, without a mere calculation of
results. Yet the action of God does create a new fellowship. It is moti-
vated in the sense that love seeks out the other. . . . Love can seek
reconciliation without assurance of fulfillment.[105]

I find Williams' work powerfully suggestive but somewhat unclear.
In a sense one feels more sure about his results than about his method.
One wonders if that is because faith and reason are here on such familiar
terms that the wisdom delivered no longer reveals clearly the distinct
sources that flow together in this maturity. But this makes it difficult to
follow Williams, to build on him in a way which retains a capacity to
criticize his impressive achievements. While he himself makes his way
along the winding trail of dialectic with sureness and persuasiveness, he
seems to offer relatively little guidance to those who must proceed on
their own. Lamenting his untimely loss, one turns to a contemporary
working within the same perspective, John B. Cobb, Jr. Perhaps here the
interplay of faith and reason will be displayed more distinctly; or perhaps simply having a look at these dynamics "one more time" will provoke a clarification.

That Cobb joins Williams in his dialectic is apparent in his effort to
produce a "Christian natural theology." By theology Cobb means

any coherent statement about matters of ultimate concern that recognizes that the perspective by which it is governed is received from a
community of faith.[106]

Thus a Christian theologian will acknowledge dependence upon participation in the community of faith when speaking of Jesus' decisive significance for humankind. In that task the theologian will find the services
of philosophy useful, perhaps even essential. This is not to say that faith,
"the appropriate, primal response to what the divine is and does," [107]
shares that dependence. But confessional theology (addressing and appealing to the community of faith alone) and dogmatic theology (addressing
the human situation as such, but appealing only to the revelatory events
recognized in the community) do.[108] Such efforts, after all, make assumptions "about the nature of language, of reality, of history, or of nature." [109]
In a time like ours when

the diversity of assumptions inhibits communication, and if many of
the assumptions militate against any adequate expression of the gospel,
then the frontal assault on natural theology becomes the systematically
prior task of adequate theological construction.[110]

The task of adequate theological construction calls for the theologian
to "adopt and adapt" philosophical resources. In doing so, the Christian
may well be guided by two criteria which reflect the interplay or overlap
of the "Christian" and the "natural." "Intrinsic excellence of the structure
of thought" (consistency, coherence) is to be valued quite "naturally." But
congeniality to Christian faith is also a value—philosophical forms otherwise being equal and none being clearly supreme. Here, then, faith does
bid for understanding without, it would seem, ceasing to be faith. At the
very least there is "a fundamental vision of reality" given with the perspective of the community which will continue to guide as questions are
put and pressed.[111]

In his *A Christian Natural Theology* (1965) Cobb set about his announced task with an emphasis on "intrinsic excellence of thought" so
rigorous as to place the criterion of "congeniality to the faith" in an apparently subordinate role. Some readers found the subtitle ("based on
the thought of Alfred North Whitehead") to be so true that the title
itself could well be abbreviated. Thus Langdon Gilkey wrote:

> Since this book is . . . almost entirely about Whitehead's view of the
> world, man, and God, it is in effect an argument for Whitehead, not for
> Christianity or even for peculiarly Christian notions about things.
> Cobb seems in other words to assume that if a philosophical interpre-
> tation on "Christian subjects" is presented by a man who lives within
> the community of Christianity, the resulting set of ideas will be Chris-
> tian . . . surely, *some* appeal to such classical Christian authorities and
> sources as Scripture, traditional theology either Catholic or Protestant,
> or the general mind of the contemporary church is in *some* sense called
> for if the word "Christian" is to be used descriptively.[112]

In calling for a Christian *appeal* Gilkey seems to be calling on Cobb to
reveal the reasoning which brought him to *adopt* this philosophy with
respect to "congeniality to the faith." One wonders, though, whether the
vision of reality that would be proffered in this case would not seem to
Gilkey to be *so* basic, so general, as to fail to satisfy his concern.

The Christian theologian adopts and *adapts* philosophical materials. Thus Cobb might object that his major revisions of Whitehead (in "a Whiteheadian doctrine of God," Chapter 5, as distinguished from the preceding chapter, "Whitehead's Doctrine of God") implicitly serve Christian intuitions. It remains true, however, that his principal explicit appeal is to greater coherence.

Most probably Gilkey can best be understood as calling for an explicit appeal to the particular Christian perspective *within* the work of theological construction. That is, he would seem to be calling Cobb beyond "natural theology" to something resembling either confessional or dogmatic theology. Thus in subsequent writings Cobb undertakes the clarification and illumination of Christian themes to which he had himself looked ahead in *A Christian Natural Theology*. But while the agenda and appeal of faith may be more explicit now, reason is not dismissed. So in *The Structure of Christian Existence* (1967) he develops an argument for the "finality" of Christ "intra-psychically," set within a careful study of other structures of human existence.[113]

Cobb's most extensive effort to speak reasonably of the distinctive concerns of the Christian community must be his *Christ in a Pluralistic Age* (1975). While the "natural" pole already asserts itself in the title's reference to the pluralistic context, the book begins with the recognition that

> for Christian believers and even for Christendom as a whole Christ has been the central image of saving power in the present as well as in both past and future.[114]

The central section of the book builds on an attempt to state the message of Jesus through a comparison of the results of four historians: R. Bultmann, N. Perrin, E. C. Colwell, and M. Machovec. While historical reason is not a peculiarly Christian possession, surely here the agenda is controlled by the Christian particular!

As one proceeds through Cobb's christology, such control is not as clear as one might have supposed. That may be due partly to Cobb's conviction that the Christ image "has passed from our basic vision," descriptively, and from his emphatic acceptance of relativism and pluralism:

> The question the Christian hears in this situation is whether there is a Way through the chaos of our time so that we can be brought to-

gether with others rather than try to run roughshod over them. This book proposes that for us Christ is the Way that excludes no Ways.[115]

Cobb's basic argument is to align Jesus with the primordial nature of God (or *Logos*) through the intermediary image of "the Christ":

"Christ" is understood as the power of transformation, redemption, unification, and order as that power has been apprehended through Jesus and his historical effects.[116]

Now there is an advance here. Faith's vision exceeds reason's reach. When the Logos is known as Christ, creative transformation is recognized as "love."[117] The Logos is now incarnate. As such:

. . . "Christ" names the logos as dynamic, trustworthy, loving. If the Logos were shown not to be dynamic, trustworthy, or loving, then the name "Christ" could not be used.[118]

But the stronger emphasis seems to be to use the historically recognizable *Kairos* to claim the universally working Logos:

. . . Christians can name as Christ the unrecognized or misunderstood working of the logos in the world if they thereby mean to identify what they name with what they intend to serve. In this sense Christians can name as Christ creative transformation in art, in persons of other faiths, and in the planetary biosphere.[119]

*Faith* illumines reason's realm: the world, where God is now seen to work.

In Chapter 4 I will introduce some of the conceptual help Cobb's mining of process thought provides for an attempt to understand the Christian Kairos. I consider his contributions in the area of christology helpful. In these matters faith seeks understanding of its own special concerns. But here I wish to make the point that for Cobb the work of God in Jesus not only illumines but also is drawn back into the universal work of God as Logos. The advance which faith in the incarnate Logos represents seems to be mainly a matter of knowledge, of insight. As such it permits "recognition" of the universal work of God.

Thus, while Cobb's descriptive summary of the message of Jesus includes forgiveness as a prominent element,[120] the constructive statement strikes a different emphasis:

*We are drawn into Jesus' field of force by the belief that in that field
of force we will be justified, or more broadly, rightly related to God.
. . .* Jesus' structure of existence as described above was one in which
the tension of self and Logos was overcome in coalescence. It was,
therefore, one that made possible a unique cumulative richness and
aliveness of experience in which intense suffering and joy were united.
It is understandable that such experience, culminating on the cross,
should produce a field of force of truly unusual magnitude sustained
and extended through repeated acts of remembrance. That this field of
force tends *to justify those who are drawn into it or more generally to
open them to the Logos* has been shown. . . .[121]

The stronger pull here seems to be the more general one. From this
Kairos emanates a field of force which opens us to the Logos. Moreover,
it is precisely the naming of the Logos as "Christ" which "makes possible
and necessary the inner acceptance of pluralism."[122]

Since the Christian finds the Logos incarnate in Jesus, faith in Jesus
cannot be in tension with the interiorization of the radically different
achievements of other traditions or in opposition to their claims.[123]

Cobb does not collapse the particulars. "Some of the meanings that we
are called by Christ to enter and to appropriate are alien to him."[124]
For example:

There appears to be a conflict between the Buddhist assertion that the
ultimate reality in all things is the Buddha-nature and the Christian
assertion that the ultimate reality is the Logos; for Buddha-nature and
Logos differ.[125]

Nonetheless, "the call of Christ does not allow us to relapse from the
effort at inner appropriation of other traditions to mere objective tolera-
tion,"[126] as Cobb points the way in suggestions about "a Christianized
Buddhism and a Buddhized Christianity."[127]

Unlike Williams, then, Cobb's work with the Christian particular is
clearly keyed to God as primordial. Yet the contrast is subtle, for Cobb
joins Whitehead in speculating about God's consequent nature in speaking of Christ as hope, just as we have found Williams to incorporate the
primordial agape in his understanding of love.[128] But the contrast stands,
and the prominence of the primordial seems to give metaphysics a greater

role in Cobb's theological work. Yet he does not fit well with the Hart-shorne/Ogden appeal to metaphysics. Specifically, he has questioned the finality of the demonstration of the existence of God by logic.[129] More broadly, he has resisted any tendency to identify God with ultimate real-ity, following instead Whitehead's reference to "a rightness in things, partially conformed to and partially disregarded."[130] Precisely, *partially:*

> My interest . . . is to show that historical "progress" has not led to greater and greater virtue or improved quality of life but to greater possibilities for good and evil. Axial existence is productive of far greater good and far greater evil than primitive existence.[131]

Moreover, like Williams, it is from the perspective of stubbornly par-ticular human faith that Cobb speaks. He will not collapse the particulars in a universal primal trust. He will not appeal to a necessary God to justify a most contingent belief. Indeed, he has worried about Hartshorne's move at a related point:

> As I read some of his statements on the relation of inclusion between God and the world, I receive the impression that this inclusion is stricter than Whitehead's principle of the lack of causal efficacy among contemporaries would allow. The rejection of this Whiteheadian prin-ciple appears to me to threaten the freedom of self-determination of indi-viduals other than God, a freedom that Hartshorne cherishes as much as Whitehead.[132]

In any case, he cannot get beyond the uncertainty that comes with the human territory:

> Ogden believes, as I understand, that on the question of ultimate im-portance for our existence, we can attain certainty. I believe, without certainty, that we can be certain of nothing whatsoever and must work out our stance toward life in the midst of uncertainty.[133]

Faith and God retain the contingency of particulars, hence: *credo ut intellegam.*

This book's first chapter has perhaps already made clear that it is with-in this second tradition of appropriation that I wish to work. That work will be begun in Part IV. Of the other tradition I wondered above whether it fails to get far enough ("Can this God justify?"), though it

may get where it does too fast ("Is God—or any other metaphysical reality—strictly necessary?"). This tradition, on the other hand, surely gets
"farther"—if I may put it so clumsily—dealing quite definitely with the
particularity of Christian community and Christ event. But I do not know
if I can find the way. I complained of a certain unclarity in Meland and
Williams as to the mix of metaphysical and theological ingredients. That
problem still seems present with Cobb, though quite differently. His
acceptance of historical relativity does help him to discern the particularity of the Christian perspective, but also seems to point the way to
abandoning the normative claims of that perspective.

Ogden (who seems inclined instead to universalize the normative
claims) has put this question of abandonment to Cobb. Cobb replies:

> I want to argue *both* that our relation to our own tradition (the corre-
> lation of our faith with what has been recognized by this tradition as
> sacred) is broken *and* that when we recognize that the break was itself
> faithful, faith in a new sense is possible. . . . I am calling for the em-
> bracing of "scientific" or "objective" study of Christianity along with
> other religions, a form of study that distances us from what is studied
> in a way that is opposed to what we have meant by "faith." I am argu-
> ing that in a deeper sense this distancing expresses faith and that we
> need to recognize as Christ that in which this faith is placed.[134]

Cobb recognizes that so to talk of the "death of faith" and yet its "broken
continuity" "is confusing, and perhaps still confused."[135] While I want to
join him in theological thought about the Logos which I consider to be
desperately important, lest we collapse and celebrate in a Christian ghetto,
I confess to wondering whether his thought on this matter of "death and
continuity" is not controlled more by a general metaphysical commitment
to novelty than by attention to the structure of Logos.[136] If that is so, it
may resemble on the level of method what I have taken to be a tendency
in the area of content to conceive the work of God in Jesus within the
work of God as Logos.

The adequacy of Cobb's work at this point depends, of course, on how
one conceives the relationship of Logos and Kairos. How shall one say
both "in him all things hold together" and "in him all the fullness of God
was pleased to dwell, and through him to reconcile to himself all things,
whether on earth or in heaven, making peace by the blood of his cross"?

Within this question lies the question of the relative contributions of metaphysics and theology to understanding the work of God as Logos.

Before turning to work on these questions in Part III, where I will attempt to sort out the distinctions as well as possible, I will conclude this analysis of methodological trends with a schematic summary (see page 158) and then to add some more strictly thematic or topical observations.

## The Dominance of the Doctrine of God: Centripetal and Centrifugal Forces

That reflection about God has dominated the work of theological appropriation is clear beyond dispute. Under this heading the anthologies offer the most articles and the major authors. Moreover, when other topics appear, they are drawn into this orbit as in the section of the Lee-Cargas collection entitled, "The Christian God: His Christ and His Spirit."[137] What shall we make of this? I want to consider (1) With respect to method, what disciplines may be at work in this dominance? (2) With respect to content, what other options rival this dominance? Do those options alter the mix with respect to method?

(1) This dominance may seem quite natural and appropriate for three reasons: (a) The doctrine of God is the right place to begin, *theologically,* for it is clearly the foundation for faith's other claims, (b) The topic of God is the right place to begin, *metaphysically,* in that Whitehead seemed required to speak of "God" in the interest of metaphysical adequacy in a way unparalleled by any reference to "Spirit" or "Christ" (or "Father" for that matter). (c) The doctrine/topic of God is the right place to begin, *culturally,* because of the urgent challenge posed at this point in our time. While more remains to be said, particularly with reference to the first and third reasons, it may be clear that the dominance is appropriate.

It is not clear whether it is in fact a *doctrine* of God that is thus dominant. That is, it is not always clear whether this discussion includes the perspective of faith, whether it can be "located," theologically. Such inclusion and location may be gained by overtly including the claims of a particular faith community as full partner in the process of interaction with the metaphysical view. Or this may occur less obviously (and per-

## TWO NATURES AND TWO METHODS: (I) *Intellego ut credam*
(II) *Credo ut intellegam*

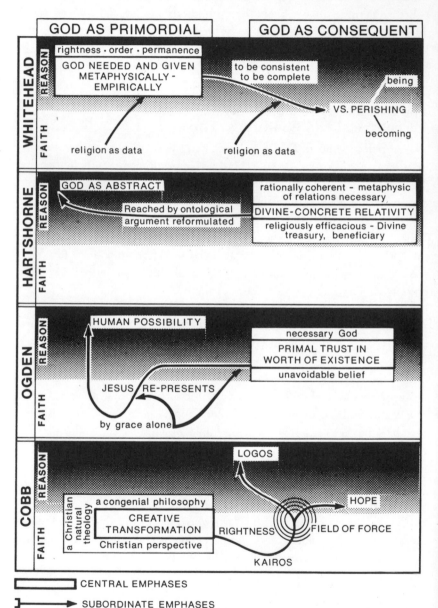

GOD AS PRIMORDIAL | GOD AS CONSEQUENT

**WHITEHEAD**

REASON
rightness · order · permanence
GOD NEEDED AND GIVEN METAPHYSICALLY - EMPIRICALLY
to be consistent to be complete
being
VS. PERISHING
becoming

FAITH
religion as data      religion as data

**HARTSHORNE**

REASON
GOD AS ABSTRACT
Reached by ontological argument reformulated
rationally coherent - metaphysic of relations necessary
DIVINE - CONCRETE RELATIVITY
religiously efficacious - Divine treasury, beneficiary

FAITH

**OGDEN**

REASON
HUMAN POSSIBILITY
necessary God
PRIMAL TRUST IN WORTH OF EXISTENCE
unavoidable belief

FAITH
JESUS RE-PRESENTS
by grace alone

**COBB**

REASON
LOGOS

FAITH
a Christian natural theology
a congenial philosophy
CREATIVE TRANSFORMATION
Christian perspective
RIGHTNESS
HOPE
FIELD OF FORCE
KAIROS

☐ CENTRAL EMPHASES

**]**━━➤ SUBORDINATE EMPHASES

haps less fully) by requiring the metaphysical view at least to address and incorporate the claims of religious experience—minimally, the quest for justification. On the other hand, it is of course possible—particularly in the first tradition of appropriation a la Hartshorne/Ogden—to conduct reflection on the topic of God in strictly metaphysical terms, and then to proceed to subsequent topics (as, "Christ," "Spirit," "Church") in a way still controlled by the metaphysical principles. But it is not clear that such a procedure represents genuine interaction between faith and reason —even "back" in the topic of God.

This issue of interaction may be illustrated by referring to the multitude of publications concerning whether God is best conceived as an actual entity or as a "person," i.e., a society of actual entities.[138] While this might appear to be a straightforwardly metaphysical issue, religious considerations come into play. The issue is exceedingly complex and defies simple summary. In Part III I will draw upon some of the discussion when I speak of conceptual and constitutive wisdom with respect to the doctrine of God. Here I introduce the matter only to illustrate the interplay of the metaphysical and the religious/theological.

That Whitehead conceived of God as an actual entity is not in dispute.[139] William Christian has made the point convincingly, and Lewis Ford has driven it home with relentless intensity.[140] Whitehead's decision on this point seems to be regarded by him to be a directly metaphysical matter. But John Cobb, following the lead of Charles Hartshorne, has argued that for the sake of coherence the view of God as a society (i.e., "person") is preferable. If God's knowledge of the actual world is to be available to render his primordial ordering freshly relevant to the emerging occasion, it must come to be so through "satisfaction" in completion. This points toward a series—a society—of such divine occasions.

Now this argument is ostensibly a metaphysical one. Yet only a little reflection will suggest how important it is to Hartshorne's religious appeal to the "divine relativity" that humankind can know that and how it is known by God. If God's knowing must at each point be complete in order for us to know his knowing through his newly formed aim for us (since we do not know strict contemporaries), then the "societal" view of God is clearly to be preferred since each entity in the series constituting the society reaches completion in turn.

Similarly, while Lewis Ford must counter the metaphysical objections, he seems to have no little interest in matters religious in doing so. To make the metaphysical response he can write:

> God, however, does not form part of that past actual world requiring unification, for he is his own ground for unification. What he provides, by way of the initial subjective aim, is not one more item to be integrated into the final concrescence, but a suggestion as to how that specific integration can be achieved. All that is required for this suggestion to be influential is that it be objectifiable, that there be something determinate in God which the occasion can prehend. . . . Now a divine conceptual feeling clearly possesses objective content, namely, that eternal object which becomes the subjective aim of the new occasion. This is all that divine causation requires.[141]

But more than metaphysics is at stake:

> Because our temporal decisions are shortsighted, we cannot adequately prepare for the vicissitudes of the future. How can we be sure that the overarching values inherent in our particular decisions of the moment will be adequate for future crises? Even human integrity may finally need a non-temporal basis, received from God's aims. Ultimately human integrity may consist in seeking to live in accordance with the divine aims, since God's inner integrity is sure. It is sure precisely because it is not based on any temporal decision or series of decisions, but on a single, unified, underlying non-temporal decision.[142]

While the topics and the options are suggested metaphysically, here as with the choice of emphasis on the respective divine natures, we seem to be asking, "Which God can justify?"

(2) Forces bid to challenge the dominance of the doctrine of God. From the standpoint of the work of theological appropriation it might be argued that a christological/soteriological interest is a centripetal force, drawing the discussion into the heart of the Christian faith's knowledge of God. A good deal of material has appeared, particularly in the area of christology, and I will make reference to some of this in Chapter 4. Here I wish only to suggest that while the topic is likely posed by faith, the handling of the topic seems largely controlled by metaphysical discussion.

I have already discussed John Cobb's christology along these lines.

Another major piece, David Griffin's *A Process Christology,* draws on the general Whiteheadian categories (the giving and reception of the aim) to discuss the distinctiveness of the Christ.[143] Indeed Griffin's empathy for the Hartshorne school within process thought (to which I alluded above in connection with his process theology) may be reflected in his choice of revelation as the controlling category. "In actualizing God's *particular* aims *for him,* Jesus expressed God's *general* aim for his entire creation."[144] Soteriology threatens to collapse into christology, and theology into philosophy. The theologian's task, according to this position, is to explicate the vision of reality revealed in Christ in metaphysical terms, and to verify that conceptuality by metaphysical criteria.[145]

While there are exceptions to the tendency I am noting (perhaps Williams' work is the most striking), the pattern is strong enough to suggest that also in christology the doctrine of God continues to dominate and that metaphysical considerations may control within that doctrine. Whether one can or should try to do otherwise remains a question to be probed in the chapters that lie ahead. Does the fact that Christian faith stakes out a claim on all reality, permit (or require) the theologian to relax (or relinquish) a method which appeals to distinctive Christian affirmations? Or is the claim made effectively only when the center is consciously held firm?

If christological interest may be spoken of theologically as a centripetal force in relation to the dominance of the doctrine of God, one may speak (with respect to content) of forces which pull away from the theological component as centrifugal. Of course, one may not find it so easy to leave the realm of God objectively. But at issue here is whether the discussion in a given extended area makes any reference to the understanding of God characterizing a Christian community, or even to what may be granted to be divine roles within the metaphysical sketch. It would be interesting, for example, to examine the conferences held under the auspices of the Center for Process Studies at the School of Theology, Claremont, with this question in mind. For example, the impressive volume *Mind in Nature,* which contains papers from such a conference, seems appropriately to bear the subtitle, "Essays on the Interface of Science and Philosophy."[146] In this neither theological agenda nor concern may be apparent. Yet here Cobb, Griffin, and Hartshorne are prominently at work.

Another centrifugal instance might be the Buddhist-Christian dialogs. Here the temptation is strong to make the exchange a matter of comparative metaphysics. That can be done by emphasizing differences, stressing particularly the process notion of the irreversibility of time. Or, caught up in the concern to come together, one may wish to stand with the Buddhist within the "eternal Now" of the concrescence.[147]

John Cobb recognizes this pressure and feels the pull, but his sense for distinction is not swept away:

> Christians can agree that what is ultimate in the metaphysical sense is dependent co-origination, the many becoming one, creativity, or concrescence as such. They can understand, therefore, why metaphysicians and mystics have so often pushed through and past God to the metaphysical-mystical ultimate which can be called Being, Brahman or Godhead. But they need not be intimidated. Buddhism teaches us that this ultimate is indeed devoid of form and beyond good and evil, as mystics have often told us. It is exemplified without discrimination in a cockroach, a human child, God, and an atomic explosion. It is not evident that this is the one ultimate that should guide our attention, our efforts, and our reflections. *If there is importance in the shape that dependent co-origination or concrescence takes, if it matters whether the universe is full of life or allowed to die, then we should attend to God.*[148]

The scope of Christian concern is indeed nothing less than the universe. But the concern reaches out from a center which does not (self-contradictorily) negate itself. The centrifugal force is being felt, but resisted.

In these final remarks regarding recent theological appropriation of process thought, I still seek more to describe than to praise or lament. Of course, criticism can be sensed at points and I have permitted myself some rather direct complaints. I have intended to venture these in the territory of theological method, as staked out in the first chapter. I have been asking, "What is going on here?" with particular attention to queries concerning the particular disciplines, kinds of evidence, nature of arguments involved. In a given formulation, for example, it will matter whether the help is offered as tactical wisdom or constitutive wisdom. Though I quest after all the help I can get from this illuminating metaphysical sketch, I want to know when the bid is raised. What help, then, is here to be had? I can put off no longer an attempt to respond personally.

# Part III

# Construction

# 4
# Proposal: Metaphysics as Faith's Colleague: Filling the Categories

In this chapter and the next a beginning is attempted. What wisdom may be found through process thought for Christian faith? With respect to each of the wisdoms I limit the discussion to a basic question. While other questions occur, I find these pairings natural. Thus to seek tactical wisdom is to seek power; one recruits means in order to be effective. Conceptual wisdom seeks a framework for the faith. If the doctrine or concept of God is foundational for faith (that remains to be argued in the second section of this chapter), it seems right that we ask what wisdom may be at hand with respect to that foundation. Christian faith and process thought combine to place the emphasis on the *action* of God. What framework may be found in which Christian truth claims about God can be coherently uttered?

Without claiming that there are no other ethical questions, it seems appropriate to underscore for Christian faith the question of what God is about in the world. With a fuller argument available in the next chapter, it may suffice here to suggest that the unity of Christian faith and life, as well as the unity of the God confessed, makes this question appropriate. In turn, the question is well suited to opening the process resources, if the God of faith has been metaphysically located in the preceding quest for conceptual wisdom. Finally, I find the question of justification to emerge from both process metaphysics and Christian faith. Without supposing the question to be identical in both cases (an examination lies ahead), I find the fit good enough to seek here constitutive wisdom for faith. Since this issue is not only a common one, but a crucial one as well, I offer it as a significant focus for the work of these colleagues.

## Tactical Wisdom and Power: How May the Christian Be Effective in the World?

I have already claimed that the logic of faith leads the Christian to aim at "mattering," at making a difference, at being effective in the world. Christian faith does not, however, guarantee such effectiveness. Some would even claim that such faith inevitably impedes effectiveness. Must the children of darkness be the wiser ones? Is it true that to be Christian is to be weak in the sense of ineffective? In Chapter 6 we will consider the atheistic form of this contention. Here I begin with the more modest task of trying to garner whatever insight may be available from a view of reality for the Christian who is called to be—but not guaranteed to be —effective in the world. That insight is in no sense reserved for Christians. It is available to Christian and pagan alike. My desire is just that: to point toward that which is available.

### The Social and the Physical

The Christian's call is social. It inevitably entails relationships with that which is outside the self. We may begin by noting that the process perspective locates that call's *ought* in an *is*. Fundamental to the being of any person is a becoming in relationship to, in dependence on, others. Both that other toward and with whom the Christian would act and the Christian's own self are being constituted in a relational field. To recognize this is to identify the prospect of acting efficaciously and to gain insight regarding the tactics of such action.

The process understanding of this "sociality of being" places a strong emphasis on the physical dimension of human being. To be sure, we have found Whitehead to hold that a living person is "canalized *novelty*."[1] As such, continuity will not be easy to come by and the self may seem more subjective than social. But the body seeks to preserve the relatedness

of the self. It does so in two respects: (1) Even that which may be said
to be the novel or non-physical dimension of the self is dependent on
that which is "given" through the body; we are, as it were, first of all
bodies. That dependence and priority is not merely temporal; our selfhood is always "embodied." By the body we are *from* the world. (2) By
the body we are *for* the world. The primary mode of action upon the
world is physical. Poet and literary critic Stanley Burnshaw is right in
writing that the body's urge to communicate may be so powerful that
not even the will can check it.[2] But we can inform and employ it.

We seem invited, then, to attend to the physical for the truest reading
of the interaction of self and world. Moreover, to those who would write
as well as read, who seek not merely to understand life but to change it,
the physical base of existence will be crucial.

It is all too easy to ignore these fundamental features of human selfhood. The intimacy of feeling found in self-awareness may not betray
to consciousness the way in which the world is given to—even *in*—the
self. The lure of the genuine novelty that is in the self may lead away
from world. To know myself from within is to suppose that you are
without—a supposition strengthened by the highly selective truth available in the reports of the world delivered by our senses. If you are without,
is it not easy to suppose that you are wholly so and thus in no sense
within me? That development in turn will strengthen the tendency to
isolate the self from the body, which so obviously is involved in a career
of transactions with the external world. Down this road damage can be
done to the self's capacity for efficacy, even if we characteristically somehow stop short of a full-fledged Cartesian dualism. We may not feel the
need to appeal with Descartes to a "pineal gland" mysteriously connecting
body and mind. Perhaps we simply do not think as clearly as Descartes
at this point. But such fuzziness will not deter us from regarding that
external world and (perhaps) even our own bodies as somehow alien,
if not optional.

Process thought with its general stress on the principles of process and
relativity and its specific critique of the sufficiency of sense-perception can
arrest and correct such disturbing tendencies.[3] It can, for example, point
the way for specific recognition and affirmation of the physical base as
simply a reality with which to reckon. It can persuade the historian to

trace the role of the non-mental—as when Frank Morley ponders the general theme of "hodalogy"—more specifically, the influence of the great North road in the history of England.[4] It can provoke the student of sexuality to ask of the import of biological differences for the meaning of the more comprehensive terms, "male" and "female." It can make us aware of the possibility that action occurs not only "without reason," but even against it.

Furthermore, if error seems particularly to arise in the "higher" mental phases of experience, there may well be reason to try to "trust" the body as a barometer of reality. To do so is not to deny that error may take place in what we regard to be physically given to us. By my "body," after all, I may mean that object delivered for all to see (including me) by the senses. But that understanding is surely a precarious one, depending as it does on how adequately that symbol-making process and the selection of sense perception have worked.[5] But it remains true that the closer we can come to "reading" the embodied interaction of the self, the better prepared we will be to act in an informed way. In this respect many body disciplines, such as Rolfing and Structural Patterning, seem to call appropriately for the reacquaintance with one's own body, learning how to listen to it.[6] (At the same time one will be alert to the possibility that a given technique depends on a severe simplification of "body" in the symbolizing process.) With respect to others (and even oneself) it will be sensible to do "discrepancy analysis" in which even apparently well-intentioned rhetoric is tested against the word of the body.[7] In trying to hear that word one may well recognize such matters as emotion and mood, not as private ecstasies, but as fundamental ways of receiving the world into the self.[8]

So to value the social and the physical is not to claim thereby an exhaustive account of human selfhood. The self's relationships, after all, are constitutive, but not determinative of its being. There is wisdom in recognizing the elusive reality of self-awareness. Robert C. Solomon asks us to consider the differences in "third person" and "first person" styles. Taking examples from literature, on the one hand we might have

Mathieu stood by the machine gun, firing through the haze and killing men he never saw. And then, it was all over.

On the other,

> I clutched the machine gun, firing into the haze, probably without re-
> sult, never knowing when a random shot might save the day, and never
> knowing when one of those whistling returns would stop me, and stop
> this horror, at least for me.

As Solomon notes, "It is not styles of writing fiction that concern us here,
but rather styles of living." [9] Process thinkers have reason to support such
an interest in the "first person." The existentialists rightly note the reality
of subjectivity, for even to share *what* another is feeling is not to possess
the *how* of feeling.

Behind the uniqueness of individual feeling lies the reality of individual
choice. While the self cannot choose to be unrelated, freedom is found in
how the fabric of relatedness is structured. Thus, to return to the matter
of the emotions as a form of world-relatedness, a process thinker can
applaud Solomon's exhortation:

> We must give up the self-excusing illusion that we *suffer* our emotions,
> even while enjoying them, and see them as our own creative activities. [10]

In recognizing the freedom of the other, one will not only gauge one's
exertion of influence accordingly, but even develop some capacity to
revel in the solitariness of the other which one cannot penetrate causally.
Thus J. Gerald Janzen finds a positive teaching in the seemingly abstract
nuance of the "non-causal relatedness of contemporaries":

> . . . once one's own solitude and the other's own solitude are accepted,
> suddenly the other as fully existing, not in the past, but in the living
> present, becomes a contemporary—and the other becomes present *to* one,
> there—*now!* What arises to intensely vivid consciousness is the fact of
> the other, not as one's benefactor, nor as one's beneficiary (as important
> as these efficacious aspects undoubtedly are), but as a person charged
> with intrinsic worth in the absoluteness of that person's own self-enjoy-
> ment, actually present-to-himself-there-now. It is the recognition of the
> other as a "Thou." [11]

Here, then, we may have a metaphysic that makes sense of Buber's
powerful but enigmatic evocation of the "I-Thou" relationship. [12]

It remains true that for Whitehead the uniqueness of the individual is most clearly seen in the development of the "mental" pole. Of that we shall speak in the next subsection when we attend to humankind's capacity for symbolism. But enough has already been said—in the more leisurely account in Chapter 2 so briefly recalled here—to note that in understanding the human person some kind of balance will be required between the objective and the subjective.[13] I *both* bear in upon the other, knowing that there are openings in this becoming one for me and the rest of the world *and* brace myself for surprises, since I recall the other is free so that the causal fit between us is only loose. The mix may well be volatile. I can make a difference; who knows what will come of it? It will not do to dismiss the behaviorist, or canonize him.

Within those boundaries, what account of human responsibility commends itself to a process thinker? If I can be clear about that, I gauge my expectations and evaluations accordingly. In turn my own strategy for action may be affected. Responsibility cannot require that my act be shown to be the complete cause of an effect in another's life, since process thought assigns some responsibility to the other in that the effect includes *how* the other person in freedom receives what I bestow. I cannot be responsible, for example, for highly "original" reactions which could not have been anticipated (*PR* 390). I can be responsible for effects which regularly follow the action I perform in a general public sense, and for effects which seem likely in the smaller scale relationship between me and a particular other.[14] That relationship may well be such that I can know that certain flags are strangely and peculiarly red for that other person.

This may still seem to minimize responsibility; my guilt seems less direct than in a simple single cause theory of action.[15] Two further comments are required:

(1) It is still possible to act toward another in such a way that the pattern of association of life constitutive of that person is unavoidably affected; murder is more than strong suggestion.

(2) While my responsibility is diffused somewhat, mingling with the acts of manifold others to constitute a world, an environment, it is deepened and broadened. Who sets out to build a slum? Who means to main-

tain it? How do acts of omission and commission come together here? While certain particular responsibilities may be assignable in such instances, general responsibility may well remain. The translation to questions of legal responsibility is obscure. Lieutenant Calley may be legally responsible for militaristic murder in a way that I am not.[16] But this view of causality should affect my attitude toward him including— possibly—my estimate of the degree of guilt and accordingly the kind of penalty deemed appropriate. Equally important, it will affect my attitude toward myself and others righteous in the land. To prevent such occur rences in the future it will not do merely to try to spot the surface pressure spots where the Calleys break through; the depths need to be reached.[17]

### The Temporal and the Linguistic

The self's constituting relationships are not limited to the environing world of what we conventionally call the present. The past does not die, but lives to bear in upon the present moment. Again we must say: the self cannot choose to be unaffected by its past; freedom is found in how the past is accepted and structured. There seems to be at least a tactical *ought* in this *is*. As a living person characterized by the capacity creatively to innovate, I can deal with my past consciously, deliberately If I do not do so, my past will deal with me all the same. Here Tillich's polarity works: destiny cut off from freedom becomes determinism.[18]

Americans are not guilty of overlearning this lesson. A romantic fascination with an idealized past (the TV western, the frontier, my personal "roots") does not represent a realistic appropriation of the rush of time toward me. Strident voices call us not merely to ignore but even to reject the past. We do not treat our aged as the repository of a wisdom that can guide us in the present. Even a prize winning historian can complete his story of *The Uncompleted Past* with these lines:

> For those among the young, historians and otherwise, who are chiefly interested in changing the present, I can only say, speaking from my own experience, that they doom themselves to bitter disappointment if they seek their guides to action in a study of the past. Though I have tried to make it otherwise, I have found that a "life in history" has given me very limited information or perspective with which to understand the central concerns of my own life and my own times.[19]

Why? Why does the past seem so lifeless, so irrelevant? Process thought suggests two reasons:

(1) Sense perception, which isolates from time, seems to leave the past emphatically behind us. Just as you are "over there" and so external (if not alien) to me, so the past is the more emphatically demoted; it is *"back* over there," if one may put it so. A metaphysics which removes the tyranny of sense perception in our knowledge of our relationships can open us as well to a new attitude toward the past. The power of personal memory and the persistence of patterns of continuity in time can persuade and enable us to act on that attitude.

(2) The "past" we suppose ourselves to "know" may be a symbolically constructed edifice, distorted in selection and frozen for permanence. To appreciate this suggestion we need to consider further the linguistic character of our existence which Whitehead found to be so decisive and distinctive. We have already cited his statement:

> ... the mentality of mankind and the language of mankind created each other. If we like to assume the rise of language as a given fact, then it is not going too far to say that the souls of men are the gift from language to mankind. The account of the sixth day should be written, He gave them speech, and they became souls (*MT* 40-41).[20]

We have examined in Chapter 2 Whitehead's account of the process of symbolic reference which is so central in human perception.[21] Language is a particularly pervasive and potent instance of such symbolic reference. We construct our own "world" through symbolic reference. Within that world (at the very least by implication) is a view about the past. If the symbolically constructed "present" so stresses what is apparently sheer presence ("presentational immediacy"), it will not be surprising that we will encourage ourselves thereby to consider the past as unrelated to us. Since it is the least significant elements of continuity that are featured in such a "present," we will not be inclined to challenge the sense of isolation suggested by the dominance of "sheerly present" entities in that world view.

We still may be inclined to examine the past—perhaps for the sake of intellectual completeness. Or we may be driven to do so by a nagging restlessness with the neatness of the isolation or by the power of personal memory. Even then the symbolism may sustain itself by identifying the past as a "model"—or, more ambitiously, as a norm. Instead of seeing the past as the stuff of the present with which we should deal creatively, we will regard the past as a potential standard for the present—not constitutive then, but controlling. Our own sense for the novelty of present claims and the artificial reading of a past in a symbolically isolated present may combine to call us to repel such a norm.

Or the process of symbolization may serve a life-defying discipline in which we waste our present creative opportunity by trying instead to replicate a real or imagined past. Both Thomas Wolfe and Richard Neuhaus are right. You can't go home again, and you surely cannot return to where you have never been.[22] But the symbol-making power of humankind makes it eminently possible to waste our years trying to do the one or the other.

Of course we do not deal adequately with the temporality of life by speaking merely of two tenses. Effectiveness in the world means mattering for the future. Again we seem to do less well than we might. "Presentism" fails to deal with the future, as well as the past. That holds true of a wide variety of folk. One person may drop out of school, eschewing long-term goals and chanting, "The future is now."[23] Another may plunge in, joining a technocratic society so engrossed in means as to lose any sight of future-relevant ends. The radical and the company man come together in forfeiting their claim on effectively constructing the future. Neither understands the character of culture. One would have the novel ideal now as sheer event, the other the present pattern forever as state. Neither sees culture as a process of continuity in change.

It is not enough to understand these errors which default on opportunity and let destiny become determinism. How might one do better? We will not do so without language. Whitehead wrote:

> The higher animals have gained a faculty of great power, by means of which they can define with some accuracy those distant features in the immediate world by which their future lives are to be determined (S 59).

The key lies in combining the precision of presentational immediacy with the power of causal efficacy. In such a combination the meanings of language are lifted into a definite effectiveness in knowledge, emotion, and purpose. As such intersections symbols serve to knit together the community and to motivate the individual.[24]

What is needed in either case is creative attention to the realities—to the potential referents, and then to the process of symbol construction. We have too easily acceded to the view that symbols simply happen, as if prepared to accept even a vacuum in broader meanings or root metaphors as a fated matter to be symbolically dignified (ironically) in turn with the awesome word "void." Against Bultmann, Stephen Toulmin has effectively argued that moderns manufacture their own myths.[25] With respect to symbol construction earlier emphases return: (1) the physical, and (2) the temporal.

(1) To recognize the power of the physical for the work of symbolism will suggest that we employ the reality of emotion as a way of receiving the world into the self. The efficacy of emotion in symbolic language is available for good or ill. Solomon notes:

> Our mythologies synthesize our views as emotional judgments into a coherent dramatic framework, organizing the dull facts of the world into the excitement of personal involvement and meaningfulness.[26]

(2) To recognize the process of symbolism as temporal is particularly to emphasize the anticipatory character of symbols. Whitehead spoke of propositions as "lures for feeling," stressing that it was more important that they be interesting than true (*PR* 395-396). We need not accept a disjunction here. Symbols speak of what may lie ahead because they speak of forces presently available to work for that future. If we tie the symbol narrowly to what is at present strictly the case, we default on an opportunity to inform the aspirations of a person or people, just as if we overstructure a social organism we doom it to an early demise as new conditions inevitably develop.[27] Thus the very structural documents of our social life—political constitutions—build in devices for change (amendment, referendum), lest the future find them with the dinosaurs. So it is the better part of tactical wisdom for Americans to let Fourth of July

oratory exceed the reach of past or present. Spokespersons for world community have more in mind than either the League of Nations or the United Nations. Attention needs to be given to symbols, to forms of meaning, in which the knower is caught up and moved ahead into the future in anticipation.[28]

This anticipatory function is but a special case of the power of symbols which work not merely to report but to create. Thus in a new context the same "report" may well create a quite different effect.[29] This will not mean disinterest in the matter of making reports but it will commend attention to the creative use of that process.[30] Indeed, quite generally, this concern to claim the temporal through the symbolic will not displace the need to speak with great precision about the present. Mythology serves us poorly in the operating room, but it makes a difference when we ask "What is health?" Clearly, to be effective is to speak both languages and to serve as translator for those who are not bilingual.

## To Counsel, To Educate

The Christian community seeks to be effective in the lives of people. Without simply repeating the material just introduced and without claiming professional competence in either field, I will seek to indicate implications for such foundational work as counseling and teaching. All four features of reality—the social, the physical, the temporal, and the linguistic —come into play.

Clearly the movement toward family counseling is consistent with the social character of the individual. Given a process view of reality, it does make sense in diagnosis to speak of an individual patient who needs to be "sick" for the benefit of the family. Brian W. Grant has extended that argument a giant step in exploring schizophrenia as a source of social insight. He writes:

> A potentially schizophrenic individual will become symptomatic in response to societal pressures that produce the same feelings as did the stresses in his family, and those stresses in turn will be highly typical of the pressures on the subgroup of which the parents are a part, hence illustrative of the structure of the society as a whole.[31]

Parenthetically, this emphasis does not deny the smaller unit(s) (individual or family) some diverse particular responsibility, as our earlier discussion should have made clear.

In any case, to treat an individual without treating the larger unit(s) would likely be self-defeating. Gestalt psychology seems to recognize this, though there may be some tendency in this school to blur the distinction between descriptive and prescriptive "wholeness." [32] But to inquire whether and how a vital, well-integrated person—that is, one who is descriptively "whole"—may be evil would lead us beyond tactical wisdom. [33]

The Gestalt movement also emphasizes that we perceive in wholes. Thus learning is understood to involve not so much quantitative accumulation as a decisive recentering which produces a new world with new relationships. This process need not be left totally to chance. To teach effectively one will seek to draw on the social as resource—which will mean that the "class" is more than an efficient form of tutorial. Social interaction will be stressed as with jurisprudential, social inquiry and laboratory T group models. [34] More simply—even apart from such rather elaborate formal arrangements—the class (this place, this time, these people) are a creative mix bidding to become in a hundred different ways for those involved. The teacher's crucial distinctive role may well be that of catalyst and orderer. The role of the relational, the place of the social, will also be important in the structure of the act of learning within the individual. Religious instruction can become the occasion for organismic development—What is God's drama with humankind? How do I make ethical decisions? The teacher will be aware that to learn is to draw upon wholes and to create wholes. [35]

In both the teaching and healing processes the relationship between the physical and the linguistic is crucial. A process therapist, knowing that "We are first of all bodies," will seek to "read the body." Talk ostensibly pertaining to the self but lacking any apparent root in experience will be worrisome. Couples need to confront their images of each other with the reality of the other—images and all. At the same time that therapist will know that in the originative mental dimension—with particular stress on the linguistic symbolic capacity—lies the distinctive element in human life. That capacity harnesses great power. Again it is not a matter of an either/or, but of the proper relationship between the two.

Thus William Gallagher's development of Whiteheadian thought mentioned above will suggest that there are genuine resources for integration and stability within the physical pole of life—one will not dismiss the message of the more habitual forms of behavior—even biorhythms, the reticular system, balance and appetite centers.[36] There are strengths here both to carry the self through a crisis and to be drawn on over the long haul in life. One will not underestimate the therapy of the physical —trying to eat together after the funeral, getting up to go to work again. But the process thinker will know too of the role of a mythic vision in channeling and focusing those strengths for conscious employment and direction. What bereaved person is alone who has the family name, the father's will, a common cause?

Surely the pastor who would teach—in the sermon, for example—will know the importance of offering the learner(s) an organizing metaphor, a centering story through which holistic appropriation can occur. That pastor will not suppose the venture to be a narrowly cerebral one, and thus will not disdain the communicative power of the body nor fear the force of emotion in the effort to tell the story. What matters is that a *true* story is *effectively* told. The matter of framework for the cognitive claims of the story awaits us just ahead in the next subsection.

To understand that human life is temporal is to affect one's teaching in both content and method. To teach is to take special responsibility for the bestowal of the past. A process perspective will prize this role, since to be human is here seen to entail a conscious appropriation of the past. The continuity of identity is won in the process of deciding how to receive that which will inevitably—in some way or other—be there for the self.

But one appropriates the past precisely in order to move ahead effectively in the future. The symbolic vision both claims the past and anticipates the future. Learning is always contextual and it is a new future for which the resources of the past are being mobilized. As Whitehead put it, ideas themselves have adventures, and surely historical energies do. To educate anticipatorily may be to give a greater role to method, though it may not be supposed that method is a timeless matter either. A sense for the temporal will surely involve the student taking responsibility for learning, developing a sense of an agenda upon which to work and resources with which to work. Since education would only mistakenly

seek to replicate or report about a completed world, there will be more emphasis upon the fruitfulness of education in an actual developing world.[37]

Similarly, to counsel effectively it will be necessary to attend to the
temporal. Again this wisdom is neutral regarding the future—both fear
and hope are real and may be well founded. But at the very least the coun-
selor will resist the tempting delusion of a "state" of health. The real is
change, growth, novelty. Health, therefore, will not array itself against
the flow of reality. This would seem to caution against a psychoanalytic
method which so dealt with the past as the basis for sickness and healing
as to assume a homeostatic version of wholeness, allowing only occasional
novel "discharges" to maintain equilibrium.[38] It would seem to suggest
support for an Eriksonian emphasis on growth "as a lawful biological
system which can, at any point, be psychologically negated by the refusal
to accept oneself as having grown." [39]

Here, again, we come close to the normative, to what I have called
"ethical wisdom," as we do in Abraham Maslow's helpful distinction
between "deficiency motivations" and "growth motivations." [40] It is difficult to discuss growth in merely descriptive terms. We seem on the verge
of value, of recommending *how* a person should develop. For is not some
development, some growth, inevitable? Hardly. The many may become
one and be increased by one remorselessly, but the fragile balance of novelty and continuity that is personal life does not necessarily develop.
Moreover, it is possible for people to array themselves against the flow of
reality—if not fully and finally, at least enough to be ineffective. Thus if
a person would survive and matter, some attention to tactical wisdom
concerning such affairs will be helpful. That is not yet specifying the
direction such development should take.

The Christian places no premium on failure in serving the gospel
story. Thus suggestions as to tactical wisdom will be valuable. I have
begun a consideration of such tactical wisdom as might emanate from a
process perspective, without wishing to claim that all process thinkers
would concur. I hope that to start is to stimulate others—you—to further
work, correcting false steps and moving much farther in effective mission.
But, meanwhile, a second task is at hand: How may we well understand
the message we seek to serve with such tactical wisdom? Without that,

we may muster our powers only to harm more than help. So it is that we turn to the question of meaning, of framework for Christian truth claims.

## Conceptual Wisdom and Truth: How Is God Actively Present in the World?

### God Acts in Relationship

The claim that God acts is foundational for Christian truth. While the Christian passion of faith may appropriately focus on the figure of Jesus, Christian theology only serves that faith well if it can speak clearly of God. It is, after all, the lamb *of God* who takes away the sins of the world. It is God of whom faith speaks. Without an intelligible concept of God all witness to Jesus as the Christ is robbed of significance. Furthermore, one cannot speak intelligibly of God—and one surely cannot connect such talk with Jesus as the Christ—unless one can speak sensibly of God *acting*. While this has always been true, it is the more emphatically clear to us in a time when we are hard put to imagine (regarding God or anything at all) what being would be without power, or identity without activity. In any case faith's own logic claims to speak of action, of events—with God as subject of that action. Thus the believer would muster the tactical wisdom just discussed to make a point: "God was in Christ, reconciling the world to himself."

This logical and theological dependence of christology on the doctrine of God may be more apparent to us than to previous periods precisely because the foundation, the doctrine of God, can no longer be taken for granted. Old Testament scholars suggest, for example, that "creation was not an article of faith, because there was simply no alternative." [41] That makes sense. Why linger long with the uncontested?

If today, on the other hand, the doctrine of God, particularly the claim of God acting, is in deep trouble, the people of faith face two alternatives:

(1) We could try for a shortcut, going to the jugular vein of human need with the message of a Savior, without clarifying the claim to authority and validity with reference to the reality of God. That strategy can produce spectacular results. Drawing perhaps on the cry for God in the human condition, some sense of connection will be managed in the hearts

if not the minds of desperate folk. Safe in the arms of Jesus, who will hesitate over definitions of God? But what will one do with the irksome outsider who wants to know what it *means* to be saved? Even for the believer, one wonders how long slogans can manage without concepts. To acknowledge the difficulty defiantly, without addressing it, is to offer anew the spectacle of the "death of God" theology. After all, the appeal to a divine work in Jesus is hardly better supported by a polite silence about the meaning of God than it was by a defiant assault on a particular form of that concept.

(2) The Christian cannot rest content with the first alternative. Faith claims knowledge—it makes a claim on the world of meaning. For example, Kent Knutson says of the modern query, "Tell us, what does the word 'God' mean?"

> This is really a Lutheran question occurring at key points in Luther's catechism. What does this mean for us, not just what does it say, but what does it mean? How shall it be interpreted? How shall it be applied? [42]

Contemporary questioning regarding the meaning of God is not, then, an irritating distraction, but an invitation to put the mind in the essential service of God. We had better take the longer, harder road of trying to frame a fresh concept of a God who acts in this world.

Why the problem? The difficulty depends on the way in which concepts introduced in this book's first section, "God," "self," "world," come together in the notion of action. On the one hand, there has been some tendency to think of God in such a way that were he to act it would have to be in a unilateral way—literally producing and controlling whatever might be said to be the effect of his action. Quite on his own he heals, destroys, saves. God does it, period. Let us speak of this concept as "monologic." I would not claim—or even grant—that this is the only theme in the tradition, but it has been rather prominent. Perhaps it is sufficient at this point simply to say that such an understanding of divine action *seems* consistent with faith's desire to worship God alone, to utter the *soli deo gloria* in an unqualified sense. In Chapter 6 I shall criticize the logic of disjunction which underlies the appropriation of that appearance.

On the other hand, "self" and "world" have come to be understood in ways hardly supportive of this view of divine action in the world. Each is related to the other more easily than either is to God, even if the relationship to the other may be disjunctive. Thus "self" may be understood autonomously—are we not self-initiating, self-establishing, self-understanding?[43] While such a view resists the threat to autonomy which a God active toward the "self" would pose, the "world" comes to be seen as matter for human making. This is surely part of the modern scenario, as the power of science and the promise of technology loom large. Or, alternately, "self" may seem overwhelmed by a "world," as a mass of forces—biological, sociological, psychological, and even genetical—career along beyond human control. That seems more the postmodern vision.[44] "Self" and "world," in any of these understandings, struggle against each other, but room is hardly made thereby for the third reality, "God." Such a self and such a world seem still to need a truncated other, but neither needs nor suggests a God as described above, if indeed any at all.

I spoke of the difficulty residing in the way certain concepts of "God," "self," and "world" came together in the concept of action. They come together—if one may so use these words—antagonistically, competitively. Each tends to be conceived monologically—whether the stage be theism, romantic or despairing existentialism, or behaviorism. But if come together they must, as when a believer would speak of God acting toward the self and in the world, an exacerbating effect is achieved. "God," "world," and "self" cancel out each other's claims.

Imagine, for example, how one may try to understand the place of such a monologic God in relation to the self and the world, similarly conceived. It will not do to juxtapose "God" and "self," "world." That could yield an "interventionist" view in which God occasionally interrupts in worldly rhythms or subjective soliloquies. But faith will rightly object to such a stress on miracle and mystery that leaves most of life aside. Or the tactic of juxtaposition differently fashioned could yield a "deterministic" view in which God is the real power behind and in world and self. But do I —does the world—suggest a fitting mechanism? Such juxtapositions hardly survive even as candidates today. How can the interventionist cordon off the self-sufficient divine acts? How can the determinist defy the self's sense of agency? Moreover, in either case—whether God does all these highly uneven things in self and world or only certain "good" ones—God is highly capricious and unfair.

If these understandings of "God," "self," and "world" are accepted as the terms of the discussion, even the resourcefulness of the theologians will not suffice to find a way out for us. To offer a special "inner history" is to appeal again to the interventionist model with its difficulties.[45] To appeal to all of history as a "master act of God" is to join the determinist in defying human agency, as well as to pose the question of the unity of direction in the presumed act.[46]

To refer the action of God to an eschatological future with determinative power *now* seems a mixture of both methods.[47] The "power of the future" escapes issues of evidence as if to intervene with special privilege. It defies the self's sense for the irreversibility of time in world and so challenges the conditions of the self's sense of agency. To settle for a more mystical view of God as "being" or even "Being-Itself" is to give up both specific divine action in the world and human interaction with God. At best action and interaction would be radically other than our ordinary meaning of these terms. In any case believers would say more than that God "lets be."[48] It is better to be done with such scrambling and look to the premises of the discussion, the understandings of "God," "self," and "world" as they come together in the meaning of action.

In this section I am asking after conceptual wisdom, a framework for Christian truth claims. Thus we ask how "self" and "world" are understood in a process perspective, looking to how the Christian claim of God acting in relation to self and world may be understood. What options are available to the believer who would speak of God acting in relationship to self and world? Whether a full understanding of "self" and "world" in the process viewpoint itself suggests talk of God becomes a concern of that section of Chapter 5 dealing with "constitutive wisdom."

By this point in the book it should come as no surprise to hear the author ceremoniously announce that action takes place "in relationship." In Chapter 2 a metaphysics of relationships was described. Now I am suggesting that acting—gaining effects—must be understood in relationship. One might better speak of "*inter*action." A threefold set of distinctions should help. They can be gathered up in the maxim: (1) The many (2) become (3) one.

(1) The *many* become one. There is the quantitative interaction suggested by the fact that it is always a *"many"* which come to be one. The principle of process reminds us that being—let it be the being of an effect —is constituted by its becoming. The principle of relativity provides the many for that becoming by stressing that any particular being (itself constituted by its becoming) becomes a potential bearing in upon every subsequent act of becoming. Thus multiple factors flow together toward the "one" effect. To specify a single "cause" is to stop short of a full account. That God acts might mean that God is such an external efficient cause, but not that he is the only one.

(2) The many *become* one. We have already spoken of how in addition to the data for an event some attention must be given to *how* the data comes together. In what form does the world gather itself for the self? We have already seen that Whitehead speaks of both "God" and "creativity" in trying to give a full metaphysical account of this matter.[49] A Christian might appropriate such an option to say something which Christian faith would utter regarding God's action. But such talk would clearly be talk of interaction—of action in relationship. There would be the matter of sorting out the relationship of God to "creativity." Beyond that one might speak of "qualitative" interaction, where the reference is not to a plurality within one kind of factor (as data in option one, or God and creativity here), but to different kinds of factors in the coming to be of an effect. For example, God may bear some unique responsibility (as Whitehead suggests) in the coming together of the data, but that God would still be acting with a world other than himself and toward a self other than himself.

(3) The many become *One*. Within this kind of qualitative interaction, a special relationship deserves attention. In Whitehead's understanding every entity is an intersection of the world's efficient causality and its own final causality. To become is at once gift and task. By the principle of relativity, I may bring myself to bear ever so emphatically on another whose becoming is open to me by the principle of process. But my gift becomes the other's task; my action invites the other's response. By the ontological principle, all action, all explanation, is to be so understood.

Thus all action toward another—and presumably God's as well in this model—is "in relationship" to the self-creative dimension of that other. Long before we come to speak of divine action process thought has challenged any monologic concept of action as unilateral production and control. Part of that challenge is a complex account of how we can construct—via presentational immediacy and symbolic reference—a view in which the terms (let us say "God," "self," and "world") are understood monologically and competitively. That is, Whitehead does show how monologic models mistakenly come to seem plausible. Of course to stress relationships is not to dissolve distinctions. Thus, for example, final causality is not merely another form of efficient causality. In considering how God might be spoken of as an efficient cause for (in) the world, we should not forget that every entity acts toward itself, according to this perspective. One may well concentrate on such distinctions for certain purposes—possibly with respect to claims Christians would make of God. In section two of Chapter 5 I will speculate as to clues Whiteheadian thought may give us for unique divine action regarding the world but in and for himself. But here my concern is action in the world where, it is clear, we must speak of action in relationship.

The interrelatedness will make a difference. "Self" and "world" are no longer understood monologically and competitively. Self's sovereignty is checked; my self-constituting project depends on the gift of world. Self's surrender is checked as well. The chaos called world churning toward me is gift after all. If self and world are so to be seen together, "in relationship," it seems right to set aside at least for the time being the disjunctive reading of "God" to consider how what faith would say of God can be heard in the framework of self and world which process thought provides.

### Divine Action as Intentional, Universal, Internal, and Free

Christian folk say things like this:

> God *cares for all things* . . . his love wills something in everything that happens and . . . the man of faith may therefore confidently place everything in his hands.[50]

If God is in the world—"in daily life, in public events, in all history"— how is he there?[51] If God *really* acts—that is, if he acts in the realm of reality encompassing self and world, I shall need to understand the action in the terms which apply in that realm. Whatever God may be in and for himself (and I shall suggest later that that does matter for the believer), he does not reach me by remaining in himself. I wish to draw on our understanding of action and the options—even suggestions—available in process thought to offer a framework for faith's claims regarding divine action. I believe that this metaphysic—which may be commended on independent grounds—does address the difficulties which seem to confront us in speaking of divine 'action.

In working on this question we may well cast a sideways glance at other prominent descriptions of what it is to act. The process contribution can be connected and commended if that dialog goes amicably. Recent work in linguistic philosophy suggests that an action be understood as activity ordered by intention. The intent is the unifying element in the bodily activities. Thus to describe a person acting it will not do merely to identify certain bodily movements; the intent must be specified.[52] Now we have already seen that Whitehead finds that a full account of reality not only permits but even requires that the giving of an initial aim is essential to the becoming of entity. We have noted that he draws that gift back to the unity of a "primordial" decision by a non-temporal actual entity. I suggest that the Christian, who would speak of God in the manner cited in beginning this subsection, has reason to let Whitehead call that entity "God," indeed to join him in such speech. That the divine will aims at something in every entity, that here we have the intentional element so crucial to action—this seems clear gain in a quest for conceptual wisdom concerning what it means to say that God acts.

But have we not celebrated too easily? The linguistic writers, whose insights I have mined rather greedily just now, might well object: intent is necessary, but not *sufficient* to constitute action. We need as well some reference to observable behavior—to events in the world. Thus Stuart Hampshire gathers the "essential features of an action":

(a) that it is something done at will and
(b) at some particular time,
(c) that it constitutes some recognizable change in the world.[53]

It is with (c) that the rub lies. I identify the student acting with inten-

186                                                    CONSTRUCTION

tion as I observe his hand waving and his face contorting. But what if I
discern no divine body bearing the divine intent? Can I still intelligibly
claim divine action? [54] This is not an idle challenge for me or anyone else
who cannot lay claim to unambiguous action of a *deus nudus.*

Here the process metaphysic can be helpful. A first step is to recognize
that the giving of the aim is held to happen *universally.* (One may pause
to note that Christians talk similarly of God's presence in all things.) But
we observe by the method of difference—a method poorly suited to discern an aspect in which no realities differ. Whitehead had to muster the
method of imaginative generalization for his metaphysical task. [55]

A second step is to follow up on the theme of "action in relationship"
by noting the *internality* of the event in question. Robert H. King has
suggested that such internality is required if God's action is to be universal
in scope:

> For God's action to be universal in scope, he must be in a position to
> intend for each agent from within the agent's own particular perspective
> and for each in relationship to the whole. The interrelatedness of agen-
> cies being what it is, that is the only way in which he can effectively
> act on a universal scale. [56]

King's categories come from linguistic thought and within that framework he seems forced to grant that "this ideal of agency is not entirely
conceivable to us." [57] It does become conceivable within a process metaphysic—or at least that is what I wish to claim. If that claim can be made
good, we will have a clear gain in conceptual wisdom. The process notion
at this point does provide what is sought. The giving of the initial aim to
the emerging occasion is about as internal as one could imagine—it is
none other than this occasion's (now beginning to become) own aim,
after all.

Perhaps such a notion of mediated action, action from within, in relationship, rhymes reasonably well with Christian sense about God's work
in the world. That work is said to have to do with so unreligious a reality
as the physical world about us. Thus Albert Outler comments:

> Christian monotheism does not propose to displace all other accounts of
> existence. . . . It holds that it is rationally conceivable . . . to think of
> *nature as given* . . . , as a configuration of finite processes, contingent

and interdependent but neither self-contained nor self-explanatory. It regards it as at least theoretically admissible to think of nature as a sort of "parenthesis," the full meaning of which is supplied "from beyond" without negating the significance of what lies "inside." [58]

If divine action from within can make sense in connection with a Christian claim about general divine action, what of the more specific? John Baillie even reaches out to encompass miracles in such a framework:

> And who shall say that . . . God did not indeed accomplish these more striking manifestations of his purpose, as he accomplishes the more familiar, through the agency of created things? Who shall say that even the most exalted final causes, as well as the humbler ones, are not served by the operation of efficient causes? Whatever happens in the phenomenal world becomes part of nature as soon as it happens, however far it carries us beyond what we had previously known about nature.[59]

It should be noted that such internality does not demean the status of an action, as if the outer side with its prominent particularity were the only element of the relationship worthy of being designated as action. Rather the giving of the aim not only directly conveys the desired sense of intention, but also points toward the priority and *freedom* of such action. King talks in such terms in considering what it would mean to speak of God as the ultimate actor:

> Where God is the Agent, nothing is exempt; everything comes within the compass of his action. Moreover, his agency is prior to every other. It is not conditional on the action of any other agent. One way of expressing this priority would be to say that God's action is foundational to every other. Everything that is, is active in some way; his action alone is the basis of every other action.[60]

Again King acknowledges that "it may be impossible to conceive of such an action." [61] And again, I have tried to show that process thought offers such a conception within a general description of reality.

Whether process thought can speak of God in relationship to the very "is-ness" of things is a question to which I wish to turn in the last chapter. But process thought does speak of God in relationship to the "such-ness" of things. That is, one must speak of God to understand why anything is *as* it is, even if it is not clear whether process thought permits an appeal to God to understand why there is anything at all. Moreover, in clarifying the "such-ness" of things, process thought speaks of an entity whose primordial decision is unconditioned, unfettered, free.[62] In the last chapter I want to ponder the question whether anything more than that —such as something pertaining to the very "is-ness" of things—can be reasonably expected of a metaphysical view.

Of course I can well understand that the theologian's applause may be somewhat hesitant. Thus Gustaf Aulen quickly qualifies his affirmation of "an effective divine presence in the human world":

> But this does not imply that the divine can be contained within or confused with the human. It is perfectly clear to faith that the divine presence at the same time accentuates the separation between the divine and the human.[63]

While Aulen hurries on to secure this point by appeal to the separation that is sin, I find it better to pause longer with the otherness which is creaturehood. Such otherness is not threatened by a process understanding of divine action as universal and internal. Distinctions do not collapse in a divine-human fog. In a metaphysics in which internal relationships are ignored or denied, it may well seem that to talk of God acting from within us would jeopardize the divine otherness. In such a view a divine work *contained* within the human (though the choice of that word is unfortunate, if it de-emphasizes divine activity and initiative), might indicate a God *confused* with the human. But in process thought it is not so. Indeed, this inner actor is, as inner, characterized by priority and freedom, though such prior and free action does not diminish the freedom of the self within which it occurs. Such complexity, such distinctions, make sense within a metaphysic of relationship—entities are internally related to each other and yet self-formative. Relationships are constitutive but not exhaustive of the self. Efficient and final causality both abide.

Now I grant that God is something of a special case in this metaphysic. The giving of the initial aim is internal and prior in a way different from the relationships we have as data for each other.[64] This will not seem an offense to the Christian who speaks of God's primacy by mention of different levels of action. But should the hard-headed student of reality bridle over this matter as an unwarranted favor for the religious? Process thought about what is real and how we know the real does prepare for this special case by its emphasis on internal relationships and its account of the distorting character of the sense perception which pictures us as only externally related. And the special case is not introduced as a gratuity for the Godly-minded, but as a factor needed to account adequately even for the activity of electromagnetic occasions.

Indeed this presence of God is not a matter of persons being Godly-minded at all—even the occasions making up the person are characteristically not conscious of God. It seems more to be the kind of point that Gustaf Wingren has sought to make so tirelessly on the theological front —that to be related to God is not necessarily to know God, that God 'works in the world apart from Christians. The first article is not cancelled by the second. Despite the radicality of sin we are still creatures. To speak so is not to speak of special endowments but of a universal relationship: "Life itself is the other side of God's continuing creative activity." [65] This metaphysic may be one in which Tillich's quest for an alternative beyond autonomy and heteronomy makes sense. Here God can be seen theonomously, uniquely as an "inner other"—as the general reality of internal relationships holds off the specter of pantheism. This God, while "other" than I, is no threat to my selfhood, but freely active in the very possibility of becoming a self.

Will this do? Of course not every understanding of "free" can be made to fit within this conception. The unilateral or monologic conception of divine action which we considered in the previous subsection would violate the relational character of reality. If such violation is not to occur, two limitations to divine freedom must be recognized. (1) The given, the past, must be dealt with—and God (in this view) aims to do so. His aim is precisely one which addresses the entity as it seeks to gather all that which flows in upon it. In that aim God is not limited to the possibilities present in the past—novelty of response was of course a major consideration for Whitehead in constructing an adequate descriptive account. But the past—which in process thought includes what we conventionally call the contemporary world—must be dealt with. This may seem to limit God too severely. Thus Langdon Gilkey, who draws significantly on White-

head at a number of points, objects to the process distinction between God
and creativity in this connection:

> To separate God from the origination of the totality of the being which
> is ours, and so in ontology from the creativity and the flux out of which
> we arise, is first of all to reduce God to *one* metaphysical factor balanced
> by others, and thus to qualify his supremacy and holiness and our own
> monotheism. Secondly, it is to relinquish the essential sacrality of
> existence, of life, of being—the dynamic vitality which is fully as sacred
> as is form itself.[66]

This is a weighty consideration. The Christian may want to claim for
God the custodianship of the past. But to do so is to accept another problem, given the evil that descends on us. Gilkey seems right in speaking
about creativity as not neutral but rather as "sacred or demonic," but
shall one go on to say that *"thus . . .* are they the work of creative providence"? [67] Perhaps it is a question of how radically one understands the
reality of divine self-limitation to which Gilkey eloquently appeals against
what he takes to be the finitude of God in process thought. If one grants
that divine self-limitation is genuinely creative of non-divine freedom—as
Gilkey does—does not one need to say that God also gives the gift of consequence to such freedom? Perhaps the notion of self-limitation permits
one to combine Gilkey's concern for God as the ultimate source of that
which is not God (as an issue which "precedes" metaphysical analysis—
see Chapter 6) with a concern to honor the full freedom of deeds—good
or evil—as they bear in upon us (as an issue which does invite metaphysical analysis).

(2) There is as well the divine relatedness to the emerging occasion, as
Ian Barbour notes:

> In the Whiteheadian scheme every entity must *respond for itself,* and
> nothing that happens is God's act alone. . . . God interacts with the
> world in time, rather than determining it in his eternal decree. He
> respects the freedom of his creatures.[68]

Will this do? Does this degree of divine freedom hold the fulness faith
seeks? That depends. It will not do if the reality of that which is not God
must somehow be finally unreal for believers. But the people of faith do

not seem to intend that. Biblical scholars speak otherwise. Thus Westermann finds biblical faith to hold that

> The creation of man in God's image is directed to something happening between God and man. The Creator created a creature that corresponds to him, to whom he can speak, and who can hear him. . . . mankind is created so that something can happen between God and man. Mankind is created to stand before God.[69]

Or Brueggemann characterizes the conception of sovereignty in the wisdom literature as follows:

> The lordship of this God is witnessed in his relaxed delight, in his confidence about the well-being of the world, in the buoyancy to give his creatures considerable latitude because he has no anxiety or concern about the general direction of the emergence of life and health in his world.[70]

Again, a Reformation theologian can insist that:

> The Reformation said that the finite *is* capable of the infinite, that God is really here and he is here in such a way that the integrity of the world has not been abandoned or changed. Man should not fear the world in itself.[71]

Faith, then, may seek to worship only God, but it does not deny the reality of that which is not God.

Two further issues need to be addressed if this view of divine action is to be found acceptable as a framework for faith's claims:

(1) Some accounting of faith's certainty or assurance needs to be made. How can we get from Baillie's "God has something to do with all that is done in his world, though assuredly much is done that is not in accord with his will" all the way to his "the whole of history stands under an ultimate divine control"?[72] Or how can we come from Aulen's "faith does not deny that suffering and want are in themselves evil. . . . Suffering and want are not in themselves an expression of the divine will" to his confidence in a "God who is sovereign even in relation to evil."[73] Or at least how can we come to that *kind* of confidence, which surely does seem to characterize living faith? Presumably these questions confront one

who would think theologically, whatever be the conceptual framework involved. I propose to address this question in process terms in the section on constitutive wisdom in Chapter 5.

(2) To return to Hampshire's analysis of action, can we speak of "some recognizable change in the world" in relation to divine action? One may grant that we have qualified "world" by calling for a deeper reading than sense perception would allow. One may also grant that we have shown that "recognizable" cannot be limited to that accessible to the method of difference which in principle fails to discern the universal. What remains? Does God's action yield anything?

Two things can be said: (a) God's intention is to be discerned in the ordering of life. Here it seems necessary to speak of something more comprehensive than the ordering of individual occasions. Perhaps Christian faith and process metaphysics can come together to do so. Gerhard von Rad speaks of the biblical faith in an ordering power which bears on both nature and humankind:

> But this primeval order does not exist only in creation; it is oriented towards man, offering him help; it is concerned about him, indeed addresses him directly. This address is not a mystery which can be deciphered only by man; it is uttered with full publicity "in the noisiest places" (Prov. 1:20f.).[74]

And Walter Brueggemann adds:

> Transcendence is the affirmation that there is a given to the ordering of life which we cannot eliminate. Transcendence is the recognition that there is a mystery to life that is not confined to our ignorance, incompetence or abdication. There is mystery in our best knowledge, in our greatest skill, and in our most passionate concern. The wisdom teachers . . . did know and affirm that life has an order and direction which is larger than human effort and which is not knowable to us. Faith means coming to terms with that direction and order for the sake of those entrusted to us.[75]

While Whitehead's understanding does stress the individual occasions, it may be possible to move—as he does in *The Function of Reason* and elsewhere—to consideration of "some tendency upwards, in a contrary direction to the aspect of physical decay" suggested by the entropic dimension of reality (*FR* 89). Thus Richard Overman writes:

> God's aim toward beauty in that larger society of human personalities is his aim toward a social background able to encourage the production of organisms harboring personalities in which increasingly beautiful experience may happen. The relevant future for God's experience is infinitely long and infinitely inclusive, so that he can provide for individual occasions just those initial aims which are harmonious with movement toward far-distant kinds of beauty as yet envisioned only by him. This is the reason that we have intuitions of a general providence, the reason that evolution appears as a movement toward higher kinds of societies. . . . [76]

In the next section of this chapter we shall be considering the content of God's work in the world, and shall be examining the Whiteheadian concept of beauty here employed by Overman. But this account does seem correct formally, and does suggest that God's intentional action in relationship does make a difference in life, even if that is true only indirectly by God working patiently but persistently through secondary causes.

(b) It may be that the intentional action of God comes distinctively into view—albeit still in the incognito of relationship—in particular strands of reality. This seems to be the "sense of God" of which John Bowker would speak, for example. He worries with A. J. Ayer over possible appeals to invisible entities and invisible worlds, but adds:

> . . . perhaps it is in relation to the sense of God that the purest of the pure acts of consciousness are possible, in an intentionality towards that which does *not* appear as other appearances (varied and different as *they* are in themselves), but which is nevertheless constitutive of distinct and publicly recognizable sequences of existential construction. . . . This *sui generis* mode of appearance constituted in the intentionality of faith which in turn is suggested as worthwhile by certain focal qualities or persons—the person of Christ, for example, and the consequent quality of life in the case of the Christian.[77]

The Christian would speak of God in Christ as some such "appearance." But to speak of Christ and of the Christian in relation to God's action is to enter into matters sufficiently particular and conscious that the boundary marking of a new subsection seems appropriate.

### Christ, the Christian, and the Christian Religion

A Christian who would speak in the framework of process thought will speak of God's action in relationship, of action which is universal, internal and free. There is value in such speaking, as Richard Overman makes clear:

> God is the Father of all these creatures—rocks, sheep, and men—the reason for their existence and the One whose love defines their possibilities. . . . The beauty in each present moment is enriched by the way God's purposes crowd into the aims of his creatures, but the "stone of stumbling" remains—God's love does not push rudely into the world. It acts not by suspending the effectiveness of other agencies, but by the steady urging of harmony, spreading through creation by "overcoming" the world.[78]

In the next chapter we shall be exploring the apparent content of the divine purpose with attention to categories such as beauty and harmony as understood by Overman. Here the focus is still on the formal issue of a framework of meaning for Christian truth claims. We have taken the issue of God's action in the world as a central matter in this connection. Process thought helps us to understand the assertion that God is active in relation to all that is—or so I have claimed. But Christians speak a more particular language as well—their dialect is Galilean. Can the message of Kairos find place in this word that is Logos?

These preliminary remarks are in order:

(1) What Christians say about God's relationship to Jesus and what they say about God's relationship to the world should be mutually consistent. Consistency is not identity, of course. There may well be something special to be said about God's relationship to the human with respect to Jesus. Moreover, we are speaking about *speaking* here. That is, we are not here addressing the matter of knowing God. Thus we are not addressing the question, which comes first—knowledge of God in Jesus or knowledge of God apart from Jesus. Rather our interest here is in the *meaning* of what we know.

(2) I limit myself to the area of the person of Christ, holding the discussion of his work to the next chapter. While I am uneasy with any full

separation of these topics, there does seem to be value in a consideration of *how* God may be said to be present in Christ, apart from the direct control of the question of *what* that God so present did. The logical priority of the christological to the soteriological question seems clear.

We cannot speak significantly of *what* God did in Jesus, unless we can say meaningfully *that* God was actively present in him. But there is a danger that faith, caught up in its desire to praise the work, may be swept along to emphases that cannot be intelligibly supported with respect to the person. In the next chapter I shall ponder what God did in Jesus in relation to the issue of justification, as that arises from within both metaphysical and religious concerns. We prepare the way for that more advanced discussion by asking here how faith's claim that God acts in Jesus can be formulated within a process point of view.

(3) In treating christology before soteriology I may seem to align myself with an approach like Wolfhart Pannenberg's "christology from below" which "is concerned first of all with Jesus' message and fate and arrives only at the end at the concept of the incarnation." [79] Yet, I do assume—as will quickly become apparent—that the Christian is looking for a framework in which to utter *vere homo, vere Deus* of Jesus of Nazareth. I want to join Pannenberg in his concern for close attention to the "distinctive features of the real, historical man, Jesus of Nazareth" as basic for christological work.[80] But I take heart from the fact that such attention rendered by him and others does not dislodge the basic ingredients of the theological task, though it may significantly rearrange them. I offer here considerations which seek to help only at the very basic level of the Christian's intent somehow to say that this one person Jesus was true God, true man. Conceptual wisdom is sought in the service of this conviction. That the conviction might be given up is of course conceivable, but I do not see how one could then claim to be Christian.[81] If it is not to be given up, we had better know what the mustering of the concepts mean together. That is a matter of framework and that is my present task.

Can that which the Christian would say of Jesus be said meaningfully today in the terms of "natures"—divine and human? In a paragraph under the heading "The Death of Substantialist Philosophy" Kent Knutson wondered:

> ... can modern man understand the Christian faith communicated with the presuppositions of reality into which the classic Christian confession was cast? ... Modern man lives in a world of protons, electrons, energy, matter, not in a world which understands or accepts the language of substance, divinity, universal, ideas, spirit and being. Can he find the statements of faith in this latter world and put them to use in his life today? That is his challenge. The church must help him.[82]

Three specific difficulties with the two natures approach may be identified, together with possible process resources as alternatives.

(1) Natures seem non-relational. We say, "It was not his nature to break a promise," "We all know human nature." The notion of "nature" may carry associations of that which is determined, given—hence, true at any time and in any situation. Since others do seem to affect us that which is unaffected in us must be the closed or self-contained. If we begin with the idea of two such self-contained realities—thing-like givens —we will face uphill going in trying to think of them truly coming together to form one person. On the other hand, for process thought being is intrinsically relational, so that the conception of human reality includes —Whitehead would say requires—openness to the divine. Process thought would clarify and expand Pannenberg's point:

> Openness to God is the radical meaning of that human "openness in relation to the world" that constitutes man's specific nature in distinction from all animals.[83]

To be open is to be accessible, even vulnerable. But it does not follow that the divine will be received or served by the human. Openness does not dictate that all are or will be Christian, or that God would have us all be Christs. But it does make clear that to be is to be internally related to others—world and God—and so to offer some preparation for Christian speech about the relationships constituting the person of our Lord.

(2) Natures seem non-temporal. A "nature" may suggest that the self-contained is such by being completed. One's "being"—one's essential na-

ture—is given. There remains a career of interactions with other beings, to be sure, but the nature as such will not be affected thereby. To speak of two such natures—divine and human—together in Jesus is to risk offering a dilemma: either they have always been together or they can never come to be so. That they never will be together will be the burden of the non-relational understanding (point 1 above). Further support for that bleak verdict will be found in the strongly opposed attributes assigned to the two natures. The eternal and the temporal, the absolute and the relative—whatever be the case with natures abstractly, two such could never come together.

Still, if faith would somehow say of Jesus that he is truly God and truly man, Christians may feel driven to speak of the two natures constituting the one person of Jesus even though that goes against the grain of meaning we have lodged in the natures. We may acknowledge, if not address, the logical problem at this point by an appeal to paradox. At least the note of opposition or contradiction sounding in the word *paradox* seems in place if we mean to bestow the blessing of the notion of non-temporal natures on Knutson's modern person who lives in a world of protons, electrons, energy, and matter. Robert Jenson, in commenting on the challenge of the new in Reformation thought, appropriately questions whether all that can be covered by the fine word *paradox:*

> . . . so long as God is defined by timelessness and creaturehood is understood as inwardly akin to "materiality," the Lutheran christological innovations were indeed intolerably paradoxical. So long as the discussion is conducted in the traditional metaphysical language—and it mostly was, by all parties—the Lutheran concerns indeed create a metaphysical monstrosity.[84]

Process thought may provide a framework in which that monstrosity can be avoided. Here to be is to become. Identity is won within temporality, not against it. Similarly Christian theologians have manifested an interest in moving in this direction in christological discussion. Thus Pannenberg specifies as a first condition for relating Jesus' unity with God to our understanding of God, that:

> . . . God in all his eternal identity is still to be understood as a God

who is alive in himself, who can become something and precisely in so doing remain true to himself and the same. . . . The change cannot be held remote from God's inner being. But this does not necessarily affect his identity.[85]

We withhold to the next chapter, under constitutive wisdom, the discussion of the relationship between the constant and the changing in God, a topic which Pannenberg so well introduces. But it is important to mention the possible resource to be had in conceiving the human as temporal, as becoming. Thus Knutson asks, "What kind of an event is a person?" and proceeds to speak of the person as a most complex unity with many forces at work. He then wonders whether this human experience could be used

> to suggest that God was at work in Christ as a transcendent self, controlling, instructing, leading Jesus as well as permitting the inner self to relate freely and wholly to the transcendent self.[86]

These authors make a promising bid to avoid the benumbing logic of timeless natures. Process thought may helpfully provide a framework in which their talk of becoming in the self makes good general sense.

(3) Natures seem competitive and disjunctive. That both the divine and the human in Jesus are "natures"—there thus being two of them—may suggest that the divine and the human in the person are of the same logical and existential order. That would seem to encourage the thought that they might compete for credit in performing particular functions within the one person. If person is understood non-relationally (point 1 again), that sense of competition will be strengthened. As the mind strains to hold such competing forces together, there may follow compromises of the "natures" in the interest of non-contradiction. While theologians have sensed the incommensurability of the divine and the human, the "two natures" formula threatens to erode the christological significance of the distinction for the theologian and may even prevent the less reflective from recognizing any such distinction at all. But, ironically, apart from the christological discussion the concepts "God and man" may still retain their qualitative uniqueness. We will then seem invited to choose between a Jesus who is not quite both truly God and truly human and

a Jesus who is that in a directly contradictory way. As Piet Schoonenberg has written:

> . . . theologians have pointed out . . . the fact that divine and human nature do not merge as parts to form one great whole, since the divine cannot be inserted into a greater whole; the fact also that the number "two" does not then have the proper function of numbers, namely, to indicate the multiplicity of like quantities. Yet it remains a task for those who proceed from the two-nature patterns, to reflect constantly on the dissimilarity of these "two." If the idea had always prevailed that because of this dissimilarity the divine and the human never appear in a competitive relationship, then the theories on the anhypostasia of Christ's humanity as the real absence of a created perfection would never have arisen.[87]

The general process possibility of understanding God's action as internal and prior points the way to a christological formulation which can resist the pressure to conceive the divine and the human in Jesus competitively. John B. Cobb, Jr. has offered such a formulation. With respect to Jesus, he emphasizes a contrast to the ordinary human situation, while drawing nonetheless on the structures underlying that situation. I have said that process thought would help us understand that God acts toward all reality as an inner other—or theonomously, in Tillich's phrasing. Cobb's argument suggests that typically the inner divine act is indeed perceived as *other*:

> . . . "I," or the organizing center of human existence, is usually constituted by conformal continuity with the "I" of preceding moments of the same personal life. . . . Similarly in ordinary Christian existence the call to conformation to Christ . . . is experienced as coming to the self from without.[88]

But this is not the only possible structure of existence:

> In another possible structure of existence the presence of the Logos would share in constituting selfhood; that is, it would be identical with the center or principle in terms of which other elements in experience are ordered. In that structure the appropriation of one's personal past would be just that ideal appropriation made possible by the lure . . . that is the immanent Logos. If this occurred, the usual tension between

the human sin and the ideal possibility of self-actualization that is the Logos would not occur.[89]

In formal terms this sounds much like an amplification of Knutson's effort to see "that God was at work in Christ as a transcendent self, controlling, instructing, leading Jesus as well as permitting the inner self to relate freely and wholly to the transcendent self." In any case Cobb proceeds to align this view to what we know of Jesus—for example, "it is appropriate to the confidence with which he acted in ways condemned by the tradition and law of his time"—and to the "Christ of the creeds." [90]

Such a process of alignment is complex. The predominant direction of the process mentality seems to stress the finally determinative reality of the human in response to the divine. As such it would seem to join with contemporary efforts to speak of the "indirectness" of Jesus' identity with the Son of God.[91] But it then becomes difficult to avoid saying that the divine becomes hypostatic in the human person rather than that the human becomes hypostatic through assumption by the divine.[92] One wonders whether the ancient talk of assumption and enhypostasia derive merely from confusion regarding the non-competitive character of the "two natures." May not such phrases stammer to say something of the priority of the divine in Jesus? Still, even those who talk in these terms want to say that the human lacked no perfection and indeed received the perfection of the divine.[93]

Perhaps help can be had at an earlier point—in describing what it is to be a person. One view is that

> a person is formally constituted in its being by a subsistence altogether complete, and therefore unity of person is to be determined from unity of subsistence.[94]

Given that understanding, and concerned to resist the divisive framework of two subsistences, one may understandably be inclined to the view that the person of Jesus must reside in the "altogether complete" divine nature alone. But it might be possible to think one's way into this question armed with a more relational temporal sense of the personal. Then the personal might be found precisely in the unitive. Thus one might seek to associate the person in a Kierkegaardian sense with the "positive third" of will, and note the tradition's insistence that Jesus did have a human will.[95] That what took place in Jesus witnesses to the priority of the divine will to any human will is a task I wish to take up in the next chapter in speaking of the work of Christ. But perhaps enough has been said to suggest that the process understanding of action may point the way toward a less competitive reading of how the divine and the human were together in Jesus than tends to be found in a "two nature" framework.[96]

A framework for Christian claims will also need categories which can express God's relationship to (action toward) the Christian person and the Christian community. Christian talk of intimate communion with God is precisely talk of a relationship, despite the tendency of mystical strains to replace communion with union. This relationship is a conscious one, though I may well be unaware of a work of God in me, for example, that prepares the way for the conscious relationship. Neither the divine nor the human poles in the Christian relationship need be supposed to be exclusively a matter of consciousness. Thus many would say that they do not consciously decide to accept or reject God. But it does not follow that in the complex organism that is the person there is not the responsibility that goes with relationship.

Nonetheless we may do well to concentrate on the conscious form of the relationship, since we have already dealt rather extensively with the way in which God works in relationship to entities, quite without consciousness on their part. To speak of the human pole in the conscious relationship to God is to suggest we take seriously (1) religious experience, in which human receptivity is emphasized, and (2) human response, in which human activity is emphasized.

(1) Of course to take religious experience seriously is not to take it uncritically. The self is active in receiving, and may emphatically distort what is there to be known. But while we must recognize the presence of human perversity, we must not be blind to the reality of a human location for the knowledge of God. Thus Walther von Lowenich hardly finds Luther soft on sin, but still writes:

> . . . faith maintains itself in man's reality. It is not only the suggestion of human possibility, but its realization as well.[97]

Theological skepticism about experience is best understood as precisely a defense of the divine-human relationship, even if the enthusiasm of that skepticism may at times overreach its mark. Three targets of that defense can be distinguished.

(a) There is the error to be found in a view which so conceives of God as to deny the possibility of a relationship at all. A common religious form of this error offers a God who lacks the definiteness needed to enter into personal relationships. Luther waged war against such a view. Unfortunately he speaks of such a view as "metaphysical," though I should wish to plead that it is a particular metaphysic, one of Being or Being itself, which is the actual target. But beneath what may be confusing phrasing, Luther's defense of the divine-human relationship is helpful. Von Loewenich puts it so:

> Metaphysics stands in opposition to religion. Once the category of being becomes the one that controls everything, then the difference between God and man coincides with the difference between the infinite and the finite. The idea of personality cannot be realized. Therefore the goal of the religious process is oneness, not fellowship.[98]

(b) There is the error to be found in a view which so conceives of God's presence as to miss the indirect character of God's action toward the Christian person. In this case one claims immediate knowledge of a *deus nudus*. While there may be some sense that can be made for such a claim within a process perspective, such an unmediated relationship to God would seem far from the clearest resource available in this mentality.[99] In giving the initial aim God works precisely through the stuff of the world available to the self, even though he does that work within the self. That rings well with a theological emphasis on the divine incognito. God acts through means that are not divine—whether in the human desire for the good, the book and bread precious to the community of faith, or in a truly human Jesus.

(c) There is the error to be found in the view which denies the divine priority in the relationship. One can so talk about human discovery in experience as to ignore or even deny the divine initiative. A disjunctive, competitive, understanding of the divine and the human (to which we alluded above) may lead both liberal and conservative to suppose that human discovery and divine disclosure cannot well comport together. But we have been arguing that process thought helps us hear faith's insistence that the relationship is not disjunctive. Indeed, it would be counterproductive to make of divine priority a denial of relationship.

Thus Ozment finds Luther stressing "simple expectation on the basis of God's promise and . . . full recognition and confession of one's utter discongruity with God and the things of God." But I wonder if he does not go too far in writing:

> What correlates and "congrues" from man's side with the "bonitas" and "gratia dei" are not good works and merits, but sinful works and un- righteousness.[100]

That is well said regarding the matter of divine priority and initiative, but the character of the relationship so initiated does suggest such human realities as "expectation, recognition and confession," after all. John Reumann has discerned this defense of relationship within Luther's attack on Erasmus:

> Erasmus' view is actually a very mechanistic one. In the synthesis of scriptural authority and human reason it thinks in terms of "forces" not persons and subjects man to the church in such a way that he loses his conscience and true humanity. The personal character of the divine-human encounter is thus lost. By the use of the term "election" Luther seeks to break Erasmus' deterministic, mechanistic world view.[101]

Divine priority is exercised, then, in relationship.

In sum, to defend a conscious relationship with God by resisting views of a God of being, a naked God, a demoted God, is in fact to find a place for religious experience appropriately conceived.

(2) In affirming the relationship of the human person with God faith calls for the recognition of the element of human activity in response. But faith has been notoriously troubled in knowing how to formulate this matter. Process thought may ease the difficulties somewhat by offering a framework in which four dimensions of that response can be emphasized.

(a) We have already spoken of how this metaphysic of internal related- ness invites a non-disjunctive reading of divine and human roles in the person of the Christ. That account may well be applied here as well as in relation to theological uneasiness over human response.

(b) In beginning this discussion we alluded to the fact that a process understanding makes available considerable resources for recognizing the unconscious dimension of the person. That we are "first of all bodies" may well speak to the anthropological contention that while we do willingly worship God, we do not often move one step back to speak of *deciding* to will.[102]

(c) Process thought helps us recognize more clearly that the response to God must be set within the temporality of reality. This can help to disabuse us of the illusion of an "eternal decision" for God. Bernard Lee has written persuasively:

> . . . one is never a Christian for all time on the basis of any single commitment. Only when that commitment is a central one . . . is my personal process a Christian process, and my personal reality a Christian reality.[103]

(d) Finally, process thought can help us understand the complexity of human response. It is not first or only with matters of faith that the human person knows the presence of an often conflicting many within the self. But that complexity understandably characterizes the relationship to God. Again, Lee puts it well:

> Someone may be doing some wrong and un-Christian actions, and all the while know deep within himself that things are not right; and it could be the presence of a Christian form of definiteness in his committed pattern of personhood, which he moves against, that makes him know his own dis-ease.[104]

Some Christian thinkers would want to place a greater emphasis on faith and confession in relationship to God than on the deeds which Lee stresses. But the issue of complexity returns as soon as we say, "I believe, help Thou my unbelief." What process thought does is to make sense of these inner struggles. I believe that process thought can also be said to permit some notion of a basic disposition which will appear as a central stance within the complex of processes making up the person. While faith may seek no "ghost within the machine," it does call for such a unifying reality in the person. Process thought can find such a reality only within the flow of time. We have considered the problem of continuity in Chapter 2, and will resume that discussion in Chapter 5 when we consider the meaning of having a history within the value of order. While process thought may seem to err on the side of undervaluing the continuity of the self, one may prefer to work with that empirically located problem instead of accepting the task of rendering a timeless substance-like self intelligible in a world experienced as through and through temporal.[105]

*How* is God present to the Christian, so experiencing and so responding? A process viewpoint will stress the data which derive from the reality of the presence and work of God in Jesus. In a process understanding those data are not dead, but living—bearing in on the self and available to God's present work with the self in question. Indeed one may go beyond the general metaphysical point of "objective immortality" to speak with John Cobb of a "field of force" emanating from the event of Jesus Christ or with Bernard Lee of the *disponibilite* of the event.[106] Moreover, it may be possible to adapt the general relationality and temporality of the self to account for Pauline talk of "Christ in me":

> For Paul the coconstituting agent of his personal "I" was the salvation occurrence of Jesus Christ. Paul experienced himself as most fully what he willed to be as conformation to Christ constituted his personal selfhood. Thus all conflicting fields of force emanating from his own past, his body, and his world were experienced as alien to what he truly was, namely a bearer of Christ's life. As a bearer of Christ's life, he was open to being continuously creatively transformed by the Logos.[107]

In addition J. Gerald Janzen seeks to employ the process distinction between causal efficacy and presentational immediacy to illumine not only a divine "presence *in*" the communion of saints, but also a "presence *to*." Pleading that "the Spirit is not imprisoned in the Church," he writes:

> This arises out of the fact that Jesus is not just our historical Pioneer. He is our contemporary. This, surely, is the testimony of the Book of Acts and of the early church—that the Jesus whom they serve, and indeed worship, is *there-now*. And this is not idolatrous worship, because as there-now he transcends settled forms of the past.[108]

It is not clear to me that process categories bring us quite as far as Janzen has come. Presentational immediacy does not seem to yield the active presence of the contemporary other to knowledge, but rather at best only the inferred knowledge of that other through correct recognition of pattern and extensive location.[109] To claim personal knowledge of the Jesus of history now present to us seems to overreach the process categories. Indeed process thought would not welcome the notion of action (much less knowledge of that) in the present by a person from the past, if that action suggests that the past person still lives in the sense of being self-deciding and self-aware.[110] But process thought does make available categories for a strong emphasis on the mediated presence of Christ in the church and would suggest to us that it is through word and sacrament, claiming continuity in proclamation and worship, that God calls people to Christian faith.

As God's relationship with the Christian person leads us to speak of experience and response, so the communal reality of faith takes the form of human religion. Again here Christian faith can welcome resources process thought makes available. Thus the Christian religion will attach itself readily to the temporal character of reality, and indeed offer comment on its direction and destiny. Of course religion can array itself consciously against the flow of reality, and regularly does so as the voluminous studies of Mircea Eliade indicate.[111] But Christians speak of a God who calls them out ahead, "beyond Eden." In that speech two themes call for recognition:

(1) The future does hold the promise of something more than a return to a golden age. In Chapter 6 I will contend that an analysis of the structure of reality may not be expected to yield any direct knowledge of that qualitatively other future. Yet the general process emphases on the irreversible character of time and the constant birth of novelty do provide a helpful preparatory framework for this theme.

(2) The hope in the future is tied together with a claim about a decisive time in the past, as the casting of the eschatological vision as "second coming" suggests. Whether process thought can accommodate a once-for-all uniqueness will concern us in Chapter 5. Again, however, the general framework of the view of reality is congenial in that the future

is not created out of nothing, but is born in dependence on what has gone before.[112]

The temporality of the Christian religion also bears implications for theological method. Timeless certainties fade in the face of the need constantly to re-contextualize the text.[113] Authority is understood as authority for an authentically responding self.[114] In thinking about the faith we shall have to return again to the reality of experience. Alan Richardson well says,

> All Christian doctrine arises from experience. The first formulations of doctrine were merely an attempt to tell others about this experience, so that they too might understand and share it.[115]

Perhaps the authority/commitment relationship may be said to specify the efficient/final causality structure of reality, though it surely intensifies it as well. I am free, but not apart from that which is given to me. The Reformation emphasis on the authority precisely of the Word well suggests this relationship, since a word is addressed to a center of understanding and freedom. One does not cower before the sacred presence, but considers a word. But the individual is not left in princely isolation; commitment to the community of the word makes very specific sense within a metaphysic affirming the sociality of being.

It will make sense too to stress the discriminate Word and the Christian community in connection with the sacraments, lest this religion of history relapse into awe before the pre-verbal Presence.[116] To affirm the community in a sacramental meal is not to evict divine presence, any more than the divine and the human are to be understood competitively with respect to the person of Christ.[117]

This Christian religion will accept its being in the present, its call into the future gladly. It will be concerned with continuity and contemporaneity.[118] Continuity will be found—with fear and trembling—in a pattern representing a prevailing sense of importance within the historical development of Christianity. But the Christian quest is not only to name the name anew. It is to be faithful to God in the living of life—to "do everything in the name of the Lord Jesus." If faith has spoken well of God's present action in all of life, the faithful person may well study that reality in a quest for ethical wisdom.

# 5

## Proposal: Metaphysics as Faith's Servant: Filling the Categories

### *Ethical Wisdom* and Goodness: What Is God About in the World?

#### The Place and Peril of Looking

Our quest is not a direct query after God's single purpose, his ultimate aim. Were it that, the Christian might well respond: "God is seeking the people of all the earth for himself," or "God is bringing the full redemption for which all creatures—human and otherwise—groan!" With such answers the Christian's correlative responsibility (beyond believing it) would simply be to tell the story of God's activity to this end. The Christian does have that responsibility and may well employ whatever tactical and conceptual wisdom is available for the task. But I am asking a different question. It is a question that invites metaphysics to play a more intimate role for the people of faith.

Three Christian affirmations lie beneath this quest for wisdom: (1) God is at work in the world.[1] Even for and with those who resist him, God works. Life itself is still from God. (2) The Christian is, as it were, with God in that world. At the very least the life of the person and people of faith does not escape earth, whether that living is "with" or against the work of God. (3) The Christian has some responsibility—as Christian—in the general human quest to live life well. Even theology rooted in Reformation skepticism about human competence can say:

The Reformation theology did not mean to say that man ought to be deprived of his potential for making this earth a good place to live. In fact, God expects men to use their power to do this.[2]

The Christian who makes these affirmations will want to know what God is about in the world. That interest is more than theoretical. To learn of God's work may be to learn about the Christian's work. After all, this quiet work of God in the world may sensibly be understood to be "in relationship"—like the specific "spoken" work in the Christ which we have just been considering. At the very least the Christian would offer a life that does not impede or obstruct God's work. More than that, there may be instruction to be had for the Christian's responsibility, if the way of God's work can be traced.

Where shall one look? People of faith have not sought special religious illumination at this point, but have repaired instead to their ordinary experience of life in the world. Gerhard von Rad speaks of how the wisdom literature points toward the treasure ordinary experience holds for the living of life:

No one would be able to live even for a single day without incurring appreciable harm if he could not be guided by practical experience. This experience teaches him to understand events in his surroundings, to foresee the reactions of his fellow men, to apply his own resources at the right point, to distinguish the normal from the unique and much more besides.[3]

Lest that seem merely tactical wisdom, von Rad proceeds to show how the "much more besides" includes "rules for behaviour."[4] So to look to ordinary experience would make sense to a Christian who heard a call to work with all humankind to the end that life may be lived well. Christians do hear such a call:

. . . God's will reaches us as a concrete demand via the world, and . . . we must therefore join with all men in a common effort to solve the problems of our time. Only in such a dialogue between the church and the world, involving faith, reason, and experience, can we arrive today at meaningful statements about man, humanity, and the human.[5]

Ordinary experience, then—that common to Christian and pagan alike— seems a proper place for the person of faith to look for ethical wisdom.

While the Christian claims no special access to that experience, faith does provide the very particular motivating quest for a life that aligns itself to what God is about in the world.

Perils await the one who would look there. Can one ever hope to learn what is to be done? The diversity of human experience (despite the claim to that held in common) would seem to leave the Christian squarely with the naturalist, who declines any invitation to derive *ought* from *is:*

> There emerges a consensus among authorities. No one of them considers the moral order derivative from the natural order. Neither by causal relation nor by logical deduction do these thinkers assert that we can begin with gravitational force, chemical bonds or DNA molecules and end with obligation of person to person. In a word they all defend the irreducibility of the moral order.[6]

If Christians do not agree even among themselves on matters special to them, what hope may be held out when all human claims must be heard?

To know the real is not necessarily to know the ideal—the Christian knows this. Faith teaches that evil is other than the good, but it is surely real. A most strange blend of "gifts," for example, is carried to the self by the sociality of existence. Relationships hurt and help, but how shall we sort them out? How, then, may one trust experience as the place to know the way of God in the world?

These perils must be acknowledged and addressed. Still, for two reasons, the Christian will persist in the effort to follow the way of God in the world:

(1) To the logic of the call outlined above there may be added the cry of human need. Thus perhaps the most active area in the law currently is that of the meaning of rights. Rights cry out for moral backing, a backing somehow to be found somewhere within the reality of the human. As one ethicist puts it:

> Rights have their initial form in morals, and the legal rule is the official recognition and the technical means of enforcement of rights. That is the meaning behind the phrase: "to secure these rights, governments are instituted." The Law does not invest a human being with the qualities of worth and dignity and the other values that flow from these; these values are intrinsic to human nature, when viewed from the point of view of morals.[7]

(2) The Christian notices that even persons who loudly proclaim that *ought* cannot be derived from *is* do not fail to prescribe for the human condition. The Christian will not abandon the quest for ethical wisdom to those outside the household of faith. But the going would seem to be uphill. Perhaps these difficulties suggest that the surer way to ethical wisdom at this point is an indirect, longer route. Rather than asking what Christian *ought* may be had in ordinary experience, we ask, "What does experience suggest God is about in this world?" If that can be found out perhaps we can then make out what we must do.

Faith has not supposed that the link of life with the living God is totally obliterated by sin. Perhaps nothing in our lives fully escapes being affected by sin. But along with the judgment of the cosmic range of sin's effects, faith has added a second word, which Paul Ricoeur formulates well:

> . . . evil is not symmetrical with the good, wickedness is not something that replaces the goodness of a man; it is the staining, the darkening, the disfiguring of an innocence, a light and a beauty, that remain. However *radical* evil may be, it cannot be as *primordial* as goodness.[8]

Even the Reformers, who can hardly be accused of being soft on sin, refused the Flacian suggestion that sin had become human substance, as if to deny the doctrine of God as creator any present significance.[9] Rather, as Edgar Carlson puts it:

> The relationship of God to the world defined by the term "creation" is no less enduring and contemporary than the relationship defined by the term "redemption." God confronts man the creature as well as man the sinner.[10]

If, then, we would persist in this perilous venture, where shall we look? One will seek as comprehensive a scope as possible, if one believes that a consistent God is at work in all that is. That scope may serve to correct the distortions of particularity and perversity. To look there is not to deny the possibility of distinctions in God's work—God's work with humankind may be significantly different from (though presumably not contradictory to) his work with that which is not human, for example. The differences may arrange themselves within a more general structure of God's way in the world. But it seems important to take the broadest context possible for a discussion of any distinctive working. Even if one does not affirm that objectively "nature is less fallen than man," [11] one may well recognize the tendency for sinful self-interest to distort the human perceptive process, subjectively. One casts the net widely for one would not have the quest for ethical wisdom be a rationalization of a particular human order. Similarly, one may intend to seek a distinction of the moral good (as a category applying to humankind) from the metaphysical good (as a category applying to all that is real), but one will seek to understand the first within the frame of meaning provided by the second, as surely as both depend on the will of a God who does not work at cross purposes with himself. [12]

We are in effect asking the metaphysician to join us as colleague in the quest for ethical wisdom. Clearly, to choose such a companion for the journey of faith is not to travel light. After all, to look for something so general is, ironically, more difficult than to pounce upon the particular— if Whitehead is right that we are accustomed to perceiving by the method of difference. But perhaps faith does not expect this quest to be an easy matter. Von Rad, for all his emphasis upon the immanence of wisdom, can acknowledge:

> This wisdom, immanent in creation, was differentiated in the three great didactic poems (Job 28, Prov. 8, Sir. 24) from the "real" works of creation (wind, springs, sea, mountains, etc.). This ontological separation of the phenomena within creation is the most interesting element. Obviously what the teachers perceived as a "summons from creation," as the "self-evident nature of its order," was not simply identical with the "real" works of creation. [13]

Since the quest is not thought to be an easy one, we would be glad for any more particular help that might be available. I have in mind two such guides:

(1) To plead for metaphysical scope in this quest is not to suppose that what God is about in the world can simply be identified with the fundamental shape of reality. Some ingredients in that sketch may reveal the mark of purpose more readily than others. Specifically, if Whitehead's description of what he terms the action of God has seemed to serve well as a framework for *how* faith may talk of God's active presence, that

description may also be helpful when we ask *what* God is about in the world.

(2) At the same time the Christian will keep one ear cocked to faith's distinctive dialect. There may not be a distinctive set of "Christian values" to be gained there, if it is general human need which defines the Christian's call. But there is more than what we have called Christian authorization, motivation. For faith does have a special account of God's work in the world. The way we are taking to ethical wisdom for human life is the long one of trying to discern the work of God in the world in order to win some lesson there for our living. Here faith and metaphysics will meet as colleagues.[14] Since my purpose is to mine whatever resources metaphysics may hold for faith, I will give major attention in this chapter to the first of these guides. In Chapter 6 I will return to the question of a distinctive component in Christian life.

### Creativity: Life and Novelty

Following the first guide, we can appropriately open our discussion with Whitehead's view that

> . . . the purpose of God is the attainment of value in the temporal world (*RM* 97).

The Christian will not wish to say *less* than that of God's purpose.

Where, then, is value to be found? Perhaps some clue can be found in recognizing that values are *valued*. Whitehead so proceeds and makes bold to claim value in valuing. While he will have more to say, he will begin his analysis of value with this elementary point. The point is foundational not only as elementary, but as universal in reference. Given the fact that every entity has "for-itself-ness," "self-reference," or "inwardness," it will not surprise us to encounter in Whitehead talk of each entity valuing. Thus does Whitehead lay a universal base for the discussion of value:

> Value is inherent in actuality itself. To be an actual entity is to have a self-interest. This self-interest is a feeling of self-valuation; it is an emotional tone. . . . It is the ultimate enjoyment of being actual (*MT* 109).

We pause to note that this point undergirds a theme in Whitehead's thought that has endeared him to ecologists: nature possesses value independently of humankind and indeed the human and the natural cohabit one community.[15] This theme no doubt poses a major challenge to the contemporary Western consciousness which regards "nature" as a distinct —and lower—realm designed for human control. Still, care must be taken in reaping this harvest. For example, a mystic personalism is no more justified toward mountains than toward automobiles. These are aggregates of primary entities, but they betray no coordinated originality of response. Whitehead's account does not require us to assume a unity of experience and valuing in such instances. Recognizing that the intrinsic value of such aggregates "is simply that of the sum of their lowly members," David Griffin proposes a helpful distinction:

> . . . while there is no *ontological* dualism between some things that are subjects of experience and other things that are mere objects, there is an *organizational* duality. Those things which *seem* to be mere objects are still affirmed by process thought to *be mere* objects. . . . The only value that needs to be considered (beyond the value of the lowly members, which in most nonliving cases do not depend importantly upon the continued existence of the aggregate) is the instrumental value.[16]

This goes far to "save the appearances" of genuine differences which experience suggests. Yet it remains true that the four forms of aggregates— the inorganic, the vegetable, the animal, and the human—together with their constituent entities indwell a single world.[17]

Recognizing the universal scope of God's creative work, we have begun to mine the categories Whitehead finds suggested by all reality. The valuing/value of self-awareness, self-enjoyment, was the place to begin. Entities are *processes* of valuing. A second nuance is noticed when we recall that entities are also instances of the *increase* of reality. "The many *become* one and are *increased* by one." Here we have not only the internal process of valuing in concrescence, but the external process of transition to new instances, which amount to increase. One might try to make something of that ethically. At least process thinkers have done so. R. B. Mellert writes that "the first business of morals is to safeguard experience and to continue the process,"[18] and Bernard Lee finds a way for us to share this work of God:

God desires for the world its openness to becoming more than it is, and its responsiveness to the call to be more. He invites increase upon everything. He invites transcendence. It matters to him that the world be more, that every person I know be more, that I be more. I may will this "more" for myself and my world without my desire being an act of personal union. It becomes shared life—union with God—when my energies are pledged to caring for "more." . . .[19]

While these comments do characterize an attitude which may be commended to the Christian, obscurities remain. One must not leap too quickly via process categories to the argument that any particular entity is called by God to be "more." At least all we can show up to this point is that the many are regularly increased by one. Other considerations would be needed to show that a particular organization of the many ("I," " every person") should be perpetuated in this increase. Indeed, one might argue that the most economical interpretation of "and are increased by one" would call for us to expect *another one*. This might cause us to sit loose to any particular confronting us; we expect the inevitable: another one. Surely there is some wisdom in this, since we do manage inefficaciously to array ourselves against the flow of reality. Some of that wisdom may sound in the word "more," but I detect a call for greater continuity than a flow of other ones would provide. I would second that call, since it would seem to be the business of ethical wisdom to guide choices among alternatives, rather than merely to advocate attitudes toward the inevitable. But if the advance to more specific value (and surely to the one Lee's "more" represents) is to be had on process terms, other categories will have to be introduced.

As it turns out the process does not drone along, endlessly producing dull repetitions. In this universe—in this cosmic epoch, at least—process has spelled *qualitative* change. Out of the rush of creativity there have come truly *other* ones. Specifically, process has yielded *life,* with its characteristic emphasis on originality of response.[20] Life is a contingent—even a precarious—affair and as such could qualify as a candidate for an ethical value to be supported by human freedom. Something may be at stake here in a way the inevitable would not allow. Thus a Christian calling this wisdom might join so unlikely an ally as Erich Fromm in his attack on the "necrophile," who:

. . . loves all that does not grow, all that is mechanical . . . is driven by the desire to transform the organic into the inorganic . . . as if all living persons were things.[21]

Or, more positively, one might join William Beardslee in his bold affirmation of the procreative phase of sexuality as "the biological basis for hope." [22]

The Christian may hear a familiar ring in this emphasis on life. At least Claus Westermann directs attention—a la Beardslee—to the notion of organic life:

> The act of creation, by directing itself to the living being, includes the capacity to propagate one's kind. That is the basic meaning of the word *bless;* the power to be fertile. The life of the living being, whether man or beast, clearly includes the capacity to propagate. Without it there would be no real life.[23]

Westermann further notes that even after the expulsion from the garden, the woman is named "Eve," meaning "mother of the living," so that

> . . . despite man's disobedience and punishment, the blessing given with the act of creation remains intact. . . . Man who is now far from God is always man blessed by God, and man's life remains open to the future just because of the power of God's blessing.[24]

Somewhat more broadly, Old Testament scholars emphasize that

> Law in Israel seems characteristically to be derived from the situational practice of the wisdom teachers who shrewdly and patiently observed the *actions which made for life.*[25]

Thus the Whiteheadian emphasis on the cosmic novelty that is life looks promising as a candidate for filling out Christian ethical intuitions. Yet the notion badly needs clarification and amplification. Without that we risk a narrow reading of the theme, as when biological growth dominates personal identity or economic growth national identity. But perhaps that need is what process thought can address: the filling out of the theme. What actions "make for life"? Or, more basically still, what life is there to be chosen and served?

Without disavowing the biological element, it is clear that by life White-head intends a wider scope. In "science and art," for example:

> . . . the finite consciousness of mankind is appropriating as its own the infinite fecundity of nature (*AI* 272).

One may suppose that taking God's concern for life as our own will affect our fundamental attitude in personal relationships. Thus David Griffin calls on us to let the other live:

> . . . since persuasion and not control is the divine way of doing things, this is the way we should seek to accomplish our ends. Much of the tragedy in the course of human affairs can be attributed to the feeling that to control others, and the course of events, is to share in divinity.[26]

We have been examining the originality of life. But "stagnation is the deadly foe of morality" (*AI* 269) also with respect to method. Accordingly, our attitude toward novelty will reflect itself also in the method of ethical reflection. It does not follow that we will contradict ourselves by turning against the value of life for a novel death. But we will recognize that the life we value morally is pointed toward the future. That about which we are deciding is itself a process bidding for qualitative novelty.[27] The nature of the life to be sought is not settled once and for all. Thus some kind of contextual element is clearly introduced into ethics.[28] To try to hold back from that is to defy the work of God in the world. Continuity for (with) the future may be won more in consistency in the process of decision making than in strict perpetuation of previous decisions. A theory of law heeding this metaphysical hint, for example, might perhaps make more of "due process" guarantees than of the specification of a material table of "rights." [29]

We have been developing the association of life with qualitative novelty. In that association as bearing on the future the note of originality emphasizes adventure.[30] If the emphasis is more on the present, there may well follow the stress on festivity and fantasy—as William Dean has suggested.[31] Or, more wryly, Whitehead observes that in a decadent society

> the last flicker of originality is exhibited by the survival of satire (*AI* 277).

But all these—satire, fantasy, festivity, adventure even—are expressions of life. At its core, according to Whitehead,

Life is a bid for freedom. . . . (*PR* 159).[32]

Robert C. Neville has produced an outstanding treatment of this theme in *The Cosmology of Freedom*.[33] While the richness of Neville's treatment defies simple summary, it may be helpful at least to cite his list of four personal and four social dimensions of freedom. Personal freedom is interpreted in terms of external liberty, freedom of intentional action (freedom to "do what one would"), freedom of choice, and creativity. Social freedom requires freedom of opportunity, social pluralism granting genuine options, an integral social life won through a pluralistic life style, and the social order of a participatory democracy in which "persons influence the conditions under which decisions are made to the extent they are potentially affected by the decisions." [34]

Neville's study offers rich resources—for example, a truly lovely classification of levels of value-comprehensiveness.[35] Every ethicist must adjudicate disputes in which claims are made from personal, interpersonal, public and social-order levels. Neville's contributions are particularly important in specifying the formal relationships involved in any ethical wisdom.

But to plead for freedom is to go on to content—it is to say *what* God is about in the world, as Neville clearly recognizes. In his reading of "freedom," Neville stays close to the linkage of life with novelty, of freedom with spontaneity. He roots those linkages in the reality of creativity. Thus for the freedom of integral social life:

> . . . the pluralistic sense of self gives rise to a heightened sense of the importance of creativity. . . . Where the literate style took unbridled imagination to be a threat to patterned behavior, the pluralistic style takes it to be a sign of both success and opportunity. . . . Where the literate style took good action to be that which contributed to the valued order of society, the pluralistic style appreciates creativity as "doing your own thing." Each agent is the center of his own creative action, and that action constitutes his identity. There is a new appreciation for privacy.[36]

Is this the freedom which is God's way in the world and wisdom for us as well? A candidate it surely is. But that some caution should be exercised in endorsing this candidate as such is suggested by the following considerations: Neville draws his understanding of freedom back into the metaphysical ground of creativity (even though the scale of the discussion is in the sphere of more particular, contingent affairs). A Christian who holds that God acts quietly and universally will have reason to probe any convincing metaphysical view for ethical wisdom. Yet the pervasive reality of evil continues to caution against hasty judgment in these matters. In Chapter 2 I offered an argument to distinguish God and creativity in the metaphysical sketch process thought represents.[37] In the present discussion I still want to ask if it is possible to draw ethical wisdom more distinctively from Whitehead's characterization of God.

We perhaps cannot expect Neville to help here, since he is critical of what he takes to be a loss of transcendence in Whitehead's God.[38] In Neville's view to regard God as a factor in the cosmic process—no, more than that, even to make bold to stand with him in common cause—is to lose the sheer reality of God. But a Christian who finds that Whitehead's description of divine agency fits as a framework for something (if not everything) that faith would say of God's activity in relation to the world (conceptual wisdom) may well look to Whitehead's discussion of God for possible ethical wisdom.

The emphasis Neville places on novelty as originality is checked by explicit warnings in Whitehead. Thus in *Process and Reality* Whitehead wrote:

> . . . novelty may promote or destroy order; it may be good or bad (*PR* 284. Cf. *RM* 129).

Is "freedom" as the development of novelty and originality the best formulation we can manage of ethical wisdom? Without appealing to Whitehead as authority, but remembering the fit faith found here for the action of God, we may wish to follow Whitehead's apparent advance to a more specific value order. It is ironic that Neville, who criticizes Whitehead pointedly for an insufficient account of personal order, seems to move away from an inclusion of social order as a material value for ethical wisdom.[39] But the question does haunt one. Does the free flowing reality of creativity represent a life-giving stream or a death-dealing flood? How we answer seems to rest on a matter of proportion—that is to say, of order. Without intending to leave behind the theme of life, we advance to the question of the relationship of order to life in the quest for ethical wisdom.

### Order: History and Harmony

We are seeking a value which would be the fitting object for human choice. That value must be characterized by contingency, if it is to be chosen significantly. As such we seek to move beyond the inevitable reality of self-feeling, self-enjoyment which goes with being actual. That value is, as it were, too intrinsic. Novelty, originality—as linked with life—suggest the needed contingency. They can be significantly chosen as Neville's work makes clear. But I posed our quest for ethical wisdom in dependence on a theological framework: What is God about in the world? Whitehead does not link novelty as such with God, but with a specific development of creativity. What then, does Whitehead consider to be the content of the divine aim?

> What is inexorable in God is valuation as an aim towards "order," and "order" means "society permissive of actualities with patterned intensity of feeling arising from adjusted contrasts" (PR 373-374).

What does this mean? In another formulation Whitehead says that "the teleology of the universe is directed to the production of beauty" (AI 265). I turn to Whitehead's discussion of beauty as a helpfully concrete specification of his notion of God's aim.

In two senses beauty is a matter of "mutual adaptation." The "minor" form of beauty refers to the avoidance of painful clashing of components and hence the absence of inhibition felt in receiving that which clashes. In the "major" form of beauty the coming together of components introduces "new contrasts of objective content with objective content" (AI 252). As these new contrasts are felt there is an increase in the weight with which the original components themselves are received, are "felt."

How is such beauty the order at which God aims? In alternate formulations, Whitehead has said that God's aim "is the intensification of formal immediacy," and that "God's purpose in the creative advance is the evocation of intensities" (PR 161). What has beauty to do with intensification? The link with "immediacy" may be seen in the reality of a many *coming together* in beauty. To come together, to "concresce," is integral to every entity, as surely as "unification" took its place with "becoming" and "novelty" in the cast of three basic notions we used to introduce Whitehead's view of reality.[40] To be is to be a togetherness of relations. To speak of such integration is not to add a statement to the fundamental account of being, then; rather, it is "immediately" true of each entity. On Whitehead's view unification cannot be avoided. But it can be intensified. The many come together to be felt.

The constitutive relations in immediacy are held together in a feeling of being actual. We have already traced Whitehead's thinking about how this self-relatedness of feeling may be regarded as representing an intrinsic value at the base of actuality itself.[41] Whether this is an adequate criterion of value in Whiteheadian terms, it clearly is fundamental in his description of reality. Beauty "intensifies" this immediate togetherness of felt relationships. We may understand how this is so by seeing Whitehead's discussion as making specific sense out of the cliché that the whole is more than the sum of its parts. As Whitehead puts it:

> Thus the parts contribute to the massive feeling of the whole, and the whole contributes to the intensity of feeling of the parts (*AI* 252).

Thus Monroe Beardsley writes of order in art:

> . . . there are at least two levels of quality . . . the local qualities of the elements (the patches of color, the notes of the melody) that are the ultimate ingredients of art, and the regional qualities that emerge from complexes of them. Similarly, there are at least two levels of form: textural form, or comparatively small-scale interrelationships; and structural form, or large-scale interrelationships.[42]

Thus there is an increase or intensification of feeling. The parts do not merely accumulate. They come together (the immediacy of unification) to constitute a qualitatively new relationship to be freshly felt (intensification).

Beauty in its major form might also be spoken of as the intensification of life. In Chapter 2 we followed Whitehead's account of how life occurs when conflict is dealt with not by elimination of diversity, but by "mental" initiative which introduces a conciliating synthesis.[43] In beauty we find that kind of synthesizing at work (*AI* 260-261). We have already noted Whitehead's critique of novelty which destroys order. That can be paralleled by the sense in which the order to be chosen is precisely a "living" one—one, indeed, which intensifies life. Thus in a strikingly explicit passage Whitehead writes of God:

"Order" and "novelty" are but the instruments of his subjective aim which is the intensification of formal immediacy (*PR* 135).

An order which arrayed itself against life would stultify rather than intensify immediacy.

Thus the advance within the metaphysical sketch to God's ethical wisdom can be traced. (1) We move beyond the continual, and indeed inevitable, birth of "another" one, though we may say that in the valuing of self-feeling of each such one there is value. (2) We move beyond the development of truly novel and original *other* ones though the contingent reality of novelty is prized as an instrument in God's aim. (3) We move toward the notion of order as beautiful harmony, for here both the immediacy of togetherness in feeling (1) and the synthesizing originality of life (2) may be "intensified."

This kind of ethical schema corresponds well to the kind of distinctions Whitehead makes in speaking of a threefold urge at work in human reason's attack on the environment:

(1) To live, (2) to live well, (3) to live better. In fact the art of life is *first* to be alive, *secondly* to be alive an a satisfactory way, and *thirdly* to acquire an increase in satisfaction (*FR* 8).

(While Whitehead here places the distinction within the realm of life, I am suggesting that the same kind of advance can be stretched to incorporate the full value scale for reality—with, of course, any number of subordinate classifications as well.) Or, Whitehead aside, this view may provide a framework for understanding our human and Christian sense that while life itself is precious and good, we are called beyond sheer existence and mere survival. It seems right to say that life is an art to be promoted, though that may be the function of more than reason (*FR* 8).[44] Still, it is reason with which we are now engaged, and our more specific question presses: What does order—as illumined by metaphysical reason—call for from human beings, such as Christians who would seek ethical wisdom in learning what God is about in the world?

A little more exposition is needed. Whitehead defines beauty in terms of harmony. The key to harmony is "variety of detail with effective contrasts" (AI 252-253).[45] Similarly, the account in *Process and Reality* emphasizes how the order which makes for intensity must steer between the twin perils of the trivial—in which the components are uncoordinated and tend toward chaos—and the vague—in which the coordination is so strict as to eliminate contrast (PR 168-172).[46] It is essential that the individuality of the components not be lost in the ordering (AI 262-263).[47]

What ethical wisdom, then, may be found for the Christian in this concept of order? Clearly we will need to deal with an expansion of order beyond the microcosmic occasion. Whitehead recognizes this need:

> Thus the problem for Nature is the production of societies which are "structured" with a high "complexity," and which are at the same time "unspecialized." In this way intensity is mated with survival (PR 154).

With that recognition we are on the way to the scale needed, even if it needs to be remembered that Whitehead's "societies" may hardly qualify for sociological scrutiny. In moving to this scale of order we need not commit the "fallacy of composition"—appealing to a whole with arguments that apply only to the parts.[48] There is a new reality, a whole, here though this whole does parallel the structure present in the parts. The parts do not merely accumulate, but are intensified. With the concept of an intensifying whole that is more than the sum of its parts in place, then, we turn to examine two such more extensive forms of order: (1) the harmony to be sought in an individual life over a time span, (2) the harmony to be sought between and among individual lives.[49]

(1) At first blush the interest in such temporal stretch may seem against the grain of Whitehead's thought. After all, did he not write that "Care for the future of personal existence, regret or pride in its past, are alike feelings which leap beyond the bounds of the sheer actuality of the present" (AI 291). But the atomistic character of Whitehead's philosophy does not prevent him from recognizing and affirming such durative elements. Indeed, it belongs "to the civilization of consciousness, to magnify the

large sweep of harmony" (*AI* 291). The tendency in reality toward endurance in complexity against entropic forces may well suggest that what God is about in aiming at intensifying order in the universe is related to the making of human histories.

Such a theme finds resonance in Claus Westermann's concept of the uniqueness of the biblical reflection on Creation:

> In the first eleven chapters of the Bible the inquiry about the whole is compressed out of millenia-long tradition into an inquiry about the beginning and the end, and is bound up with the question of the history of mankind which is centered in the history of God's people.[50]

But Westermann is well ahead of us, the scale of his statements would lead us into this chapter's last section and this book's last chapter as well. Freshly encouraged by the biblical interest in the large sweep of history, let us put the simpler question to process thought: What wisdom may here be commended regarding the living of a single human life?

(a) The individual is called to *make* history. To say that is not first or necessarily to speak of publicity, but precisely of the privacy of self-understanding. The Christian person who hears ethical wisdom here will refuse the model of a timeless self. That person will rather share James Gustafson's strong hunch:

> . . . that to be human is to have a vocation, a calling; that it is to become what we now are not; that it calls for a surpassing of what we are; that apart from a telos, a vision of what man can and ought to do, we will flounder and die.[51]

Thus one will plan, one will intend, one will anticipate. One will spend little time with experiences that leave the self stillborn in the present. From such a viewpoint F. David Martin launches a critique of rock music:

> There is no revelation of a subject matter, no content. Thus "rock" music . . . can be experienced with great intensity. But this kind of intensity fails to thrust us into an awareness of ecstatic temporality, because the tensions and resolutions of the embodied meanings are trivial and monotonous. The presently sounding tone anticipates, more or less, the succeeding tone and maybe a few after that, but there is no "stretch," no far-reaching references. . . . The embodied meanings are trite because they make no significant demand upon our imaginations.[52]

In the pursuit of such "stretch" there will be concern for continuity, but always within change. Along the way one will beware of the apparently safe harbour of too rigid or narrow a personal order.[53] At the end of the way self-transcendence may replace self-fulfillment, as David Tracy suggests:

> One lives authentically insofar as one continues to allow oneself an expanding horizon. That expansion has as its chief aim the going-beyond one's present state in accordance with the transcendental imperatives: "Be attentive, be intelligent, be reasonable, be responsible, develop, and if necessary, change!"[54]

(b) The individual is called to *have* a history. The self, ignoring the lure of the timeless present, bears on the future only by purchasing the power of the past. At the simplest level this speaks of personal consistency, of "owning" one's memories, of taking responsibility for one's past. But the simply individual level is *too* simple; to have a history is to be a participant in a *people's* story. Of this matter Robert Neville has written with great insight. There is a kind of dialectic of mutual dependence between individual and community. The great accomplishments of the historic few are dependent on the development of the historical community, of the culture. Thus I may find my sense of identity dramatized by those few through my continuity with the community's development. In turn, Neville points out, the individual who has a cultural history, has a "public face" which must be taken into account by others in the interactions of society. In those interactions the basis exists for mutual enrichment.[55]

(2) Our attempt to trace the harmony to be sought in an individual life over a time span has ineluctably drawn us into the matrix of relationships—of order or harmony—between and among individuals. That fits the facts. Our lives will be lived out in the terms of some social order. Moreover, we recognize that the particular form of the social order matters importantly—for good or ill. We could use counsel in such a matter of consequence. Christian writers have recognized this dimension and have even assigned the faithful responsibility in this sphere. Thus Gustaf Aulen writes:

When Christian faith speaks of the law of creation, or rather the law of the Creator, it does not refer to any collection of laws, fixed commandments, or statutes. The reference is to that divine will which maintains creation and preserves it from disaster and destruction. . . . God's will as law urges and even compels men to actions which advance and further the purposes of God. In this sense God makes men his partners in the continuing work of creation, which is intended to create in human society order instead of chaos, fellowship instead of dissension and dissolution, and mutual service instead of injury.[56]

What social order makes for harmony—for the true promotion of life? Following the clues available in the basic discussion of order, we will be questing after "variety of detail with effective contrast." One will be seeking a society which encourages and enables the self to "grow" in the sense of entering increasing numbers and kinds of relationships without losing the central thread of identity.[57] I-Thou and I-You relationships will both be stressed.[58] One will try to win a conscious recognition of the internal character of these relationships. That should serve to check the claims of self-possession. If I and the other(s) simply do not have our selves in separation from each other, we may be more hesitant to stake out claims. It will not do to talk easily of individual rights in isolation from talk of responsibility.[59] I shall have to ask, for example, how my right over my body correlates with my responsibility for my body in relationship. It may be that even such a "right" as privacy will be best understood as a necessary element in relationships of love, trust, friendship and the like.[60]

This ethical wisdom stresses qualitative contrast within those relationships. To that end the human community may well take a page from nature more generally and seek to avoid the temptation of inbreeding:

Inbreeding reduces the effectiveness of exploratory behavior, appetitive and aversive learning, and motility. Thus a decline in appetitive initiative on the reproduction level has a "snowball" effect, which might be described as follows: the second generation suffers from decreased ability to face a novel environment, a low tolerance for challenging situations, a low level of adventuring on several levels.[61]

This orientation not only suggests "the folly of a social system that includes no proscription against incest."[62] It will suggest as well the lack of (ethical) wisdom in a cellular model of city planning in which allowance is not made for modification of the cells in their interaction with other units.[63] If we spoke earlier with Neville of the human need to have a culture, we hear now of the need to appreciate an alien culture.[64]

In this relatedness there should be place to welcome not only the alien other who shares our present, but also the strange temporal "new" with which the future bears in upon us both. This will make sense to the person of faith who affirms:

> . . . that the God of creation is the continually active, working and creative God who makes his will known and effective anew in the various contexts and situations in the world.[65]

If that be so, it would seem to follow that:

> "Orders of creation" are not to be viewed statically, ontologically, but in terms of ordering and, some say, even in a historicized way so that what is really meant is man's responsibility for the world.[66]

What order God might have us be making in this new time will not be clear without a penetrating scrutiny of our situation. Can we, for example, advance to a post-personal community which corrects individualism's poor stewardship of the planet's dwindling resources without collapsing in a pre-personal tribalism? [67]

To the believer who asks, "What is God about in the world?" process thought responds: God is about the making of order that is history and harmony. Still questions remain. What height of interpersonal harmony can process thought accommodate? Can it, for example, offer genuine speech about sacrifice? Process thought can trace the following advance: (1) To recognize my relatedness to the other(s) is to recognize that I will always be limited by the other(s). (2) To recognize that there will always be such highly relevant other(s) may be to suggest that the other(s) should not be inhibited in development.[68] (3) To recognize that my relatedness is precisely internal, may be to move beyond "balance" to the more intrinsic sharing, which we perhaps particularly associate with moral good:

> Like the aim at self-creation, the aim at self-expression is final causation, but it is also the anticipation of oneself as sharing in the creation of the future, and hence as an efficient cause. Accordingly, an occasion of experience in creating itself does not aim solely at its own private enjoyment; it also aims to create itself in such a way as to make a definite

contribution to the enjoyment of others . . . absolute egoism is ontologically ruled out.[69]

I say intrinsic sharing "may" be available as ethical wisdom here since
I am not clear why I might not respond to this situation by forcing all
the stuff of relationships within the frame that organizes my present self.
"I need you even now," and "I can't freeze my own future for myself"
might add up to "I'll take you now for all you're worth!" [70] Yet, perhaps
if I really understood my personal good to be the harmony that derives
from "variety of detail with effective contrast," I would resist that addition. I would reach out to those left out of the structure; I would seek
to heal.[71]

The Christian has reason to be glad for this ethical wisdom. Faith may
well suppose that to work for such order is to "serve the will of love
under the conditions of sin," in the words of Aulen.[72] There may well be
a sharpening of this wisdom in the context of the Christian particularity.
Gustaf Wingren puzzles over the combination of continuity and discontinuity:

> The commandment which follows the Gospel and baptism and which
> is heard in the exhortation of the New Testament . . . is simply the
> natural law with love for the neighbor as its center, though since this
> law is grounded in the Gospel and baptism, the assumption now is that
> those who hear it and do what it commands are *on the way to the
> resurrection of the dead*. But this same "evangelical" assumption means
> that we shall find *a willingness to suffer and die* in those who here and
> now obey this law. This is what is meant by the accentuation, newness,
> and heightening of the law.[73]

That may be so. Yet perhaps Reinhold Niebuhr was right in recognizing in "common grace" capacity for performance as well as perception
of the good.[74] Responsibilities and affections do draw the self beyond
itself inexorably. The Christian "sharpening" at this point may well be
precisely a capacity, even a motivation, to follow the logic and lure of
life all the way. Perhaps even that transcendence is hinted at in the strange
transcendence which characterizes authentic aesthetic experience.[75] We
will examine that question briefly in Chapter 6.

But meanwhile the Christian may have another question. Whether or
not this wisdom gives the last word, how *surely* does it speak at all?

Could it be that faith finds here an independent (if not exhaustive) witness to the one God and Father of us all? May metaphysics offer more in the conceptual sphere than framework—which receives the sense of faith for expression? One might say that in this section we have assumed something more than framework regarding ethical matters. While faith told the Christian to look for God's work in the world, the advance in the claims concerning *what* God is about seems to have emerged within the metaphysical sketch itself: value inherent in actuality, novelty, freedom, history, harmony. If these values can be recognized as such by people who make no claim to faith, if they can be affirmed by the Christian as well, one wonders whether still more may be gained. Two questions are particularly pressing: (1) Can the process account of reality amount to an argument *that* there is indeed a God before whom one's life is lived? (2) Can the process account of reality suggest *what* is to be said of that God toward or for us?

Here we reverse the ethical question. We ask not what we might do to share the work of God. Rather we want to know what God might do in relationship to the work that is our life. Without a word about that, one may wonder whether ethical wisdom itself can be complete. At least Whitehead thought that

> . . . the peculiar character of religious truth is that it explicitly deals with values. It brings into our consciousness that permanent side of the universe which we can care for (*RM* 120).

Is not religion "explicit" precisely insofar as it offers a word which can ground the quest for value—whether pagan or Christian? We are, after all, in quest of God. Is there a God before and in whom our little harmonies and our stumbling histories make sense? How surely, how suggestively, may the student of reality respond? To ask of that is to quest after constitutive wisdom.

## *Constitutive Wisdom* and Holiness: How Can the Worldly Be Justified?

### On the Concepts "Constitutive" and "Justification"

Our metaphysical discussion has employed the term "constitutive" to describe an entity's effect(s) on other entities. In Whitehead's view of reality A is constitutive for B, when B takes account of, deals with, some-how incorporates A in itself. We have spoken several times of how per-vasive this theme is in process thought. We hear it in Whitehead's witness to efficient causality, to "objective immortality," to the "superjective" aspect of entities. But final causality is also real. Thus A and all other efficient causes may be said to be constitutive of—but not strictly deter-minative of—B.

I intend this same pattern to apply when we move to speak of a meta-physical wisdom which is "constitutive" for some Christian interest. Here the interest is specified as the concern to be "justified"—a concept to which we return momentarily. What I am asserting is that metaphysical wisdom provides something "to be taken account of," "to be dealt with," "to be somehow incorporated" in understanding how the worldly may be justified. It is not suggested that faith's account on this matter is "ex-hausted" by metaphysics' contribution; only that there is an independent contribution on a matter of which faith would speak.

That much could not be strictly claimed for tactical wisdom or con-ceptual wisdom. There metaphysics seems cast more in the role of servant. Faith has a mission and a message intact, but the extension of the given (in action and thought) calls for assistance in which metaphysics can play a significant role. In the case of ethical wisdom, the servant relation-ship does seem to have given way to one of partnership. The concepts there considered—actuality, life, novelty, order, history, harmony—are not the filling out of a content already given. Perhaps the word "constitutive" would be in place there. Still, the partners are hardly equal. While there seemed to be a genuine sharing in the development of these "values"— we kept an ear cocked in each direction—the authorization for the whole project came from the side of faith. It was faith that told us where to look, even though it did not tell us what to see. Of course, Whiteheadian thought readily accommodated that inspection, through the emphasis on value, and the distinction between God and creativity. But the authorizing impetus came from faith.

The wisdom to be discussed in this section most clearly deserves to be characterized as "constitutive" for two reasons: (1) The issue to be addressed—how can the worldly be justified—emerges equally from the community of being and the community of faith. (2) In addressing that issue metaphysics offers content to be dealt with, just as the affirmations of faith address this issue. Thus the "initiative" of metaphysics—already granted in the shared starting point of (1)—is maintained. This wisdom would advise faith in its most fundamental efforts to understand how the worldly may be justified. The advice is offered *to faith*—that is, after all, how I have constructed this entire project. Faith, thus, does not cease to be faith. But it finds itself facing a strange bedfellow. Its question turns out to be public property—as if, indeed, it is the worldly and not merely the Christian that seeks to be justified.

I shall be suggesting that this metaphysical wisdom speaks freshly to faith in three senses: (a) It *reminds* faith of what it may have forgotten; (b) It *recognizes* a resource which faith might otherwise fail to see; (c) It *recommends* a coherence which faith might otherwise fail to construct. If these offerings can in fact be received, we would have in hand constitutive wisdom.

The interest in justification does emerge from both process metaphysics and Christian faith. In Chapter 3 we followed the way in which this view of reality links religion with universality which is interpreted as the "endeavor to find something permanent and intelligible by which to interpret the confusion of immediate detail." [76] We dealt there with the dynamics of solitariness and universality and with the primordial and consequent natures of God. What is at stake in this is not merely a metaphysical account of religion conceived as a casual historical development. Rather Whitehead so understands reality that the quest to be justified is a natural—if not an inevitable—development. Thus he notes how science in many ways has played the part of a theology "by reason of the answers which it gave to current theological questions":

> Science suggested a cosmology; and whatever suggests a cosmology suggests a religion (*RM* 136).[77]

We have cited Whitehead's conviction that "justification is the basis of all religion" (*RM* 15). But the people of faith hardly need to learn that from Whitehead. They speak this language on their own. Thus there is the Lutheran insistence that the doctrine of "justification by faith alone, without the works of the law" is the one doctrine by which the church stands or falls.[78] Luther himself summed up the importance of the matter in the Smalcald Articles:

> On this article rests all that we teach and practice against the pope, the devil and the world.[79]

Moreover, John Calvin spoke of justification as "the principal hinge by which religion is supported." [80] Nor can Protestants claim this territory as their private preserve, when Hans Küng's study of justification focusing on Karl Barth's work can with Barth's approval *and* a Catholic recognition that

> . . . the real acceptance of justification as God's act of sovereign grace is understood by all as truly Catholic.[81]

Of course I do not wish to argue that all people of faith—not to mention the metaphysicians—means the same thing by "justification." Even within Lutheran circles, for example, Krister Stendahl has provoked a stir by his contention that:

> Paul's thoughts about justification were triggered by the issues of divisions and identities in a pluralistic and torn world, not primarily by the inner tensions of individual souls and consciences. His searching eyes focused on the unity and the God-willed diversity of humankind, yes, of the whole creation.[82]

These debates among Christians about justification are clearly important. I do not wish that any reader be misled by the mesmerizing power of the sheer word, justification. But here I am suggesting that there is something common about the quest which is at work in connection with this word. The responses to the quest vary widely, to be sure. Within that variety are metaphysical responses, and I propose that people of faith may well ponder these responses. The variety of responses makes it desirable to outline the content of the concept of justification, before we begin our investigation of what may be found by faith or reason in this quest. What, then, would do? What is the justification for which the anxious and weak turn to God?

(1) Justification is "free," in two senses:

(a) The freedom of that which is not God must be recognized. These particular, contingent ventures are what call out for justification.

(b) The freedom of God in relation to the freedom of that which is not God must be recognized. If God justifies, that is a matter of freedom in relation to freedom. To be God is not tantamount to justifying.

(2) Justification is "sure," in two senses:

(a) Justification must be subjectively sure, with respect to God. While the notion of God does not itself entail justification, that notion in its categoreal structure must permit a sure resolution or determination with respect to the justification of the worldly. The decisiveness of the divine act must not be threatened from within by a free God (1 b). Divine freedom is expressed in divine commitment which is sure, quite apart from the action or reaction of any being other than God.

(b) Justification must be objectively efficacious, with respect to that which is not God. It must make a difference, it must "matter" somehow with respect precisely to the worldly which is to be justified.

(3) Justification is "good"—the response must include the sense that the word of justification is "good"—sweet, right, blessed. In this, justification materially specifies the structure which is formally outlined in (1) and (2). What God does is not only free and sure; it is good.

So much is needed, if one is to speak properly of justification! I submit that the Christian and the metaphysician (in this case in the process mode) can accept these stipulations. Both can speak of that which is free, sure, and good, and both come to speak of God. Of course one can define justification differently. While a very extensive argument could be anticipated regarding the components of this outline, I make bold to offer these rather bare sentences as a structure to guide us as we ask what wisdom a process metaphysics may hold for the believer who would speak of the God who justifies. If the concept of justification has been poorly shaped in this outline, that will become apparent in the more concrete discussion to follow. But, in my view, if something so free, sure, and good could be found (intelligible and existent), we would have come a long way indeed.

### Recall in the Intermediate: God for All

A metaphysician might well remind a theologian of assertions which are foundational to the faith "once delivered to the saints." This notion depends on only two assumptions: (1) The content of faith, its body of cognitive claims, is not confined within the walls of the sanctuary, but becomes intelligibly available to others, and indeed represents part of the data with which a metaphysician must deal. Thus the church's treasure is held in a very strange vessel indeed—by folk who may not at all intend to confess the faith, though they would understand it. Again the *fides quae creditur*—the claims of faith—are not to be reduced to the *fides qua creditur*—the claiming of faith.[83] (2) A theologian might well need "reminding," since there is no clear safeguard against a "fall from truth" in the work of reflection.

I am fully prepared to make these assumptions and in connection with the first of them take note of the considerable attention Whitehead directed to the phenomenon of the Christian religion.[84] That is enough.

Accordingly, I do *not* make either of two other assumptions: (1) Whitehead is to be understood as consciously affirming the truth of Christianity. Such a claim would need to display something approximating a commitment on his part to the living center of Christian conviction in its particularity of perspective. That claim exceeds the evidence available. (2) Whitehead's thought is so informed by Christianity as to represent all its essential claims—albeit in philosophical dress. This thesis is more arguable, but its acceptance would collapse the principled distinction between faith and metaphysics as far as cognitive claims are concerned. The Christian's cognitive perspective includes concern for matters which may be said to be pre-metaphysical (the special particularity of one called Jesus) and trans-metaphysical (the "whence" and "whither" of the realm available in metaphysical analysis or at least the possibility of such a "whence" and "whither"). I find that Whitehead usually acknowledges the distinction between faith and metaphysics,[85] and proceeds to offer his thought from the metaphysical side. I am proposing that we accept this self-understanding. The difference in perspective is important, as I shall try to make clear in the last chapter of this book. But that difference does not constitute a chasm over which no contribution can come.

The contribution for which we now look will be in the "intermediate," where Christian claims intersect with that which is properly "metaphysical," in the sense of universally applicable categories. That the contribution is, after all, a "reminder" suggests that the act of recognition occurs on faith's side in this dialog, even though the word spoken is itself a metaphysical one. Such reminding is apt to occure precisely at those entry points where the particular Christian claims have lodged themselves most stubbornly in the metaphysical view. As one moves farther into the general claims of the metaphysic, it will not do blithely to claim that the metaphysical contribution is to "remind." The source and support in such matters are of a more general sort. The principles of relativity and process, for example, do not depend on Christian confession for their perception or their persuasiveness. The more intermediate realm involving the anchoring of the system in experience will provide a more likely field for relearning the lessons of faith from a metaphysical schoolmaster.

Whitehead set himself to scrutinize the full range of experience:

> Philosophy may not neglect the multifariousness of the world the fairies dance, and Christ is nailed to the cross (*PR* 513).

In so doing he saw something about the Christian religion which might well be called forward for our remembrance: God is for all. This insight has several components:

(1) God is *for* all. Whitehead is making this point, whether more abstractly in saying "the limitation of God is his goodness" (*RM* 147) or more concretely in saying that to speak with Christians of God as Father is to imply with St. John that "God is love" (*RM* 70). Clearly this theme becomes important for Whitehead. It lies within his quasi-analytic judgment that religion

> . . . runs through three stages, if it evolves to its final satisfaction. It is the transition from God the void to God the enemy, and from God the enemy to God the companion (*RM* 16).

Indeed Whitehead seems to wish to *commend* such a view when he writes:

> If the modern world is to find God, it must find him through love and not through fear, with the help of John and not of Paul (*RM* 73).

Whitehead himself warns that this statement is a superficial one, and the distinction between the biblical writers may indeed seem too simple to one who has read the eighth chapter of Romans, for example. But I take it that Whitehead is essentially right in this: Christians do claim God wills to bless; their news is good. It may be helpful to be reminded of this, if the people of faith seem to be drawn toward a God of whom one cannot speak or a God whose word is against us.[86] Neither no news nor bad news would seem to make a gospel.

(2) God is for *all*. Whitehead recognizes in Christianity the movement to transcend a tribal deity. There is, indeed, one God and Father of us all. Pluralism is not equivalent to relativism. The Christian can acknowledge—indeed insist—that genuine differences exist in perspective, that no synthesis can be made of all religious claims. But the Christian still confesses no family deity, but a God for all. If this assertion is forgotten, the basis for ecumenics and missions alike is removed. With this assertion in place, the need to distinguish between the universal and the relative aspects of faith comes to the fore.

God is (1) for (2) all. Each of these statements suggests a subordinate point. (a) The God who is for *all* people is not to be cordoned off into some limited sphere of the life of all people. Rather,

> . . . the final principle of religion is that there is a wisdom in the nature of things, from which flow our direction of practice, and our possibility of the theoretical analysis of fact (*RM* 137-138).

Whitehead's casting of this is abstract and metaphysical, but it may well serve to remind the Christian that faith focuses in one in whom all things hold together. If that be so, it would make sense to "do everything in the name of the Lord Jesus." [87]

Again, it may well be that the Christian will have reason and means to make subordinate distinctions within this "doing." But it is helpful to be reminded of the range, the reach, of the Christian commitment. That range also serves to suggest a connection between justification and the issue of meaninglessness. How could a word justify and still leave a person's existence devoid of meaning? Would not such strategy seem unlikely in any case for a God whose claims are so cosmic? From this perspective, then, it would seem that Tillich has done well to stress the religious significance of the problem of meaninglessness, whether or not he is right in his historical judgment that this is the dominant problem of the twentieth century.[88] We address this connection of justification and meaningfulness in the next section. The way in which justification transcends (while requiring) the bestowal of meaning will concern us in the last section of this chapter.

(b) The God who is *for* us works *with* us. That would seem to make good sense. If freedom is essential to being human, to be actively for such beings is to have to do with their freedom. In any case, Whitehead clearly was deeply impressed at this point with "Christian beginnings"— if not with all that followed. Thus, on the one hand, he writes:

> The life of Christ is not an exhibition of over-ruling power. Its glory is for those who can discern it, and not for the world. Its power lies in its absence of force (*RM* 56).[89]

But, on the other:

> The brief Galilean vision of humility flickered throughout the ages, uncertainly. But the deeper idolatry, of the fashioning of God in the image of the Egyptian, Persian, and Roman imperial rulers, was retained. The Church gave unto God the attributes which belonged exclusively to Caesar (*PR* 520).

Of course, Whitehead might be wrong in his historical judgment. But it surely is possible that a Christian person or Christian church might become restless with the patience of God and resort to the overt coercion or the subtle manipulation that wage war on freedom. One might even introduce a doctrine of God to serve such tactics. The monologic concept of God discussed in Chapter 4 would serve well. Given these dangers, it is helpful to be reminded that the God who is for us is actually *with* us, honoring human freedom even at the end. In considering the possible conceptual wisdom available in process thought we suggested that such a God who works "in relationship" might very well work as no "other other" does.[90] In comments to come we will ask how faith may speak also of God acting apart from that realm of relationships, of creaturely freedom.[91] But any such talk will qualify rather than abrogate that realm.

This bears on the issue of justification. However much it may be true that God is the author—even the agent—of justification, he is not its object. Whatever is to be said about justification will have to deal with that which is not God. The justifying word speaks good to one who is free and does so surely. What, then, is to be said about justification by the metaphysician? So far, Whitehead seems simply to be reading to the people of faith from their own book—even if the words combine familiarity with surprise in the shock of recognition. But what constitutive wisdom can the metaphysician offer from the writing which is to be found in the nature of things?

### Recognition in the Universal: The Sure Will of God

What would serve to justify the worldly? In Whitehead's understanding the religious quest for justification is associated with universality which is interpreted to be:

> . . . an endeavour to find something permanent and intelligible by which to interpret the confusion of immediate detail (*RM* 42-48).[92]

Sure it is that human beings do seek order. Moreover, the connection between order and religion is well demonstrated by the researches of Eliade and others, according to which performance of the ritual secures a sacred world against the threatening forces of chaos.[93] If one prefers, one may de-emphasize the "back-to-Eden" theme in such order seeking and opt for a more temporal stress. Thus John Bowker writes of religions as

> . . . route-finding activities, routes by which men and women are able to trace a path from birth to death and through death.[94]

It is plausible to find in this the quest for justification. In Eden and Zion the fragile and contingent life of the individual is indeed brought into relationship with something that is perceived to be both intelligible and permanent. Why should one want this? At least part of the answer lies in the very nature of being. Thus Paul Ricoeur speaks of the ethic of the desire to be or of the effort to exist which is prior to any ethic of obligation:

> . . . at the core of this ethic is the identity between effort, in the sense of the "conatus" of Spinoza and desire, in the sense of the "Eros" of Plato and Freud. . . . By "effort" I mean the affirmative power of existing, which is articulated in the most fundamental expression of affirmation: I am, ich bin, je suis. . . . Because our power to be has been alienated, the effort to exist remains a desire. . . .[95]

Process thought places this penetrating existential insight in a metaphysic of relationships. How does the drive for order seek to justify my being? If to be is to have effect, to be for (to bear upon) others—then, I seek to align my living with some general order which already represents connectedness within reality generally and so promises to carry my choices beyond myself. The general (universal?) scope of such order not only serves to provide the sense of effectiveness needed for justification, but also suggests that the relationship is "sure." If the order does not call me away from time, but rather accommodates each new decision and perhaps even guides me within the realm of time, the justification seems to honor my freedom. Thus there come together many of the ingredients that are needed if the worldly is to be justified.

The Christian faith seems to endorse this common human quest. Thus in the concern for consequence one may hear an echo of the Christian emphasis that life is to be preserved as the gift of God.[96] More broadly, von Rad writes:

> This conception of the good as a force which promotes both the individual life and the community life can be described as common to the whole of the ancient world. . . . In its "teaching about the good things" this ethic is, in fact, astonishingly realistic. It never criticizes man's search for happiness and fulfillment, even in its excesses. It simply presupposes this search as a fact. This desire for happiness—we ought, rather to say in more restrained terms: this desire to survive without

coming to grief and to know that life is secure within an order that is
beneficial—is planted deep within man and is accepted without
question.[97]

Catholic theologians have been particularly active in writing of the theological significance of the human drive to connect with others. Thus
Bernard Lonergan stresses the gift of God's love that lures us in diverse
ways:

> The question of God is epistemological, when we ask how the universe
> can be intelligible. It is philosophic when we ask why we should bow
> to the principle of sufficient reason, when there is no sufficient reason
> for the existence of contingent things. It is moral when we ask whether
> the universe has a moral ground and so a moral goal. It finally is reli-
> gious when we ask whether there is anyone for us to love with all our
> heart and all our soul and all our mind and all our strength.[98]

Others may wonder whether such talk is too ambitious in its tendency
to anticipate affirmative answers to these questions. But to acknowledge
that the odds are against one is not to deny the *quest* for justification. As
Jürgen Moltmann writes:

> Even in deep skepticism and with men who have resigned themselves
> to the failures of this life there burns at bottom the demand for true
> human existence and for a more human life.[99]

What particular contribution can process thought make in connection
with life's search for order as justification? That contribution lies in
affirming with Whitehead the work of God as primordial as providing
a justifying order. There are two aspects to that contribution: (1) This
*concept* of God's primordial decision considerably enriches the dimensions
of freedom and sureness associated with any justifying order. (2) This
approach sets the concept within an *argument,* which bids to reduce the
arbitrariness of an appeal to justifying order. Both points loom large in
our setting, when we are tempted to suppose that any available order is
a matter of human fabrication or the artifice of accident.[100]

(1) Without conducting a full review of Whitehead's discussion of the
primordial nature of God, it is still possible to indicate that the order

yielded is both "free" and "sure." We speak here of a divine decision among genuine alternatives. There is surely divine freedom of a sort here:

His unity of conceptual operations is a free creative act, untrammelled by reference to any particular course of things (*PR* 522).[101]

That free act yields an order that is sure, precisely in the universality of its application. The free yields the sure, then. In the Whiteheadian framework, one will not trade that "sureness" for the dubious prize of a free God who may renege on commitments. But the divine decision need not be conceived as a "past" reality imposing itself heteronomously on a grudgingly obedient God of the present. Unlike other entities God's final freedom is always the first word to be spoken about him. "His heart is in it," indeed. Thus Lewis Ford writes:

The non-temporal envisagement constitutes the underlying subjective unity of God, such that all his values, whenever temporally emergent, will fully cohere with one another. Therein lies the faithfulness of God, his steadfast, sure love.[102]

(2) This sure order need not be a secret. Thus process thought does not win universality for this order by retreating within an inaccessible self as if to require mystical exertion from us all. Though not coercive, God's ordering is effective—it has effects. The divine ordering that justi fies takes tangible shape in existence. Thus Whitehead links God as primordial with the determination of the regional standpoint for occasions and with the viability of statistical probability.[103] Of course the reference to God in such a move is not an irresistible one. We do stop short of a *deus nudus* whose reality could not be denied. But, while human discernment may be needed, mystical vision is not. Proof may not be available, but an argument is at hand.

To seek to identify a general human quest for order is *not* what the argument for God amounts to in Whitehead. I have been concerned with that quest here since our present topic is positioned at the level of humankind in that the issue is the human quest for justification. But while some process theologians have attempted to argue from the alleged psychological inevitability of such a human quest to the objective existence of

God, Whitehead's approach is different.[104] Whitehead might fairly appropriate the language of piety to say that such a God would be "too small." Whitehead's God is posited to account for the novel order which (in differing degrees) characterizes all that is. If Whitehead is criticized often enough for the positioning of his discourse at the level of electro-magnetic occasions, he should not be denied that range of reference at this point. It is less psychology than physics which forms the battleground of this argument.

Of course the argument remains a human act. It is human beings who make the claim to recognize God in the universal. While I find that argument convincing, it is important to recognize that its persuasiveness depends on the metaphysical system in which it is located. Throughout this study I have argued that this metaphysical view is not to be understood as one that wins assent by the force of analytic self-evidence. Rather it is commended as the most adequate account of experience. As an account, an interpretation, it may of course be in error. Moreover, there is always a tentativity about the metaphysical proposal—for experience continues to report to us, after all. Whitehead recognized these limitations to certainty more clearly than others in this tradition of process thought.[105]

Accordingly, intelligent persons will probably disagree about the adequacy of this view of reality. The argument for God cannot be supposed to carry weight where its supporting system is not accepted. Moreover, even within the process point of view, there are those who disagree with Whitehead's argument—as Donald Sherburne and Robert Neville do, for example. I still think the argument has weight; I have commented on Sherburne's critique in Chapter 2 and will offer a response to Neville in Chapter 6.[106] That their objections are significant should not surprise the reader of *Process and Reality* who remembers that "God" is a "derivative" notion.[107] An argument offering as its conclusion a sure divine act will still have to make its way uncertainly through the premises.

Will this do? My sense of insufficiency with the argument for God as primordial is not directed at how strongly this can be claimed, but at how much is claimed here. Even if every step of the argument is accepted with enthusiasm, have we come far enough? Process thought in its development of the primordial activity of God does—to my way of thinking—construct a plausible argument that a sure will of God is at work in the world.[108] (It is harder to be sure *what* God is about, despite what ethical wisdom can be mined here.) But is such a sure will of God sufficient to justify me? It is not the argument *for* the primordial God, but the argument *from* that concept that troubles. My problems are twofold:

(1) While a will for the world honors temporality in that it does not call us back from the project of existence, can I properly speak of justification unless my life in its *outcome* finds the permanent? To give my life—in each day and at the end of my days— to the cause of God *is* deeply meaningful. But if God is about the making of history, can my story be justified without some sense of the end? God as primordial does not yet grant any permanent resolution of the course of my life; I do not know how (or even if) my life comes to rest. If God's will is always there as I begin, what awaits me as I end? It will not do simply to talk about beginning again with God. I need to know what is the resolution, the definition, as it were, of my doing in relation to some reality that does not pass away. My past is mine as true legacy and present prospect. I want to know—I *need* to know—how it is God's as well.

(2) The specific content of my course of life may add anguish to this sense of the inadequacy of God's primordial will. This is not to attack that sure will in itself. To be aware of my failure, to know my sin, is not to attack the law, but it is to ask a second time whether law can justify. Even if God's primordially sure will for me could somehow reach out ahead to receive my response, that judgment would hardly be justification. Langdon Gilkey has put the same question on a more than individual scale:

> Because of the ironical and tragic drama of providential possibility, human creativity, sin and then catastrophe—and beyond that a new historical creativity on a higher level—the divine work of providence as possibility, as the principle of creativity and the new in history, is *not enough*. Even with all its manifest creativity of the new, history remains ambiguous, however great and apparently cumulative the creativity of history—and what culture in history does not sense its own creativity?—that ambiguity itself accumulates and the potential nemesis grimly reappears.[109]

But the same issue insinuates itself into one's understanding of the history of one's own days. If justification requires a sense of "good," will not my disharmony and failure leave me short of what is sought?

I need a free response to my freedom and one that is sure, if I am to be justified. That was the first point. If such a response is to be "good," if it is to bless, it must somehow deal effectively with the pattern of *dis*conformity with the sure will of God which my life reveals. This is the second point. Thus with an anxiety in which fear and hope mingle does the quest for justification ask of the judgment of God.

### Recommendation for the Particular:
### The Singular Judgment of God

Religion is the quest for a justification which is free, sure, and good. The self wonders whether there may be some such response to its contingent career—some response other than the abiding presence of the will in relation to which that career came to be.[110] When faced with such human questing, such wondering, Christian faith is not mute. Faith knows what to say. It goes like this:

> What then shall we say to this? If God is for us, who is against us? He who did not spare his own Son, but gave him up for us all, will he not also give us all things with him? Who shall bring any charge against God's elect? It is God who justifies; who is to condemn? Is it Christ Jesus, who died, yes who was raised from the dead, who is at the right hand of God, who indeed intercedes for us? Who shall separate us from the love of Christ? [111]

That the Christian goes on from "naming the name" to asking "What went on here?" is not an attack upon faith. Rather, faith would possess its truth as amply as possible; it would dwell on it in order to take full possession of the truth confessed. But it is in this task of amplification that the speech of the Christian becomes troubled. If faith has in some respects been able to claim the God of the (process) philosophers for Abraham, Isaac, and Jacob (according to our argument), may it not hear in that concept hints which can help it make its testimony more amply and so more surely? [112]

But what is it that faith would state amply and yet coherently? Two basic dialectics may be identified. The difficulties come in maintaining the dialectics.

(1) The Dialectic of the Eternal and the Historical:

Our justification is rooted in the concrete, the particular, the historical —but that is not to impugn the universal creative love of God for the world. William Wolf well stresses the historical when he writes:

> Far too often atonement has been regarded primarily as an *idea* of reconciliation between God and man or as a *theory* about their relationships. . . . The Atonement is primarily a saving *event*, something that God did upon the plane of history.[113]

Yet Christians sense as well the need to say that "the biblical revelation of the oneness of God makes it clear that a single, undivided will lies behind our many words."[114]

(2) The Dialectic of the Divine and the Human:

Our justification is by God, from God—but that is not to impugn the significance of human response. It is God who acts. God's primal will calls for action and it is God who acts.[115] Yet one would recognize that we are dealing with a personal relationship which cannot be treated in the monologic concepts of cultic or juridical models.[116]

These two dialectics meet for faith in the one called Jesus the Christ. The tensions are intensified in the meeting. This one illustrates the dialectic of the divine and the human. If the dialectic of the eternal and the historical is then superimposed, the historical figure may seem to represent the reality of human freedom in relation to the eternal divine will. On the other hand, inasmuch as the historical figure is transcendent, settled, I may sense here the reality of the divine deed over against my freedom. Can we do better than saying simply that in this one "a sufficient salvation is made possible [actual?] for us. God is fully involved and man is fully involved."[117] One wonders if we must settle for saying:

> The sacrifice at the center of history was once-for-all and complete. Yet as within the total organismic development of the universe a process of ritual enactment led up to it, so a further "process goes forth from it."[118]

We can do worse—that is clear. It is easy enough to go wrong in the adjustment of these themes, and the aberrations can be ghastly. Obviously one may so stress the particular, the man from Nazareth, as the source of bliss, that the God of the Old Testament—and of all the universe—becomes a tyrant, despite all testimony to the contrary. Or one may so stress the universal creative love of God for the world, that it only remains for the Christ to announce that truth, albeit somehow with a new decisiveness.

Thus "revelation soteriologies" conflate the problems of the two dialectics—imperiling at once the historical and the human. We then approach the issue of the decisiveness of the historical Jesus through the image of a "Godfather" God, who makes humankind an offer in Jesus which it cannot refuse. But in such a formulation the decisiveness of God is saved only at the price of human freedom. That price is too high, whether it is to be paid in the softer currency of universalism or in the hard cash of double predestination.[119] To be told that "there is no justification without faith" is to be offered a difficult dilemma.[120] Either God's hands seem tied by human freedom; he cannot bring his will to completion in any significant sense. It is not such a long step to the notion that it is we who make it possible for God to justify. Or faith becomes irresistible and human freedom (and so selfhood) a sham.

The difficulties identified in the preceding paragraphs may be caused, or at least exacerbated, by the absence of a sufficiently ample set of distinctions at the disposal of faith. Here process thought can be helpful in pointing toward a coherent statement of the concerns of faith. Two process notions regarding God will be found to be particularly helpful: (A) the reality of relationships for God—a notion Whitehead develops particularly in the concept of the "consequent" nature of God, and (B) the reversal of the "poles" in God—a notion developed by Whitehead in the service of general explanatory concerns.[121] These affirmations hold importance for faith already in regard to the basic doctrine of God. The first serves so to link us with God as to make faith's claims conceptually intelligible; the second serves so to distinguish God from us as to make these claims conceptually distinctive. But these process notions hold particular hints for the Christian who struggles to say as fully and as clearly as possible what Paul set out to say to the Romans regarding the divine justification. With these categories now available to faith, we resume our consideration of the dialectics of justification.

*The Eternal and the Historical:*

We have already indicated how Whitehead's conception of the primordial action of God may serve the theologian by bringing a sense for the constant, the sure, will of God freshly relevant to each developing temporal situation. Whitehead's concept of the "consequent nature" of God understands God as "internally" related to the world, as surely as all actual entities are related to each other. We do not hurry ahead to the way in which God's receiving the world informs his primordial will. We pause over that act of receiving and the decisiveness characterizing it. In this metaphysical notion a preparation is made for the theological concept of the judgment of God, which would represent a response other than the abiding presence of the will of God. Such a concept of a judgment, a response, by God need not threaten the reality of the creative will of God. Rather it seems a natural, if not necessary, development of that will. Love cares for what it creates. The creation is good—for itself and for God. Indeed, the two themes come together as Westermann writes:

> Because everything that God created was good, the history of the cosmos and of mankind has been given an indestructible meaning, inasmuch as it is something good in the eyes of God.[122]

The world invites judgment. God's creative will for the world is not a solitary fiat, but a dialogic call to freedom. Life is good, and it is *to be* good—to be treasured, preserved, enhanced. Before God life is gift, but it is task as well. To affirm in these terms the contingency of a free human response that matters to God is to raise the question of God's response to that which comes to him from the world. There is something here with which God must deal; the reality of the world and of the will of God come together to require it. The dealing will be a real event for God, just as every entity "judges" what is given to it.[123]

And yet there is a difference. The reversal of the poles entails that the first word to be spoken of God is that of independence, of final causality—unlike all other entities of whom it must be said that they are first of all dependent products of efficient causality. This theme is already important in protecting the sure will of God for the world, as our discussion in the previous section suggested. Now the theme comes freshly into play when we seek to understand God's response to the world. The priority of the independent, the free, in God—which (I say again) Whitehead came to posit in the service of general explanatory concerns—is now to be understand with reference to God's reception of the world. Whitehead makes that quite clear:

> God is primordially one, namely he is the primordial unity of relevance of the many potential forms: in the process he acquires a consequent multiplicity, which the primordial character absorbs into its own unity (*PR* 509).

Such an emphasis helpfully stresses the freedom and the unity of God. Such freedom and such unity are suggested by the biblical teaching that only God can judge, just as only God can create.[124] But while this "judgment of consequence" in Whitehead seems sure and free enough, it is not clear that it is "good," that it blesses. Whitehead's formulations do not convey the genuine "over-againstness" in quality of a justification in which God acts freshly to love that which has spurned his love. Perhaps that lack is not surprising, since Whitehead's discussion is keyed to the problem of "perpetual perishing" (which hardly seems a matter of contingent—and so potentially culpable—human response) and is not conducted in the light of the role of any historical cause, any "Christ," for the justifying action of God. Whitehead's reflection may aid us in understanding the relationship between the eternal and the temporal in God. But more is claimed by faith; its dialectic depends on the historical particular, the event. Christians gather around a cross and a word. Attention to that particularity can serve to advance the discussion of what takes place when a God who is truly related and uniquely constituted freely responds to all the stories that make up the world's history.

What faith says of the Christ in the work of justification points to the fact that justification entails more than the historical revelation of an eternal will. Christians speak here of the faithful obedience of one who was like us in all respects, save without sin. And the talk is not trivial. In this singular one was something done so surely that Paul may claim that nothing can now separate the Christian from the love of God in

Christ Jesus.[125] Faith would add to its word that only God can judge. Only a suffering God can forgive. Dostoyevsky expresses this Christian intuition with characteristic insight:

> . . . Alyosha suddenly, with flashing eyes, "But, Ivan, you asked just now, is there a person in the whole world who has the right to forgive and can forgive? But there is a Being and He can forgive everything, all and for all, because He gave His innocent blood for all and everything. You have forgotten Him, and on Him is built the edifice, and it is to Him they cry aloud: 'Thou art just, O Lord, for Thy ways are revealed!' " [126]

That this conviction has often been put very badly by Christians does not invalidate its credentials for faith. How may we put it well? If that is to occur, two tasks confront us: to understand that the work of this Jesus is both human and divine without indulging in contradiction and to understand this new work of God in such a way as not to sunder the unity of God. Our dialectics do not disappear.

To address the first task we can follow the direction evident in conceptual wisdom's reflection on the relationship of the divine and the human in the person of Christ.[127] In that section we outlined an approach in which the divine and the human are not understood competitively, as can be encouraged by a non-relational concept of human identity. In following that approach it will be important to stress the priority of the divine willing in Jesus—an emphasis fully consistent with what was said above concerning God's action generally as internal and free.[128] Thus these general process themes prepare the way for a distinctive statement about the divine and the human at work in Jesus which faith seeks to make. In the final chapter we will return to the topic of how these perspectives come together to do this.

To hold both the decisiveness of what transpired in the life of Jesus and the unity of the eternal God seems as difficult as it is important. The believer would give up neither Kairos nor Logos, but how shall the two be held together? Up to this point I have suggested that from the eternal God comes the range and sureness of the divine response. Only a God so primordially free can judge. From the historical particular it comes that the response is relevantly "good." Only a God so freely suffering can forgive. But this is at best a distinction of emphasis, for faith calls the Creator good and the Christ sure. Faith holds these themes together with passionate ambiguity:

> Blessed be the God and Father of our Lord Jesus Christ, who has blessed us in Christ with every spiritual blessing in the heavenly places, even as he chose us in him before the foundation of the world that we should be holy and blameless before him. He destined us in love to be his sons through Jesus Christ, according to the purpose of his will, to the praise of his glorious grace which he freely bestowed on us in the Beloved. In him we have redemption through his blood, the forgiveness of our trespasses, according to the riches of his grace, which he lavished upon us. For he has made known to us in all wisdom and insight the mystery of his will, according to his purpose which he set forth in Christ as a plan for the fulness of time, to unite all things in him, things in heaven and things on earth.[129]

Here come together creation and redemption, plan and destiny—justification, sanctification and unification. While the beauty and power of the passage is beyond improvement, perhaps the coherence of what is said is not as clear. We have been moving our categories into place long enough. What suggestions are available from the process mentality?

(a) God's eternal will is not "finished" in the sense of being a "once-upon-a-time" past act. His one will reaches out actively to every time.[130]

(b) In that living confrontation with the world, God "receives," knows, the disconformity of the world in a way that is personal and painful. The sinner frustrates God's purpose, including the good sought for the neighbor(s). Jürgen Moltmann well says:

> What the Old Testament terms *the wrath of God* does not belong in the category of the anthropomorphic transference of lower human emotions to God, but in the category of the divine *pathos*. His wrath is injured love and therefore a mode of his reaction to men. . . . He suffers in his passion for his people.[131]

(c) The divine receiving of the world unifies itself, quite as every entity's process of decision has subjective unity (*PR* 340-347).[132] J. Gerald Janzen has shown how Whiteheadian categories of God as primordial and consequent can be employed to interpret the divine speech in Hosea 11:

. . . the wrath which arises in the world in the form of mutually discordant, eccentrically-misdirected efficacious actions *becomes* the wrath of God. . . . God's wrath, then, arises from the world through his perfect conformal feeling of the world. . . . To lose . . . either the totality of the determinate vectors of the world inclusive of its wrathful components; or the aboriginal divine aim of which the world has been made a constituent member—would be . . . to "set aside his divinity." . . . Therefore, an act of *transformation* is called for, by means of which the disparate ingredients in the divine wrath are incorporated into a wider deeper vision which is consonant with the aboriginal vision and to which they may ultimately contribute.[133]

One might expect that the predominance of the primordial would suffice, but it is to be remembered that Whitehead says of God's primordial nature:

It is God in abstraction, alone with himself. As such it is a mere factor in God, deficient in actuality (*PR* 50).

While the primordial will for the world is sure, it seeks the concrete unity to be found in the receiving of the world.

(d) The concrete unity is won in that God chooses to receive the world "in Christ." In this one the loving divine initiative and the freely obedient human response come together to constitute the form which will characterize the divine love become concrete. The God who judges becomes the God who justifies. The divine pathos (b) and human "obedience unto death" come together in what may well be called sacrifice. That notion should be understood not as splitting God into an angry Father and a loving Son, but precisely as the winning of concrete historical unity for the one divine love.[134]

(e) The divine will to love, become concrete in Christ, abides. This is not only true in the sense that all entities yield themselves objectively to the ongoing process of life. God does not perish. His life—unified in principle in the divine decision to love and unified in history in the one called Jesus—goes on in every time (a). That the principle of God's judgment is "once-for-all" settled bestows an unending significance on the world. But it does not cancel the living character of God's continuing relationship to the world. The reversal of the poles does not deny the reality of relationships. Primordially and historically, it is decision and not coercion of which we speak. It is, after all, his own will which gives the unity.[135]

Problems remain, of course. But here at least is a considerable set of categories which may come together to suggest how faith can say coherently that God made peace by the blood of a cross on one who was "before all things." Or even that "he chose us in him before the foundation of the world."

*The Divine and the Human:*

Both the eternal and the historical may seem to threaten human freedom in its existential dimension. What can be said of human response, what of faith and obedience? It hardly helps to leave unbelievers to their own deserts, if we understand the response of faith to be strictly produced by God. To do that is to try to retain meaning for human sin at the cost of forfeiting divine goodness. At least such a God does not seem to love all equally, despite the fact that Christ came because God so loved the *world*.

In reaction to such a threat to freedom, one may veer into the other ditch by compromising the certainty of God's work in Christ, and then one gets the sorry picture of God emphatically negotiating with candidates for forgiving love. Can process thought offer any hints to faith in its concern to preserve both divine decisiveness and human significance?

Process thought recognizes the reality of relationships, of efficient causality, as well as the reality of final causality in the self so related. Relationships are the data—but not the agents—of decisions by entities. This distinction can be applied helpfully at two points in the drama of God and humankind. (a) While the stuff of our lives provides the occasion and the object for God's act, it is he who decides to receive the world in Christ. He does not seek the sinner's permission to love. Here, then, is a conceptual framework in which faith's talk of imputation, of the "forensic" character of justification, makes good general sense.[136] Within that sense is the recognition that the divine freedom has a unique priority (the reversal of the poles) and range. Only the divine decision is so sure. While the objects of this decisive love do matter—it is love of which we speak, after all—they do not motivate. While I may not, then, understand *why* God does choose so to love, it is helpful to be able to entertain some idea of *how* the divine decision (whatever it might have been) can be so sure. It goes with being God—"it is God who justifies!"

(b) With the divine decisiveness so surely granted, it becomes possible to welcome the theme of human response. Since God's work in Christ does not depend on our response, it need not be supposed to be threatened by a recognition of that response.[137] That response does make a difference *to us*. As one entity lives by taking account of the decisions of others, so our lives will be affected by how we respond to what God has done independently of us. In the relationship to God we are invited to receive. Thus Luther in the Large Catechism commends the petition for forgiveness without compromising the divine decisiveness:

> Here again there is great need to call upon God and pray, "Dear Father, forgive us our debts. Not that he does not forgive sin even without and before our prayer; and he gave us the Gospel, in which there is nothing but forgiveness, before we prayed or even thought of it. But the point here is for us to recognize and accept this forgiveness.[138]

In a comment on this passage, William Hordern writes:

> God seeks a personal relationship with his children. When the relationship is broken by the sin of the children, God freely forgives them. His love for them does not waver, and he refuses to give up on them. He seeks them out where they are. But because God seeks a personal relationship with us, the relationship depends upon our free response to God's forgiving love. The father has forgiven his son even in the far country, but the son cannot be reconciled so long as he stays there.[139]

Clearly such human response matters *to God* as well. Doubly so, for without faith and obedience God's love suffers in vain and his will for the world through us is impeded. The unity of God is to be preserved here too. While God's decisive act in the Christ is independent of our response, God does continue to call us to a good not our own, as surely as justification and justice are to be held together.[140] They may, for example, be together in the sphere of the ethical, as the Christ event enables and even informs the wisdom available to the one who studies what God is about in the world.[141] But our freedom to resist God does not undo the divine decision in the Christ. That means much for the believer. For the eternal freedom of God and historical givenness of the Christ come together in a divine decision which is both sure and good, however faltering faith may be.[142] The Christian must fight the good fight, to be sure —but not without the knowledge that "nothing can separate. . . ."

In these pages we have been considering the quest for justification which is recognized by both Christian faith and process thought. Two agendas come together to constitute the concerns of this section. Yet I have given far more direct attention to faith's concern with guilt than to process thought's concern with death, with "perishing." I have paid little attention to the latter, partly because of the difficulties to be found in the proposals available, as I suggested in Chapter 3.[143] Moreover, in Chapter 6 I want to raise the question whether metaphysical analysis can be reasonably supposed to offer a solution to the problem of perishing, despite Whitehead's own efforts to do so.

But in leaving aside this process agenda and turning to faith's casting of the issue of justification, it may seem that we have not made good on the claim that here metaphysics may function constitutively as colleague. Still, that seems not too much to claim if process thought can remind the Christian that God is for all (b, above) and offer an argument for a will sure and good at work in the world (c, above). Moreover, even in these last paragraphs what process thought may be seen to provide is a construct which offers coherence to the believer. Faith will be served in a system where the eternal and the historical and the divine decision and the human response in justification can be coherently distinguished and related. That becomes a constitutive contribution to a central Christian statement. God justifies freely because of Christ through faith.[144]

Distinction and relationships require each other. We have come to see that in this chapter in the work of appropriating the insights of process thought for faith. It remains to step back from such specific work to ask how metaphysics and theology may be distinguished and related in their spheres of relevance. Then we seek to step ahead to ask what the relationships here identified may require of us.

# Part IV

# Continuance

# 6

# Faith and Process: The Principles and Practice of Dialog

Among the meanings assigned "continuance" are (1) the act or process of continuing in a state, condition, or course of action, and (2) adjournment of court proceedings to a future day.[1] I seek the first through the second for this project in faith and process. I have sought to put certain materials at the disposal of faith and have offered a beginning in the work of appropriation. Throughout I have pleaded—probably ad nauseam —for whatever methodological clarity can be mustered in this area. It matters whether the issue before us at any time is to be considered tactical, conceptual, ethical or constitutive. While such distinctions are no guarantee of success in thinking straight, without them one is always in a muddle. Now I seek continuance. That is, I would commend to you the conduct of this dialog in any of these four spheres. Of course, your consideration of that proposal cannot be uncritical; thus this last chapter supposes that a continuance is granted, looking toward your judgment in the proceedings of your days.

I am not as brave as Søren Kierkegaard who could send out his books to his "solitary reader" without instructions and even with occasional poetic mystifications.[2] Even at the end I still admonish and lecture. Yet only a little needs to be done. First, I muse again over how the disciplines come together without collapsing into each other. Particularly I want to

257

note how even the grand sweep of metaphysics fails to cover certain concerns of faith, though the intersection of interests which has been the book's subject is not denied. But certain qualifications should be in place as we turn to mine the resources in the intersection. Second, I bid to identify three principles as major directions to be followed in the act or process of continuing this affair. The first task is to remember distinctions, the second is to discern relationships. Third, I show myself unwilling (or even unable) to let the dialog rest, for I turn to the task of responding to unbelief. That has not been the concern of this book—faith's identity as one of the partners in the dialog has been assumed but not defended. Perhaps, then, it is in order to ask what assistance process thought can provide as we set about to give a reason for the hope that is in us.

## Qualifications: Remembering Distinctions

### The Particularity of God

Ironically, "general ideas which are indispensably relevant to the analysis of everything that happens"[3] become limited in their service to faith by the very generality of their scope of application. The distinction to be remembered at this point has to do with the *particularity* of faith. If evil is real, but God good—then a convincing analysis of reality in its most general structure will not reveal what distinguishes God in his goodness from the fully real evil.[4]

That evil is real is not to be doubted. Faith does not doubt that, but it does diagnose evil's reality as parasitic. To become, to be, to exist is—as such—good. One account of that claim of faith—a metaphysical account —is contained in our discussion of the ethical wisdom available in process thought.[5] To say that evil is parasitic is not to say that it is merely a privation of good. John Hick well argues:

> When we turn from the realm of nature to that of moral personality, an interpretation of the privatio boni doctrine as a description of experience would be even less adequate. For a corrupted will does not always tend to disintegrate and to cease to exist as a will or personality. On the contrary, it may retain its degree of mental integration, stability, coherence, intelligence, lucidity, and effectiveness.[6]

Or Saul Bellow puts the positive claim of evil to reality in these terms:

> Mr. Sammler himself was able to add, to basic wisdom, that to kill the man he ambushed in the snow had given him pleasure. Was it only pleasure? It was more. It was joy. You would call it a dark action? On the contrary, it was also a bright one. It was mainly bright. When he fired his gun, Sammler, himself nearly a corpse, burst into life. . . .[7]

It is not a matter of the novelist's fiction or the theologian's abstraction. One turns from Hick's

> Cruelty is not merely an extreme absence of kindness, but is something with a demonic power of its own. Hatred is not merely lack of love, or malevolence merely a minimum of goodwill.[8]

to the newspapers' account of the good sense murder makes to one who writes:

> Nothing is lower than blacks and Jews, except the police who protect them.[9]

While the problem of evil poses the issue of the particularity of God most dramatically, the reality of that which is *not* God sounds that note still more fundamentally. Faith clings to the particularity of God because it would resist a pantheistic muddle in which the real replaces God.

To recall the distinctions implicit in the particularity of God is not to deny metaphysics' significance for faith. Faith has reason enough to be interested in whatever metaphysics can say about the power that flows in that which is evil as well as in that which is good. Moreover, I have tried to show how Christian faith and process metaphysics come together in assigning a unique metaphysical function to God.[10] Faith stands ready to appropriate whatever specific contributions metaphysics can make in the description of God. It may be expected that those contributions will come more readily on formal questions—*how* God acts—than on material ones—his ultimate purpose in acting. In the continuing dialog remembering the distinction will serve to restrain the Christian from the genuine temptation to identify the good and the powerful, the creative and the Christian. It may also serve to suggest that any proof which depends on the metaphysical material will be hard put to demonstrate the goodness of God.[11]

## The Priority of God

A second distinction to be remembered has to do with the *priority* of God. We might speak of it as the *eternality* of God, were that word not in such a poor state of repair. Or we might speak of God as Christians speak of God as Alpha and Omega. Now such speech does not deny the meaning of those many words to be spoken between the First and the Last. Indeed, that God as Omega is not reducible to God as Alpha already witnesses to the meaning of that which lies within the cosmic boundaries. The development in God takes place in relation to that which is not God. But in speaking of the beginning of things, and of their end, Christians assign a peculiar priority to God.[12]

Harold Ditmanson appropriately finds a more than chronological sense in this priority:

> The priority of God is called "transcendence." This means that in contrast to beings whose lives are derived and dependent, God is the self-sufficient and independent source of all things. He "exists" in a different way than do all the objects and persons we know. He is eternal and cannot gain or lose existence as we do through the passage of time. . . . The "difference" or "distance" of God from the world is the basis of his power to launch it into existence and to come into it as One who rules and redeems it.[13]

I agree, though care must be exercised in the use of the word "rule." At any rate, "beginning" and "end" should not be limited to meaning the extremities of a temporal series.

How does remembering this priority affect the dialog between faith and metaphysics? If certain aspects of the particularity of God proved too concrete to hold within the grand grasp of metaphysics, the priority of God witnesses to that which lies outside the reach of the philosopher. This may serve to remind the Christian that metaphysics may not be expected to give an exhaustive account of any such priority as absolute beginning or absolute end. That is particularly the case with a descriptive or empirical metaphysics, where no claim is made that the categories identified are necessary in the sense that alternative formulations can be ruled out on entirely non-empirical grounds. Such necessity might be thought to reveal the perfect mind of the maker. But the categories discussed in Chapter 2 were introduced as candidates for universal empirical reference. I do not at all suggest that alternatives can be ruled out on grounds of self-contradiction. Whatever might have been so—and a number of worlds, of systems, are conceivable—this is how matters empirically appear (to me) to be. That has been our approach.

Such a metaphysics, then, will not try to rule exhaustively on statements which seek to refer beyond this realm of reality, this scheme of things, while obviously being launched from within this realm. Christians do speak so. For example, they speak of God as inherently or intrinsically triune—quite apart from God's economy of activity in the world.[14] Or they may speak of God's creative work in ways (ex nihilo) which exceed the crucial ordering of existing components.[15] They speak of a future with (or against but before) God as an End which is not in simple continuity with the life we all share.[16] In the dialog with metaphysics such speaking will not be the subject of direct assessment.

What keeps the remembering of such a distinction from amounting to a double-truth dualism in which the dialog is rendered trivial? Christians do not only speak of matters beyond the reality known to us. They —we—speak as well, and I should say the more emphatically, of this earth, of human history and organizations. At the very least Christians seek a coherence in their speech: specifically, they would not let their reference to what is hidden gainsay their testimony to what is revealed. More ambitiously, if they would speak of the "prior," they do so in the service of what is "here." Thus three checks against a double-truth position emerge. Reaching for the positive relation, one may say that these checks suggest the way in which metaphysics may influence what the Christian wishes to say concerning that which lies beyond this realm, if indeed anything is to be said of that sort at all.

(1) Perhaps the Christian will no longer be inclined to make certain claims about the "prior," if God can be claimed clearly and convincingly in this realm. For example, I may find that the concepts available in process thought concerning God's work within the world as "a condition; a critic and an ideal" (RM 62) provide the range of definiteness and certainty which I may have sought for the this-worldly action of God by appeal to another realm. Thus the flexibility of roles available in a metaphysic of internal and external relationships may permit the meaningful

assertion of claims which in a simpler view of reality seemed to call for further buttressing by appeal to something qualitatively other or prior. If the tyranny of sense perception has been broken by a metaphysic which makes it possible—indeed probable—to speak of God as universally active *here,* I may be less inclined to place so much stress on divine activity *there*—however that "there" might be conceived.

(2) Even where statements beyond metaphysical reach are not generated by this worldly truth (and so be subject to replacement by a fuller grasp of what we do know here), they may be subject to correction by such truth. These statements may place the truth of this world in a far more comprehensive context but they may not be permitted to contradict that truth. Thus whatever one may say about the internal divine triune life, one shall not contradict the claims made concerning the this-worldly divine economy of salvation.[17] Similarly, the world as now created is clearly not *nihil.* Divine self-limitation is real limitation.[18] The world may be the gift of sheer divine freedom, but it now exists over against God. One need not suppose that this demeans God. Rather the reality of divine limitation provokes Søren Kierkegaard to sing:

> O wonderful omnipotence and love! A man cannot bear that his "creations" should be something directly over against him; they should be nothing, and therefore he calls them "creations" with contempt. But, God, who creates out of nothing, who almightily takes from nothing and says "Be!", lovingly adds, "Be something even over against me." Wonderful love, even his omnipotence is under the power of love! [19]

Again, while faith may well decline to be helped or hindered by metaphysical ruminations as far as Christian conviction about the absolute future is concerned, such conviction shall not be permitted to ignore the reality of this life with its decisions and distinctions. Clearly, to ignore the distinctions and decisions of this life is to ignore the reality of this life, as that becomes apparent in a process account of reality. Moreover, the unity of reality and the oneness of the divine will would be sundered as well. The language of faith abounds with recognitions of this theme of continuity: judgment, *second* coming, new heaven and new *earth.* In sum, the future may be God's, but we believe his word that it is for us.

(3) The relationship between the two kinds of statements may be found to be a supportive one—one, for example, in which hints and help may be had from the analysis of this realm for the other. Thus Christians may turn with particular attention to a doctrine of the intrinsic trinity in which the plurality is a matter of internal relationships, if they find conceptual preparation for that notion in what they know of this present reality in process thought. Thus Karl Rahner urges:

> But relations are as absolutely *real* as other determinations; and an "apologetics" of the "immanent" Trinity should not start from the false assumption that a lifeless self-identity without any mediation is the most perfect way of being of the absolute existent.[20]

In a process account of reality such pleading will not seem special.

Or a process analysis of present reality may well suggest a choice between options. Thus it seems better to speak of the goodness of God, rather than his glory, as the cause of creation. Given the lavish presence of freedom in what is created, it seems better to talk of the expansive goodness of a God who, since "he wished to communicate the highest good, most freely communicated himself" than of the more monopolar glory of a God who "wishes to be recognized and revered as the great God that he is."[21] Generally, the people of faith may well find their view of reality supported by a metaphysics which identifies a divine reality in which each moment has its beginning and end. To try to go farther than that by argument and analysis seems unnecessary and perhaps unwise, for it suggests that one may have forgotten that a God who has linked his life with ours decisively is still other than we.[22]

### Jesus the Christ and the Christian

Both the *particularity* and the *priority* of the perspective of faith are to be found in Christian speech about Jesus of Nazareth. Clearly, metaphysics —left to its own general pursuits—could not be expected to identify any particular in its unique significance. Moreover, the Christian may find reason to speak of divine priority with respect to this person in a way paralleling (with respect to "new" creation) what was said regarding creation. But again any such talk—as regarding the "assumption" of the human nature by the divine—must not violate the integrity, including

the freedom, of that human nature.[23]. Similarly, while faith does not
receive the figure of Jesus from the metaphysician, general analysis may
well be supposed to apply in the analysis of his career. Life and work in
the world are just that. Process, Relativity, and all the rest do not go on
holiday. Indeed, under conceptual wisdom we have suggested how attending to the general nature of relationships may help one to identify conceptual possibilities for expressing the uniqueness of this particular
relationship.[24]

Such distinctions as we have been discussing may also apply to the
Christian person and the Christian community—though in a derived
sense. In the sphere of method the Christian by definition will acknowledge a commitment to a particular source of insight and truth, though
that commitment does not resist (but requires) an interest in a thinking
on "whatever is true, whatever is honorable, whatever is just, whatever
is pure, whatever is lovely, whatever is gracious." [25] Moreover, thinking
on Christian themes is still thinking and the rules for making sense
continue to apply.

Perhaps a certain kind of otherness or priority comes to characterize
Christian existence in relationship to God and humankind. There does
seem to be a kind of Christian abandon carried in the rhythms of piety
of the Negro spiritual or in the person of a Martin Luther King, for
example. Such abandon—as in heedlessness with regard to self-interest—
does seem truly other than what we expect from a normal human life.
Perhaps that otherness is hinted at in the general human recognition that
"is" does not easily yield "ought." Thus it is not a theist but rather Walter
Kaufmann who sees the leap involved in an advance beyond sheer autonomy to love as an ethical goal:

> An autonomous person might lack love. Any claim that all who are
> rational and use the canon would end up with the same code—mine—
> would be moral rationalism. Love is compatible with rationality, but it
> is not entailed by rationality.[26]

The Christian can match Kaufmann's candor and can add a material testimony to the wonder of agape.

Still, faith is not caught in the trap of defining the good negatively as
self-sacrifice.[27] Process thought may help faith resist the selfish ineffective-

ness of such a view, through its stress on the sociality of being. While I may more obviously err by developing my selfhood in such a way as to harm the other, usurping the world that is there for us both, I hardly help the other by presenting only an atrophied self for appropriation. In our section on ethical wisdom we have tried to accept faith's invitation to "read reality" in the interest of joining the creative work of God in the world. Similarly, the Christian, even in crying *soli deo gloria,* will not refuse God's blessing. To accept God's blessing is not to dethrone a God who rules through mercy.

## Directions: Discerning Relationships

### God and Humankind: Against a Theology of Disjunction

To discern the relationship between God and humankind is to become aware of power and direction for the life of faith generally, including its dialog with the world view represented by process thought. We end as we began—recognizing the theme of the categorical uniqueness of God.[28] But in the dialog with process thought faith is invited to recognize that logical otherness does not require existential opposition. God is for us! Two points emerge: (1) God is for us *existentially:* not only does he will to bless us, but our work and success can genuinely serve and please him. (2) God is for us *epistemologically:* we do know God and can give our best conceptual efforts to the service of this God.

(1) God is for us existentially! Faith does not need process thought to learn that the deity of God does not depend on human sin or human creatureliness. Moreover, a God who creates free beings is not threatened by them, though he may well have something at stake in his aim for them. Thus the logic of faith is not disjunctive: it need not suppose that one must curse humankind in order to praise God. But a strange temptation persists at this point. The people of faith seem lured to interpret God's categorical uniqueness in existential disjunctions. If God is to be other than we, he must be against us. If, then, we are to be for him, we must be against ourselves.

This tendency manifests itself in a number of ways. Christian folk may deny themselves the sense of self-worth to be had in affirmation of one's creatureliness. Their only joy may be found in the guilt which sets the stage for God's glorious redemption. Yet they may even deny themselves the joy to which that gospel of redemption invites them—or at least the expression of that joy. Or—moving from the sphere of feeling to that of doing—they may suppose that any human achievement somehow diminishes the divine glory. In such a mentality one will worry about doing well and cast a justifying religious halo over all-too-familiar experiences of failure. After all, one is told, God does not call us to be successful but only faithful.

I do not desire to ridicule, but to correct. Faith itself should teach us that this logic of disjunction is to be resisted. The wholly-other is wholly for us! God grants freedom and seeks service. What we do matters to him directly and personally. Without denying our sin, we can affirm that we are God's creatures. We fail often enough without trying to do so. We are called to serve God and to enjoy him forever!

These insights do not depend on Whitehead. They come to the people of faith from their own scripture. As Richard Neuhaus writes:

> At the risk of being misunderstood, we can say that the whole of the biblical message is premised upon sanctified self-interest. That is, it is sometimes necessary, through the mysterious and circuitous ways of history, that we abandon ourselves—our common sense, our moral responsibilities, our apparent self-interest—in order to submit to the will of God. But that submission is always premised upon the promise that God's will is to vindicate the human struggle of which we are part. *For the Lord's sake* we must seek our own vindication. This is the logic in the psalmists' incessant plea that the Lord grant peace, prosperity and victory to the children of Israel. For if the children of Israel become a "byword and laughing stock among the nations," the God of Israel would be brought into disrepute. . . . God had inextricably tied his glory to their vindication. . . . Neither did Jesus call for *ultimate* self-abandonment. . . . If his abandonment on the cross had been ultimate, if it had been the last word, then the covenant would have been broken, his trust fatally misplaced, and we would have no reason to celebrate him as Lord.[29]

While Neuhaus moves very quickly over some very complex matters, his judgment is essentially correct. The lingering guilt or suspicion we may feel over his claims may well reveal again the presence of disjunctive thinking. It is there that the process of thought may be helpful. To affirm human effort and human satisfaction is not to rob God (or neighbor, as we shall see). But that has been difficult to see in a metaphysic where identity and relationships are juxtaposed to each other competitively. Then human achievement can in no way be a tribute or joy to God. Process thought can confirm and clarify faith's true intuition that the relationship is not disjunctive. God's transcendence is in relationship. God acts in relationship, seeking secondary causes to serve him.

Obviously, the corrective which process thought provides does not amount to saying "everything is wonderful." Rather the bid is raised; the significance of our sin and failure is in no way minimized, but we are not called to such, but to service and joy. While that call is important and risk-laden, we are not paralyzed by panic. We have shown how this metaphysics of relationships offers categories such that neither the sure will nor the singular judgment of God depends on our response. That seems right on Christian grounds, and it is helpful to have a framework in which human significance and divine decisiveness can well come together.

(2) God is for us epistomologically! We do not honor God by clothing our claims in obscurity. We can acknowledge that his revelation is a matter of divine freedom. We can wonder at what is revealed—that he is so surely and fully for us. We can acknowledge that there are indeed significant cognitive objections to the claim that God exists—as our discussion of atheism will indicate. But we do not back away from the claim to knowledge, as if professions of ignorance would honor God the more.[30] Rather here, too, our efforts can be supposed to serve God. It is right that we take responsibility for our claims by reflecting about them as coherently and comprehensively as we can.

Within that reflection there should be an effort to relate our knowledge of God to the rest of our knowledge. In that effort the dialog with process thought will continue. Christian people need to claim this promise—not the least in a time when a new surge of fundamentalism threatens to enshrine disjunctive thinking in the form of authoritarianism.[31] To enter this dialog is not to slip into the quicksand of subjectivity, but to recognize that knowledge itself is a relationship in which the knower is active and bears responsibility. Discerning the relationship between God and humankind can provide the conurage needed to bear the risk involved in moving in this direction.

### Identity and Change: Against an Anthropology of Eden

What, then, is this self which is to be affirmed on theological grounds? At this point a second relationship begs to be noticed: that of identity within change. Again there is need to make this point. We are lured to consider change a threat to identity, so that our conscious relationship to change is one of guarded and grudging concession. While such an attitude may in fact amount to an assault on the inevitable, it does manage to deny the self a significant role in shaping the development of identity within development. This mentality diminishes one's capacity for self-affirmation throughout the aging process—one has changed, after all. In the short range, it impoverishes the mix which makes up the self, for it routinely chooses stability at the risk of triviality, rather than growth at the price of conflict.

A religious form of this anti-time, anti-change view of identity is found in the call to "return to Eden," to the golden age. That view is the one which dominated primitive religion (as analyzed by Mircea Eliade). In myth and ritual one abolishes time to return to that sacred age when God laid the foundations of the earth.[32] This view may also be discerned in contemporary appeals to return to assorted Edens: "old-time religion," "the real America," pre-technological primitivism.[33] At the very least such appeals, whether in religious or secular dress, serve to eviscerate the self's understanding of the challenge and promise of present and future reality.

The call to resist change or to return to Eden is not Christian. But it may have gained support from Christian thinkers like Thomas Aquinas who have prized the image of the circle as a symbol of God for there "a return is made to the beginning." [34]

If there is no gain for God in time, who can wonder that creatures in his image will fail to prize the prospects the process of living holds? At this point attending to a process reading of reality may be more helpful than a direct onslaught on the view of God involved. In that context we can learn with Galileo once again that it is motion-time and so change which is natural, not rest. We can appreciate the psychotherapeutic insight that the basic direction of the human organism is forward.

Such insight can open us to appreciate anew the positive view of time that lies within the logic of the Christian faith. We can join Albert Outler in the call to the Christian person to "grow up":

> The aim and pattern of this forward motion is maturation, understood as fulfillment at every level of the organism's capacities. Men are born to grow up, to develop, to become mature and productive persons, capable of object love and rational management of their lives, without phobias and anxieties, without regressions and illusions.[35]

Faith *and* process thus combine to bid the Christian person and the Christian congregation to seize the opportunities for growth to be found in each new time. That is not to argue for an atomistic view of change in which continuity of direction and integrity of commitment would be compromised. The ethical wisdom considered in the last chapter commended the making of history—the gaining of continuity through time. We do seek identity with integrity, but that is to be found within the reality of change.

There is a lesson in this relationship for the task of theological reflection. The elusive matter of theological identity does not escape the reach of temporality. We cannot expect to carry forward the delivered results of another time as if only cosmetic changes were required. It is not at all clear that we meaningfully possess the tradition apart from our own traditioning struggle. It becomes increasingly clear that the conceptual framework common to Judaism and Christianity can no longer be simply assumed. Jaroslav Pelikan suggests that the cost of such a simple assumption is to be paid in public currency:

> . . . the heritage of values bequeathed to us by Judaism and Christianity is being spent, but not replenished, because the faith upon which these values were based no longer animates many of those who profess the values.[36]

To address this situation faith will struggle for new understanding. It is not surprising that reason is distrusted as an ancient enemy of contemporaneity,[37] but it is high time for faith to put the gift of reason into responsible service in the working out of what it means to be Christian today.[38] If we do not accept that task, we end in unwitting acquiescence in the unreliable fashions of the time, while still losing any effective purchase on the faith delivered to the saints. In accepting that task, we commit ourselves to dialog with other students of reality in the "descriptive" disciplines. The emphasis on relationships, on time and change, in the natural and social sciences suggests that some consideration of the process viewpoint can contribute to working out what it means to be God's people in this world. To discern the relationship between identity and change, then, is to become aware of both power and direction for the task before us.

### Self and Other: Against an Ethic of Individualism

A resilient individualism continues to diminish our efforts to enrich the human condition. This mentality takes many forms. In its most direct expression it may take the form of blatant competitiveness in which God helps the self-serving person or nation. I may define myself in such a way that I not only seek to be "at the top of the heap," but apart from it.[39] Yet, strangely, there is a kind of objectifying consciousness which is only a subtle variant on the "do your own thing" subjectivism.[40] In either case selves are not considered to be essentially related *and* essentially independent. In fact the two phenomena may conspire to coexist. A romantic subjectivity, after all, does not effectively challenge the authoritarian mind but only provides a superficial irritation which leaves the strictly channeled public flow of power undisturbed.

Christian faith has called its adherents away from such individualism. The obligation to the neighbor is clearly intact in Christian teaching. Process thought amplifies this teaching by a line of reflection which may help us know better why and how to seek the neighbor's good.

Perhaps the first step in this line of reflection is to remind ourselves of the strong emphasis we have noted on the immanence of God.[41] This does not reduce God to a human other. It does remove any sense of the self left adrift in a Godless sea, threatened by the hungry advances of others. God is at work in that other and in me. We are not left to personal one-up-manship or to divide the planet's spoils. Moreover, God has good in mind for each of us through the other. That bestowal of good for each other does not depend on, but can be enhanced by, conscious cooperation. While there are competitive goods, life can be more than an athletic contest (and that more than victory or defeat). We are invited to think of human relationships (and relationships to nature [42]) not merely in terms of armed neutrality or positive obligation even, but rather in terms of an essential collegiality of existence and so to quest for goods that are common. Again, it is not a matter of sharing a fixed sum of "good." It is other than that with relationships. In my wife's loving relationship with our children she and they do not steal from me but become more, also for me. This is not to deny that we do steal from each other, that we employ the structure of relatedness to harm each other. But the cure for such abuse is not to withdraw within a "fortress" self, thereby exacerbating the loss of full human development in relationship.

If there is thus motivation in process thought for resistance to an ethic of individualism, there is also direction for an alternative. Given the risks identified, direction is needed. I need the neighbor precisely as *other* than myself. We have tried to hear the ethical wisdom available in this viewpoint, and found the theme of contrast a major note. Thus we are called beyond the alternatives of unrelated freedom and regimented connection to work for the potentiation of variety within relationships, the development of differences but not disjunctions. The social arrangements that are required to serve that principle may not be fully clear. Shall we, for example, follow the call to seek some kind of post-personal community on this planet in this post-modern time? [43] But the critique of individualism in its several forms is clear and should not be attacked or defended as if it were a matter of divine arbitrariness. The principle of relatedness on which the critique is based is given with the reality of our humanness, as process thought makes clear.

There is an intellectual dimension to this ethic of relatedness. The Christian community should not seek protective isolation from the human community—also as far as its intellectual self-understanding is concerned. The Christian will rather join the secularist in a struggle for a self-understanding that is responsible, given the deliverance of human experience. That experience is not available in prefabricated "secular" or "Christian" models. Rather we largely live and die together, and are alike as well in what we must be and do alone. Perhaps the explicit dialog between Christian faith and process thought can itself find a modest place within the intellectual sphere of this ethic of relationships. A convincing metaphysical sketch will serve such dialog partners well. The social "ought" dare not be offered in isolation from an understanding of what "is" the case—presently and permanently.

Some of the partners in this dialog specifically decline to identify themselves as Christians. It is one thing to identify and address common human problems together. But how shall Christians comport themselves, when the human other specifically declines to "name the name"? While my remarks have been addressed to Christians, I really do not seek to weave a cocoon around Christian existence. It seems better to give some sentences—even if they be the book's very last—to possible process contributions to the Christian response to unbelief.

## Case in Point: Responding to Unbelief

### A Perspective on the Problem

The people of faith might be tempted to take heart from the fact that contemporary unbelief seems less strident than earlier versions. A more accurate assessment of the fact might well be that to many there no longer seems pressing need to shake one's fist in the face of what is increasingly regarded as a fiction. Thus Alasdair MacIntyre asks:

> Is the cultural irrelevance, the marginal character, of the contemporary debate between atheism and theism merely due to the fact that the main advances of the secular disciplines no longer happen to be in areas in which a direct confrontation with theism occurs? My answer is that the lack of confrontation is due not only to the directions in which secular knowledge is advancing, but to the directions in which theism is retreating. Theists are offering atheists less and less in which to disbelieve.[44]

A second check on optimism derives the fact that it seems harder to engage this enemy in a fair fight. The appearance of tolerance seems to rule out combat as less than courteous conduct. Thus Philip Rieff can conclude his account of "the triumph of the therapeutic" by writing:

> The therapeutics must be understood precisely in their efforts to go beyond the analytic attitude, as the articulate representatives of a sharp and probably irreparable break in the continuity of the Western culture. None of their doctrines promises an authentic therapy of commitment to communal purpose; rather in each the commitment is to the thera-

peutic effort itself. As Jung insisted the therapeutic cannot claim more than a private value for his moral science.[45]

Thus if unbelief shows a softer face in our time, it does so as the measure of its success and as the promise of further triumph.

While the language of combat may seem somewhat florid, I consider it appropriate. But can one not claim the atheist as ally? I do not deny the descriptive observation—made by Herbert W. Richardson, for example—that public atheism may be the voice of new concerns pressing for a radical cultural change.[46] In some fashion these concerns need to be addressed. Or the atheist can render service to the people of faith by exposing stupidity and sloth in their thought and life. But atheism remains atheism as surely as it does not accept the truth claims of the Christian faith. Since that is the decisive issue, I shall employ the stronger, clearer form of outright atheism as representative of the region of contemporary unbelief. Whatever the degree of conscious opposition may be, the region is unified by the fact that here Christian truth is not affirmed.

Central to that truth is the doctrine of God. The very word, a-theism, helpfully reminds us that there are those who do not believe in God. It seems patently wrong to christen these by decree—as if they did not know their own mind. Neither one's own enthusiasm for God (as if unchecked by an atheism within) nor one's desire to be humane (as if the atheist would welcome such generosity) should be permitted thus to confuse the distinction between faith and unfaith. But what, then is faith? Corresponding to the intellectual (notitia and assensus) and the volitional (fiducia) aspects of faith, atheism takes cognitive and volitional forms.[47] The cognitive atheist claims that there is no God; the volitional atheist that God is not to be trusted or worshiped. The distinction should not be pressed too far, as if there were no volition in cognition, for example. Both forms may be present in a single book, even if the first should logically exclude the second. Nonetheless, it is helpful to have the distinction in mind so that one's response can be to the point.

But how is atheism—in either form—possible? Atheism is possible because the relationship between God and humankind presupposes a distinction—which is to say a distance—between the two. Against the claims of some mysticism, it must be said that God remains other for the self. The opening chapter's discussion of the triadic self already makes that claim, and subsequent chapters have reaffirmed it. Human freedom—and with it the possibility of volitional atheism—is clearly a major, if not an uncontested,[48] theme in process thought. While God may act toward me in a way other entities cannot—from within, as it were—I am still not God and may well resist him.

Process thinkers seem less eager to acknowledge that cognitive atheism can actually occur. Thus David Griffin writes:

> . . . we all know, at the prereflective level, that there is a sacred reality, whose existence is supremely valuable, that our lives finally have meaning because of our relation to this holy reality.[49]

Yet cognitive atheism seems fully conceivable, given the distance between God and humankind. Here, ironically, the special character of God's action toward us—taken along with the universal scope of that action which proves so elusive to observation by a method of difference—may prove supportive of cognitive atheism. It is easier to take an *inner* other as *none* other than the self. Of epistemic distance John Hick has written convincingly:

> God must set man at a distance from Himself, from which he can then voluntarily come to God. But how can anything be set at a distance from One who is infinite and omnipresent? Clearly spatial distance means nothing in this case. The kind of distance between God and man that would make room for a degree of human autonomy is epistemic distance. In other words, the reality and presence of God must not be borne in upon men in the coercive way in which their natural environment forces itself upon their attention. The world must be to man, to some extent at least *etsi deus non daretur,* "as if there were no God." God must be a hidden deity, veiled by His creation. He must be knowable, but only by a mode of knowledge that involves a free personal response on man's part. . . .[50]

One may detect in Hick's argument a tendency to collapse volitional atheism into cognitive atheism, as if no sheer defiance of a God fully known as God were possible.[51] My concern is to keep both forms before us as a set of categories which well correspond to the actual situation in which faith must live today.

It seems important to take cognitive atheism seriously on its own terms. While cognitive atheism may be vanquished only to have volitional atheism remain, it still seems necessary to respond to the problems of cognitive atheism directly, lest the more advanced tactics aimed at volitional atheism simply misfire. While some process thinkers so stress the universal action of God as to deny the possibility of cognitive atheism, Whitehead's distinction between God and creativity—with God claiming only the status of a "derivative notion"—would seem to take seriously the atheist who simply asserts: There is no God! [52] What shall one say to that person?

### Responding to Cognitive Atheism

Three forms of cognitive atheism may be distinguished. Process thought holds resources for Christian response to each of these forms. I have in mind objections to Christian claims regarding God with respect to (1) method, (2) content, and (3) efficacy.

(1) At the core of the argument are the questions: What counts for evidence? and, What constitutes adequate evidence? With respect to the former question Anthony Flew notes that criticism of the argument from religious experience challenges

> . . . just the vital assumption that having religious experience really is a kind of perceiving.[53]

In the analytic challenge to the meaningfulness of religious statements much is made of refutability "as a necessary character of warrantable belief at every point in the study of history, in science, and in ordinary life." [54] Refutability is most readily at hand in repeatability. Thus does the experiential collapse into the experimental, as we prepare to run another set of tests.[55] Matters of faith have not managed too well when subjected to this procedure.

At this point it is the metaphysics of process thought itself which is most helpful. This view of reality removes us—and not merely in matters religious—from the tyranny of a standard of evidence which limits itself to the deliverances of sense perception. In sketching that view in Chapter 2 I emphasized that sense perception must be accounted for and indeed included in a full account of perception.[56] Thus we do not escape into mysticism, but reformulate the analytic challenge as one calling for the Christian to show how an appeal to experience—including but exceeding sense experience—does not amount to saying "anything goes."

What would constitute adequate evidence? We may agree with William Clifford that:

> It is wrong in all cases to believe on insufficient evidence; and where it is presumption to doubt and to investigate, there it is worse than presumption to believe.[57]

But what *is* sufficient evidence? How much is enough? How would "enough" announce itself? Here a metaphysics of relationships with its recognition of freedom and distance, stresses the need to respond. We may well be suspicious of any view which makes knowledge a matter of sheer necessity. This, of course, is the point in William James' response to Clifford:

> *In concreto,* the freedom to believe can only cover living options which the intellect of the individual cannot by itself resolve; and living options never seem absurdities to him who has them to consider. When I look at the religious question as it really puts itself to concrete men, and when I think of all the possibilities which both practically and theoretically it involves, then this command that we shall put a stopper on our heart, instincts and courage and *wait*—acting of course meanwhile more or less as if religion were *not* true . . . this command, I say, seems to me the queerest idol ever manufactured in the philosophic cave. Were we scholastic absolutists, there might be more excuse. If we had an infallible intellect with its objective certitudes, we might feel ourselves disloyal to such a perfect organ of knowledge in not trusting to it exclusively, in not waiting for its releasing word. But if we are empiricists, if we believe that no bell in us tolls to let us know for certain when truth is in our grasp, then it seems a piece of idle fantasticality to preach so solemnly our duty of waiting for the bell.[58]

Christian enthusiasm at this point should not blind us to the fact that James' point cuts both ways. Thus process thought may open the door for leaps of faith in its acknowledgment of the role of human freedom even in perception and knowledge, but it ought also remind us that we are leaping and liable to error. Clearly, the Christian who acknowledges that it is such a world in which faith so occurs will resist the development by which

> ... irrefutability has been written into the content of the beliefs themselves, and is not just a characteristic of the manner in which they are professed and acted upon.[59]

It remains possible that someone may object not with respect to the announced meaning, but with respect to the alleged truth, of Christian faith. Both questions we have considered—what counts as evidence, and as adequate evidence—bear on the issue of the meaning of the faith. In asking them one wants to know what kind(s) of assertions or expressions are made by believers, and so how one may assess them. But, conceivably, one may find a faith statement clearly identified in form and cleanly presented in content—but false! Assuming good will on both sides, we must take this to involve a dispute regarding the evidence. The principle of epistemic distance recognizes this possibility. In this circumstance one can only seek a covenant to read the evidence again and together. Obviously there is no guarantee of gain or even warranty against loss in that process. But I have suggested in this work that Whitehead's understanding of reality does encourage that effort and that his understanding is a persuasive one. But to what shall one leap—and with what effects? These questions point us toward other forms of cognitive atheism.

(2) Objections concerning the basic content of Christian claims come in various forms. Perhaps most obvious is the assertion that Christian claims cannot be reasonably affirmed because they are self-contradictory. Thus Anthony Flew writes often of the "ostensible incoherence"

> between the idea of creation, as necessarily involving complete, continual and absolute dependence of creature upon Creator, and the idea that creatures may nevertheless be sufficiently autonomous for their faults not to be also and indeed primarily His fault.[60]

I have argued that the Christian faith refuses to collapse the distinction between God and humankind, and with that holds out for the reality of freedom, both divine and human. While divine freedom and human freedom differ significantly ("the reversal of the poles"), neither is absolute in the sense that would yield Flew's dilemma. But in responding to unbelief it is not sufficient to display a set of statements which remove the charge of incoherence. One must demonstrate the continuity of those statements with the targets of the objection, if one takes genuine Christian intentionality to be at work in the statements attacked. Thus it is not to be doubted that Christians have so spoken as to warrant Flew's premise about the absolute dependence of creature upon Creator. How shall one account for that?

It occurs to me to wonder whether the premise of absolute dependence (admittedly not precisely defined) may represent an effort to secure on anthropological grounds the justification which is only available on theological grounds. Faith seeks certainty. A logic of disjunction could reason from human emptiness to divine plentitude. "Absolute dependence" is then, a mistaken stab at certainty. But the quest is sound. In the section on "constitutive wisdom" the remarks concerning the sure will of God and the singular judgment of God are understood to be made about God, independently of (though of course in relation to) that which is not God. Such constitutive wisdom can serve to reinforce the intuition of faith itself and lead to a formulation of dependence which does not contradict human responsibility for evil.

Indeed the whole task of formulation invites the contribution of what we have here called conceptual wisdom in the Christian response to unbelief. To draw upon a metaphysics of relationships is to speak of how the divine and the human can interrelate. In such talk resources are to be found for the Christian who would speak of the relationships between God and others—generally, as well as quite specifically regarding Jesus the Christ.[61]

A second set of difficulties dealing with the content of Christian claims concerns what Langdon Gilkey has spoken of as "noncompossibility." The claim is

> . . . that because there is a total disrelation of the concept to experienced actuality, the concept and its system are meaningless, or . . . not compossible with our experienced world.[62]

While such a challenge is subtler than that of self-contradiction, it may be more severe. Or so Gilkey claims:

. . . the question of the *noncompossibility* and therefore the meaning-lessness of a concept or a system of language is a more radical question than is that of their *validity* since the former asserts a much more total disjunction of the word game or concept from all that we take to be the case in the world around us.[63]

Again process thought may make available conceptual wisdom to a Christian facing this charge of meaninglessness. Specifically, for example, process thought may provide a way in which dimensions of contingency, relativity, temporality and autonomy—Gilkey's "four elements of the modern Geist"—can be taken seriously in the Christian vision.[64] That will be the more likely as the framework sought for the Christian witness is to be found in the world of experience common to Christian and pagan alike. The expectation is that such a quest will again cut both ways—recasting, correcting and deepening formulations on both sides.

Such a pilgrimage is hardly apt to be an easy one for faith, but it is a far better course than to take the lofty road of incoherence or to retire from the journey altogether in a God without incoherence because without predicates.[65] Most importantly the Christian must cling to the contention that God has chosen to bless. Faith clings to a God whose will is good and whose mercy endures forever against Hume's claim that "terror is the primary principle of religion." [66]

Of course faith is still exposed to criticism. One may find faith's consolation to be the other side of faith's accusation. Should one not then choose to reject the shelter with the taboo as the "rotten points of religion"? [67] Or one may hold these elements apart—and launch the criticism at the one point or the other. Thus Walter Kaufmann seems very sure that

. . . in Christian morality, from the Sermon on the Mount to Thomas, Luther, Calvin, and beyond, guilt and fear have always been central.[68]

Or Freud finds consolation to suggest wish-fulfillment in his famous essay "The Future of an Illusion":

We say to ourselves: it would indeed be very nice if there were a God, who was both creator of the world and a benevolent providence, if there were a moral world order and a future life, but at the same time it is very odd that this is all just as we should wish it ourselves.[69]

The Christian will resist such subtle psychological intimidation, for there may be detected here the faint odor of the logic of disjunction. Why must any God be against us to be real? R. P. C. Hanson makes the appropriate response:

> . . . the fact that a person wants to believe something is no proof of the truth of that belief, but it is no disproof either. . . . If God does exist, and if he is such a God as the Christian faith represents him to be, then it is not the least surprising that people should find belief in God attractive and should derive pleasure from it.[70]

Process thought may aid in that response inasmuch as it assists the believer in finding the cosmic scope of the sure will and singular judgment of this good God. God is no personal sugar-daddy; his love is for all.

I have considered this objection as one bearing on the content of the predicate the Christian claims for God. Faith calls God good. As the criticisms are developed, the thrust of the argument tends toward what I have called the "ethical." The argument shifts its attention to the effects in life of such claiming, such calling. While the Christian will not collapse the *fides quae creditur* into the *fides qua creditur*—it is of God's goodness, not Christian pleasure, that we speak—it is fair enough to examine independently the effect(s) of Christian faith. There are objections to be heard at that point as well.

(3) Cognitive atheism may root in objections to the efficacy of Christian faith in the lives of its adherents. Three may be distinguished. With respect to the individual's integrity, Christian faith may be seen as a slavish collapse to authoritarianism—a breach of the autonomy of the human spirit. Simone deBeauvoir casts the point in existentialist language:

> When a man projects into an ideal heaven that impossible synthesis of the for-itself and the in-itself that is called God, it is because he wishes the regard of this existing Being to change his existence into being; but if he agrees not to be in order to exist genuinely, he will abandon the dream of an inhuman objectivity. He will understand that it is not a matter of being right in the eyes of a God, but of being right in his own eyes.[71]

Second, with respect to the individual's behavior, it is now a commonplace to hear faith identified with an opiate that drugs human striving and with social conservatism. Thus deBeauvoir reserves Dostoyevski's "If God does not exist, everything is permitted":

> However, far from God's absence authorizing all license, the contrary is the case, because man is abandoned on the earth, because his acts are definitive, absolute engagements. He bears the responsibility for a world which is not the work of a strange power, but of himself, where his defeats are inscribed, and his victories as well. A God can pardon, efface, and compensate.[72]

Third, to abandon integrity in belief may affect the behavior of others as surely as one sets a fatal example of self-deception.[73]

The Christian may find in the dialog with process thought reminders and other resources for response to this complex of ethical objections. Foundational is the insight into the fundamentally relational character of life. Both moral obligation and salvific blessedness are, after all, forms of relatedness. It is not surprising that an existentialist who cannot agree that we humans are made for each other will not share the view that humankind is made for God.[74] But the first point can prepare the way for the second for the Christian. *Imago Dei* and "male and female he created them" come together in Genesis 1:27. Moreover, one is committed to a God who is emphatically for us! The relationship turns the other way as well. Thus the Christian cannot agree with deBeauvoir's description of the religious premise, that "this earthly stake has no importance." [75] Our lives matter importantly to God, though (because) his sure will and singular judgment abide.

As for the charge of social conservatism, the distinction between God and creativity in process thought, as well as the recognition of the vast array of non-divine causes, should once again serve to caution against baptizing the status quo. In any case the Christian must stake out claims regarding ethical motivation and content. These will surely be set within the context of some kind of world view. The direction in which process thought points has been suggested in our section under "ethical wisdom." If, for example, James Gustafson is right in arguing that the Christian may derive "reasons" for moral action through faith's account of such matters as a sense of dependence, finiteness, and possibility—then process thought offers a view of reality in which such a testimony of faith makes good sense.[76]

I do not at all mean to suggest that these very considerable challenges to Christian belief can be dispatched by strict attention to a few paragraphs penned by a Christian who once read Whitehead. That would be to resort to magic. But I do mean to suggest that process thought does provide resources to the Christian who would respond to the challenge of cognitive unbelief—whether that has to do with the "how," the "what," or the "so what" of belief. But perhaps all of this only raises the bid, as it were. For if Kierkegaard is right that the crucial Christian problem lies "not in the intellect but in the will," [77] what shall one say to volitional unbelief?

### Responding to Volitional Atheism

*(1) The Problem of Evil*

A transitional form of volitional atheism still offers an argument against faith as trust and worship, though it acknowledges the existence of God. The attack on Christian claims is directed not against the reality, but the morality, of God. That God is not to be trusted. Thus Anthony Flew charges religious intellectuals with "doublethink" mustered "in order to retain their faith in a loving God in the face of the reality of a heartless and indifferent world." [78] Strictly at the point of "doublethink" the problem of evil poses itself as a setting for cognitive atheism directed to the content of the faith—with particular attention to the air of self-contradiction alleged to be found here. Thus one attends to the argument presented. I cannot agree with Flew's conclusion, since I do not accept his premise of unqualified divine omnipotence.[79]

Refusing doublethink, one is faced with the choice of limiting either the goodness or power of God. Once one has made the choice, the issue presents itself as a moral one for the will: shall one trust, given the limitations? Given the options, it seems better to limit God's power. That is the view I have been presenting throughout this book. John McTaggart puts the point so:

> . . . when believers in God save his goodness by saying that he is not really omnipotent, they are taking the best course open to them, since

both the personality and the goodness of God present much fewer difficulties if he is not conceived as omnipotent.[80]

While we wish to resist the lures of doublethink, must we accept McTaggart's inference:

> But then they must accept the consequences of their choice, and realize that the efforts of a non-omnipotent God in favor of the good may, for anything they have yet shown, be doomed to almost total defeat. It is not a very cheerful creed, unless it can be supplemented by some other dogmas which can assure us of God's eventual victory.[81]

McTaggart has rightly identified the problem. Has the logic of faith outlined here rescued the goodness of God at the price of forfeiting his power to save? It helps a little to employ process categories to make the goodness of God not merely an abstract notion, but a testimony to the God who suffers with us. But that is not enough. It helps more to show that a limited God is still able to bring himself to bear on the world with a flexibility and relevance unparalleled by other entities. But faith wants more. What is at stake is the quest for a response that is free, sure and good. I have discussed this issue under "constitutive wisdom" as the issue of justification. There process categories were employed to illumine the notion of the singular judgment of God in the person of Jesus. While God's decision calls for human response, it does not depend on such response. Clearly many problems remain. Yet it may be argued that this "finitely perfect Deity"—to use the phrase of Hume's Cleanthes —may appropriately elicit the believer's *fiducia,* for this God (while limited in power) can and does justify.

But will God win? The notions which distinguish God—the reversal of the poles and the universality of scope—do serve to supply something of the kind of supplementary help McTaggart sought—and do so within rather than at the expense of the view of reality at hand. Moreover, carlier in this chapter we considered another kind of supplementation, by which the particularity and priority of God might be seen to elude but not destroy the reach of the metaphysical sketch. Still, neither of these avenues yields an assurance that God will win—such that a full-orbed faith in those whom he seeks is the only sensible response. The very element of uncertainty on the cognitive issue of future victory opens the full

question of volition. One cannot pretend to settle the issue of the trust-
worthiness of God on rational grounds. How may one then respond to
one who simply will not trust God?

*(2) Defiance and Tactical Wisdom*

The Christian apologist does well to remember the innerrelatedness of
the human person. We have already spoken of how will is active in the
way in which reason receives the world. So, too, reason may be supposed
to act on and within the process of decision. Process thought does not isolate the will in some lonely inner citadel. Rather the world and reason as
its broker are internal to the process of decision. Somehow the data must
be dealt with, as they continue to press their claims. If this be true, the
Christian apologist will never be done reasoning, persuading. After all,
that one to whom he speaks cannot actually emigrate from reality by
force of will. Indeed the Christian grounds this persistence theologically
as well as metaphysically. For faith confesses the Christ as the one in
whom all things do still hold together, despite the destructive reality of
sin. Error—even sinful distortion—in perception cannot actually rid the
unbeliever of the real world. The world remains one, the unbeliever remains accessible within that world, the unbeliever's will cannot completely
evict Christian gospel and counsel.

Thus perseverance is commended. The temptation to write off the
atheist as a lost cause needs to be resisted. Perseverance in aim mixes well
with flexibility in means. After all neither the person to whom the message is once more communicated, nor the situation in which the communication now occurs, is the same as the "last time." A full repertoire
of means needs to be employed. Notably Christian apologists may have
been inclined to limit themselves to the clear but narrowly cerebral tool
of reason, giving little conscious attention to the subtle but powerful in-
strument(s) of imagination. Process thought warns against such a strategy, for the affective domain is an essentially relational one and the cognitive domain itself may represent the distortions introduced and maintained in the "originality" of the individual's mental pole.

While the will of God cannot be evicted, it can be refused or rejected.
Defiance does remain a possibility, and indeed may be considered as the

highest potentiation of unbelief.[82] No word from Whitehead will dispel such defiance; we are not hawking magic in this book. Rather, it is the case that the counsel of faith and process thought would be to warn against holding such high expectations that the unbeliever comes to be destroyed in the process of being saved. The word is directed to a center of freedom—unless sheer pressure or subtle manipulation come in to destroy. Thus to the guidelines of perseverance and flexibility is added that of patience. We are called to serve; we hope to succeed. But like God —indeed with God—we act in relationship and seek a free response. We would have no hollow victory with half-selves reciting mechanical testimonies. We are prepared to fail. One can say in this way:

> Always be prepared to make a defense to any one who calls you to account for the hope that is in you (perseverance), yet do it with gentleness . . . (patience).[83]

## (3) The World in Common

Two matters remain. First, there is a final word here about the Christian response to unbelief. Even with the volitional atheist, as already with the cognitive atheist, the Christian will work. I speak of working "with" not "on"—the atheist. Christian and atheist have the world in common, after all, and it is there God's work is to be done. Since faith claims that God works even through those who do not affirm him, there is a call to Christians to join the work in that common world. Since Christians do not claim a monopoly on what is just and humane, there is reason to join the atheist in the struggle to know and to do what is right in this world. Thus the mining of the "ethical wisdom" sketched in the previous chapter itself comes to constitute a step in the Christian response to unbelief.

Secondly, there is a final word here about the book's venture. This dialog was launched supposing that the world is common ground for the self in its relationships to God and itself. Thus the Christian person studies the world better to know and serve God, as the human calls for consistency in the self's relationships to God, world and self.

We share a common world with each other. A book can be written because the author believes the world goes on; words do not arrive at utterly alien terrain. Readers can know whereof the author speaks. Thus it makes sense to try to continue (to write for you) and to seek a continuance (to leave it with you).

Common worlds are not identical. Moreover, faith and metaphysics are not the same activity; they do not amount to a single perspective. Thus your reading of the human situation or of the Christian claim—or both—may differ from mine. But I have come upon a faith and a world view which make sense to me—indeed, make better sense together. I make bold to commend such wisdom to you.

# Notes

## Preface

1. Bernard Lonergan, *Philosophy of God and Theology* (London: Darton, Longman and Todd, 1973), p. 56.
2. Webster's *New International Dictionary of the English Language*, 2nd ed., unabridged (Springfield, Massachusetts: G. and C. Merriam Co., 1961), "wisdom."
3. In *AI* 295. Whitehead draws this wisdom from Cardinal Newman's *Grammar of Assent*.

## 1: Prospect: The Case for Faith's Interest in Metaphysics: Finding the Categories

1. Charles Hartshorne clearly articulates this "categorical supremacy" which he appropriately understands to be essential to both his own "dipolar" view and to the "monopolar" tradition. In *Philosophers Speak of God*, ed. by Charles Hartshorne and William L. Reese (Chicago: University of Chicago Press, 1953), p. 7, he writes:

   "God" is a name for the uniquely good, admirable, great, worship-eliciting being. Worship, moreover, is not just an unusually high degree of respect or admiration; and the excellence of deity is not just an unusually high degree of merit. There is a difference in kind. God is "perfect," and between the perfect and anything as little imperfect as you please is no merely finite, but an infinite, step. The superiority of deity to all others cannot (in accordance with established word usage) be expressed by indefinite descriptions, such as "immensely good," "very powerful," or even "best" or "most powerful," but must be a superiority of principle, a definite conceptual divergence from every other being, actual or so much as possible. We may call this divergence "categorical supremacy." Now our suggestion is that there is a monopolar and a dipolar way of conceiving such supremacy.

It is most helpful that Hartshorne so clearly distinguishes his analytic comment from his constructive suggestion so that the logic of faith's agenda is seen to be property common to both traditions. One could show at length that theologians as diverse as Augustine, Luther, Schleiermacher, Barth, and Tillich speak of God in a similar way.

2. I am deliberately casting this point in very broad terms to accommodate a great variety of specification. What must not be lost, if we are to maintain contact with the Christian tradition, is the insistence that the God who is radically other than we is for us. Karl Barth, who cannot easily be charged with underestimating the "otherness" of God, clearly sounds the note of gospel:

> . . . The God of the Gospel is no lonely God, self-sufficient and self-contained. He is no "absolute" God (in the original sense of absolute, i.e., being detached from everything that is not himself). To be sure, he has no equal beside himself, since an equal would no doubt limit, influence, and determine him. On the other hand, he is not imprisoned by his own majesty as though he were bound to be no more than the personal (or impersonal) "wholly other." By definition, the God of Schleiermacher cannot show mercy. The God of the Gospel can and does. (*Evangelical Theology: An Introduction,* trans., Grover Foley [New York: Holt, Rinehart and Winston, 1963], p. 10.)

Cf. the succinct formulation, "The content of God's Word is his free undeserved Yes to the whole human race, in spite of all human unreasonableness and corruption" (Ibid., p. 69). Barth does point to a difficulty in Schleiermacher's formulation which is intensified by Schleiermacher's concern for consistency which indeed contrasts with Barth's felicitous freedom at this point. Yet Schleiermacher surely struggles to make the message for humankind one that is good and in fact adds another note necessary to Christian sentiment—that Christian piety finds everything related to faith in Jesus of Nazareth as redeemer. (*The Christian Faith,* trans. H. R. Mackintosh and J. S. Stewart from the second German edition [Edinburgh: T. & T. Clark, 1948], p. 52.) My omission of this undeniably crucial christological element may be excused, if it is understood that the attention in the argument in the text is directed to the concept of God involved in Christian existence.

3. For a different view see Barth's insistence that "the living God" who acts in "a history that is always freshly in motion . . . does not allow the theologian to mistake any one point for the center itself, or to create an epicenter competing with the primary center, or to fashion an ellipse out of the circle and in this way succumb to sectarianism, heresy, or perhaps even apostasy. 'Everything is yours,' but 'He who does not gather with me scatters.' " (*Evangelical Theology,* pp. 89-90.)

While Barth is speaking of the specific work of the theologian, the contrast seems to remain intact with respect to the larger sphere of Christian existence in the world. In this respect I find myself drawn more toward Tillich and his method of correlation, and I find it not surprising that Barth would whisper warnings into Tillich's ear (Ibid., p. 131). Yet the specific discussion to follow of the relationship between metaphysics and theology cannot be identified with Tillich. Perhaps that is because Tillich's concept of God tends to pull back from the second theme of relatedness in blessing to emphasize the first theme of otherness in holiness.

4. Søren Kierkegaard, *The Sickness Unto Death,* trans. W. Lowrie (Princeton: Princeton University Press, 1941; Doubleday Anchor Edition):

> Man is spirit. But what is spirit? Spirit is the self. But what is the self? The self is a relation which relates itself to its own self, or it is that in the relation that the relation relates itself to its own self. Man is a synthesis of the infinite and the

finite, of the temporal and the eternal, of freedom and necessity, in short it is a synthesis (p. 147).

5. C. Walther von Loewenich, *Luther's Theology of the Cross*, trans. H. Bouman (Minneapolis: Augsburg, 1976), p. 64: "Faith maintains itself in man's reality. It is not only the negation of human possibility, but its realization as well."

Cf. Gustaf Wingren, *Creation and Law*, trans. Ross Mackenzie (Philadelphia: Muhlenberg, 1961), p. 22: "The statement that God exists means in Biblical terms that God helps, governs, or creates man, and here the activity on God's side is always related to receptivity on man's. If there is no such relationship, then what exists is not *God*." (Italics his.)

It does not follow that the relationship need be conscious, of course. It is interesting to observe that even that alleged disciple of discontinuity, Søren Kierkegaard, could write, "Faith is a miracle, and yet no man is excluded from it; for that in which all human life is unified is passion, and faith is a passion." (*Fear and Trembling*, trans. W. Lowrie [New York: Doubleday, 1955]), p. 77. Cf. Paul Tillich on "ecstasy" (*Systematic Theology* [3 vols.; Chicago: University of Chicago Press, 1951-1963]) where only the demonic—as distinguished from divine possession—destroys the self.

6. Harold Ditmanson well expresses this comprehensiveness in *Grace in Experience and Theology* (Minneapolis: Augsburg, 1977), pp. 66-67:

Nature, world, universe, creation—these are all comprehensive words. By "world" we mean the total environment that all men have in common. We use the word "nature" to designate the whole economy or system of observable phenomena and things, including man, existing in time and space and held together in a field or web of cause-and-effect relationships. When we speak of the "universe" we have in mind the ultimate context of life, an encompassing reality of stupendous proportions and of incredible age.

I collapse these distinctions in "world," reserving with Ditmanson "creation" for theological use.

7. A helpful specification of options chosen historically is available in James M. Gustafson's *Christ and the Moral Life* (New York: Harper & Row, 1968). An interesting case in this connection is the "Man come of age" theme in the thought of Dietrich Bonhoeffer. Even in the *Letters and Papers from Prison* (London: SCM, 1953) Bonhoeffer is opposing a separation which would not find Christ "at the center of the village." In so doing he is following the clue of the *Ethics* (ed. Eberhard Bethge, trans. N. H. Smith, New York: Macmillan, 1955) in which one seeks "participation in the reality of God and of the world in Jesus Christ today, and this participation must be such that I never experience the reality of God without the reality of the world or the reality of the world without the reality of God" (p. 62). To affirm "the natural," as Bonhoeffer does, is not therefore to isolate the presence of God to some religious preserve. On the other hand, "the 'ethical' as a theme is tied to a definite time and a definite place. That is so because man is a living and mortal creature in a finite and destructible world and because he is not essentially or exclusively a student of ethics. . . . To confine the ethical phenomenon to its proper place and time is not to invalidate it; it is, on the contrary, to render it fully operative. Big guns are not the right weapons for shooting sparrows" (pp. 232-233).

8. Perhaps Stephen Pepper (*World Hypotheses* [Berkeley: University of California Press, 1942], p. 1) puts the point most forcefully in writing: ". . . the peculiarity of world hypotheses is that they cannot reject anything as irrelevant. . . . Every consideration is relevant to a world hypothesis and no facts lie outside it." Thus Aristotle begins his *Metaphysics* (trans. Richard Hope [Ann Arbor: University of Michigan Press, 1968], pp. 6-7) by assuming "first . . . that the wise man knows all so far as possible,

though he does not know anything in particular . . ." and so comes to his identification of the "science" "of first principles and reasons."

F. H. Bradley (*Appearance and Reality: A Metaphysical Essay* [London: Oxford, 1969], p. 1) accepts the formulation of metaphysics as ". . . the study of first principles or ultimate truths, or again the effort to comprehend the universe, not simply piecemeal or by fragments, but somehow as a whole."

Similarly Hegel opens his *Phenomenology of Mind* (Torchbook edition, trans. by J. B. Baillie [New York: Harper, 1967]) with the observation that ". . . philosophy has its being essentially in the element of that universality which encloses the particular within it . . ." (p. 67), and goes on to insist that philosophy ". . . does not deal with a determination that is nonessential, but with a determination so far as it is an essential factor" (p. 105).

Spinoza's concurrence may be discerned in the geometric demonstration of the *Ethics* (trans. R. H. M. Elwes [2 vols.; New York: Dover, 1955], Vol. II) though that method incorporates as well the materially specific denial of contingency. Paul Weiss presumes this understanding of metaphysical scope in pleading so for the discipline:

> Some, and perhaps even all of a given discipline's certified truths might have to be altered if they are to be brought into accord with the certified truths of other inquiries. Unless we can somehow stand outside all disciplines, unless we can somehow use common principles, categories, values, we cannot hope to adjudicate authoritatively the claims which each discipline makes even within its own framework; we can therefore have no surety that its results will ever form part of a single harmonious body of knowledge. (*Modes of Being* [Carbondale: Southern Illinois Press, 1958], Arcturus edition, p. 5.)

My concern is not at all to erode the massive differences among these several thinkers, but merely to point out at the beginning of our task that so wide ranging a field of thinkers supports the view that Whitehead's understanding of the metaphysical task is not eccentric. This is to suggest that the terms of the investigation could be applied as well in principle to very differing metaphysical views.

9. Cf. Weiss (*Modes of Being,* pp. 6-7):

> Only if we know what it is to be a man can we engage in co-ordinate investigations into his nature; only if we know what it is to be a man can we estimate the rival contentions of doctors, biologists, psychologists, anthropologists, and the rest. Only if we know what it is to be, to inquire, to understand, can we recognize that we are all dealing with different phases of the same subject, and can know how to bring together the different results that were obtained along different routes of investigation.

For that matter, "to be a man" is too specialized a category metaphysically speaking.

10. Ian Barbour makes the point effectively in responding to R. B. Braithwaite's understanding of religious assertions as affirmations of one's intention to act in certain ways:

> Now I would agree that religious language does indeed express and evoke distinctive attitudes. It does encourage self-commitment to a way of life; it acknowledges allegiance to ethical principles and affirms the intention to act in particular ways. But I would maintain that these *non-cognitive uses* presuppose *cognitive beliefs.* To be sure, religious faith is not simply assent to the truth of propositions; but it does require the assumption that certain propositions are true. It would be unreasonable to adopt or recommend a way of life unless one believes that the universe is of such a character that this way of life is appropriate. "Useful fictions" are no longer useful if they are recognized as fictions or treated as "parables" whose truth or falsity is taken to be irrelevant. (*Myths, Models and Paradigms* [New York: Harper & Row, 1974], p. 58. Italics his.)

NOTES 291

Braithwaite's position may be examined in *An Empiricist's View of the Nature of Religious Belief* (London: Cambridge, 1955).
11. Weiss, *Modes of Being*, p. 7.
12. Kent S. Knutson, *The Shape of the Question* (Minneapolis: Augsburg, 1972), p. 121.
13. I recognize that this statement may seem to reflect a metaphysical identification of being and doing which has not yet been established. I am aware as well of the strong tradition linking piety and passivity, as with Schleiermacher's emphasis on the core religious consciousness of absolute dependence. Yet Schleiermacher came to view teleological religion as a form higher than aesthetic, so at least there is to be activity generated by the God-relationship. Barth's very complex material stresses divine priority, but not in such a way as to exclude human activity:

> Man acts by believing, but the fact that he believes by acting is God's act. Man is the subject of faith. It is not God but man who believes. But the very fact of a man thus being subject in faith is bracketed as the predicate of the subject, God, bracketed exactly as the Creator embraces His creature, the merciful God sinful man, i.e., so that there is no departure from man's being a subject, and this very thing, the Ego of man as such, is still only derivable from the Thou of the Subject God. (*Church Dogmatics* [4 vols. in 13 Parts; Edinburgh: T & T Clark, 1936-1969]; Vol. I, Part 1: *The Doctrine of the Word of God*, trans. G. T. Thomson, p. 281.)

This emphasis on human activity need not deny the independent point that the actual meaning of the human is denied at the opposite extreme where too great a role is granted to humankind.
14. Terence E. Fretheim, *Creation, Fall and Flood* (Minneapolis: Augsburg, 1969), pp. 116-117. The Apostle Paul so speaks of independent divine action that "none may boast." God may choose not many who are wise or powerful, since the sin of presumption is less apt to occur directly in such, but the worldly weak and the worldly strong —if they would boast—"must boast of what the Lord has done." See 1 Corinthians 1 With regard to the interdependent divine action, see my "Transcendence in Relationship" (*Dialog*, Autumn, 1973).
15. Kierkegaard, *The Sickness Unto Death*, pp. 213ff. Yet the sense in which the individual is alone before God cannot be pressed too single-mindedly. If the self's failure to act/choose properly were strictly and exclusively a matter of the God-relationship, Kierkegaard would have had to suppose himself divine to have the evidence needed to launch his stringent critique of Danish Christendom. His critique is often directed, not at the dogmatics of the church, but at the existence of the person. So, too, "Religion B" or the decisively Christian position in the *Postscript* does not isolate the Christian, but incorporates the human, while critiquing and transcending earlier schemes of organization in the stages toward "aesthetic," "ethical," and "Religion A." For a defense of this view see, Emanuel Hirsch, *Kierkegaard-Studien* (2 vols.; Gütersloh: C. Bertelsmann, 1930-1933), II, pp. 804-805.
For a statement of the most conventional opposing view, see Jan Sperna Weiland, *Humanitas Christianitas* (Te Assen Biij: Van Gorcum, 1951), pp. 31-35.
At this point of discussion I have aligned myself with Hirsch in *Kierkegaard on Christ and Christian Coherence* (New York: Harper & Row, 1968).
In sum: to affirm the distant character of the God-relationship is not to deny the bearing of that relationship on the rest of reality through the unity of the self. It does remain true, unfortunately, that Kierkegaard was so engrossed in making the first point that he gave little systematic attention to the second. The best treatment of the Christian ethical concern in Kierkegaard remains Valter Lindstrom's *Efterföljelsens Teologi hos Søren Kierkegaard* (Stockholm: Svenska Diakonistyrelses, 1956).

16. If asked, "What does God in his Law want with us and from us?", Barth can draw all the commandments into the first which Christ fulfilled and so reply: "You shall believe!" See *Community, State, and Church* (Gloucester, Mass.: Peter Smith, 1968), esp. pp. 71-100. But see also Vol. IV, Part Three, second half, *Church Dogmatics,* for qualifications of this motif. I have discussed this aspect of Barth's thought in *Contemporary Forms of Faith* (Minneapolis: Augsburg, 1967), pp. 71-73.

17. B. A. Gerrish, *Grace and Reason* (Oxford: Clarendon Press, 1962), pp. 10-27. Cf. Von Loewenich, *Luther's Theology of the Cross,* pp. 72ff.

18. See above, pp. 23-24.

19. Søren Kierkegaard, *Papirer,* ed. by P. A. Heiberg and Victor Kuhr (11 vols.; Copenhagen: Gyldendals, 1909-48), VII 2 B 235, pp. 199-205. (Trans. mine.) Cf. *On Authority and Revelation: The Book on Adler,* trans. W. Lowrie (Princeton: Princeton University Press, 1955), p. 168. In the *Papirer* see also X 2 A 119, X 3 A 756, and X 5 A 121. Kierkegaard may disclaim that he subjectively represents the Christian possible, but he asserts, "I know what Christianity is." See *My Activity as a Writer* published with *The Point of View for My Work as an Author,* trans. W. Lowrie (New York: Harper & Row, 1962), p. 153.

20. Again Kierkegaard provides a lucid instance of a Christian thinker who would rescue paradox from confusion with sloppy thinking:

> So the believing Christian not only possesses but uses his understanding, does not put it down to a lack of understanding if somebody is not a Christian; but in relation to Christianity he believes against the understanding and in this case also uses understanding . . . to make sure that he believes against the understanding. Nonsense therefore he cannot believe against the understanding, for precisely the understanding will discern that it is nonsense and will prevent him from believing it; but he makes so much use of the understanding that he becomes aware of the incomprehensible, and then he holds to this, believing against the understanding. (*The Concluding Unscientific Postscript to the Philosophical Fragments,* trans. David F. Swenson (Princeton: Princeton University Press, 1944, p. 504.)

See, too, Henning Schröer, *Die Denkform der Paradoxalität als Theologisches Problem* (Göttingen: Vandenhoeck & Ruprecht, 1960) for a study of Kierkegaard's thought as the paradigmatic attempt to place the thought form of the paradoxical in the service of theology. I agree with this estimate formally, though I think Schröer places too much emphasis on the ontological formulation of paradox in the writings of the pseudonym Johannes Climacus and not enough on the religious formulation in the writings of Anti-Climacus. In any case two points redeem paradox from nonsense: internal structure (entailing, in my view, at least otherness, opposition and simultaneity) and external reference (entailing some framework of meaning).

21. See the stimulating collection, *The Concept of Order* (ed. by Paul G. Kuntz [Seattle: University of Washington Press, 1968]), especially the introductory essay by Kuntz, pp. ix-xxxix. See also the distinction between naturalism and historicism in E. Troeltsch, *Historimus und Seine Probleme* (Tübingen: J. C. B. Mohr, 1922).

22. Joseph F. Wall, "The Historian's Approach to Reality," in *The Concept of Order,* ed. by Paul G. Kuntz, pp. 461-467.

Another striking literary instance is E. M. Forster's Mrs. Moore in *A Passage to India* (New York: Modern Library, 1924), pp. 149-150, who is driven to distraction by her visit to the famous Marabar caves of central India. It is the monotonous sound of the echo, *bou-oum,* that undermines her hold on reality:

> Devils are of the North, and poems can be written about them, but no one could romanticize the Marabar because it robbed infinity and eternity of their vastness,

the only quality that accommodates them. . . . She tried to go on wih her letter. . . . Out suddenly, at the edge of her mind, Religion appeared, poor little talkative Christianity, and she knew that all its divine words from "Let there be light" to "It is finished" only amounted to "boum."

Forster and Wall rightly find this "talkative faith," this religion of the Word, to "rage for order," to cite the happy phrase from the poetry of Wallace Stevens which David Tracy takes for the title in his *Blessed Rage for Order* (New York: Seabury Press, 1975).

It is not solitaire, but poetry, which occupies God, according to Paul Ricoeur in (with Alasdair MacIntyre) *The Religious Significance of Atheism* (New York: Columbia University Press, 1969), p. 97:

In its most inclusive sense, "poetry" is that which roots the act of dwelling between heaven and earth, under heaven and on earth, in the power of the Word, of discourse, of saying. "Poetry" so defined is more than the making of poems; it is *poesis*, the act of creation in the broadest sense.

23. John 1:18. (Italics mine.) Barth's very intricate discussion of "the knowability of the Word of God" (*The Doctrine of the Word of God*, Vol. I, Part I, *Church Dogmatics*, pp. 213-283) raises the question of whether it is possible to know God *incoherently*. While Barth speaks of recognizing the Word of God as

. . . an understanding, a personal sense of being touched, an affirmation, assent, and approval, a concentration of remote times in the present, an obedience, a decision, a standing still before the mystery and a stimulation by its inner life, a founding of the whole man upon this mystery (p. 250),

he warns against presuming upon this experience:

Not for one moment or in any respect, merely because he is thus in it, will he put his confidence in the fact, take his bearings by it, derive from it the measure for understanding the reality in which he stands; he will not reflect upon it at all, but still simply be in it (p. 252).

Barth seems driven to this statement by the combination of the Calvinist dicta, *finitum non capax infiniti* and *peccator non capax verbi divini*, on the one hand, and the earlier noted insistence that God has acted for us, on the other (note 2, above). The *Church Dogmatics* seems testimony that he is driven beyond the statement to a quest for a coherent pattern of reflection upon the "first order" reality of faith.

24. This is to suggest that intelligibility cannot be fully separated from plausibility, if not verifiability. See Raeburne S. Heimbeck, *Theology and Meaning; A Critique of Metatheological Scepticism* (Stanford: University Press, 1969) and also Anders Jeffner, *The Study of Religious Language* (London: SCM, 1972).

25. Barbour, *Myths, Models and Paradigms*, p. 27. Cf. Pepper, *World Hypotheses*. A theologian who was particularly attentive to this aspect of religious thought was H. Richard Niebuhr. See not only his classic *Christ and Culture* (New York: Harper & Row, 1951), but also the specific methodological remarks regarding "symbolic forms" in *The Responsible Self* (New York: Harper & Row, 1963).

26. Tracy, *Blessed Rage for Order*, p. 23. See also Max Black, *Models and Metaphors* (Ithaca: Cornell University Press, 1962).

27. For a current chronicle of such rivals, see *The New Religious Consciousness*, ed. by Charles V. Glock and Robert N. Bellah (Berkeley: University of California Press, 1976).

28. See the discussions by John Hick, *Faith and Knowledge* (Ithaca: Cornell University Press, 1957), esp. "The Logic of Faith," pp. 134-164, and *Religious Belief* by C. B. Martin (Ithaca: Cornell University Press, 1959), esp. "Life After Death," pp. 64-94.

29. See Elizabeth Schüssler Fiorenza "Wisdom Mythology and Christological Hymns," pp. 17-41, in Robert Wilken, *Aspects of Wisdom in Judaism and Early Christianity*

(South Bend: Notre Dame Press, 1975), and James M. Robinson, "Jesus as Sophos and Sophia: Wisdom Tradition and the Gospels," pp. 1-16 in the same collection.

30. Heiko Oberman, "Headwaters of the Reformation," in *Luther and the Dawn of the Modern Era* (Leipzig: Brill, 1974), p. 57.
31. Knutson, *The Shape of the Question*, p. 15. Cf. the thorough discussion by Langdon Gilkey in *Naming the Whirlwind: The Renewal of God-Language* (Indianapolis: Bobbs-Merrill, 1969), where after noting that three faces of the modern secular spirit —contingency, relativism, and temporality—leave modern man ". . . 'on his own,' an alien set within a context that is indifferent and so irrelevant to his own deepest purposes" (p. 57), Gilkey speaks of ". . . the autonomy and freedom of man, his inalienable birthright and, fortunately, his innate capacity to know his own truth, to decide about his own existence, to create his own meaning, and to establish his own values" (p. 58). He further notes the way in which

> . . . this assertion of autonomous freedom and self-direction is subversive of many of the historic forms of religion, with their traditional authorities of various sorts stemming from the distant past, their requirements of faith, obedience, submission, and self-surrender, and their insistence that man is fulfilled when he patterns himself according to the divine image. Is not—so the modern spirit declares— revelation the denial of all autonomy in inquiry and rationality; is not a divine law the denial of personal autonomy in ethics; above all, is not God, if he be at all, the final challenge to my creativity as a man? (pp. 60-61).

32. Knutson, *The Shape of the Question*, p. 17.
33. Tracy, *Blessed Rage for Order*, makes much of the post-modern critiques of Enlightenment "illusion" to be found in the likes of Freud, Marx, and Nietzsche. But he does observe:

> What remains constant in the shift from modernity to post-modernity is the fact that such contemporary critiques of modernity deepen the fundamental commitment to those purely secular standards for knowledge and action initiated by the Enlightenment. . . . The authentic person is committed above all else to the full affirmation of the ultimate significance of our lives in this world (p. 8).

34. The address was delivered in Stockholm on Sunday, December 12, 1976. See the Associated Press report of December 13.
35. Heinrich Ott, "Philosophical Theology as Confrontation," pp. 144-168, *The Future of Philosophical Theology*, ed. Robert Evans, trans. of Ott's essay by D. L. Holland (Philadelphia: Westminster Press, 1971), p. 146, writes further:

> The salvation-historical scheme assures theology a sacral zone inside the world. This sacral zone is under attack today. Here, indeed, the principle of secularization is valid! (p. 151).

Accordingly:

> We must withdraw the "salvation events" from the salvation-historical framework where one can still recite them simply as facts, and transpose them (über-setzen) (p. 149).

36. Andrew Greeley, *The New Agenda* (New York: Doubleday, 1973), p. 46. Greeley points out that the collapse is not only fundamental but thoroughgoing:

> The solid rock turned out to be shifting sand. The unsinkable boat has sprung a leak. Where there once was certainty of the most rigorous sort, there is now only chaos and confusion. We used to be able to prove everything, now we can't prove anything; and it seems as though nothing is worth proving (p. 56).

37. Glock, *The New Religious Consciousness*, p. 365.
38. Ibid., p. 361.

39. Tracy, *Blessed Rage for Order*, p. 177. Greeley nicely indicates the connection between the Christian's "contemporary" and the Christian:
   It came as a great shock in the fifties and early sixties when large numbers of Catholics began to go to the secular graduate schools to discover that the pagan and agnostic students and faculties were intelligent, reasonable men and women. Many young Catholics found the existence of the "good secularist" a heavy blow to their "faith." For if faith is based on arguments that men and women who are as intelligent as you and more sophisticated do not find persuasive, then it is obviously a very fragile faith (p. 49).
   I am suggesting that difficulties of framework place both plausibility and, more primitively, intelligibility in jeopardy.
40. At this point the same dynamic may lie beneath the more bizarre new "faiths" chronicled by Glock and Bellah *(The New Religious Consciousness)* and the presumed "return" to old certitudes. In the latter connection see the trenchant critique of Richard John Neuhaus, "Returning to Where We Have Never Been," *Time Toward Home* (New York: Seabury Press, 1975), pp. 9-21. Neuhaus examines various versions—ethnic, political, and religious—of the "homeward trek" "back to the way things were before everything started coming apart."
41. This is the formulation suggested by David B. Burrell in "The Future of Philosophical Theology as Reflective Awareness," p. 92 (*The Future of Philosophical Theology*, ed. by Evans, pp. 85-112). Burrell likens the analytic role of theology to that of a grammar with respect to working languages: "Grammar is not itself a competing language but rather a specialized type of reflection designed to show forth the structure of any particular language and so to help one master his own language or acquire another." Thus theology doesn't give a picture of God, any more than grammar writes sentences, though it may rule out some stories as unintelligible; it can't specify criteria, but it can "display" them (pp. 86-90).
42. Again, one worries about the tendency to respond to the stringent terms of the falsifiability debate by simply distinguishing intelligibility from truth. That victory is empty. We need to tell a story that not only is clear, but which could also be true for persons in this world.
43. Tracy, *Blessed Rage for Order*, p. 55.
44. Van Harvey's *The Historian and the Believer: The Morality of Historical Knowledge and Christian Belief* (New York: Macmillan, 1966) remains an excellent statement of the challenge. Tracy, *Blessed Rage for Order*, p. 7, takes the application to mean a new self-critical role for the theologian. He does acknowledge that the Christian theologian's basic loyalty to his church tradition means that he resolves to study that tradition to aid its self-understanding. But that acknowledgment seems weakened by Tracy's statement that a non-Christian could do Christian theology. Here Tracy seems to have left the terms of my discussion, *faith* and process, but this is perhaps to be accounted for by a conviction he possesses which I cannot share. He described "the faith of secularity" as "that fundamental attitude which affirms the ultimate significance and final worth of our lives, our thoughts, and actions, here and now, in nature and history" and adds that this faith is a common faith shared by secularist and modern Christian (p. 8). Yet I do agree that the methodological rigor associated with the quest for truth in the self-world relationship must impinge on the effort to state coherently and winsomely the claims associated with the self-God relationship. The Christian theologian can give up neither relationship; in turning to a metaphysics one does not find a safely transcendent "third" but merely a comprehensively common context in which the work can—but must—proceed.
45. Neuhaus, *Time Toward Home*, pp. 77-78.

46. Thomas Kuhn, *The Structure of Scientific Revolutions* (Chicago: University of Chicago Press, 1962). See also his second edition of 1970 (Chicago) and his "Second Thoughts on Paradigms," *The Structure of Scientific Theories*, ed. by Frederick Suppe (Champaign: University of Illinois Press, 1973).
    Michael Polanyi, *Personal Knowledge* (Chicago: University of Chicago Press, 1958).
47. Barbour, *Myths, Models and Paradigms*, p. 115.
48. See Errol E. Harris, *The Foundations of Metaphysics in Science* (London: George Allen and Unwin, 1965). See also Lewis S. Ford's "Can Science Provide the Foundations for Metaphysics? A Comment on Errol E. Harris's Project," *The Modern Schoolman 46* (January, 1969, pp. 148-153). Ford's more important reservations seem to be material ones, directed at what he takes to be Harris' disjunctive consideration of the status of relations (all external or all internal), but he does question whether scientific assertions can be directly helpful in the construction of a metaphysical world-picture (as distinguished from rendering assistance in empirical falsification), since a genuine metaphysical principle must be exemplified by "all possible actualities." While it is important to remember that scientific statements do not yet have the scope needed to qualify as metaphysical statements, they point the way if we understand metaphysics as empirically anchored. See below, Chapter 2, pp. 53-58, 89-90.
49. See Emil Fackenheim, *Metaphysics and Historicity* (Milwaukee: Marquette University Press, 1961):

> For historicism asserts . . . not only that all metaphysical assertions are historically relative; it adds that this is so because these assertions are part of an historically situated process of self-making. And it is then forced to concede that the assertion "historicism is true" is also part of this process of self-making. But the crux is that both statements, no matter how different in type, must be part of one and the same self-constituting process; and it is precisely this that historicism cannot account for without collapsing in self-contradiction (p. 64).

    Fackenheim's response does comprehend the derivative reflection about self-making within the process of self-making and so retains the objectivity of reference needed for metaphysics. It does not show, however, that the *meaning* of the relativist statement depends on that process of self-making. Thus a metaphysics having to do with self-making (including a self coming to be aware of historical relativity) will need to address the issue of continuity with states of reality in which self-making presumably did (will) not occur, relating the emerging historical differences to common structure, while at the same time accounting for other metaphysical versions.
50. Robert L. Wilken, *The Myth of Christian Beginnings: History's Impact on Belief* (New York: Doubleday, 1971), p. 205. Cf. Neuhaus, *Time Toward Home*, p. 127:

> An immutable God is not playing hide-and-seek. A capricious God has not staged history as a striptease show in which he exposes his purposes bit by bit. No, a suffering God has engaged his creation in a labor of love and invites us to join him in bringing his project to completion.

    I cite this as a statement of a Christian's commitment to history, though of course it could be read as a particular framework subsitution.
51. Note, for example, the way in which John Hick distinguishes between Christian theology and Christian mythology in *Evil and the God of Love* (New York: Harper & Row, 1966). While "in the past, theology and myth have been closely twined together" due to scientific ignorance, contemporary developments are seen to evoke a distinction and a selection within the theological materials: "In the light of modern anthropological knowledge some form of two-stage conception of the creation of man has become an almost unavoidable Christian tenet" (p. 291).

52. Gustaf Wingren, *Creation and Law*, trans. Ross Mackenzie (Philadelphia: Muhlenberg, 1961), pp. 28-29.

53. Ibid., pp. 101-102. Cf. H. Paul Santmire, *Brother Earth* (New York: Thomas Nelson, 1970), esp. pp. 164-170.

54. See Ivar Asheim, "Humanity and Christian Responsibility, *Christ and Humanity* (Philadelphia: Fortress, 1970), p. 13:

> . . . it must be pointed out that God's demand is perceived *within* the reality of the world. Certainly Scripture continues to be the ethical norm, although it should be noted that it is not via the church that God's law has to be brought into the world. The law is not a derivative of the gospel. God's demand already exists in the reality of the world prior to our faith, addressing every man via the concrete life situations in which he finds himself by bringing home to him through these situations the burdens and needs of his neighbor.

Cf. Wingren, *Creation and Law*, p. 31:

> Every encounter between human beings involves an unexpressed demand to be responsible for one another's life as long as we are able to do so. To receive life means to be implicated in this reciprocity of demand.

See also the most provocative study, *The Ethical Demand* by Knud Lögstrup (trans. T. I. Jensen [Philadelphia: Fortress, 1971]), who analyzes human relationships for "the demand that we take care of that in the other person's life which is dependent upon us and which we have in our power" (p. 29).

55. Knutson, *The Shape of the Question*, p. 45.

56. Thus Neuhaus, *Time Toward Home*, p. 47, holds with regard to the civil religion that "the covenant relevant to America is but a specific instance of that covenant with the creation." For a critique generated from the more particular tradition, see *Defining America* by Robert Benne and Philip Hefner (Philadelphia: Fortress, 1974).

57. Gustaf Wingren, *Gospel and Church*, trans. Ross Mackenzie (London: Oliver and Boyd, 1964), pp. 180-181. Cf. *Creation and Law*, p. 42.

58. Gerhard von Rad, *Wisdom in Israel*, trans. James D. Martin (New York: Abingdon, 1972), p. 61. Cf. Walter Brueggemann, *In Man We Trust* (Richmond: John Knox, 1972). Wingren stresses that one God is at work here:

> The "opus proprium" of God, which is to give and which is seen most clearly in the Gospel, is already operative in creation and is expressed in the primary fact of life. (*Creation and Law*, p. 30.)

See also James Gustafson, *Theology and Christian Ethics* (Philadelphia: United Church Press, 1974), especially pp. 215-228, on "The Relationship of Empirical Science to Moral Thought."

59. For an examination of this problem in current moral philosophy, see *The Is-Ought Question*, ed. W. D. Hudson (London: Macmillan, 1969). See also the comprehensive survey article, "Recent Work on Ethical Naturalism" by R. L. Franklin in *Studies in Ethics* (Monograph 7 in the *American Philosophical Quarterly* monograph series, Oxford, 1973), pp. 55-95. I have commented on this issue in "How Do We Decide? With Reality?" in *Dialog*, XIV, 1 (Winter, 1975), pp. 21-25.

60. Tracy, *Blessed Rage for Order*, p. 71.

61. Of course care must be taken to recognize elements of distortion deriving from the condition of sin, cf. above pp. 41 and 43, and below pp. 47-48. Still the desire to avoid Pelagianism should not be permitted to drive one into Flacianism or Manicheanism.

62. Whitehead, for example, is one metaphysician who seems to allow for such an appeal:

> It is characteristic of the learned mind to exalt words. Yet mothers can ponder many things in their hearts which their lips cannot express. These many things,

which are thus known, constitute the ultimate religious evidence, beyond which there is no appeal (*RM* 65).

Of course, this is no carte blanche justification, since Whitehead recognizes that the authority of religion "is endangered by the intensity of the emotions which it generates" (*RM* 81). He worries about a religion which confines itself to "moments of emotional excitement," arguing that religion must instead "find its verification at all temperatures" (*RM* 53). The question, of course, is what kind of verification at all temperatures is possible and adequate for an appeal to special experience.

63. I recognize that in these comments I seem to be assuming the non-reversibility of time which is itself a metaphysical point yet to be argued. Indeed my formulation might be said to be precisely metaphysical in the sense that Whitehead reserves that term for the most universal structures as distinguished from cosmological characterizations of particular cosmic epochs. I must defer a full consideration of this problem to Part II for analysis and Part IV for evaluation.

64. See Heinrich Schmid, *The Doctrinal Theology of the Evangelical Lutheran Church*, 5th ed. rev. by Charles May and Henry Jacobs (Minneapolis: Augsburg, 1899), pp. 166-167, 248-249. While the specific focus of the discussion concerns the creation of human souls and the transmission of sinfulness, the considerations introduced suggest a more general issue. Thus the opposing position (that souls are created daily by God) is held to imply the following "absurdity": ". . . that man does not beget an entire man, or an entire composite being, but only that part of it which does not give form to man; that he does not beget man, for man without form, i.e., soul, is not man" (p. 167).

65. Admittedly opulence will have to take its place alongside economy in the method to be used at such points. One is reminded of the dialog in Bernard Shaw's *St. Joan*, Act I:

JOAN: I hear voices telling me what to do. They come from God.

DEBAUDRICOURT: They come from your imagination.

JOAN: Of course; that is how the messages of God come to us.

We shall have to ask what it takes to best explain "the voices."

66. Hegel, *Phenomenology of Mind*, the sections on "revealed religion" and "Absolute knowledge" in particular, pp. 750-808.

67. Lewis S. Ford, "The Power of God and the Christ," pp. 79-92, in *Religious Experience and Process Theology: The Pastoral Implications of a Major Modern Movement*, ed. by Harry James Cargas and Bernard Lee (New York: Paulist, 1976), pp. 83-84. See also Ford's *The Lure of God* (Philadelphia: Fortress, 1978), pp. 26-27.

68. Depending on the degree of the hindrances, one may be required to limit such knowledge merely to formal themes.

69. Romans 8:33-34.


## 2: Data: The Claims of This Metaphysics

1. William Christian, *An Interpretation of Whitehead's Metaphysics* (New Haven: Yale University Press, 1959), pp. 168-172, marshalls convincing evidence that, while Whitehead appeals to both scientific facts and facts of immediate experience, "quantum phenomena seem to be on a level distinctly secondary to the facts of immediate experience" (p. 168).

2. Stephen C. Pepper, *World Hypotheses* (Berkeley and Los Angeles: University of California Press, 1942), p. 91.

3. *PR* 6: "Philosophers can never hope finally to formulate these metaphysical first principles. Weakness of insight and deficiencies of language stand in the way inexorably." Cf. D. M. Mackinnon, *The Problem of Metaphysics* (London: Cambridge University Press, 1974) especially Chapters 2 and 3 for a discussion of how "being metaphysically minded" involves a "thrusting against the limits of language."

4. *SMW*, Chapter 3. This is the error "of mistaking the abstract for the concrete" (*SMW* 51). Similarly, in *PR* 11, he warns that "the chief error in philosophy is overstatement" which occurs "in neglecting the degree of abstraction involved when an actual entity is considered merely so far as it exemplifies certain categories of thought."

5. Of course the consensus threatens to collapse in the trivial if one casts the net too widely. Thus I do not consider "process thought" to include the thought of Teilhard de Chardin, though Ewert H. Cousins has included readings from that school in his influential anthology *Process Theology* (New York: Newman, 1971). Nor do I include in my discussion the work of Pannenberg and Moltmann, despite the apparently similar stress on time. While in these cases some common themes can be traced, the differences stubbornly refuse to fade—notably in the area of eschatology, including the effects of the eschatological orientation on the temporal process. Lewis Ford has tried to link Whitehead and Pannenberg in the theme of God as the ultimate power of the future. In "Toward a Process Theology of Hope," a paper read in the Fall, 1975, meeting of the American Academy of Religion, Ford emphasizes that Whitehead's God rescues "the world from degeneration into chaos by the relentless provision of ever-new creative possibilities for the world to actualize" (p. 10). In a striking note (14, p. 16) he acknowledges:

> Since these possibilities may become distorted in transmission, God is not the *sole* power of the future, although he is the *ultimate* power. The perversion of the divine is the demonic. Both exercise their power upon us by the lure of the future.

See also Ford's *The Lure of God* (Philadelphia: Fortress, 1978), pp. 29-44, and "A Whiteheadian Basis for Pannenberg's Theology," *Encounter* 38/4 (Autumn, 1977), pp. 307-317 as well as his conversation with Pannenberg, "A Dialogue about Process Philosophy," ibid., pp. 318-324.

From a Whiteheadian perspective the reality of non-divine efficient causation seems undervalued in both Pannenberg and Moltmann. In Chapter 3 I will ask whether Whitehead himself may have erred in that direction with respect to the "religious" appeal of the "Consequent Nature" of God. That chapter will also suggest the range of thinkers who seem to me to fall within the field of those seeking to appropriate process thought for theological purposes. Here my concern is simply to state the position which anchors the effort to follow.

6. See Whitehead's own "autobiographical notes" in P. A. Schilpp, ed., *The Philosophy of Alfred North Whitehead* (New York: Tudor, 1961), pp. 1-14. Victor Lowe offers a sketch relating life and thought in "Alfred North Whitehead and his Philosophy," *Understanding Whitehead* (Baltimore: J. Hopkins, 1962), pp. 3-31. W. E. Hocking offers the reflections of a colleague in "Whitehead as I knew him" in Kline, ed., *Alfred North Whitehead: Essays on His Philosophy* (Englewood Cliffs, N.J.: Prentice Hall, 1965), pp. 7-17.

7. See Whitehead's own appeal to "common sense" or "naive experience" in *PR* 14, 25, 216, 220-221, 237, 266-267. The appeal to primitivity is needed since "common sense" may benumb and repress experience (13). The appeal to pervasiveness—the "recurrent" (25), the "daily" (123, 264)—is needed, since distortion through "artificial accounts" (219) can occur.

8. In the paragraph which follows Whitehead employs the categories of the One and the Many, asking, "What is the meaning of the 'many' things engaged in this common flux,

and in what sense, if any, can the word 'all' refer to a definitely indicated set of these many things?" I detect that the movement of his thought is from the primitive ("things flow") to the pervasive ("all things").

9. *MT* 71. Whitehead speaks of "the sense of qualitative experience derived from antecedent fact, enjoyed in the personal unity of present fact, and conditioning future fact," distinguishing "the sense of derivation from without, the sense of immediate enjoyment within, and the sense of transmission beyond."

10. Whitehead notes that "disorder shares with order the common characteristic that they imply many things interconnected."

11. In another schematization Whitehead writes: "I suggest to you as fundamental characterizations of our experience, three principles of division expressed by the three pairs of opposites—'Clarity and Vagueness,' 'Order and Disorder,' 'The Good and the Bad'" (*MT* 75).

12. *PR* 247. Cf. *PR* 471. Cf. *FR* 21: "The Way of Rhythm pervades all life, and indeed all physical existence. This common principle of Rhythm is one of the reasons for believing that the root principles of life are, in some lowly form, exemplified in all types of physical existence." In such a move the direction seems to be from the primitive in experience to the pervasive, though the reading of the primitive may be revised in the process.

13. *MT* 9. Cf. *FR* 5: "The problem set by the doctrine of evolution is to explain how complex organisms with such deficient survival power ever evolved. They certainly did not appear because they were better at the game than the rocks around them." He finds himself drawn to the view that "the material universe has contained in itself, and perhaps still contains, some mysterious impulse for its energy to run upwards" (p. 24). Cf. *RM* 153 regarding the "two aspects of the universe": the "physically wasting" and the "spiritually ascending."

14. Cf. *MT* 21, 159.

15. *PR* 5. The fuller phrasing is as follows: "The term 'logical' has its ordinary meaning, including 'logical' consistency, or lack of contradiction, the definition of constructs in logical terms, the exemplification of general logical notions in specific instances, and the principles of inference."

16. Whitehead acknowledges that "it is difficult to draw the line distinguishing characteristics so general that we cannot conceive any alternatives, from characteristics so special that we imagine them to belong merely to our cosmic epoch" (*PR* 441).

17. This empirical emphasis seems to differ at least in degree from Charles Hartshorne's view of the a priori character of metaphysical principles. David R. Griffin cautions against too sharp a distinction between the two philosophers at this point, noting the descriptive side of Hartshorne's view. *Two Process Philosophers*, ed. Lewis Ford (Tallahassee, Florida: American Academy of Religion, 1973), pp. 45-49. Lewis Ford suggests that for Hartshorne the principles are analytic a priori—their denial is meaningless and their contraries are all self-contradictory. He takes Whitehead to regard the principles as synthetic a priori, "i.e., although they are necessary in the sense of being exemplified in all possible actual entities, they do have non-self-contradictory alternatives" (Ibid., p. 47—Griffin's summary). This moves in the right direction and is separable from Ford's effort to view God as establishing the metaphysical principles. (On that effort, see below, p. 88.) In any case, Whitehead does not speculate as to what might be possible in some other universe, but he does hold that the "doctrine of necessity in universality means that there is an essence to the universe which forbids relationships beyond itself, as a violation of its rationality" (*PR* 6). For other statements of criteria with an empirical emphasis, see *PR* 67 and *SMW* 158. On differing kinds of order in relationship to the role of metaphysics, see the introductory essay

by Paul G. Kuntz in *The Concept of Order* (Seattle: University of Washington Press, 1968), pp. ix-xxxix.

18. Donald Sherburne has helpfully gathered the many strands of reference in his *A Key to Whitehead's Process and Reality* (Bloomington: Indiana University Press, 1966) under the title "Whitehead and Other Philosophers," pp. 126-170.

19. Above, p. 62. Cf. *PR* 42-43, regarding the appropriation of Alexander's "principle of unrest" and 65, where Whitehead associates his use of "feeling" with Alexander's use of "enjoyment."

20. John Dewey, *Reconstruction in Philosophy* (New York: H. Holt, 1920).

21. See *Principles of Psychology* (New York: H. Holt, 1890; Dover, 1950), *Essays in Radical Empiricism* (New York: Longmans & Green, 1912), *Essays in Pragmatism* (New York: Hafner, 1948) and *Varieties of Religious Experience* (New York: Longmans & Green, 1925).

22. Cf. L. D. Landau and G. B. Rumer, *What is Relativity*, trans. N. Kemmer (New York: Basic Books, 1960), p. 19.

23. John B. Cobb, Jr., *A Christian Natural Theology* (Philadelphia: Westminster, 1965), pp. 208ff. See also Gottfried Martin, "Metaphysics as *Scientia Universalis* and as *Ontologia Generalis*," in *The Relevance of Whitehead*, ed. Ivor Leclerc (London: George Allen and Unwin, 1961), pp. 219-231.

24. David Bohm, *Causality and Chance in Modern Physics* (Philadelphia: University of Pennsylvania Press, 1957), p. 147.

25. Milic Capek, *The Philosophical Impact of Contemporary Physics* (Princeton: Van Nostrand, 1961), p. 391. (Italics his.)

26. Bohm, *Causality and Chance in Modern Physics*, p. 157. (Italics his.)

27. The fuller phrasing is:
    "That every condition to which the process of becoming conforms in any particular instance, has its reason *either* in the character of some actual entity in the actual world of that concrescence, *or* in the character of the subject which is in the process of concrescence." (*PR* 36.) (Italics in both passages his.)

28. Stuart Hampshire, *Thought and Action* (London: Chatto and Windus, 1959), p. 88.

29. Whitehead points out that even such a prehension still has a "subjective form" (*PR* 35).

30. See Sheila O'Flynn Brennan, "Substance Within Substance," *Process Studies* VII:1 (Spring, 1977), pp. 14-26 where the "vector" character of feeling is stressed regarding the components of the later instance of becoming.

31. Bryant Keeling, "Feeling as a Metaphysical Category: Hartshorne from an Analytical View," *Process Studies*, Vol. VI, Number 1 (Spring, 1976), pp. 51-56. While Keeling's critique is directed against Hartshorne, Whitehead's work could also serve as target.

32. In another phrasing the mental operations are said "to achieve, in the immediate subject, the subjective aim of that subject as to the satisfaction to be obtained from its own initial data. In this way the decision derived from the actual world, which is the efficient cause, is completed by the decision embodied in the subjective aim which is the final cause" (*PR* 423).

33. Whitehead adds the immediate caution that "conceptual [mental] feelings do not necessarily involve consciousness."

34. Capek, *The Philosophical Impact of Contemporary Physics*, p. 344. (Italics his.)

35. See Edward Pols, *Whitehead's Metaphysics: A Critical Examination of Process and Reality* (Carbondale, Illinois: Southern Illinois University Press, 1967) and *The Southern Journal of Philosophy*, Vol. VII, No. 4 (Winter, 1969-1970) for a good sample of discussion of the issue by Cobb, Ford, and Pols.

36. Weiss makes this point forcefully in an unpublished interview with Lewis Ford, "Recollections of Alfred North Whitehead," January 30, 1974.
37. Thus Søren Kierkegaard can write: "The only reality that exists for an existing individual is his own ethical reality. To every other reality he stands in a cognitive relation; but true knowledge consists in translating the real into the possible." *The Concluding Unscientific Postscript to the Philosophical Fragments*, trans. by David F. Swenson (Princeton: Princeton University Press, 1944), p. 280.
38. Cecil J. Schneer, "Science and History," pp. 122-149, in *The Concept of Order*, ed. Paul G. Knutz (Seattle: University of Washington Press, 1968), pp. 127-128.
39. Colors characterize the given entity without being involved in the history of that entity; as such, they have a distinctive contingency. Cf. Hampshire, *Thought and Action*, pp. 15-36:

> In any discussion of classification, one returns always to colours, marked by the specific colour adjectives which, unlike any other adjectives seem like names of the shades they stand for. The same, indiscriminable shade, precisely identifiable by its name, may recur again in experience. . . . Specific colour adjectives, and indeed the whole system of colour descriptions are unique within the vocabulary in the conditions of the applications. There are no other sensory predicates that are entirely determinate in the same sense.

40. Lewis Ford, *Two Process Philosophers*, pp. 61-62.
41. For a helpful amplification of this argument see Lewis S. Ford, "Process Philosophy and Our Knowledge of God," pp. 85-115, in *Traces of God in a Secular Culture*, ed. G. F. McLean (New York: Alva, 1973), especially pp. 108ff.
42. Above, p. 54.
43. Cf. Lewis Ford, *Two Process Philosophers*, pp. 61-62.
44. William A. Christian, "The Concept of God as a Derivative Notion," in *Process and Divinity*, ed. by William L. Reese and Eugene Freeman (LaSalle, Illinois: Open Court, 1964), p. 183.
45. Christian, *An Interpretation of Whitehead's Metaphysics*, p. 13. Cf. Ibid., pp. 112-113, 319.
46. Gene Reeves in "God and Creativity," *The Southern Journal of Philosophy*, VII:4 (Winter, 1969-1970), pp. 377-386, worries that John B. Cobb, Jr. may have erred in this direction in his attempt *(A Christian Natural Theology*, pp. 203-214) to argue that God is *the* decisive factor in creation in a "Whiteheadian" doctrine of God, if not in "Whitehead's" doctrine of God. More recently Cobb seems to have moved clearly in the other direction. Thus in "Buddhist Emptiness and the Christian God," in *Journal of the American Academy of Religion*, XLV:1 (March, 1977), pp. 11-26, he argues that

> within process theology, but also wherever Biblical faith is primary, God must be identified with the principle of rightness rather than with the metaphysical ultimate. The problem for Christian theology is then the right understanding of this principle in its purity and distinctness instead of the effort to unite with it the metaphysical ultimate. To this task Whitehead has himself made a contribution whose full meaning has not yet been grasped or appropriated by his followers (pp. 21-22).

47. This seems to be the direction in which Robert C. Neville argues in "Whitehead on the One and the Many," in *The Southern Journal of Philosophy*, VII:4 (Winter, 1969-1970), pp. 387-394. There (p. 392) he summarizes his argument in *God the Creator* (Chicago: University of Chicago Press, 1968):

> . . . anything determinate is created, in the ontological sense. Applied to Whitehead, creativity is determinate vis-a-vis one and many in the category of the

ultimate; and therefore the ultimate category descriptive of the world and the ontological character of the world it describes, are created in the ontological sense. I am still, in this chapter, examining the metaphysical roles of "God" and "Creativity," holding in abeyance the matter of theological evaluation and appropriation.

48. Above, Chapter I, pp. 44-50.

49. Christian, *An Interpretation of Whitehead's Metaphysics*, p. 403.

50. Lewis S. Ford, "Can Whitehead Provide for Real Subjective Agency? A Reply to Edward Pols's Critique," *The Modern Schoolman*, 47:2 (January, 1970), p. 223. As this line of thought is developed, it would provide a response to the criticism of philosophers like Justus Buchler who accuse Whitehead of elevating a certain mode of being, actuality, to a privileged position as the "really real." See David M. Brahinsky's unpublished doctoral dissertation, "Metaphysical Generality and the Principle of Ontological Parity. An Examination of the Ontology of Justus Buchler in comparison with the Cosmology of Alfred North Whitehead," State University of New York at Binghamton, 1976.

51. William J. Garland, "The Ultimacy of Creativity" in *The Southern Journal of Philosophy*, VII:4 (Winter, 1969-1970), p. 366.

52. Ford, "Can Whitehead Provide for Real Subjective Agency? A Reply to Edward Pols's Critique." Later in *The Modern Schoolman*, XLIX:2, January, 1972, p. 152, Ford writes:

Only that which is either definite or determinate can be prehended, and creativity, as such, is neither. I do not see, however, that power must be either definite or determinate, and therefore understand creativity to be the power of determination which *enables* some occasion to become fully determinate. . . . To enable something to become determinate seems to me to be a perfectly good meaning for power, and we cannot require power in this sense to be fully determinate without involving us in a vicious regress (Italics his).

Garland, "The Ultimacy of Creativity," p, 368, points out that "only one principle in Whitehead's system can be legitimately cited in ultimate explanations. All other principles must finally be grounded upon specific actual entities."

53. Cf. *PR* 326-327: "To sum up: There are two species of process, macroscopic process, and microscopic process. The macroscopic process is the transition from attained actuality to actuality in attainment; while the microscopic process is the conversion of conditions which are merely real into determinate actuality. The former process effects the transition from the 'actual' to the 'merely real'; and the latter process effects the growth from the real to the actual. The former process is efficient; the latter process is teleological."

54. Capek, *The Philosophical Impact of Contemporary Physics*, p. 385 (Italics his). Earlier (pp. 206-207) Capek draws from Whitehead's *The Concept of Nature* to differentiate "the universal 'creative advance of nature' from the discordant time series which are its various complementary manifestations." Cf. Bohm, *Causality and Chance in Modern Physics*, pp. 125ff., where a causal explanation of quantum mechanics is combined with indeterminacy theory. See also Henry Pierce Stapp, "Quantum Mechanics, Local Causality, and Process Philosophy," edited by William B. Jones, pp. 173-182 and Charles Hartshorne, "Bell's Theorem and Stapp's Revised View of Space-Time," pp. 183-191 in *Process Studies*, VII:3 (Fall, 1977). Stapp notes that "spatially separated parts of reality must be related in some way that goes beyond the familiar idea that causal connections propagate only into the forward light-cone" (p. 184). Hartshorne notes that this sense of biconditioning does not entail the strict interdependence of absolute mutuality. Thus "it is time's one-way dependence, not space's symmetrical

dependence or interdependence, that is the clue to reality in general or as such" (p. 187).

55. PR 359 notes: "Prehensions are not atomic; they can be divided into other prehensions and combined into other prehensions."

56. Christian, *An Interpretation of Whitehead's Metaphysics*, p. 66. (Italics his.) Here Christian does seem to allow a second-order principle of explanation within first-order actuality, though the second sentence may suggest a merely metaphorical reading of creativity.

57. Cf. *PR* 351, for a discussion of how several percipients can share the same complex togetherness. See also the discussion by Stapp and Hartshorne identified in note 54 above.

58. Capek, *The Philosophical Impact of Contemporary Physics*, p. 222.

59. Ibid., p. 377. He adds this qualification:

> The spatial relation of juxtaposition implies a complete mutual *externality* of the *static* elements, whereas in polyphonic movement the component melodies not only proceed together toward the future but also overlap "transversally," so to speak, without losing melodic individuality and autonomy. But while the dynamic togetherness of the component melodies is different from the static relation of juxtaposition, it is on the other hand akin to what we called the *co-existence* or rather *co-becoming* or *co-fluidity* of world tubes in relativistic time-space (Italics his).

Cf. Ibid., p. 373.

60. See Cobb, *A Christian Natural Theology*, Chapter 4.

61. Cf., for example, Lewis Ford, *Two Process Philosophers*, p. 61:

> . . . all of God's conceptual entertainment of eternal objects with respect to time requires propositional feeling. The integration of his pure conceptual feelings of the eternal objects with indicative feelings derived from his consequent nature is the way in which portions of the primordial nature become temporarily emergent.

62. Thus John Hick *(Evil and the God of Love* [London: Macmillan, 1966, Fontana Library edition, 1968], p. 36) is in error in classifying Whitehead as an instance of internal dualisms "that locate the opposition to God within the divine nature itself." It is creativity that plays this comprehensive role in Whitehead's thought.

63. Lewis Ford, "Whitehead's Categoreal Derivation of Divine Existence," pp. 374-400 in *Monist*, 54, 1970, pp. 27-28. Cf. his statement in *Two Process Philosophers*, p. 69:

> Yet metaphysical principles can be created if we permit nontemporal activity accompanying the temporal process, situated neither at the purported beginning of time nor somewhere in its middle. The primordial act is not a decision amid antecedent possibility, for it is the very creation of possibility itself. I interpret the primordial envisagement to be the activity of interrelating the eternal objects as bare individual essences (sheer qualities) by providing each with its specific ·relational essence, thereby generating a domain of pure possibility. . . . The primordial envisagement is a decision in the sense that it determines which eternal objects are capable of actualization and which are not in the process of creating their relational essences. Alternatively, we may say that God nontemporally decides what the metaphysical principles are.

In *The Lure of God* (Philadelphia: Fortress Press, 1978), pp. 126-128, Ford applies this material to the doctrine of the Trinity.

64. In the next chapter Hartshorne's attempt to restate the ontological argument for God will be considered. On necessity/contingency see the pieces by Christian and Ford identified in notes 44 and 63. See also Donald W. Sherburne, "Whitehead Without

God," pp. 305-330, in *Process Philosophy and Christian Thought,* ed. by Delwin Brown, Ralph E. James, Jr., and Gene Reeves (Indianapolis: Bobbs-Merrill, 1971).
65. Cf. William Christian, "The Concept of God as a Derivative Notion," p. 189:
So the concept of God is introduced at two removes from common public facts. It is not introduced as a direct interpretation of the experienced fact of successiveness, as the notion of temporal actual entities is. It is introduced at a later point, to explain those temporal actual entities. So it is an explanation of an interpretation.
This is not to deny that in his primordial nature God as "unfettered" in his ordering of possibility (unlike all other entities) may be said to be the "one non-derivative actuality" in Whitehead's own phrasing (*PR* 48). But one reaches that concept in dependence upon others.
66. I am following Whitehead in using "atoms" to refer to the discrete irreducible units of becoming rather than to a particular scientific class—"atoms" as distinguished from "electrons." See *PR* 29, 53, 55.
67. For a summary account of a cell, see *PR* 162-163.
68. See *MT* 27-28 for an account of "four types of aggregations of actualities": the inorganic (dominated by the average), the vegetable (exhibiting a democracy of purposeful influences from the parts), the animal (including one central actuality with intricate bodily functioning) and the human (stressing novelty of functioning).
69. On "life as robbery," see *PR* 160-163: "In a museum the crystals are kept under glass cases; in zoological gardens the animals are fed."
70. David Crocker has argued for "dual membership" by which an actual occasion "can be both a member of an entirely living non-social nexus and of an enduring object because it can be both original with respect to some parts of its environment and repetitive with respect to other parts." See his unpublished doctoral dissertation at Yale, "A Whiteheadian Theory of Intentions and Actions," pp. 124-128.
71. John B. Bennett, "Whitehead and Personal Identity," pp. 510-521 in *The Thomist,* XXXVII:3 (July, 1973), pp. 519-520.
72. Cobb, *A Christian Natural Theology,* p. 77.
73. In *AI* 191 Whitehead speaks of how "anticipation of kinship with the future assumes the form of purpose to transform concept into fact." Similarly, the eighth "categoreal obligation" in *PR* 41 speaks of the aim not only at the present but at the "relevant future."
74. William J. Gallagher, "Whitehead's Theory of the Human Person," unpublished doctoral dissertation at the New School for Social Research, 1974, pp. 68-69. See also his article "Whitehead's Psychological Physiology: A Third View," *Process Studies,* IV:4 (Winter, 1974), pp. 263-274. Cf. Crocker, "A Whiteheadian Theory of Intentions and Actions," p. 109, for an argument that the living nexus need not be "regnant" vis-a-vis its inorganic apparatus, but merely "efficacious." In "Whitehead and Merleau-Ponty: Commitment as a Context for Comparison," pp. 145-160, *Process Studies,* VIII:3 (Fall, 1977) Robert Doud tries to develop a similar line by employing the notion of "sedimentation" from Merleau-Ponty.
75. In Gallagher's dissertation, see pp. 76-81, in his article in *Process Studies,* see pp. 266-273.
76. Talcott Parsons provides an interesting comment on the efficacy of the symbolizing apparatus:
The fundamental proposition here is that systems which are low in energy but high in information can control systems which are higher, much higher, in energy and lower in information. . . . I think particularly of the analysis of the mechanism of genetic inheritance, at the level of the total organism species and of the

individual set. That is, the protein molecule referred to as DNA is an information processing system, not an energy system. And it is this which enables the continuity of the organization type of the living organism to be maintained and transmitted from generation to generation. See his article "Order as a Sociological Problem," pp. 373-384, in *The Concept of Order*, ed. by Paul Kuntz (Seattle: University of Washington Press, 1968), p. 380.

77. For a succinct summary along these lines see Charles Hartshorne, "Personal Identity from A to Z," *Process Studies*, II:3 (Fall, 1972), pp. 209-215. In "Of Time, the Self, and Rem Edwards," *Process Studies*, VII:1 (Spring, 1977), pp. 40-43, Robert Fancher notes that the notion of "gaps" between occasions depends on a notion Whitehead abandons: the notion of time as an independent container for actual entities.

78. See above, p. 85.

79. See also Whitehead's *Symbolism: Its Meaning and Effect*.

80. F. David Martin, *Art and the Religious Experience: The "Language" of the Sacred* (Lewisburg: Bucknell University Press, 1972), pp. 183-184. Whitehead's suggestion that presentational immediacy is particularly dominant in visual perception is beautifully amplified by Martin's discussion of painting. In this discussion we have not appealed to causal connections within the "contemporary" world, although Bell's theorem (see note 54 above) may invite some modification of Whitehead's views of perception.

81. David L. Hall, *The Civilization of Experience: A Whiteheadian Theory of Culture* (New York: Fordham University Press, 1973), p. 95. (Italics his.)

82. For a useful summary, see A. H. Johnson's *Whitehead's Philosophy of Civilization* (New York: Beacon, 1958; Dover, 1962), pp. 121-123.

83. *AI*, Chapters 16 and 17.

84. W. Widick Schroeder, *Cognitive Structures and Religious Research* (East Lansing: Michigan State University Press, 1970), pp. 127-131.

85. Johnson, *Whitehead's Philosophy of Civilization*, p. 171. (Italics his.)

86. Whitehead, "An Appeal to Sanity," pp. 44-59 in *Essays in Science and Philosophy* (London: Rider and Company, 1948), p. 45.

87. See, for example, Hall, *The Civilization of Experience*, pp. 68-78.

88. Johnson, *Whitehead's Philosophy of Civilization*, p. 180. Yet in his other work, *Whitehead's Theory of Reality* (New York: Beacon, 1952; Dover, 1962), pp. 180-181, Johnson is troubled just at this point:

> The human subject seems to be more than the sum of integrated feelings. . . . If there is, to begin with, no center of feeling to which the feelings add content, then the feelings appear to be substantives rather than relational processes. . . . This theory seems to bear witness to a fear of substance rather than a completely accurate report of observed fact.

89. Hampshire, *Thought and Action*, pp. 21-22. Cf. Whitehead's reservations in Chapter 1 of *Process and Reality*.

90. Still, perspectives are not interchangeable and it is desirable to seek the most comprehensive order. Ian Barbour, *(Myths, Models and Paradigms: A Comparative Study in Science and Religion* [New York: Harper, 1974]) helpfully points out (pp. 113-114): (1) While data are theory-laden, rival theories are not incommensurable. (2) While theories are resistant to falsification, observation does exert some control over them. (3) There are independent criteria of assessment—simplicity, coherence, extent and variety of supporting evidence. These insights from the field of science point the way for metaphysical method as well.

91. David Tracy, *Blessed Rage for Order* (New York: Seabury, 1975), p. 67.

92. Van Harvey seems to make much of the disagreement when he writes:
    The difficulty the alienated theologian has with metaphysics as the basis for reli-
    gious belief is rooted in his dubiety about the enterprise itself, a dubiety he
    shares with a great number of contemporary philosophers. Many reasons can be
    given for this dubiety, but the most obvious one arises as one confronts the
    radical and fundamental disagreements among metaphysicians themselves regard-
    ing almost every aspect of their enterprise.
    ("The Alienated Theologian," pp. 113-143 in *The Future of Philosophical Theology*
    ed. Robert Evans [Philadelphia: Westminster, 1971]), p. 123.
    My image of "interaction" suggests more elliptical relationships than "metaphysics as
    basis for belief," as the first chapter has argued at length. More to the point is Mal-
    colm Diamond's challenge:
    The buttressing of one questionable enterprise (theology) by means of an appeal
    to the insights of another questionable enterprise (Whiteheadian metaphysics) is
    not likely to compel attention from thinkers who are not already involved with one
    or the other of them.
    ("Metaphysical Target and Theological Victim," pp. 143-170 in *Process Philosophy
    and Christian Thought*, ed. by Brown, James, and Reeves), p. 169.
    I do not propose as ambitious a "buttressing" as Hartshorne's, against whose work
    Diamond's piece seems explicitly directed. But of course I do seek aid of one sort
    or another—tactical, conceptual, ethical, or constitutive. While that aid is sought for
    the people of faith, it depends on the kind of descriptive adequacy which would be
    of interest presumably to the analytic philosophers, who launch the salvo to which
    Diamond refers. Thus I quite agree with Diamond's statement that "in philosophy
    as in science, the fruitfulness of a theory is in direct proportion to the variety of
    kinds of circumstances to which it finds application" (ibid.) and would add theology
    to his list.

93. See Pepper, *World Hypotheses*, pp. 344-347. Cf. Hans-Georg Gadamer, *Wahrheit
    und Methode: Grundzüge einer philosophischen Hermeneutik* (Tübingen: JCB Mohr,
    1965), pp. 1-39.

94. Antony Flew, *God and Philosophy* (London: Hutchison & Co., 1966), pp. 27-29.

95. Crocker, "A Whiteheadian Theory of Intentions and Actions," pp. 9-10. He also notes
    that speculative philosophy must address the issue of how these several kinds of
    "experience" are related to each other.

96. See note 4 above. Hartshorne accepts the validity of such empirical debate, even
    though his work seems particularly to stress the "rational" criteria. In fact, he makes
    such an appeal:
    My own conviction that reality is indeed an "ocean of feelings" (Whitehead's
    phrase) was reached at an early age, without conscious reference to any philo-
    sopical writer or teacher, and was based, as I know from conversation White-
    head's was, upon an attempted analysis of immediate experience, where alone
    reality can be encountered.
    *Whitehead's Philosophy* (Lincoln, Nebraska: University of Nebraska Press, 1972),
    p. 148. See also note 17 above.

97. Thus Lanis Scott Smith, "Critical Observations on Whitehead's Approach to Specula-
    tive Metaphysics in the Light of Kant's Criticisms," unpublished doctoral dissertation,
    Columbia University, 1976, argues that Whitehead's attempt to interpret every item
    of reality within a single scheme of facts fails to deal adequately with such Kantian
    distinctions as that between things as perceived and things as they are in themselves.
    This is a familiar theological criticism as well.

98. Peter F. Drucker, *Landmarks of Tomorrow* (New York: Harper, 1957), p. 4. Drucker deals with psychology, social sciences, economics and linguistics as examples.

99. See, for example, Ervin Laszlo's *Introduction to Systems Philosophy: Toward a New Paradigm of Contemporary Thought* (New York: Gordon and Breach, 1972). A considerable range of such literature is identified by Robert L. Moore in his review article "Process Philosophy and General Systems Theory," pp. 291-300, *Process Studies* IV:4 (Winter, 1974).

100. Charles Hartshorne, "Why Psychicalism? Comments on Keeling's and Shepherd's Criticisms," pp. 67-72, *Process Studies*, VI:1 (Spring, 1976), p. 72.

101. Page 73, note 31 above.

102. John S. Lawrence, "Whitehead's Failure," pp. 427-435, *The Southern Journal of Philosophy*, VII:4 (Winter 1969-1970), p. 432.

103. For example, David Bohm, *Causality and Chance in Modern Physics*, p. 148, in speaking of change in the basic qualities defining the modes of being of entities, writes:
    Such motions are not inessential disturbances superimposed from outside on an otherwise statically existing kind of matter. Rather, they are inherent and indispensable to what matter is.
    See pages 67-68 and notes 24 and 25 above.

104. Barbour, *Myths, Models, and Paradigms*, p. 170.

105. Pols, *Whitehead's Metaphysics*.

106. Ibid., p. 134.

107. Above, pp. 83-86.

108. Alfred North Whitehead, "Time" (1926), reprinted in *The Interpretation of Science: Selected Essays*, ed. A. H. Johnson (Indianapolis: Bobbs-Merrill, 1961), p. 241. (Italics mine.)
    Lewis Ford works with this passage in his article "On Genetic Successiveness: A Third Alternative," pp. 421-426, *The Southern Journal of Philosophy*, VII:4 (Winter, 1969-1970). He proposes that temporality be identified with supersession, "recognizing two species, physical and genetic time" (p. 424). John Cobb resists limiting the choices for interpreting genetic successiveness to temporal or logical order, but seems to incline toward the latter in writing:
    Whole and parts come into being together. The whole is equally the subject of the one act of becoming and the superject or outcome.
    "Freedom in Whitehead's Philosophy: A Response to Edward Pols," pp. 409-414 in *The Southern Journal of Philosophy*, VII:4 (Winter, 1969-1970), p. 413.

109. Søren Kierkegaard, *Either/Or*, trans. by David F. Swenson, Lillian M. Swenson, and Walter Lowrie (2 vols.; Princeton: Princeton University Press, 1944), Vol. II, p. 179.

110. Above, pp. 95-96.

111. Crocker, "A Whiteheadian Theory of Intentions and Actions," p. 135. See also Robert Fancher, "Of Time, the Self, and Rem Edwards," *Process Studies*, VII:1 (Spring, 1977), pp. 40-43.

112. A. R. Louch, *Explanation and Human Action* (Berkeley: University of California Press, 1966), p. 234.

113. On the interaction of efficient and final causation, see Crocker, "A Whiteheadian Theory of Intentions and Actions," pp. 68-70. See also P. F. Strawson, *Individuals* (New York: Doubleday, 1963) and Michael McLain, "On Theological Models," *Harvard Theological Review*, LXII (1969), pp. 155-187.

114. See the linkages suggested between identity and intent on the one hand, and identity and responsibility on the other, in W. Donald Oliver, "Order and Personality," pp. 309-321 in *The Concept of Order*, ed. Paul Kuntz.

115. Above, page 95.

116. Crocker, "A Whiteheadian Theory of Intentions and Actions." See also Nicholas F. Gier, "Intentionality and Prehension," pp. 197-213, *Process Studies* VI:3 (Fall, 1976). Crocker's conversation is with analytic philosophy, Gier's with phenomenology.
117. Edward Pols, *Meditation on a Prisoner* (Carbondale: Southern Illinois University Press, 1975), p. 104.
118. Ibid., p. 119.
119. See the exchange between Robert Ariel and Dean Fowler in *Process Studies*, IV:4 (Winter, 1974).
120. Bohm, *Causality and Chance in Modern Physics*, pp. 139-140.
121. Errol Harris, *The Foundations of Metaphysics in Science* (New York: Humanities Press, 1965), p. 141. Cf. pp. 200, 225. Harris finds this ordering to be the more striking because it stands against the grain of the tendency toward disorder expressed in the second law of thermodynamics (pp. 173, 197, 216, 242-243). Cf. Whitehead, *The Function of Reason*, pp. 89-90. See also Murray Code, "Toward a Whiteheadian Philosophy of Mathematics," pp. 23-65 in *Philosophia Mathematica*, XII:1 (Summer, 1975) and Granville C. Henry Jr., *Logos: Mathematics and Christian Theology* (Lewisburg: Bucknell University Press, 1976).
122. See Dale H. Porter, "History as Process," *History and Theory*, XIV:3 (1975), pp. 297-313.
123. Arnold Toynbee, "Individuality and Unpredictability of Human Affairs," pp. 43-59 in *The Concept of Order*, ed. Paul Kuntz, p. 59.
124. This summation is by Bennett in *Process Studies*, VI:2 (Summer, 1976), pp. 145-146. The full article may be seen in *Journal of Thought*, X:1 (January, 1975), pp. 24-30, under the title "Ecology and Philosophy: Whitehead's Contribution." A full-scale consideration is available in John B. Cobb's *Is It Too Late? A Theology of Ecology* (Beverly Hills: Bruce, 1972).
125. Thus Pols can conclude in his *Whitehead's Metaphysics: A Critical Examination of Process and Reality* with a chapter on "The Platonism of Whitehead," pp. 159-195.
126. See the reference cited in note 64.
127. Thus in his unpublished interview with Lewis Ford, "Recollections of Alfred North Whitehead," January 30, 1974, p. 24, Weiss states:
    I also object, of course, to the supposition that he's maintaining the ontological principle in his application of the categories to God. Since they are there applied in a reverse way and therefore strictly speaking, are not the same categories but the reverse of the initial categories applied to particular finite actualities. Cf. above, p. 79, for a tentative response.
128. While I have stressed the giving of the subjective aim, Whitehead further makes clear (*PR* 434-436) how that role bears on the occasion's "standpoint" in the extensive continuum:
    [The standpoint will be] consonant with the subjective aim in its original derivation from God. Here "God" is that actuality in the world, in virtue of which there is physical "law" (p. 434).

## 3: Projects: A Sketch of Current and Recent Theological Appropriation

1. See above, Chapter 2, pp. 78ff.
2. Above, pp. 78-79. See W. E. Hocking, "Whitehead, as I knew him," in *Alfred North Whitehead: Essays on His Philosophy*, ed. George Kline (Englewood Cliffs: Prentice-Hall, 1963), p. 16:
    Of the concept of God, primordial and consequent, he said to me: "I should never have included it, if it had not been strictly required for descriptive com-

pleteness. You must set all your essentials into the foundation. It's no use putting up a set of terms and then remarking, 'Oh, by the by, I believe there's a God.' " This would seem to give the consequent nature a stronger rootage in experience than the discussion in Chapter 2 allows.

3. In this connection Whitehead notes the occasioning significance of travel for the broadening of religious outlook.

4. Cf. *RM* 81: "Religion requires a metaphysical backing; for its authority is endangered by the intensity of the emotions which it generates. Such emotions are evidence of some vivid experience; but they are a very poor guarantee for its correct interpretation."

5. See above, pp. 85-87.

6. See above, pp. 87-90.

7. See above, pp. 87-90.

8. See above, pp. 84-85.

9. Whitehead, *Process and Reality*, p. 94. See above, pp. 68-69.

10. Lewis S. Ford, ed., *Two Process Philosophers: Hartshorne's Encounter with Whitehead* (Tallahassee, Florida: American Academy of Religion, 1973), p. 74.

11. See above, pp. 68-69.

12. Cf. *PR* 524-525:
The perfection of God's subjective aim, derived from the completeness of his primordial nature, issues into the character of his consequent nature. . . . The wisdom of the subjective aim prehends every actuality for what it can be in such a perfected system. . . .

13. See A. H. Johnson, "Whitehead as Teacher and Philosopher," pp. 351-376, in *Philosophy and Phenomenological Research*, XXIX (1969), p. 369:
. . . Whitehead commented that God's immediacy doesn't "die." There is no elimination in God's nature as such. There is, of course, elimination of some of the data presented for inclusion in God's nature.

14. Perhaps one could try to claim that the only impediments are "cosmological," as distinguished from "metaphysical." See the discussion above, p. 64. Yet the difficulty seems genuinely metaphysical.

15. Ford, *Two Process Philosophers*, p. 74.

16. Lewis S. Ford and Marjorie Suchocki, "A Whiteheadian Reflection of Subjective Immortality," *Process Studies*, VII:1 (Spring, 1977), pp. 1-13. A note indicates that the authors have subsequently separated on this issue. Suchocki has written "The Question of Immortality," pp. 288-306 in *The Journal of Religion*, LVII:3 (July, 1977) in which she argues from God's knowledge of an occasion's first ("dative" or given) and third ("determinate" or being) stages that God could "reenact" the second: the living immediacy of the occasion. To me this seems unconvincing, and suggests a troublesome reversal of the rhythm of the stages in the concrescence. Ford's position is well indicated in *The Lure of God* (Philadelphia: Fortress, 1978), p. 114ff.

17. In a student journal of theology circulated at Luther Theological Seminary, St. Paul, Jonathan Strandjord makes an intriguing attempt to respond to this difficulty by employing Whitehead's concept of shifts in cosmic epochs. See his "Do Not Go Gentle Into That Good Night, Rage, Rage Against the Dying of the Light," pp. 32-49, *Praxis*, unnumbered and undated.

18. The triadic description suggests that my discussion may have neglected the "superjective" aspect of God, by which the consequent feeling of the world ("critic") so qualifies the primordial ("condition") as to yield the ideal. See *PR* 134-135 and 531-533. For a secondary discussion, see John W. Lansing, "The 'Natures' of Whitehead's God," pp. 143-153 in *Process Studies*, III:3 (Fall, 1973) and L. Ford's "Is There a

Distinct Superjective Nature?" pp. 228-229 in the same issue. With respect to the issue of justification, the primordial and superjective come together to identify the (general or particular) will of God for the world.

19. Bernard Meland, "The Empirical Tradition in Theology at Chicago," pp. 1-62, in *The Future of Empirical Theology,* ed. Bernard Meland (Chicago: University of Chicago Press, 1969), p. 31.

20. See ibid. and Randolph Crump Miller, *The American Spirit in Theology* (Philadelphia: United Church Press, 1974). Of this tradition Miller writes (p. 17):

> It is more than an appeal to experience, which every philosopher and theologian accepts at least covertly. Even if the experience being interpreted is private or in one's solitariness, it provides data which are open to public inspection. In principle, at least, everyone can see for himself or herself what the theologian is talking about. Because the testing is open to inspection, it is self-correcting. . . . The meaning of experience in the last analysis is tested by how it works out, and thus empiricism and pragmatism remain wedded in American thought.

21. In his first work, *Religious Experience and Scientific Method* (New York: Macmillan, 1926), Wieman already shows the interest in Whitehead which persists into his own "middle period." (See, for example, *The Source of Human Good* [Chicago: University of Chicago Press, 1948.]) As an example of the late Wieman, see *Religious Inquiry: Some Explorations* (Boston: Beacon, 1968). A. H. Johnson ("Whitehead as Teacher and Philosopher," p. 372) cites Whitehead as saying that Wieman "starts off admirably, but, finally, being in an intellectual funk, divests it of all meaning." Johnson interprets the reference as one to Wieman's anti-metaphysical bent.

22. For example, among Claremont graduates are Delwin Brown and Richard Overman. Brown has contributed as an essayist ("Freedom and Faithfulness in Whitehead's God," pp. 137-148, *Process Studies,* II:2 [Summer, 1972]) and editor (*Process Philosophy and Christian Thought* [Indianapolis: Bobbs-Merrill, 1971.]) Overman has written *Evolution and the Christian Doctrine of Creation* (Philadelphia: Westminster, 1967).

23. See Miller, *The American Spirit in Theology,* pp. 14-19. See also Sidney E. Mead, *The Lively Experiment* (New York: Harper & Row, 1963), Chapter One.

24. The appropriation is guarded and selective. Thus in a later work Thornton seems more interested in Whitehead's organic metaphysics than in the "misleading half-truth that religion is what a man does with his own solitariness" (*Revelation and the Modern World* [London: Dacre, 1950], pp. 261, 304).

25. Other thematic emphases are indicated by Pittenger's titles: *God in Process* (London: SCM, 1967), *God's Way with Man: A Study of the Relationship Between God and Man in Providence, "Miracle," and Prayer* (London: Hodder & Stoughton, 1969), *The "Last Things" in a Process Perspective* (London: Epworth Press, 1970), and *The Holy Spirit* (Philadelphia: United Church Press, 1974).

26. See *Making Sexuality Human* (Philadelphia: United Church Press, 1970), *Time for Consent: A Christian's Approach to Homosexuality* (London: SCM Press, 1970), *Love and Control in Sexuality* (Philadelphia: United Church Press, 1974).

27. Peter Hamilton has written *The Living God and the Modern World* (London: Hodder & Stoughton, 1967). See also articles by David A. Pailin: "The Incarnation as a Continuing Reality," *Religious Studies,* VI:4 (December, 1970), pp. 303-327, and "Process Theology—Why and What?" *Faith and Thought,* C:1 (1972-1973), pp. 45-66. For an indication of similar interest, see the *Anglican Theological Review,* LV:2 (April, 1973).

28. See, for example, Nicholas Berdyaev, *Freedom and the Spirit,* trans. O. Clarke (New York: Charles Scribner's Sons, 1935) and Piet Schoonenberg, *The Christ: A Study*

*of the God-Man Relationship in the Whole of Creation and in Jesus Christ,* trans. Della Couling (New York: Herder & Herder, 1971).

29. For example, in the area of theology of nature we have Richard Overman's "Hat die Theologie die Natur vergessen?" (*Radius,* September, 1973), and John Cobb's *Der Preiss des Fortscritts* (München: Claudius Verlag, 1972).

30. Alix Parmentier, *La Philosophie de Whitehead et le Probleme de Dieu* (Paris: Beauchesne, 1968). A rather thorough review is available in *Process Studies,* II:2 (Summer, 1972), pp. 159-165.

31. Walter Stokes, "Freedom as Perfection: Whitehead, Thomas and Augustine," *Proceedings of the American Catholic Philosophic Association,* XXXVI (1962), pp. 134-142. We refer below to Tracy's *Blessed Rage for Order.*

32. Bernard Lee, *The Becoming of the Church: A Process Theology of the Structures of Christian Experience* (New York: Paulist Press, 1974). This synthesizing effort is apparent in the work of Ewert Cousins, who has helped to develop Fordham University as a major center of process studies.

33. Lyman Lundeen's *Risk and Rhetoric in Religion: Whitehead's Theory of Language and the Discourse of Faith* (Philadelphia: Fortress Press, 1972) is probably the most considerable work. Charles Curtis discussed process theology in *The Task of Philosophical Theology* (New York: Philosophical Library, 1967) and *Contemporary Protestant Thought* (New York: Bruce, 1970).

34. John B. Cobb, Jr. and David Ray Griffin, *Process Theology: An Introductory Exposition* (Philadelphia: Westminster, 1976), pp. 162-185; Ewert Cousins, *Process Theology: Basic Writings* (New York: Newman, 1971); Delwin Brown, Ralph James, and Gene Reeves, *Process Philosophy and Christian Thought* (Indianapolis: Bobbs-Merrill, 1971); Harry James Cargas and Bernard Lee, *Religious Experience and Process Theology: The Pastoral Implications of a Major Modern Movement* (New York: Paulist, 1976); Robert B. Mellert, *What Is Process Theology?* (New York: Paulist, 1975); W. Norman Pittenger, *Process Thought and the Christian Faith* (New York: Macmillan, 1968); and Cobb and Griffin, *Process Theology: An Introductory Exposition.*

35. William Lad Sessions argues this case convincingly in "Hartshorne's Early Philosophy," pp. 10-34, in Lewis Ford, ed., *Two Process Philosophers: Hartshorne's Encounter with Whitehead* (Tallahassee, Florida: American Academy of Religion, 1973). For a much fuller discussion see Sessions' unpublished doctoral dissertation at Yale University, "A Critical Examination of Dipolar Panentheism," 1971. Hartshorne's own comment is conveniently gathered in *Whitehead's Philosophy: Selected Essays, 1935-1970* (Lincoln: University of Nebraska Press, 1972).

36. Hartshorne, *Whitehead's Philosophy,* p. 109. Ely's celebrated critique is *The Religious Availability of Whitehead's God: A Critical Analysis* (Madison: University of Wisconsin Press, 1942).

37. Charles Hartshorne, *The Divine Relativity: A Social Conception of God* (New Haven: Yale University Press, 1948), p. 27.

38. Ibid.

39. Ibid., pp. 27-28.

40. Ibid., p. 62.

41. Ibid., p. 27.

42. Ibid., p. 25.

43. Charles Hartshorne and William L. Reese, editors, *Philosophers Speak of God* (Chicago: University of Chicago Press, 1953), pp. 3-4.

44. Hartshorne, *The Divine Relativity,* p. 44.

45. Ibid., p. 30.

46. Hartshorne, *Philosophers Speak of God,* pp. 1-15.

47. See Charles Hartshorne, *Aquinas to Whitehead: Seven Centuries of Metaphysics of Religion* (Milwaukee: Marquette University Press, 1976), pp. 50-51. In a characteristic emphasis Hartshorne adds: "I believed there was novelty in God's knowledge and that this did not imply any defect in that knowledge."
48. David R. Griffin, "Hartshorne's Differences from Whitehead," pp. 35-57 in Lewis Ford, ed., *Two Process Philosophers*, p. 40.
49. Hartshorne, "What did Anselm Discover?", pp. 321-333 in John Hick and Arthur C. McGill, *The Many-Faced Argument; Recent Studies on the Ontological Argument for the Existence of God* (New York: Macmillan, 1967), p. 330. (Italics his.)
50. Hartshorne, *The Divine Relativity*, pp. 20-21.
51. Hartshorne, *A Natural Theology for Our Time* (LaSalle, Illinois: Open Court, 1967), pp. 51-52. For a full discussion of the way in which "the concrete" includes "the abstract," see Ralph E. James, *The Concrete God* (Indianapolis: Bobbs-Merrill, 1967).
52. See above, p. 88.
53. See Sessions in Ford, *Two Process Philosophers*, p. 27.
54. Hartshorne, *The Divine Relativity*, p. 124.
55. Hartshorne, Review of John Blyth, *Whitehead's Theory of Knowledge* in *Philosophy and Phenomenological Research*, III:3 (March, 1948), p. 374.
56. Hartshorne, *A Natural Theology for Our Time*, p. 56.
57. Hartshorne, *The Divine Relativity*, p. 58.
58. Ibid., p. 142. See the discussion by Lewis Ford in *Two Process Philosophers*, pp. 77-79. Thus on the epistemological level, Hartshorne regularly argues that it is descriptions of God that are truly literal. See ibid., pp. 36-40.
59. See above, Chapter 2.
60. Hartshorne, *A Natural Theology for Our Time*, p. 56.
61. James, *The Concrete God*, p. 190.
62. In his Yale doctoral dissertation already mentioned, Sessions (p. 261) makes these points in criticism of Hartshorne:
    (1) Intentionality (a triadic relation) is irreducible to inclusion (a dyadic relation). (2) Qualitative superiority requires some irreducibly triadic relation. (3) God's perfection is expressible only in terms of qualitative superiority. (4) Hence any doctrine of God requires some irreducibly triadic relation such as intentionality.
    *The Southern Journal of Philosophy* carries a conversation between Sessions ("Charles Hartshorne and Thirdness," XII:2 [Summer, 1974], pp. 239-251) and Hartshorne ("Synthesis as Polyadic Inclusion: A Reply to Sessions," XIV:2 [Summer, 1976], pp. 245-255).
    See also Frederic F. Fost, "Relativity Theory and Hartshorne's Dipolar Theism," pp. 89-99 in Ford, *Two Process Philosophers*. In the same work David Griffin traces the development by which Hartshorne has given up his strict view of inclusion for the view "that it is enough if each state of the world is necessarily destined to be included in God" (p. 51). But he seems to cling to the notion nonetheless, if the (unknown or unincluded) occasions contemporary to God are to be identified merely as "nascent" and denied actuality until they are known by God. See Hartshorne, *Creative Synthesis and Philosophic Method* (LaSalle, Illinois: Open Court, 1970), p. 151, ". . . actual being is what God does perceive." A similar collapsing distinction is the target of John Hick's critique of Hartshorne's ontological argument, when he writes, *The Many-Faced Argument*, p. 348:
    . . . logical necessity is not a case of ontological necessity, nor vice versa. . . .
    From the concept of God as ontologically necessary we can derive the analytic

truth that if God exists, he exists eternally and *a se*, but we cannot deduce that it is a logically necessary truth that God exists. . . .

63. Schubert Ogden, "Response," pp. 45-57 in *The Perkins School of Theology Journal*, XXVI:2 (Winter, 1973), p. 55. (Italics his.)

64. Schubert Ogden, *The Reality of God and Other Essays* (New York: Harper & Row, 1963), pp. 42-43. As recently as 1978 Ogden seems still to maintain this position. Thus in "Theology and Religious Studies," *Journal of the American Academy of Religion*, XLVI:1 (March, 1978), pp. 3-19, he writes (p. 7): ". . . to be human at all is both to live by faith and to seek understanding." Appealing to acceptance of the environment as a conscious act involving "certain principles of truth, beauty, and goodness" in the case of humans, he contends: "Necessarily implied by this understanding is the confidence that these norms have an unconditional validity and that a life lived in accordance with them is truly worth living."

65. Ibid., p. 69.

66. Ibid., pp. 23, 40.

67. Whitehead, *Process and Reality*, p. 519. Ogden, "The Point of Christology," pp. 375-395 in *The Journal of Religion*, LV:4 (October, 1975), p. 393.

68. Ogden, "The Point of Christology," p. 392. (Italics his.)

69. Ibid., pp. 377-379.

70. Ogden, *The Reality of God*, p. 173. (Italics his.) Cf. Schubert M. Ogden, *Christ Without Myth: A Study Based on the Theology of Rudolf Bultmann* (New York: Harper & Row, 1961), p. 144.

71. See Herbert Braun, "Der Sinn der neutestamentlichen Christologie," *Gesammelte Studien zum Neuen Testament und seiner Umwelt* (Tübingen: J. C. B. Mohr, 1962), pp. 243-282. See also Russell Pregeant, "Matthew's 'Undercurrent' and Ogden's Christology," pp. 181-194 in *Process Studies*, VI:3 (Fall, 1976).

72. Ogden, *Christ Without Myth*, p. 145. (Italics his.)

73. Schubert Ogden, "God and Philosophy: A Discussion with Antony Flew," pp. 161-181, *The Journal of Religion*, XLVIII (1968), p. 170.

74. Ibid., pp. 172-173. Cf. Hartshorne's denial—on logical grounds—"that the experience of evil implies the nonexistence of God" in Hick and McGill, *The Many-Faced Argument*, p. 332.

75. See Frederick J. Streng, "The Task of Theology in the Context of Religious Man," pp. 20-25, in *The Perkins School of Theology Journal*, XXVI:2 (Winter, 1973), pp. 23-24. Regarding such *dis*trust, see the comments by Donald Evans and Michael Novak as reported by Donald M. Mathers, "Dialogue on the Future of Philosophical Theology: A Report," pp. 169-187 in *The Future of Philosophical Theology*, ed. Robert Evans (Philapedphia: Westminster, 1971).

76. Schubert Ogden, "Falsification and Belief," pp. 21-43 in *Religious Studies*, X:1 (March, 1974), p. 40.

77. Ibid., p. 41.

78. Ibid. Ogden has a three-fold distinction. In addition to the strictly metaphysical, he distinguishes propositions bearing on the external sense perception of ourselves and the world ("empirical"), on the one hand; and propositions having to do with an "inner nonsensuous perception of our own existence as mutually related to others and to the inclusive whole of reality as such" ("the existential"), on the other (Ibid., p. 40).

79. David Ray Griffin, *God, Power and Evil: A Process Theodicy* (Philadelphia: Westminster, 1976), especially Chapters 17 and 18. Griffin's position seems an elaboration of Ogden's rejoinder to Anthony Flew (see note 73 above), p. 173:
The very idea of "power," so far as it has any meaning through experience, is

through and through a social idea, connecting capacity to act on or influence the action of others who also are and therefore cannot be simply powerless. Consequently, "omnipotence" cannot possibly mean all the power there is, but only all the power that could conceivably belong to any one individual consistent with there being other individuals on whom omnipotent power is exercised and who also have power, however minimal. But since divine power makes sense at all only in relation to other non-divine powers, which as such could not conceivably act with infallible goodness, the existence of evil in some form and to some degree is only what one should expect. Cf. Hartshorne in note 74 above.

80. David Tracy, *Blessed Rage for Order: The New Pluralism in Theology* (New York: Seabury, 1975), p. 10.
81. Ibid., p. 93.
82. See above, p. 64.
83. Again, this seems to be Hick's objection to Hartshorne's mingling of ontological and logical necessity. See note 62 above.
84. Such would be a succinct statement of Whitehead's understanding as he begins his metaphysical airplane flight in *PR,* Chapter 1.
85. Bernard E. Meland, "Can Empirical Theology Learn Something from Phenomenology?", pp. 283-306 in *The Future of Empirical Theology,* p. 290.
86. Ibid., p. 291.
87. Bernard E. Meland, *Fallible Forms and Symbols: Discourses of Method in a Theology of Culture* (Philadelphia: Fortress, 1976), p. 78.
88. Bernard E. Meland, *The Realities of Faith: The Revelation in Cultural Forms* (New York: Oxford University Press, 1962), p. 257.
89. Ibid., p. 195.
90. Meland, *Fallible Forms and Symbols,* p. 96.
91. Ibid., vii.
92. Meland, *Fallible Forms and Symbols,* p. 100.
93. Ibid.
94. Ibid.
95. Daniel Day Williams, "Truth in Theological Perspective," pp. 242-254, in *The Journal of Religion,* XXVIII:4 (October, 1948), p. 248.
96. Ibid., p. 252.
97. Daniel Day Williams, "How Does God Act?: An Essay in Whitehead's Metaphysics," pp. 161-180, in *Process and Divinity,* ed. by William L. Reese and Eugene Freeman (LaSalle, Illinois: Open Court, 1964), pp. 161, 180.
98. Williams, "Truth in Theological Perspective," p. 250.
99. Ibid., p. 251.
100. Ibid.
101. H. Richard Niebuhr in collaboration with D. D. Williams and James H. Gustafson, *The Purpose of the Church and Its Ministry* (New York: Harper, 1956) and James M. Gustafson, H. Richard Niebuhr and D. D. Williams, *The Advancement of Theological Education* (New York: Harper, 1957).
102. Daniel Day Williams, *The Spirit and the Forms of Love* (New York: Harper & Row, 1968), pp. 114-122.
103. Ibid., pp. 154, 186, 173.
104. Ibid., p. 160.
105. Ibid., p. 38.
106. John B. Cobb, Jr., *A Christian Natural Theology, Based on the Thought of Alfred North Whitehead* (Philadelphia: Westminster, 1955), p. 252.

107. John B. Cobb, Jr., *Christ in a Pluralistic Age* (Philadelphia: Westminster, 1975), p. 88.
108. Cobb, *A Christian Natural Theology*, pp. 279-281.
109. Ibid., p. 12.
110. Ibid., pp. 12-13.
111. Ibid., pp. 264-267. In *John Cobb's Theology in Process*, edited by David Ray Griffin and Thomas J. J. Altizer (Philadelphia: Westminster, 1977) Cobb continues to cling to this dialectic, writing (p. 167):
    . . . the relativity of belief is compatible with strong convictions. Conviction is not certainty about the truth of particular propositions but the sense that a system of belief generally survives well in the encounters with alternatives.
112. Langdon Gilkey, "A Christian Natural Theology," *Theology Today*, XXII:4 (January, 1966), p. 531. (Italics his.)
113. John B. Cobb, Jr., *The Structure of Christian Existence* (Philadelphia: Westminster, 1967), p. 143.
114. Cobb, *Christ in a Pluralistic Age*, p. 17.
115. Ibid., p. 22.
116. Ibid., p. 43.
117. Ibid., p. 87.
118. Ibid.
119. Ibid.
120. Ibid., pp. 104-105.
121. Ibid., pp. 145-146. (Italics mine.)
122. Ibid., p. 203.
123. Ibid.
124. Ibid., p. 204.
125. Ibid., p. 206. Cf. *John Cobb's Theology in Process*, p. 152.
126. Ibid., p. 204.
127. Ibid., pp. 209-220.
128. Ibid., pp. 225-226.
129. John B. Cobb, Jr., " 'Perfection Exists': A Critique of Charles Hartshorne," pp. 293-304 in *Religion in Life*, XXXII:2 (Spring, 1963).
130. See above, p. 124. This is most apparent in Cobb's "Buddhist Emptiness and the Christian God," *Journal of the American Academy of Religion*, XLV:1 (March, 1977), pp. 11-26.
131. John B. Cobb, Jr., "Response to Ogden and Carpenter," pp. 123-129, in *Process Studies*, VI:2 (Summer, 1975), p. 128.
132. Cobb, " 'Perfection Exists': A Critique of Charles Hartshorne," p. 304.
133. Cobb, "Response to Ogden and Carpenter," p. 126.
134. Ibid., p. 123. In responding to his critics in *John Cobb's Theology in Process*, p. 157, Cobb writes:
    I agree . . . that my effort to identify the essence of each structure of existence with the form of its first appearance is misleading. It exaggerates the abruptness of change and the degree of constancy in the periods between what I called threshold crossings. More seriously, it tends to make a past and given form of a movement normative for its further development. Today I would prefer to accept Koch's counterproposal that the "essence" of a thing is its history, or, as I have been more inclined to say, a historical movement has no "essence."
    So to Wolfhart Pannenberg Cobb can respond that the Christian
    . . . movement is not bound to preserve any specifiable doctrine, even of Jesus, although its identity is constituted by the primacy of its memory of that history

of which Jesus is the center, and its healthy continuance depends on constant re-encounter with Jesus and with the earliest witness to his meaning for the church (Ibid., p. 187).

135. Cobb, "Response to Ogden and Carpenter," p. 123.

136. Cobb's comment (in personal conversation) regarding this specific speculation on the controlling force in his thought is: "I think it is based on my perception of modern history." Thus Cobb can distinguish his work from a colleague's as follows:

Neville's approach is primarily philosophical. Mine is more historical or eschatological. That is, Neville seeks unity through the mind's universal grasp of value and through a philosophical anthropology. I look for a movement toward unity through the actual encounter of two highly diverse structures of existence, each being modified by its specific appreciation for the other. Instead of directly seeking a universal structure that synthesizes all, I hope for a transformation of the Christian structure through Buddhism and a transformation of the Buddhist structure through Christianity. *(John Cobb's Theology in Process, p. 161.)*

While modern history cannot be the peculiar province of either faith or reason alone, I tend to link this response with Whitehead's empirical understanding of metaphysics. Wolfhart Pannenberg seems to make a similar judgment in "A Liberal Logos Christology: The Christology of John Cobb" (Ibid., pp. 133-149), when he argues that

. . . the concept of "creative transformation" or "creative formation" is by no means simply identical with the concept of the logos, because it signifies God's creative activity altogether, working together in the Father, Son, and Spirit. To that extent it is more encompassing than the Logos concept, which in turn is to be defined as a partial aspect of creative transformation or creative formation (p. 148).

137. Cargas and Lee, *Religious Experience and Process Theology*, pp. 79-136.

138. Gene Reeves and Delwin Brown provide an introduction to the debate in the volume they have edited with Ralph James, *Process Philosophy and Christian Thought*, pp. 39-40. The basic positions are well represented by Cobb, *Christian Natural Theology*, pp. 176-185 (the societal view) and Lewis Ford, "The Non-Temporality of Whitehead's God," pp. 347-376 in *International Philosophical Quarterly*, XIII:3 (September, 1973). (The entitative view.)

139. See above, pp. 87-90.

140. See Part III of William Christian's *An Interpretation of Whitehead's Metaphysics* (New Haven: Yale University Press, 1959). Among the many articles by Ford bearing on this point are: "Process Trinitarianism," *The Journal of the American Academy of Religion*, XLIII (1975), pp. 199-213, and "Boethius and Whitehead on Time and Eternity," *International Philosophical Quarterly*, VIII:1 (March, 1968), pp. 38-67.

141. Ford, "Boethius and Whitehead on Time and Eternity," p. 65.

142. Ford, "The Non-Temporality of Whitehead's God," p. 376.

143. David R. Griffin, *A Process Christology* (Philadelphia: Westminster, 1973), especially Chapter 9, "God's Supreme Act of Self-Expression," pp. 206-232. See also Lewis Ford's appreciative criticism of Griffin in "The Possibilities for Process Christology," *Encounter*, XXXV:4 (1974), pp. 281-294.

144. Griffin, *A Process Christology*, p. 220. (Italics his.)

145. Ibid., pp. 154-157.

146. John B. Cobb, Jr., and David Ray Griffin, *Mind in Nature: Essays on the Interface of Science and Philosophy* (Washington, D.C.: University Press of America, 1977).

147. For the distinction between "concrescence" and "transition," see above, pp. 76-77.

148. Cobb, "Buddhist Emptiness and the Christian God," pp. 23-24. (Italics mine.)

## 4: Proposal: Metaphysics as Faith's Servant: Filling the Categories

1. See above, p. 93.
2. Stanley Burnshaw, *The Seamless Web* (New York: George Braziller, Inc., 1970), p. 30.
3. See above, pp. 63-71, 96-102.
4. Frank Morley, *The Great North Road* (New York: Macmillan, 1961). For a principaled statement see *AI* 184-185:
    . . . any doctrine which refuses to place a human experience outside nature, must find in descriptions of human experience factors which also enter into the descriptions of less specialized natural occurrences. If there be no such factors, then the doctrine of human experience as a fact within nature is a mere bluff.
5. See above, pp. 98-99. Whitehead's account of error at this point does assign responsibility to the body in the "mixed mode of symbolic reference." Thus in *PR* 274 Whitehead writes:
    In the mixed mode, the perceptive determination is purely due to the bodily organs, and thus there is a gap in the perceptive logic—so to speak. This gap is not due to any conceptual freedom on the part of the ultimate subject. It is not a mistake due to consciousness. It is due to the fact that the body, as an instrument for synthesizing and enhancing feelings, is faulty, in the sense that it produces feelings which have but slight reference to the real state of the presented duration.
    Thus in "trying to trust" the body, it will be important to try to get back behind the mixed mode to the more fundamental mode of causal efficacy. One may recognize such an effort in the work of Fritz Perls. See, for example, his *The Gestalt Approach and Eyewitness to Therapy* (Palo Alto, California: Science and Behavior Books, 1973), p. 64.
    It does seem to be the case that effectiveness is impeded—both on the scale of the individual and on that of the group—when in the originality of reflection the organism is not permitted to act on the natural wisdom of the body. Alexander Lowen seems to have an intuitive grasp of this point in *The Betrayal of the Body* (New York: Macmillan, 1967), though he lacks the discrimination which the Whiteheadian distinction between causal efficacy and presentational immediacy can provide. For a discussion of "the mysterious and polymorphic relation between 'context' and 'content'" in both anatomy and linguistics, see Gregory Bateson, *Steps to An Ecology of Mind* (New York: Random House, 1972), Ballantine edition, pp. 154ff.
6. See the discussion by Donald Stone in "The Human Potential Movement," pp. 93-115, in *The New Religious Consciousness,* ed. Charles Y. Glock and Robert N. Bellah (Berkeley: University of California Press, 1976).
7. See Shirley Luthmann, *The Dynamic Family* (Palo Alto, California: Science and Behavior Books, 1974), p. 20. One thinks of "hostile love" as an instance inviting such discrepancy analysis.
8. For a discussion of the role emotion plays in listening, see Donald W. Sherburne, *A Whiteheadian Aesthetic* (New Haven: Yale University Press, 1961), pp. 153ff.
9. Robert C. Solomon, *The Passions* (New York: Anchor/Doubleday, 1976), pp. 52-53.
10. Ibid., p. 428.
11. J. Gerald Janzen, "Modes of Presence and the Communion of Saints," pp. 147-172, in Harry James Cargas and Bernard Lee (editors), *Religious Experience and Process Theology* (New York: Paulist, 1976), p. 159. (Italics his.) This theme has also been effectively developed by William D. Dean, particularly in *Love Before the Fall* (Philadelphia: Westminster, 1976). In "Bell's Theorem and Stapp's Revised View

of Space-Time," *Process Studies* VII:3 (Fall, 1977), pp. 183-192, Charles Hartshorne argues that despite recent modifications entailed in Bell's work in physics, "for many practical purposes the idea of mutually independent contemporaries retains its significance" (p. 186). Indeed a truly unqualified teaching of the causal independence of contemporaries might make very difficult the kind of relatedness of which Janzen speaks, despite the effort to speak of that relatedness as "non-causal."

12. Martin Buber, *I and Thou,* a new translation with a prologue "I and You" by Walter Kaufmann (New York: Scribner's, 1970).
13. See Solomon, *The Passions,* pp. 64-65: "Subjectivity without objectivity is blind; objectivity without subjectivity is meaningless. The first is madness, the second meaninglessness."
14. See *PR* 227 for the recognition that what is given for the self is not a determination of that self.
15. See, for example, Richard Taylor, *Action and Purpose* (Englewood Cliffs: Prentice Hall, 1966).
16. On the basic issue of responsibility requiring an abiding self, see above, Chapter 2, pp. 111-113. As for responsibility in the moment, Emil Fackenheim, *Metaphysics and Historicity* (Milwaukee: Marquette University Press, 1961), p. 83, sounds very much like a Whiteheadian, though he offers his comment in explicit dependence on Kierkegaard:

> Human being must be understood as something more than a mere product, and yet as something less than a self-making. Instead of a self-constituting, it must rather be the accepting or choosing of something already constituted, and yet also not constituted, because the accepting or choosing is part of its essence.

Cf. John B. Cobb, Jr., *A Christian Natural Theology* (Philadelphia: Westminster, 1965), pp. 92-98.
17. In this discussion of responsibility I have been heavily influenced by the article, "Contours of Responsibility: A New Model," by Harold F. Moore Jr., Robert Neville, and William Sullivan in *Man and World,* V:4 (November, 1972).
18. Paul Tillich, *Systematic Theology* (3 vols.; Chicago: University of Chicago Press, 1951-1963), Vol. II, pp. 62-64.
19. Martin Duberman, *The Uncompleted Past* (New York: Random House, 1970), p. 356.
20. See also David Crocker, "A Whiteheadian Theory of Intentions and Actions," unpublished doctoral dissertation, Yale University, 1970, p. 143.
21. Above, pp. 98-99. See also Gregory Bateson, *Steps to an Ecology of Mind,* p. 453, for his elaboration of the Kantian point that the most elementary aesthetic act is the selection of a fact."
22. Richard John Neuhaus, "Returning to Where We Have Never Been," pp. 9-21, *Time Toward Home* (New York: Seabury, 1975).
23. Margaret Mead, *Culture and Commitment* (New York: Doubleday, 1970).
24. Cf. *S* 66:

> The response to the symbol is almost automatic but not quite; the reference to the meaning is there, either for additional emotional support or for criticism. But the reference is not so clear as to be imperative. The imperative instinctive conformation to the influence of the environment has been modified. Something has replaced it, which by its superficial character invites criticism, and by its habitual use generally escapes it. Such symbolism makes connected thought possible by expressing it, while at the same time it automatically directs action. In the place of the force of instinct which suppresses individuality, society has gained the efficacy of symbols, at once preservative of the commonweal and of the individual standpoint.

25. See Stephen Toulmin, "Contemporary Scientific Mythology," in *Metaphysical Beliefs,* with Ronald W. Hepburn and Alasdair MacIntyre (London: SCM Press, 1957), pp. 13-84.
26. Solomon, *The Passions,* p. 279.
27. See Bernard Lee, *The Becoming of the Church* (New York: Paulist, 1974), pp. 200-201, for a development of this dialectic.
28. See F. David Martin's discussion of "embodied meaning" in *Art and the Religious Experience: The Language of the Sacred* (Lewisburg: Bucknell University Press, 1972), p. 96. With reference to this entire theme of the linguistic see Lyman T. Lundeen, *Risk and Rhetoric in Religion: Whitehead's Theory of Language and the Discourse of Faith* (Philadelphia: Fortress, 1972).
29. One might speculate, for example, regarding the effect of a report regarding divine predestination in differing contexts, or of how a given word of Scripture can function either as "law" or "gospel."
30. For one such effort see David Tracy, *Blessed Rage for Order* (New York: Seabury, 1975).
31. Brian W. Grant, *Schizophrenia: A Source of Social Insight* (Philadelphia: Westminster, 1975), p. 89. Grant follows Whitehead in combining this notion with a recognition of individual responsibility.
32. See Perls, *The Gestalt Approach and Eyewitness to Therapy,* pp. 15, 28, 42.
33. See below, pp. 258-260, 284.
34. See the useful summary available in Bruce R. Joyce and Marsha Weil, *Models of Teaching* (Englewood Cliffs: Prentice-Hall, 1972), Part I.
35. For a discussion in process terms of communal reflection and evaluation see Gloria Durka and Joanmarie Smith, *Modeling God; Religious Education for Tomorrow* (New York: Paulist, 1976), pp. 33ff.
36. See William Gallagher, "Whitehead's Theory of the Human Person," unpublished doctoral dissertation, The New School for Social Research, 1974. A summary is available in Gallagher's "Whitehead's Psychological Physiology: A Third View," pp. 263-274, *Process Studies,* IV:4 (Winter, 1974).
37. See Eugene Fontinell, "Process Theology: A Pragmatic Version," pp. 23-40 in Cargas and Lee, *Religious Experience and Process Theology,* for a rather one-sided stress on this theme.
38. See the fourth chapter of William Gallagher's dissertation (note 36) for a critique of Freud, who "has limited higher levels of intensity of experience to a series of dodges in the interest of homeostasis" (p. 185). For an extended warning at this point, see William R. Rogers, "Order and Chaos in Psychotherapy and Ontology: A Challenge to Traditional Correlations of Order to Mental Health and Ultimate Reality, and of Chaos to Mental Illness and Alienation," pp. 263-284 in Peter Homans, ed., *The Dialogue Between Theology and Psychology* (Chicago: University of Chicago Press, 1968), especially pp. 259-260.
39. Grant, *Schizophrenia: A Source of Social Insight,* p. 226.
40. Ibid., p. 151.
41. Claus Westermann, *Creation,* trans. John J. Scullion, S.J. (Philadelphia: Fortress, 1974), p. 5.
42. Kent S. Knutson, *The Shape of the Question* (Minneapolis: Augsburg, 1972), p. 17. If the response is to appeal that "the domain and character of the religious faith is such that the faith cannot be expressed or communicated in any way," Knutson in turn responds:

> This, to me, is a very unsatisfactory answer. If God is completely inexpressible Christianity becomes a mystical religion where you can think but not talk. . . .

One has no idea of whether what one believes or thinks is illusion or reality unless one is able to talk about it (p. 29).

43. Ibid., p. 16.

44. See the trenchant analysis by Charles Glock quoted above, p. 35.

45. See, for example, Richard Niebuhr, *The Meaning of Revelation* (New York: Macmillan, 1941). For the erosion of the interventionist model, see the worried comment by Heinrich Ott on pp. 34-35 above.

46. See Gordon D. Kaufman, *God the Problem* (Cambridge: Harvard University Press, 1972), especially Chapter 6. For a detailed critique of Kaufman from a process perspective, see David R. Mason, "Can We Speculate on How God Acts?", *The Journal of Religion*, LVII:1 (January, 1977), pp. 16-32.

47. I worry about the theology of hope movement at this point. For example, I find Jürgen Moltmann's assertion that God creates the future out of nothing posing a possible threat to the reality of the present. See his *Theology of Hope*, trans. J. W. Leitch (New York: Harper & Brothers, 1967), p. 226.

48. This theme is foundational in John Macquarrie's *Principles of Christian Theology* (New York: Scribner's, 1966). Thus, p. 183: God's essence is Being, and Being, in turn, is letting-be. So it is of the essence of God to let be.
While Macquarrie gets very considerable mileage out of this theme, I am arguing that faith speaks of a more directly and specifically active God.

49. See above, pp. 77-90.

50. Gustaf Aulen, *The Faith of the Christian Church*, trans. Eric H. Wahlstrom (Philadelphia: Fortress, 1960), p. 174. (Italics his.)

51. Knutson, *The Shape of the Question*, p. 119.

52. Ian Barbour provides a useful summary of this line of thought in *Myths, Models and Paradigms* (New York: Harper & Row, 1974), p. 158.

53. Stuart Hampshire, *Thought and Action* (London: Chatto and Windus, 1959), p. 154.

54. Kai Nielsen, *Contemporary Critiques of Religion* (New York: Macmillan, 1971), Chapter 6.

55. See above, pp. 56-58.

56. Robert H. King, *The Meaning of God* (Philadelphia: Fortress, 1973), p. 90.

57. Ibid.

58. Albert Outler, *Who Trusts in God* (New York: Oxford University Press, 1968), p. 39. (Italics his.)

59. John Baillie, *The Sense of the Presence of God* (New York: Scribner's, 1962), pp. 215-216. In a like manner, Piet Schoonenberg, S.J., writes:

. . . God does not oppose a natural law, but his grace evokes modifying factors from within the world itself, so as, for example, to give man new powers through his faith. The miracle is a special work of God, not because he eliminates earthly forces, but precisely because he enlists as many of them as possible as signs of the eternal life that he will give in the new heaven and the new earth. (*The Christ*, trans. Della Couling [New York: Herder & Herder, 1971], p. 25.)

60. King, *The Meaning of God*, p. 80.

61. Ibid.

62. *PR* 522. See David A. Fleming's discussion of the "giftedness" of life in "God's Gift and Man's Response: Toward a Whiteheadian Perspective," pp. 215-230 in Cargas and Lee, *Religious Experience and Process Theology*. Cf. Schoonenberg, *The Christ*, pp. 29-30.

63. Aulen, *The Faith of the Christian Church*, p. 132.

64. Though this would seem to be true, John B. Cobb, Jr., has speculated regarding the

possibility of also regarding God as datum in a Whiteheadian schema, *A Christian Natural Theology,* pp. 232, 248. See also Gerald Janzen, "Modes of Power and the Divine Relativity," pp. 374-406 in *Encounter* XXXVI:4 (Fall, 1975), for an attempt to incorporate both coercive and persuasive elements. Eugene TeSelle offers a discussion of divine agency which draws in part on Whitehead in *Christ in Context* (Philadelphia: Fortress, 1975), especially pp. 132, 142.

65. Gustaf Wingren, *Creation and Law,* trans. Ross Mackenzie (Philadelphia: Muhlenberg Press, 1961), p. 46.

66. Langdon Gilkey, *Reaping the Whirlwind; A Christian Interpretation of History* (New York: Seabury Press, 1976), pp. 248-249. Gilkey also raises the objection that the distinction between God and creativity strains the coherence of the Whiteheadian system in view of Whitehead's own emphasis on the ontological principle with its appeal to actual entities as the principle of explanation. We have discussed this internal Whiteheadian debate above, pp. 77-90.

67. Ibid. (Italics mine.)

68. Barbour, *Myths, Models and Paradigms,* pp. 162-163. (Italics his.)

69. Westermann, *Creation,* p. 56. See also Bernhard Lohse, "Conscience and Authority in Luther," pp. 158-183, in Heiko Oberman, *Luther and the Dawn of the Modern Era* (Leiden: Brill, 1970).

70. Walter Brueggemann, *In Man We Trust* (Richmond: John Knox, 1972), p. 119.

71. Knutson, *The Shape of the Question,* p. 121. Cf. Wingren, *Creation and Law,* p. 45.

72. Baillie, *The Sense of the Presence of God,* p. 225.

73. Aulen, *The Faith of the Christian Church,* p. 173.

74. Gerhard von Rad, *Wisdom in Israel,* trans. James D. Martin (Nashville: Abingdon, 1972), p. 162.

75. Brueggemann, *In Man We Trust,* p. 62.

76. Richard H. Overman, *Evolution and the Christian Doctrine of Creation* (Philadelphia: Westminster, 1967), pp. 273-274. Elsewhere (p. 238) Overman contrasts Hebrew and Greek thought. Of the Old Testament understanding he writes:

> The order of nature is therefore not that of the Greek *kosmos,* maintained by its own indwelling rationality, and we hear nothing of "natural law." Instead, the regularities of nature are based entirely on God's faithful keeping of his covenant promise to Noah.

While Overman seems to be particularly appreciative of the Hebrew view, Maurice Wiles would incline toward the Greek when he writes in *The Remaking of Christian Doctrine* (London: SCM, 1974), that a genuinely religious sense of purpose arises "by pointing to a purposiveness within the world as a whole" (p. 38).

77. John Bowker, *The Sense of God* (Oxford: Clarendon, 1973), pp. 178-179.

78. Overman, *Evolution and the Christian Doctrine of Creation,* p. 292.

79. Wolfhart Pannenberg, *Jesus-God and Man,* trans. Lewis L. Wilkins and Duane A. Priebe (Philadelphia: Westminster, 1968), p. 33.

80. Ibid., pp. 34-35. See also his discussion of how various views of the work of Christ carry implications for understanding the person of Christ, ibid., pp. 39-57.

81. Maurice Wiles, *The Remaking of Christian Doctrine,* p. 43, criticizes Karl Rahner and J. P. Jossua for assuming the vere homo, vere deus as a starting point, since the substance of belief changes with the grounds for belief, and the grounds for belief do change.

82. Knutson, *The Shape of the Question,* pp. 78-79.

83. Pannenberg, *Jesus-God and Man,* p. 344. Process thought would have great difficulty going on to Pannenberg's further contention, p. 345:

> Jesus is the true and real man precisely as the "God-man," only because unity

with God, "sonship," is *man's eternal destiny, even though it became historical reality only* in Jesus' activity and fate. (Italics mine.)

To claim that seems to be to deny human freedom and human history the seriousness of decisiveness.

84. This is Robert W. Jenson's analysis in *Lutheranism: The Theological Movement and Its Confessional Writings*, with Eric W. Gritsch (Philadelphia: Fortress, 1976), p. 108. The specific focus of Jenson's discussion is the Lutheran notion of *communicatio idiomatum*, but the comment would clearly apply as well to the theologically prior issue of the two natures.

85. Pannenberg, *Jesus-God and Man*, p. 320. He adds:

To be sure, such identity can be conceived together with a becoming in God himself only if time and eternity are not mutually exclusive. This is the critical point for the question of God's sameness if one may reject the idea of a purely conceptual, timeless becoming as a mere chimera.

Cf. ibid., p. 157. A process parallel will come into view in the last section of this chapter.

86. Knutson, *The Shape of the Question*, pp. 84-86.

87. Schoonenberg, *The Christ*, pp. 62-63.

88. John B. Cobb, Jr., *Christ in a Pluralistic Age* (Philadelphia: Westminster, 1975), p. 139.

89. Ibid., pp. 139-140.

90. Ibid., p. 141. See his summary discussion, pp. 170-173.

91. Pannenberg, *Jesus-God and Man*, p. 334.

92. See Schoonenberg, *The Christ*, p. 87. In *The Lure of God*, pp. 49ff., Lewis Ford notes that for process christologies it is not subjectively, but objectively, that God can be incarnate in Jesus. Pannenberg, *Jesus-God and Man*, p. 341, notes distrust of the notion of the impersonality of Jesus' humanity and of a realistic communication of attributes in such writers as I. A. Dorner, Paul Althaus, Donald M. Baillie, and Emil Brunner.

93. Thus Heinrich Schmid, *Doctrinal Theology of the Evangelical Lutheran Church*, trans. Charles A. Hay and Henry E. Jacobs (Minneapolis: Augsburg, 1899), pp. 300-308.

94. Ibid., p. 300.

95. Søren Kierkegaard, *The Sickness Unto Death*, trans. W. Lowrie (Princeton: Princeton University Press, 1941), Doubleday Anchor ed., p. 147. See Schmid, *Doctrinal Theology of the Evangelical Lutheran Church*, p. 299, for the tradition's repudiation of the monothelite tendency.

96. For an interesting suggestion by someone who hardly identifies himself with process thought, see John Hick, "Christology at the Cross Roads," pp. 137-166, in *Prospect for Theology*, ed. F. G. Healey (Welwyn Garden City: James Nisbet & Co., 1966). For example:

Let us proclaim the *homoagape* rather than the *homoousia!* For we know, at least ostensibly (and what better way could there be?), what we mean by *agape*, but we do not know what we mean by substance. . . . (Italics his.)

Hick retains reference to "nature" and holds that Jesus

had one nature, and this nature was wholly and unqualifiedly human; but the *agape* which directed it was God's (Ibid., p. 164).

One wonders whether the defense of human nature is threatened by the absence of human fredom.

97. C. Walther von Loewenich, *Luther's Theology of the Cross*, trans. H. Bouman (Minneapolis: Augsburg, 1976), p. 61.

98. Ibid., p. 150.

99. In *A Christian Natural Theology*, p. 232, John Cobb has a go at making sense of such claims for immediate experience of God.
100. Steven Ozment, *Homo Spiritualis* (Leiden: Brill, 1969), p. 177.
101. John Reumann, "The Scope of Christ's Lordship," pp. 61-118, in *Christ and Humanity*, ed. Ivar Asheim (Philadelphia: Fortress, 1970), p. 82.
102. See William Gallagher's discussion of subordinate centers of organization in the persons above, pp. 95-96.
103. Bernard Lee, *The Becoming of the Church*, p. 256. Lee also pleads that Christian formation should follow the natural terrain of the human.
104. Ibid., pp. 256-257.
105. For the notion of such a unifying disposition, see H. H. Price, *Belief* (London: Allen and Unwin, 1969), pp. 248-251, and Kaufmann's employment of Price, *God the Problem*, pp. 88-94. Harold Ditmanson expresses some misgivings about trying to conceive the Christian relationship to God in subpersonal terms in *Grace in Experience and Theology* (Minneapolis: Augsburg, 1977), pp. 41-42: ". . . it is quite incredible to think that the immediate drama of our own existence is the misinterpretation of a more than usually complicated kind of impersonal process." See above, pp. 95-96, 112-113.
106. Cobb, *Christ in a Pluralistic Age*, p. 125; Lee, *The Becoming of the Church*, p. 219.
107. Cobb, *Christ in a Pluralistic Age*, p. 125.
108. Gerald Janzen in Cargas and Lee, *Religious Experience and Process Theology*, pp. 168-169.
109. See above, pp. 97-99.
110. While it may be said that the past presently "aims" (Cobb, *A Christian Natural Theology*, p. 248), a remote historical figure—of itself—could not be supposed to represent a vivid and effective presence, or so it seems to me.
111. For a concise discussion see Mircea Eliade's *Cosmos and History*, trans. W. R. Trask (New York: Harper, 1969), pp. 12-17.
112. It may be noted even here that mainstream Christian teaching does not consider either the decisive event in the past or the "coming of the future" to abrogate the significance of present freedom.
113. See William Beardslee, "Narrative Form in the New Testament and Process Theology," pp. 301-315, *Encounter*, XXXVI:4 (Autumn, 1975) and Theodore Weeden, "The Potential and Promise of a Process Hermeneutic," pp. 316-330 in the same issue.
114. See Joseph M. Hallman, "Toward a Process Theology of the Church," pp. 137-146 in Cargas and Lee, *Religious Experience and Process Theology*. See also Lorenz Nieting, "The Otten-Preus Heresy," pp. 192-201, in *Dialog, XV:3* (Summer, 1976).
115. Alan Richardson, *Creeds in the Making* (London: SCM Press, 1935), pp. 14, 16.
116. I have this formulation from a public lecture by Paul Ricoeur in Claremont, California, February 15, 1977.
117. See Lee Snook, "Luther's Doctrine of the Real Presence: Critique and Reconstruction from the View of Process Thought." Unpublished Th.D. dissertation, Union Theological Seminary in New York, 1971.
118. This is a major concern of Bernard Lee's in *The Becoming of the Church*. See also John Cobb's appreciative criticism in *Process Studies*. The contrasting view is well suggested in Jaroslav Pelikan's comment on Eastern Christendom:

> Underlying this definition of divine truth as changeless was a definition of the divine itself as changeless and absolute. Because God transcends change, the truth about him also had to do so. (Pelikan, *The Spirit of Eastern Christendom* [Chicago: University of Chicago Press], pp. 14-16.)

For a Lutheran comment on the "event" character of the church, see Ditmanson, *Grace in Experience and Theology,* p. 124.

## 5: Proposal: Metaphysics as Faith's Colleague: Filling the Categories

1. See, for example, Martin Luther's comments in *Luther's Works,* ed. Helmut Lehmann (54 vols.; Philadelphia, Muhlenberg, 1958-67), Vol. XXXVII, pp. 58, 68.
2. Kent Knutson, *The Shape of the Question* (Minneapolis: Augsburg, 1972), p. 46.
3. Gerhard von Rad, *Wisdom in Israel,* trans. James D. Martin (Nashville: Abingdon, 1972), p. 3.
4. Ibid., pp. 89-90.
5. Ivar Asheim, "Humanity and Christian Responsibility," pp. 1-60, in Asheim, *Christ and Humanity* (Philadelphia: Fortress, 1970), p. 31. See also Knutson, *The Shape of the Question,* p. 45, and B. A. Gerrish, "Luther's Belief in Reason," pp. 10-27, of *Grace and Reason* (Oxford: Clarendon, 1962). As a biblical model one might have in mind the succession narrative. Of that von Rad, *Wisdom in Israel,* p. 98, writes:
   It represents a piece of genuine, secular history without in the least curtailing God's share in it. Therein lies its real theological achievement.
6. Paul G. Kuntz, *The Concept of Order,* ed. Paul Kuntz (Seattle: University of Washington Press, 1968), xxvii. See also the literature identified in note 59 in Chapter 1. Or perhaps the problem is that one does not like what one seems to find in the "is." Thus Charles Birch, while seeking "A Biological Basis for Human Purpose" (*Zygon,* 1975, 244-260), finds himself pressed to say:
   There is after all no problem in deriving characteristics that aid in self-survival from evolution, though it is extremely difficult to ascribe altruistic tendencies to genetic evolution (p. 253).
   See also Donald Campbell, "On the Genetics of Altruism and the Counter-Hedonic Components in Human Culture," pp. 21-37, *The Journal of Social Issues,* XXVIII:3 (1972).
7. Samuel E. Stumpf, "The Moral Order and the Legal Order," pp. 385-404 in Kuntz, *The Concept of Order.*
8. Paul Ricoeur, *The Symbolism of Evil* (Boston: Beacon, 1967), p. 156. (Italics his.) Similarly, Alan Richardson writes of "Second Thoughts: Present Issues in New Testament Theology," *The Expository Times,* January, 1964, p. 111:
   According to the classical tradition of Christian philosophy (which, of course, goes back to Greek thought), evil is essentially the unreal, the absolutely nonexistent. Therefore it can be demythologized with plausibility. But God is defined as "He who is," the One in whom essence and existence coincide. A possible way, therefore, of characterizing God in our contemporary thought-forms would be to say that He is the uniquely undemythologizable One. . . . The historic Christian faith involves the metaphysical assertion that good and evil are not of equal ontological status.
   I accept Richardson's conclusion, but find his premises claim more than is needed.
9. See Article I, Solid Declaration, the Formula of Concord, in *The Book of Concord.*
10. Edgar M. Carlson, *The Reinterpretation of Luther* (Philadelphia: Westminster, 1948), p. 207.
11. Gustaf Wingren, *Creation and Law,* trans. Ross Mackenzie (Philadelphia: Muhlenberg, 1961), pp. 37, 101.
12. David R. Griffin works with such a distinction in *God, Power, and Evil: A Process Theodicy* (Philadelpha: Westminster, 1976), p. 307, when he writes:

Hence, while moral good is not of the essence of intrinsic goodness (since there can be intrinsic goodness in those beings who are incapable of moral goodness or evil), or even of the intrinsic goodness of human life, it *is* of the essence of that type of intrinsic good which God seeks to promote in us; and this promotion involves God's enlistment of our deliberate support in the drive to overcome evil in the world by maximizing good. (Italics his.)

13. von Rad, *Wisdom in Israel,* pp. 172-173.

14. No one has pursued this issue with more insight than James Gustafson. See, for example, both his *Theology and Christian Ethics* (Philadelphia: United Church Press, 1974), especially pp. 216-229, where he lists the development of moral norms as one of the areas in which empirical science can assist ethics, and his *Can Ethics Be Christian?* (Chicago: University of Chicago Press, 1975.)

15. See John Cobb, *Is It Too Late? A Theology of Ecology* (Minneapolis: Bruce, 1972), and J. B. Bennett, "Ecology and Philosophy: Whitehead's Contribution," *Journal of Thought,* X:1.

16. John B. Cobb Jr. and David Ray Griffin, *Process Theology: An Introductory Exposition* (Philadelphia: Westminster, 1976), p. 129. (Italics his.)

17. On these categories see above, pp. 91-93, and Chapter 2, note 68.

18. Robert B. Mellert, *What Is Process Theology?* (New York: Paulist, 1975), p. 116.

19. Bernard Lee, *The Becoming of the Church* (New York: Paulist, 1974), pp. 268-269.

20. See above, pp. 69-71, 91-96.

21. Erich Fromm, *The Heart of Man* (New York: Harper & Row, 1968), p. 41.

22. William A. Beardslee, *A House for Hope* (Philadelphia: Westminster, 1972), especially Chapter 1.

23. Claus Westermann, *Creation,* trans. John J. Sullivan, S.J. (Philadelphia: Fortress, 1974), p. 46. (Italics his.)

24. Ibid., p. 104.

25. Brueggemann, *In Man We Trust* (Richmond: John Knox, 1972), pp. 87-88, quoting Erhard Gustenberger. (Italics mine.)

26. Griffin, *Process Theology: An Introductory Exposition,* p. 53.

27. See D. D. Williams, "Moral Obligation in Process Philosophy," pp. 263-270, in *The Journal of Philosophy,* LVI (1959).

28. See Delwin Brown, "Hope for the Human Future: Niebuhr, Whitehead, and Utopian Expectations," *Iliff Review,* XXXII.3.

29. This is Barbara Ann Swyhart's emphasis in *Bioethical Decision-Making* (Philadelphia: Fortress, 1975), see especially pp. 67, 116.

30. See Lee, *The Becoming of the Church,* pp. 187-188. This is strongly emphasized by Charles H. Reynolds in an unpublished paper, "Somatic Ethics: Joy and Adventure in the Embodied Moral Life."

31. Thus William D. Dean, *Coming To: A Theology of Beauty* (Philadelphia: Westminster, 1972), p. 22:
    If festivity is participation in a broader context through activity, fantasy is participation in a broader context through "envisionment."
    See also Stephen Greenfield's unpublished doctoral dissertation, "A Whiteheadian Perspective of the Problem of Evil: Whitehead's Understanding of Evil and Christian Theodicy," Fordham University, 1973.

32. See above, p. 92, for a fuller quotation and discussion.

33. Robert C. Neville, *The Cosmology of Freedom* (New Haven: Yale University Press, 1974).

34. Ibid., p. 14.

35. Thus, ibid., pp. 214-217, Neville specifies personal values, interpersonal values, public

values, social-order values, values of civilization—with opulent subordinate specifications.

36. Ibid., p. 329.

37. Above, pp. 77-90.

38. For a full presentation of the argument, see Robert C. Neville, *God the Creator: On the Transcendence and Presence of God* (Chicago: University of Chicago Press, 1968).

39. For Neville's critique and proposal of the concept of a "discursive individual," see *The Cosmology of Freedom*, pp. 40-51.

40. See above, pp. 63-71.

41. Above, pp. 213-214.

42. Monroe C. Beardsley, "Order and Disorder in Art," pp. 191-218, in Kuntz, *The Concept of Order*, p. 217.

43. See above, pp. 91-92.

44. On different orders of value in Whitehead, see A. H. Johnson, "Truth, Beauty, Goodness in the Philosophy of Alfred North Whitehead," pp. 9-29, in *The Philosophy of Science*, XI (1944).

45. I have featured here what Whitehead calls the component of "massiveness" in "strength of beauty." The other component is termed "intensity," "comparative magnitude without reference to qualitative variety."

46. In *God, Power, and Evil*, pp. 282ff., David Griffin provides an excellent discussion of the criteria of intrinsic good, harmony and intensity, and, in turn, of the criteria of intrinsic evil, disharmony and triviality.

47. See the application of such considerations in Rudolf Arnheim, "Order and Complexity in Landscape Design," pp. 153-166, in Kuntz, *The Concept of Order*.

48. See the trenchant criticism Donald Sherburne directs at Robert Neville's *Cosmology of Freedom* in Sherburne's review in *Process Studies* VI:4 (Winter, 1976), pp. 279-292. Thus he contends, (p. 286):

> . . . The assumption which now goes with our distinction is that, just as "continuous creativity" was essential to the creative individual, so "continuous creativity" with all its baggage of social instability, constant revolution, emotional immersion in change, etc. is essential for a creatively free society. But here we are on the brink of the fallacy of composition. Just because all the rooms in a building are small, it does not follow that the building is small! Just because certain conditions hold in connection with freedom at the level of the individual, it does not follow that these very same properties must characterize the social whole these individuals make up if that social whole is to be creatively free!

The fallacy is here avoided first in that the whole is controlled in its character by the coming together of the parts and second in that the whole does directly double back to maximize the value already located in the parts.

49. Our concern is to inquire into the ethical form(s) of harmony. For another use of the notion of such a whole, see Burnshaw, *The Seamless Web* (New York: George Braziller, 1970), on the significance of poetic equilibrium.

50. Westermann, *Creation*, p. 14.

51. James Gustafson, *Theology and Christian Ethics*, p. 244. Cf. Neuhaus, *Time Toward Home* (New York: Seabury, 1975).

52. Martin, *Art and the Religious Experience* (Lewisburg, Pa.: Bucknell University Press, 1972), p. 131. Another way to state this point would be to say that persons are more affected by processes than by sheer events, despite our rhetoric about the quick change or instant lunch. Yet I do not wish to deny that the moment cut off from continuity may have great power. But to the degree that such power exerts its pull, the human self is held back from building a history.

53. William R. Rogers, "Order and Chaos in Psychopathology and Ontology: A Challenge to Traditional Correlations of Order to Mental Health and Ultimate Reality, and of Chaos to Mental Illness and Alienation," pp. 263-284 in Peter Homans, ed., *The Dialogue Between Theology and Psychology* (Chicago: University of Chicago Press, 1968), pp. 250, 252.
54. Tracy, *Blessed Rage for Order* (New York: Seabury, 1975), p. 96. Tracy acknowledges the influence of Bernard Lonergan at this point.
55. Neville, *The Cosmology of Freedom*, pp. 227-235.
56. Aulen, *The Faith of the Christian Church*, trans. Eric W. Wahlstrom (Philadelphia: Fortress, 1960), p. 163. Cf. von Rad, *Wisdom in Israel*, p. 92; Brueggemann, *In Man We Trust*, p. 42.
57. See Brian W. Grant, *Schizophrenia: A Source of Social Insight* (Philadelphia: Westminster, 1975), p. 227. In *The Civilization of Experience* (New York: Fordham University Press, 1973), p. 180f., David Hall identifies two threats to identity: "the falling away of the past," and the excess of novelty which produces a sense of uprootedness due to being confronted with a vast array of possibilities.
58. Janzen stresses the I-Thou relationship in Cargas and Lee, *Religious Experience and Process Theology*, p. 167; Norman Pittenger the I-You relationship in the same volume, p. 14. *
59. Charles Malik writes of this theme as one who has reason to know the significance of responsibility. See his "An Appreciation of Professor Whitehead With Special Reference to his Metaphysics and to his Ethical and Educational Significance," pp. 572-582, *The Journal of Philosophy*, 45 (1948).
60. See Charles Fried's discussion of this connection in "Privacy: A Rational Context," pp. 21-33, in Richard Wasserstrom, ed., *Today's Moral Problems* (New York: Macmillan, 1975), especially p. 21. Similarly, Donald Sherburne in *A Whiteheadian Aesthetic: Some Implications of Whitehead's Metaphysical Speculation* (New Haven: Yale University Press, 1961), pp. 156ff., interprets aesthetic experience in connection with the proposal to "create a world."
61. William Gallagher, "Whitehead's Theory of the Human Reason," unpublished doctoral dissertation at the New School for Social Research, 1974, p. 45.
62. Gallagher draws on G. Lindzey, "Some Remarks Concerning Incest, the Incest Taboo, and Psychoanalytic Theory," *American Psychologist* 22 (1967), p. 1054.
63. This is the concern of Gilbert Herbert, "The Organic Analogy in Town Planning" in *American Institute of Planners* Journal, XXIX:3 (August, 1963), pp. 198-209.
64. Neville, *The Cosmology of Freedom*, pp. 235ff.
65. Aulen, *The Faith of the Christian Church*, p. 163.
66. So Reumann in Asheim, *Christ and Humanity*, p. 84f., stresses that the "orders" of creation are not static, but are indeed a human responsibility.
67. See John Cobb's discussion in *Christ in a Pluralistic Age*, p. 220. Cf. E. F. Schumacher, *Small Is Beautiful: Economics As If People Mattered* (New York: Harper and Row, 1973).
68. Thus in *PR* 424 Whitehead speaks of the

　　. . . urge towards the realization of the maximum number of eternal objects subject to the restraint that they must be under the conditions of contrast. But this limitation to "conditions of contrast" is the demand for "balance." For "balance" here means that no realized eternal object shall eliminate potential contrast between other realized eternal objects. Such eliminations attenuate the intensities of feeling.

69. Griffin, *Process Theology: An Introductory Exposition*, p. 27. Cf. Griffin's discussion of moral evil as involving the *"intention* to be destructive of the potential intrinsic good

of other actualities" in *God, Power and Evil*, p. 292. (Italics his.) Hartshorne writes of God in *Creative Synthesis and Philosophic Method* (La Salle, Illinois: Open Court Publishing Co., 1970), pp. 309-310:

> God cannot benefit another without benefiting himself. In his case self-interest and altruism are indeed coincidental, but not because he is clever enough to do us good so as to satisfy his own egoistic desires. He has no egoistic desires, if words are properly used. He wants only to enjoy creaturely good, seeking for the creatures the happiness they seek for themselves.

Similarly, Robert Solomon—without dependence on process categories—can claim:

> We all know . . . that sense of unity that defines an afternoon spent walking with an old friend, those vibrant moments of *we* that secure our friendships and our love . . . there is no confrontation of Selves but rather a *sharing* . . . in short, a sharing of Selves. (*The Passions* [New York: Doubleday, 1976], p. 104. Italics his.)

70. Hall, *The Civilization of Experience*, p. 203.
71. See Gustaf Wingren, *Gospel and Church*, trans. Ross Mackenzie (Edinburgh: Oliver and Boyd, 1964), p. 4. Cf. Asheim, *Christ and Humanity*.
72. Aulen, *The Faith of the Christian Church*, p. 166. Cf. Wingren, *Creation and Law*, p. 165.
73. Wingren, *Gospel and Church*, p. 181. (Italics his.) Cf. Wingren, *Creation and Law*, p. 42:

> Christ's command is at one time as old as Creation, and as new as salvation. . . . To care for one's children and to sacrifice oneself for one's enemies may appear to be two different things from the point of view of a barren ethical system. From the point of view of murder, however, they merge into one another in the commandment, "Thou shalt not kill" . . . In obeying this sharpened demand of Jesus the disciple is not breaking away from the natural law.

Cf. Aulen, *The Faith of the Christian Church*, p. 166.
74. Reinhold Niebuhr, *Man's Nature and His Communities* (New York: Scribner's, 1965), p. 125.
75. Ralph Norman comments on this transcendence as a basis for morality in "Steam, Barbarism, and Dialectic: Notations on Proof and Sensibility," *Christian Scholar*, 50 (1967), pp. 184-196.
76. See above, pp. 120ff.
77. Note Whitehead's contrast between Buddhism and Christianity (*RM* 50):

> It [Christianity] has always been a religion seeking a metaphysic, in contrast to Buddhism which is a metaphysic generating a religion.

Cf. *RM* 31.
78. Thus Robert Jenson and Eric Gritsch understand their study of the Lutheran Confessions to be centered in this doctrine. *Lutheranism: The Theological Movement and Its Confessional Writings* (Philadelphia: Fortress, 1976), vii.
79. Theodore Tappert, ed. and trans. *The Book of Concord* (Philadelphia: Muhlenberg, 1959), p. 292.
80. John Calvin, *Institutes of the Christian Religion,* trans. John Allen (Presbyterian Board of Christian Education, n.d.), Book III, ch. x, para. 1.
81. The statement quoted is by Karl Rahner in Hans Küng, *Justification: Doctrine of Karl Barth and a Catholic Reflection,* trans. Thomas Collins, Edmund E. Tolk, and David Granskou (New York: Thomas Nelson, 1964), xi. See Karl Barth's letter, ibid., xix-xxii.
82. Krister Stendahl, *Paul Among Jews and Gentiles* (Philadelphia: Fortress, 1976), p. 40.

This volume concludes with Stendahl's responses to a number of his critics, notably Ernst Kasemann's *Perspectives on Paul* (Philadelphia: Fortress, 1971), pp. 60-78.

83. See above, pp. 53-54.

84. *Religion in the Making* is the most striking instance, but see the range involved in Frederic R. Crownfield's collection in "Whitehead's References to the Bible," *Process Studies*, VI:4 (Winter, 1976), pp. 270-278.

85. At times he comes near collapsing the distinction, as when he writes (*RM* 31) that "the doctrines of rational religion aim at being that metaphysics which can be derived from the supernormal experience of mankind in its moments of finest insight." But we have found the same work to recognize the possible viability of special claims from the side of faith. See pp. 45-47 above and Chapter 2, note 62.

86. von Rad, *Wisdom in Israel*, p. 66, cautions us in our reading of the biblical material: The modern reader must, therefore, eliminate, in the case of the word "fear," the idea of something emotional, of a specific psychical form of the experience of God. In this context, the term is possibly used even in a still more general, humane sense, akin to our "commitment to," "knowledge about Yahweh."

Similarly, Karl Barth, who can hardly be charged with consciously endorsing human projections regarding God, insists that the divine No be placed within the divine Yes. See his *Evangelical Theology: An Introduction* (New York: Holt, Rinehart and Winston, 1963), p. 11 and note 2 in Chapter 1.

87. Colossians 3:17.

88. Paul Tillich, *The Courage to Be* (New Haven: Yale University Press, 1952), pp. 46-51. Cf. H. Thielicke, *How Modern Should Theology Be,* trans. George Anderson (Philadelphia: Fortress, 1965), Chapter 1.

89. Cf. *PR* 525-526.

90. See above, pp. 188-189.

91. See below, pp. 260-261.

92. See above, pp. 117-130.

93. See the article by Joseph Kitagawa, "Chaos, Order and Freedom in World Religions," pp. 268-289, in Paul Kuntz, *The Concept of Order.*

94. Bowker, *The Sense of God*, viii.

95. Paul Ricoeur (with Alasdair MacIntyre), *The Religious Significance of Atheism* (New York: Columbia University Press, 1969), p. 76.

96. See, for example, Wingren, *Creation and Law*, p. 99.

97. von Rad, *Wisdom in Israel*, pp. 80-81.

98. Bernard Lonergan, *Philosophy of God and Theology* (London: Darton, Longman and Todd, 1973), pp. 54-55. Cf. Karl Rahner, *Geist in Welt* (München: Kosel, 1957), pp. 181f., 387ff.

99. Jürgen Moltmann, *The Gospel of Liberation,* trans. H. Wayne Pipkin (Waco, Texas: Word, 1973), p. 124. For an ample and sensitive reading of this quest, see F. W. Dillistone, *The Christian Understanding of Atonement* (Philadelphia: Westminster, 1968), especially Chapter 1.

100. See the characterization of this mentality in Chapter 1 above, note 31.

101. In "The Viability of Whitehead's God for Christian Theology," pp. 141-151 in the *Proceedings of the American Catholic Philosophical Association,* 44 (1970), especially pp. 145-146, Lewis S. Ford nicely shows how the attribute "infinite" can be appropriately employed at this point. Cf. the discussion by David Griffin in Ford, ed., *Two Process Philosophers,* p. 56.

102. Lewis S. Ford, "The Non-Temporality of Whitehead's God," pp. 347-376 in *International Philosophical Quarterly*, XIII (1973), p. 376. For a slightly different view, see

Delwin Brown, "Freedom and Faithfulness in Whitehead's God," *Process Studies*, II (1972), pp. 137-148.

103. For a gathered discussion of this matter see John B. Cobb, Jr., *A Christian Natural Theology* (Philadelphia: Westminster, 1965), pp. 151-154.

104. Cf. the discussion of Hartshorne, Ogden and Tracy in Chapter 3 above. I find forceful Van Harvey's question to David Tracy in "The Pathos of Liberal Theology," pp. 382-391, in *The Journal of Religion*, LVI:4 (October, 1976), p. 388:

> What if someone like Ernest Becker were to argue . . . that what informs human existence is not a fundamental confidence but a fundamental terror from which we shield ourselves through art, neurosis, and religion?

Whitehead's more cosmological approach reminds me of von Rad's account of how wisdom attempts to explain "on her own terms, the phenomenon of Torah . . . in very untraditional terms." *Wisdom in Israel*, p. 166. For a combination of approaches, see Bowker, *The Sense of God*, pp. 115, 166.

105. Contrast Whitehead's position as described above, pp. 55-58, 90, with the tradition represented by Hartshorne and Ogden, as described above, pp. 134-145.

106. Above, pp. 114-115, and below, Chapter 6, note 18.

107. See above, p. 90, and the discussion by Lewis Ford and William Christian sketched in Chapter 2, notes 63 and 65. What is being discussed is an argument, not a proof. In the interchange that makes up argument Sherburne and Neville would consider the kind of empirical considerations collected by Errol Harris in *The Foundation of Metaphysics in Science* (New York: Humanities, 1965).

108. Faith will not be surprised by the argument. On the natural knowledge of the existence of God and "something" of his attributes, see Schmid, *The Doctrinal Theology of the Evangelical Lutheran Church*, trans. from 5th ed., Charles A. Hay and Henry E. Jacobs (Minneapolis: Augsburg, 1899), pp. 103-111, and Roland D. Zimany, "The Enduring Value of Luther's Approach to Knowing God," pp. 6-26, in *The Lutheran Quarterly*, XXVII:1 (February, 1975). In *The Future of God* (New York: Harper, 1969) Carl Braaten laments the collapse of the whole enterprise of natural theology and writes:

> Nature, history, moral conscience and numinous experience mediate an awareness of their own lack and their openness to a power which can promise unity, wholeness and fulfillment beyond negativity (p. 63).

Similarly, Harold H. Ditmanson in *Grace in Experience and Theology* (Minneapolis: Augsburg, 1977), p. 25, notes that

> we do not raise the question of the ground of being because we are Christians, but because we are human beings.

While these contemporary statements may reflect a Lutheran skepticism in limiting themselves to language of "openness" and "questioning," they do provide the point of contact for the argument developed independently of Christian faith.

109. Langdon Gilkey, *Reaping the Whirlwind: A Christian Interpretation of History* (New York: Seabury, 1976), p. 276. (Italics his.) I do not precisely follow Gilkey in his statement of the response to this need, as when he suggests that "the autonomy which combines with providence in actualizing possibility must itself be transformed by grace. . . ." Thus John B. Cobb, Jr. criticizes Bernard Lee's conflation of Teilhard and Whitehead:

> Lee presents the creative advance into novelty as more progressive than it is in Whitehead. . . . The only place in Whitehead's view where there can be confidence of progress is in the Consequent Nature of God.

See Cobb's review of Lee's *The Becoming of the Church* in *Process Studies*, IV:4

(Winter, 1974), pp. 303-304. For Cobb's own views, see *A Christian Natural Theology*, Chapter 3, especially p. 132, and *Christ in a Pluralistic Age*, Part 3.

110. Such wondering may be suggested by Whitehead's striking reference to the ruthlessness of God as primordial (*PR* 373-374). His own effort to respond is, of course, represented in the last part of *PR* and the last chapter ("Peace") in *AI*. To wonder and respond so is not to demean the primordial—for example, it is not to deny that the will for the world is completely fitted to the realities of the world, since Whitehead sees to that with his concept of the "superjective" aspect of God. It is more the kind of point that W. C. Maclagan makes in *The Theological Frontier of Ethics* (New York: Macmillan, 1961), pp. 178-179, when he says that the ethical demand must be impersonal, while a response sought to life may be personal.

111. Romans 8:31-35a. We now return to a theme introduced already in Chapter 1, p. 49.

112. It is the task of conceptual wisdom to help make the testimony more clearly. If it is made more surely through a metaphysical contribution, we are dealing with constitutive wisdom. Insofar as incoherence as something counting against the claims of faith can be addressed in the metaphysical contribution, we can be the more sure.

113. William Wolf, *No Cross, No Crown* (Garden City, New York: Doubleday, 1957), p. 130. (Italics his.) Wolf adds:

> From this perspective it would probably be better not to speak of "the Cross of Jesus Christ," not to generalize in the phrase "The Atonement," but to keep its concrete meaning by such words as "the atoning work of God in Jesus Christ."

See F. W. Dillistone's treatment of this dialectic in *The Christian Understanding of the Atonement*, Chapter 10, "The Idea and the Event."

114. Thus Ditmanson, *Grace in Experience and Theology*, p. 60. He continues:

> The Christian idea of God is not a mere jumble of contradictory elements. It is centered about the grace of God that is known to us in Jesus Christ, and all else that we say about God should be united to and expressive of this central concept of love.

115. Wolf, *No Cross, No Crown*, p. 65. Thus Frances M. Young, *Sacrifice and the Death of Christ* (London: SPCK, 1975) is driven to speak of the divine costly act of "self-propitiation" (p. 95).

116. For a critique of the cultic (but a defense of the juridical), see Markus Barth, *Was Christ's Death a Sacrifice?* (Edinburgh: Oliver and Boyd, 1961), p. 32. F. R. Barry would seem to go farther in *The Atonement* (London: Hodder and Stoughton, 1968), p. 132:

> Forgiveness is a relation of persons, and to tell us that God's justice has been vindicated is not to tell us that we have been forgiven.

117. Knutson, *The Shape of the Question*, p. 67.

118. This is F. W. Dillistone's summary of Lionel Thornton's emphasis in *Revelation and the Modern World* (London: Dacre, 1950). See Dillistone's discussion in *The Christian Understanding of the Atonement*, Chapter 2.

119. This statement of the matter troubles a wide range of discussions. Thus Paul Tillich's *Systematic Theology*, Vol. 1 (Chicago: University of Chicago Press, 1951), pp. 144-147, derives universal fulfillment from universal revelation. In *The Meaning of God*, pp. 91-93, Robert H. King tries to employ the category of "word" to get omnipotence without coercion. The tendency to confuse the decisiveness of God and the significance of human response creates a pressure which would elide the middle term, Jesus the Christ. His revelatory work may have been needed to "thematize" our knowledge of God (Rahner), but the biblical constant is a theological anthropology, the understanding of humanity as existing in the presence of a gracious God (Herbert Braun). Or one may indeed exalt the kairotic moment, but do so in such a way as to make faith

inevitable. Thus Ozment in *Homo Spiritualis* (Leiden: Brill, 1969), p. 174, tends toward such exaltation when he writes of Luther's understanding:

Because of Luther's awareness of the *historical* character of the gospel and of the uniqueness of the objective context which it alone establishes, the reconciliation of peace and righteousness, theologically and existentially, is christocentric and fidelic, rather than theocentric and synderetic (Gerson) or "gemeutlich" (Tauler). Luther does not speak of the exaltation of the highest powers of the soul to a form of generic similitude with God (Gerson), nor of the absorption of the ground of the soul in the uncreated Ground (Tauler). He speaks of Christ's coming to men "where they are" and the effective presence of righteousness, peace, mercy, and salvation in and through faith in Christ. (Italics his.)

Here historical decisiveness is purchased at high cost to human freedom.

120. In *Justification of the Ungodly*, trans. Eric W. Gritsch and Ruth C. Gritsch (St. Louis: Concordia, 1968), p. 114, Wilhelm Dantine cites numerous Pauline passages to reach this conclusion.

121. See above, pp. 86-87, 114. More than anyone else Lewis S. Ford has developed the theme of the reversal of the poles. See particularly his "The Non-Temporality of Whitehead's God," *International Philosophical Quarterly*, XIII (1973), pp. 347-376, and "Whitehead's Categoreal Derivation of Divine Existence," *Monist*, LIV (1970), pp. 374-400. See also Marjorie Suchocki, "The Metaphysical Ground of the Whiteheadian God," *Process Studies*, V:4 (Winter, 1975), pp. 237-246.

122. Westermann, *Creation*, p. 64.

123. See "The Temporality of Divine Freedom" by James W. Felt, S.J., in *Process Studies*, IV:4 (Winter, 1974), pp. 252-261. Felt employs Whitehead's categories of qualitative pattern and quantity of emotional intensity to reach toward significant temporality without compromising the primordial nature.

124. von Rad, *Genesis*, p. 49.

125. To speak so would be to place oneself within the "transactional" type in George Rupp's typology in his *Christologies and Cultures* (Mouton: The Hague, 1974). But I am seeking a set of categories sufficiently supple to accommodate what he calls for under the "processive," as well—that is the significance of human response.

126. Fyodor Dostoyevsky, *The Brothers Karamazov*, trans. Constance Garnett, ed. by Manuel Komroff (New York: New American Library, 1957), pp. 226-227.

127. See above, pp. 196-201.

128. Above, pp. 185-189. In that consistency the humanity of Jesus is protected. Elisabeth Schussler Florenza in "Wisdom Mythology and Christological Hymns," pp. 17-41, in Robert Wilken, ed. *Aspects of Wisdom in Judaism and Early Christianity* (South Bend: Notre Dame Press, 1975), p. 37, stresses that Paul "emphasized the humanity of Jesus Christ by stressing his death on the cross" to ward off the danger that the human Jesus would be swallowed up by the mythical. If (lest) this connection of cross and humanity is lost, other instruments may be needed to the same end.

129. Ephesians 1:3-10.

130. See Lewis S. Ford, "The Possibilities for Process Christology," *Encounter* XXXV:4 (1974), pp. 281-294.

131. Jürgen Moltmann, *The Crucified God*, trans. R. A. Wilson and John Bowden (London: SCM, 1974), p. 272. (Italics his.) Moltmann is following a lead he has found in the work of Abraham Heschel who speaks of God as "free in himself and at the same time interested in his covenant relationship and affected by human history" (Ibid.). Such a dipolar theology of the divine pathos again suggests that a Whiteheadian structure is not an alien imposition as far as the vision of faith is concerned. Faith sees and wonders how to say coherently what it sees.

132. At this point the theological advantages of the "entitative" view of God—as distinguished from the "societal" view—begin to become clear. See the discussion above, pp. 159-160.

133. J. Gerald Janzen, "Metaphor and Reality in Hosea 11," *Society of Biblical Literature 1976 Seminar Papers,* ed. George MacRae (Missoula: Scholars Press, 1976), pp. 413-445, 436.

134. Markus Barth, *Was Christ's Death a Sacrifice?* p. 51, states well the need to stress the divine—and indeed the trinitarian—character of the sacrifice:

> The sacrifice of Christ shows that the gift of redemption is not a work of Jesus alone, or a fiction of human belief in that Jesus. A sacrifice must be acceptable to Him to whom it is brought. And to be acceptable and revealed as accepted, there must be the right ("eternal," Heb. 9:14; "holy," John 1:32f.) Spirit given to a chosen servant. . . . If, however, the concept of sacrifice is eschewed, we are left with a Christomonism, like the Gnostic Marcion's or with a "Jesusism" of more recent origin and character. This in turn means that man is left alone with "knowledge" of a way to the soul's salvation or with his deified idea of an ideal man.

Cf. Dillistone, *The Christian Understanding of Atonement,* pp. 250-251, on sacrifice as the expression of the very being of God.

Both Lewis Ford (in Cargas and Lee, *Religious Experience and Process Theology,* pp. 83-84) and Eugene TeSelle (in *Christ in Context: Divine Purpose and Human Possibility,* pp. 134-145) try for christological novelty, using Whiteheadian categories. What I am seeking to add to their themes (which stress the primordial nature) is a sense of the significance for God of what the divine and the human come together to do in Jesus. Cf. my question of Cobb's christology, above, p. 156. Process thought does helpfully remind us that we cannot get back behind the reality of freedom—divine or human—as if to ask "why Jesus?"

135. Heinrich Ott seems to be reaching in this direction when he suggests that

> . . . we might further examine the three dimensions, namely past, present, and future, in their interpenetration, their perichoresis.

See his discussion in "Philosophical Theology as Confrontation," pp. 144-168, *The Future of Philosophical Theology,* ed. Robert Evans (Philadelphia: Westminster, 1971), trans. of Ott's essay by D. L. Holland, p. 104. Another instance of such an effort is offered by John Baillie in *The Sense of the Presence of God* (New York: Scribner's, 1962), p. 202:

> . . . the eternal Christ who was made *flesh* in Jesus of Nazareth, and the Eternal Atonement which was made *event* on Calvary, were and are the source of every "saving process" which has at any time proved to be for the healing of the nations. (Italics his.)

It must be said that such efforts beg for clarification. I am suggesting Whiteheadian metaphysical categories be possessed as part of the equipment needed to answer that call.

136. See Schmid, *The Doctrinal Theology of the Evangelical Lutheran Church,* p. 424.

137. Lutherans, for example, regularly point out that the doctrine of election is intended as existential consolation, and they seem to be following master Martin in making such assurances. It is to be regretted, however, when such consolation usurps the role of human response. Is such a healing worth having? For a discussion of the election controversy of the 1880s within American Lutheranism, see Eugene L. Fevold, "Coming of Age," pp. 255-358, in *The Lutherans in North America,* ed. E. Clifford Nelson (Philadelphia: Fortress, 1975), pp. 313-325.

138. See Tappert, ed., *The Book of Concord,* p. 432. Cf. Schmid, *The Doctrinal Theology*

*of the Evangelical Lutheran Church,* p. 342, for Lutheran dogmatic teaching on "the redemption of the human race." For a contemporary witness to this theme, see Jürgen Moltmann, *The Gospel of Liberation,* p. 39:

> And if it is true that God has reconciled "the world" with himself, who then is excluded? Who then is not in Christ as long as he belongs to this world? It is not up to our faith or to our unfaith, our high or low feelings. God reconciled the world in Christ. Thus all who live and die in this world are included. No one is excluded. Indeed, before we believe or doubt, before we are grasped by it or even feel nothing, this reconciliation has happened in us and for us. For God— God himself—was in the forsaken Christ and became the forsaken God and Father.

See also the effort of the Lutheran World Federation to articulate this theme at the fourth Assembly in Helsinki, 1963, in *Justification Today,* supplement to *Lutheran World,* No. 1, 1965, especially page 4, Section II, paragraph 5, on the theme that "Jesus Christ is the act of God in which God has created salvation for all men."

139. William Hordern, *Living by Grace* (Philadelphia: Westminster, 1975), pp. 77-78. Cf. Philip S. Watson, *The Concept of Grace* (Philadelphia: Muhlenberg, 1959), p. 38:

> The gospel does not say "Unless you have faith, God will not love you," but rather "God loves you, therefore have faith, believe in his love for you." Faith, in the Christian understanding of it, is a human response to the forgiving love of God.

140. A succinct statement of this concern is available in Joseph M. Shaw's *If God Be For Us* (Minneapolis: Augsburg, 1966), especially pp. 78ff., where the danger of severing imputation from regeneration is stressed. The emphasis on response characterizes the employment of the category of "reconciliation." For a strong affirmation of that theme, see Ditmanson, *Grace in Experience and Theology.* I appreciate the effort Ditmanson makes to state the delicate distinction between the forensic and transactional character of justification and the personal character of reconciliation. I wonder, though, whether the distinction is compromised if one goes on to say (ibid., p. 223) that "it is clear that the reconciliation was effected by the exercise of divine forgiveness." Other Christian thinkers have tried to employ a chronological distinction. See Dillistone, *The Christian Understanding of the Atonement,* pp. 289-292, and Wolf, *No Cross, No Crown,* Chapters 7-9.

141. I have discussed this relationship throughout the section on ethical wisdom, above, pp. 208-229. See especially note 73. Barth, *Was Christ's Death a Sacrifice?,* p. 49, traces the biblical understanding of how the ethical character of Christian sacrifice is dependent on the cultic character of Christ's sacrifice.

142. In this sense one could appropriate the theme that the gospel frees us from preoccupation with our own salvation.

143. Above, pp. 125-130.

144. On this as a summary of Lutheran teaching on justification, see Shaw, *If God Be For Us,* p. 48, and Charles S. Anderson, *Faith and Freedom* (Minneapolis: Augsburg, 1977), p. 44.

## 6: Faith and Process: The Principles and Practice of Dialog

1. *Webster's Seventh New Collegiate Dictionary* (Springfield, Mass.: G. and C. Merriam Company, 1972), p. 180.
2. I have discussed Kierkegaard's use of "indirect communication" in *Kierkegaard on Christ and Christian Coherence* (New York: Harper, 1968), pp. 28-42.

3. For a consensus on this conception of metaphysics see above, Chapter 1, note 8.
4. Even in making this presuppositional link between God and moral goodness we part company with a theologian like Tillich who warns in his *Systematic Theology* (3 vols.; Chicago: University of Chicago Press, 1951-1963) Vol. I, pp. 217-218, against such a link since then "the holy loses its depth, its mystery, its numinous character." More specifically, Robert C. Neville has criticized Whitehead at this point in "The Impossibility of Whitehead's God in Christan Theology," *Proceedings of the American Catholic Philosophical Association*, XL (1970), pp. 130-140. Neville protests (p. 140):

> . . . the assimilation of worshipfulness to admirable moral character or redemptive service. . . . I would say we worship the creator both transcendent of us and creatively present in us. As to redemption, if experience reveals that God does indeed redeem, create beauty and bring peace, then God is to be worshipped as the supreme creator of those things, as he is the creator of all things. If God creates evil and suffering, our worship, although not our moral sensibility, still says, Blest be the Name of the Lord.

I find that Neville's discussion has a confusing abstractness about it, for it seems to call us back behind God's loving will to create and forgive in order to face us with a purer choice. Given that will—and its decisiveness has, of course, been a major theme in this study—I believe my distinction applies.
5. Above, pp. 215-229.
6. John Hick, *Evil and the God of Love* (London: Collins, 1966), p. 62.
7. Saul Bellow, *Mr. Sammler's Planet* (New York: Viking, 1969), p. 140.
8. Hick, *Evil and the God of Love*, p. 63.
9. The statement is by Frederick Cowan who killed five persons—three blacks, one East Indian, and himself—on February 14, 1977. Cowan was a member of the States Rights party which is thought to include about a thousand members.
10. Above, pp. 186-193.
11. See above, p. 141 on Hartshorne's thought in this connection. See note 74 in Chapter 3 for Hartshorne's view of the logical compatibility of evil and God.
12. Claus Westermann, *Creation*, trans. John J. Scullion, S.J. (Philadelphia: Fortress, 1974), p. 22, notes how biblical thought about the Beginning is linked with confidence about the End.
13. Harold Ditmanson, *Grace in Experience and Theology* (Minneapolis: Augsburg, 1977), p. 70.
14. See, for example, Bengt Hägglund's account of the Cappadocian contributions at this point in *History of Theology*, trans. Gene J. Lund (St. Louis: Concordia, 1966), pp. 84-85.
15. Gerhard von Rad, *Genesis*, trans. John H. Marks (Philadelphia: Westminster, 1961), p. 47, finds such testimony in the biblical speech about creation.
16. Thus in traditional dogmatic language, "not a transformation of the world, therefore, but an absolute annihilation of its substance is to be expected." See Heinrich Schmid, *The Doctrinal Theology of the Evangelical Lutheran Church*, p. 656.
17. For an extended expression of this concern, see Karl Rahner, *The Trinity*, trans. Joseph Donceel (New York: Seabury, 1974).
18. Thus God now works through secondary causes—in relationship, we have said—as is suggested by the dogmatic position that human souls "by virtue of the divine blessing, are propagated, per traducem, by their parents." (Schmid, *The Doctrinal Theology of the Evangelical Lutheran Church*, pp. 166-167). In God's use of the created to create lies a suggestion of the reality for God of that which God creates.
19. Søren Kierkegaard, *Christian Discourses*, trans. Walter Lowrie (London: Oxford, 1939), pp. 132-133.

20. Rahner, *The Trinity*, p. 103. (Italics his.)
21. Schmid, *The Doctrinal Theology of the Evangelical Lutheran Church*, pp. 162, 160.
22. This is the impression I have as I read the debate between Robert Neville and Lewis Ford in the Proceedings of the *American Catholic Philosophical Association* cited above in note 4. My ironic reaction to Professor Neville's bold speculations is that what he attempts is at once too much and too little. I find it too much in that I do not see that we should expect the qualitative otherness of God to be turned up by analysis and argument of (in) this world, beyond the very considerable ruminations of Ford on the Whitehead theme that God "at once exemplifies and establishes the categoreal conditions" (*PR* 522). See above, pp. 87-90. Yet Neville's argument—even if it works —seems to yield too little, for the creator must be "indeterminate" to account for what is created. See *God the Creator* (Chicago: University of Chicago Press, 1968), p. 73, for example:

> We have seen that all of the determinations together need a creator and that therefore the creator must create them all. If the creator were itself determinate essentially, then it would need a creator itself, and on ad infinitum.

It seems better to say that existentially—and essentially—God has chosen to be for us —already in creation. But it is in the very decisiveness of that choice that the Christian finds adumbrated the otherness which so radically distinguishes God from all other entities.

23. See Schmid, *The Doctrinal Theology of the Evangelical Lutheran Church*, pp. 295, 298.
24. See above, pp. 195-201.
25. Philippians 4:8. Thus Langdon Gilkey argues that

> . . . surely *some* appeal to such classical Christian authorities and sources as Scripture, traditional theology either Catholic or Protestant, or the general mind of the contemporary church is in *some* sense called for if the word "Christian" is to be used descriptively.

(See his review of John Cobb's *A Christian Natural Theology* in *Theology Today*, XXII:4 [January, 1966], p. 531.) See my comment above, pp. 151-152. I also wish to associate myself with David Tracy's emphasis on such commitment including a critical element. In *Blessed Rage for Order* (New York: Seabury, 1975), p. 7, Tracy pleads accordingly for an

> . . . open-ended inquiry, a loyalty to defended methodological canons, a willingness to follow the evidence wherever it may lead.

I take this to be simply a matter of what is inevitably entailed in the human striving for truth. See also Delwin Brown's "What Is Christian Theology," ed. Harry James Cargas and Bernard Lee, *Religious Experience and Process Theology* (New York: Paulist, 1976), pp. 41-52.

26. Walter Kaufmann, *Without Guilt and Justice: From Decidophobia to Autonomy* (New York: Delta, 1973), p. 185. Cf. p. 180. The formal uniqueness of the ethical is adumbrated by the sense of leap in this move. Perhaps a more positive suggestion of the same otherness is to be found in the transcendence characterizing an aesthetic experience. Of this Stuart Hampshire writes in *Thought and Action* (London: Chatto and Windus, 1959), pp. 119-120:

> It is important that we are capable of a type of experience, aesthetic experience, in which thought of the possibility of action is for a time partly suspended. The recognized value of aesthetic experience is partly a sense of rest from intention, of not needing to look through this particular object to its possible uses. This type of "pure" experience, when it exceptionally occurs, does in fact give a sense of timelessness, just because it is contemplation which is as far as possible divorced from the possibility of action.

F. David Martin understands this type of reference via Whitehead's category of presentational immediacy, but also has aesthetic categories for the elucidation of causal efficacy. See his *Art and the Religious Experience: The "Language" of the Sacred* (Lewisburg: Bucknell University Press, 1972), pp. 183-184 and 96. Cf. Chapter 2 above, note 174, and Chapter 3, note 29.

27. Gene Outka in *Agape: An Ethical Analysis* (New Haven: Yale University Press, 1972), pp. 276-278, points out how self-sacrifice leads to self-contradictory circumstances if everyone were so to act, and that this theme can at best be incorporated as a subordinate feature in neighbor-regarding considerations.

28. See above, page 19 and Chapter 1, note 1.

29. Richard John Neuhaus, *Time Toward Home* (New York: Seabury, 1975), pp. 61-62.

30. In "To the Unknown God: Luther and Calvin on the Hiddenness of God," pp. 263-293 in the *Journal of Religion*, LIII:3 (July, 1973) B. A. Gerrish argues for the contemporary viability of Luther and Calvin's thought regarding the hiddenness of God outside his revelation. But his closing plea is:

> In the passage from the *abyss* of the Unknown God to the *mystery* of faith assailed by doubt lies the efficacy of the Christian story (p. 292. Italics his.)

31. Robert Bellah outlines this ascending tendency in *The New Religious Consciousness*, ed. with Charles Y. Glock (Berkeley: University of California Press, 1976), pp. 333-352.

32. See, for example, Mircea Eliade, trans. Rosemary Sheed *Patterns in Comparative Religion* (New York: Sheed and Ward, 1958), pp. 393-394.

33. See Richard Neuhaus' critique in *Time Toward Home*, pp. 9-21.

34. Thomas Aquinas, *Summa Theologica*, trans. Father of the English Dominican Province (London: R. & T. Washbourne, 1912), pt. 1 Q. xlviii, art. 5.

35. Albert Outler, *Psychotherapy and the Christian Message* (New York: Harper, 1954), p. 102.

36. Jaroslav Pelikan (with G. Weigel and E. Fackenheim), *Religious Responsibility for the Social Order* (New York: National Conference of Christians and Jews, 1962), p. 7.

37. Saul Bellow's Nobel lecture in December, 1976, opened with such an expression of distrust, for example.

38. This, of course, is a slight paraphrase of Dietrich Bonhoeffer's famous question ("What is the meaning of Jesus Christ for us today?") in *Letters and Papers from Prison*. I believe my concern is consistent with Bonhoeffer's, though I grant that it differs in form, since the "metaphysical" was so defined by him as to be part of the problem, not part of the solution.

39. I have in mind a "privatism" which accepts anonymity, seeks anomie, and exults in "frontier freedom." Philip Rieff's analyses are insightful at this point, whether cast more cheerfully *(The Triumph of the Therapeutic: The Uses of Faith after Freud* [New York: Harper & Row, 1966]) or more wistfully ("Fellow Teachers," pp. 5-85, *Salmagundi* X [Summer-Fall, 1972]).

40. See Robert L. Heilbroner's analysis of the capacity for authoritarianism in *An Inquiry into The Human Prospect* (New York: Norton, 1974). On the polar character of these dynamics, Kierkegaard *(The Sickness Unto Death)* and Tillich *(The Courage to Be)* continue to be convincing.

41. Above, pp. 184-193.

42. Above, pp. 108ff. and 113-114.

43. See John B. Cobb's consideration of this question in his *Christ in a Pluralistic Age* (Philadelphia: Westminster, 1975), pp. 190-220. For a different approach to the post-Cartesian predicament, see Herbert W. Richardson's speculations regarding the "socio-

technic age" in *Toward An American Theology* (New York: Harper & Row, 1967), pp. 1-30.

44. Alasdair MacIntyre (with Paul Ricoeur), *The Religious Significance of Atheism* (New York: Columbia University Press, 1969), p. 24.

45. Philip Rieff, *The Triumph of the Therapeutic: Uses of Faith After Freud*, p. 261.

46. Richardson, *Toward an American Theology*, pp. 5-6.

47. On the elements essential to faith, see Schmid, *The Doctrinal Theology of the Evangelical Lutheran Church*, pp. 410-411.

48. See above, pp. 139-141, for my querulous reaction to Hartshorne at this point.

49. David Ray Griffin (with John B. Cobb, Jr.), *Process Theology: An Introductory Exposition* (Philadelphia: Westminster, 1976), p. 32. Cf. p. 31.

50. Hick, *Evil and the God of Love*, p. 317. (Italics his.)

51. That tendency may also be reflected in the fact that Hick looks to an ultimately universal salvation, ibid., pp. 398-400.

52. See above, pp. 77-90, on the distinction between God and creativity, as well as the amplification of this distinction in "ethical wisdom", pp. 213-229. I much prefer to work with this distinction in accommodating cognitive atheism (which cries out to be taken seriously) than to revert to either an ontological distinction between entity and person or an epistemological distinction with regard to consciousness.

53. Anthony Flew, *The Presumption of Atheism* (New York: Harper & Row, 1976), p. 26.

54. Alasdair MacIntyre, *The Religious Significance of Atheism*, p. 14.

55. On the distinction between the experiential and the experimental, see Paul Tillich, *Systematic Theology*, Vol. I, pp. 100-106. My topic in this section is the modest one, "respond*ing*" to unbelief, not the more ambitious one, "response to unbelief." Were it the latter—were I seeking directly to defend the faith and answer the unbeliever, I should have to try now to cite the evidence—the empirical and (Hartshorne) logical evidence. That would lead me back over much of the ground considered earlier, notably, pp. 79-90 and 238-240.

56. Above, pp. 97-99.

57. William Clifford, "The Ethics of Belief," pp. 201-220, in *Religion from Tolstoy to Camus*, ed. Walter Kaufmann (New York: Harper & Row, 1961), p. 220.

58. William James, "The Will to Believe," pp. 221-238, in *Religion from Tolstoy to Camus*, p. 237. (Italics his.) Flew in *The Presumption of Atheism*, p. 39, seems to misunderstand James' response:

> First: it would be grotesque to suggest that the basic beliefs in God, Freedom, and Immortality are such as can be made true by our determinedly thinking so. Second: to act upon an hypothesis with decision and effect it is by no means necessary to hold that hypothesis to be a known truth. I always welcome the chance to quote again words of the hero Stadtholder William the Silent: "It is not necessary to hope in order to act, nor to succeed in order to persevere."

The first point seems clearly wide of James' meaning. With the second we would agree, if one may grant that one may hold something to be true without claiming to "know" that it is so. Cf. John Smith, *Experience and God* (New York: Oxford, 1968), p. 151.

59. MacIntyre, *The Religious Significance of Atheism*, p. 10.

60. Flew, *The Presumption of Atheism*, p. 30.

61. See above, pp. 179-207.

62. Langdon Gilkey, *Naming the Whirlwind: The Renewal of God-Language* (Indianapolis: Bobbs-Merrill, 1969), p. 19.

63. Ibid. (Italics his.)

64. Gilkey's second chapter in *Naming the Whirlwind* is a most impressive delineation of these dimensions. For a summary, see above, Chapter 1, note 31.
65. Ludwig Feuerbach, *The Essence of Christianity*, trans. George Eliot (New York: Harper Torchbook, 1957), pp. 21-28.
66. David Hume, *Dialogues Concerning Natural Religion*, ed. Henry D. Aiken (New York: Hafner, 1948), p. 93.
67. Paul Ricoeur (with Alasdair MacIntyre), *The Religious Significance of Atheism*, p. 60.
68. Walter Kaufmann, *Without Guilt and Justice*, p. 234. Cf. also pp. 64, 107.
69. Sigmund Freud, "The Future of an Illusion," pp. 272-289 in Kaufmann, *Religion from Tolstoy to Camus*, p. 278.
70. R. P. C. Hanson, *The Attractiveness of God: Essays in Christian Doctrine* (Richmond: John Knox, 1973), p. 2.
71. Simone de Beauvoir, *The Ethics of Ambiguity*, trans. Bernard Frechtman (New York: Philosophical Library, 1948), p. 14. This reminds one of the stress on self-hatred in the Christian religion, according to Friedrich Nietzsche's analysis. See his "The Antichrist," pp. 191-200, in Kaufmann, *Religion from Tolstoy to Camus*, p. 192.
72. DeBeauvoir, *The Ethics of Ambiguity*, pp. 15-16. Cf. Alasdair MacIntyre, *The Religious Significance of Atheism*, p. 34.
73. Clifford makes this point forcefully in Kaufmann, *Religion from Tolstoy to Camus*, p. 204.
74. Langdon Gilkey makes a related but more comprehensive point in charging Schubert Ogden with the "fallacy of misplaced intellectualism" in Ogden's diagnosis of secularism. See Gilkey's "A Theology in Process: S. Ogden's Developing Theology," *Interpretation*, XXI, pp. 449-450. Thus he writes:
    . . . the dynamic factors responsible for secularism lie far deeper than particular philosophies of the past, which expressed rather than created these cultural moods. . . . As they say over and over, it is the category of *God*—dynamic or static, independent or dependent, unrelated or related, ontological and impersonal and "out there" which is radically questioned by the modern mind.
    The issue is joined, then, when we consider the relationship(s) of the self to that which is other than the self.
75. DeBeauvoir, *The Ethics of Ambiguity*, p. 16.
76. James M. Gustafson, *Can Ethics Be Christian?* (Chicago: University of Chicago Press, 1975), p. 93.
77. Søren Kierkegaard, *The Sickness Unto Death*, trans. W. Lowrie (Princeton: Princeton University Press, 1941), Doubleday Anchor Edition, pp. 227-231.
78. Anthony Flew (with Richard Hare and Basil Mitchell), "Theology and Falsification," pp. 470-479, in Kaufmann, *Religion from Tolstoy to Camus*, p. 479.
79. Ibid., p. 478.
80. John McTaggart, "God, Evil, and Immortality," pp. 455-469, in Kaufmann, *Religion from Tolstoy to Camus*, p. 462.
81. Ibid.
82. Kierkegaard, *The Sickness Unto Death*, pp. 200-207, 255-262.
83. 1 Peter 3:15. I have tried to expound this beautiful text in "A Gentle Journey of Reasoning Hope" in the *Luther Seminary Review*, Fall, 1975, pp. 30-34.

# Index of Subjects

341

346

# Index of Names

Alexander, S. A. 65
Althaus, P. 323n.92
Anderson, C. S. 335n.144
Anselm 137
Aquinas 268, 279
Ariel, R. 309n.119
Aristotle 23, 65, 69, 104, 289n.8
Arulicini, R. 327n.47
Asheim, I. 297n.54, 325n.5, 329n.71
Augustine 288n.1
Aulen, G. 188, 191, 225, 228, 321n.50, 328n.65, 329n.73
Ayer, A. J. 193

Bachelard, G. 68
Baillie, D. M. 323n.92
Baillie, J. 187, 191, 334n.135
Barbour, I. 31, 38, 108, 190, 290n.10, 306n.90
Barry, F. R. 332n.116
Barth, K. 27, 37, 232, 288n.1, n.2, n.3, 291n.13, 292n.16, 293n.23, 321n.52, 330n.86
Barth, M. 332n.116, 334n.134, 335n.141
Bateson, G. 318n.5, 319n.21
Beardslee, W. 216, 324n.113
Beardsley, M. 221
Becker, E. 331n.104
Bell, J. S. 303n.54, 306n.80, 318n.11
Bellah, R. N. 259, 295n.40, 338n.31
Bellow, S. 34, 338n.37
Benne, R. 297n.56
Bennett, J. B. 94, 114, 309n.124, 326n.15

Berdyaev, N. 133
Bergson, H. 65, 68
Birch, C. 325n.6
Black, M. 293n.26
Blythe, J. 313n.55
Boethius 317n.140
Bohm, D. 67-69, 113, 303n.54, 308n.103
Bonhoeffer, D. 289n.7, 338n.38
Bowker, J. 193, 238, 331n.104
Braaten, C. 331n.108
Braithwaite, R. B. 290n.10, 291n.10
Bradley, F. H. 23, 290n.8
Brahinsky, D. 303n.50
Braun, H. 314n.70, 332n.119
Brennan, S. O. 301n.30
Brueggemann, W. 191-192, 297n.58, 326n.25, 328n.56
Brown, D. 134, 311n.22, 317n.138, 326n.28, 331n.102, 337n.25
Brunner, E. 323n.92
Buber, M. 169
Buchler, J. 303n.50
Buddha 119
Bultmann, R. 37, 143-144, 152, 174, 314n.71
Burnshaw, S. 167, 327n.49
Burrell, D. B. 295n.41

Calvin, J. 232, 279, 338n.30
Campbell, D. 325n.6
Capek, M. 68, 75, 84-85, 303n.54, 304n.58, n.59
Cargas, H. J. 157

**347**